Regionalism and Rebellion in Yemen

Like other Arab revolutions in 2011, it is said that Yemen's rebellion was modeled on street protests in Tunis and Cairo. As this erudite new study explains, however, what happened in Yemen is far from being a mere echo of events elsewhere. In fact, the popular uprisings that came as a surprise in Tunisia, Egypt, Libya, and Syria were already well under way in Yemen. As early as 2007, this country on the southern tip of the Arabian Peninsula was embroiled in sit-ins, demonstrations, and open rebellion against the government. The author ably demonstrates how Yemen's political upheaval is rooted in divisions and conflicts of the past, especially the country's troubled national unification in 1990. Based on years of in-depth field research, this book unravels the complexities of the Yemeni state and its domestic politics with a particular focus on the post-1990 years. The central thesis is that Yemen continues to suffer from regional fragmentation, which has endured for centuries. En route the book discusses the rise of President Salih, his tribal and family connections, Yemen's civil war in 1994, the war's consequences later in the decade, the spread of radical movements after the U.S. military response to 9/11, and finally developments leading to the historic events of 2011. Politics in this strategically important country is crucial for many reasons, not least on account of its links to al-Qaeda terrorism. The United States and Western allies have good reason to regard Yemen as a security risk. This book sets a new standard for scholarship on Yemeni politics and is essential reading for anyone interested in the modern Middle East, the 2011 Arab revolts, and twenty-first-century Islamic politics.

Stephen W. Day is Adjunct Professor of Middle East Politics at the Hamilton Holt School at Rollins College. He has written for many journals, including *Middle East Journal*, *Middle East Policy*, and Publications of the *Carnegie Foundation*.

Cambridge Middle East Studies 37

Editorial Board

Charles Tripp (general editor)
Julia Clancy-Smith
F. Gregory Gause
Yezid Sayigh
Avi Shlaim
Judith E. Tucker

Cambridge Middle East Studies has been established to publish books on the nineteenth- to twenty-first-century Middle East and North Africa. The aim of the series is to provide new and original interpretations of aspects of Middle Eastern societies and their histories. To achieve disciplinary diversity, books are solicited from authors writing in a wide range of fields, including history, sociology, anthropology, political science, and political economy. The emphasis is on producing books offering an original approach along theoretical and empirical lines. The series is intended for students and academics, but the more accessible and wide-ranging studies will also appeal to the interested general reader.

A list of books in the series can be found after the index.

Regionalism and Rebellion in Yemen

A Troubled National Union

STEPHEN W. DAY

Rollins College

CAMBRIDGE
UNIVERSITY PRESS

CAMBRIDGE UNIVERSITY PRESS
Cambridge, New York, Melbourne, Madrid, Cape Town,
Singapore, São Paulo, Delhi, Mexico City

Cambridge University Press
32 Avenue of the Americas, New York, NY 10013–2473, USA

www.cambridge.org
Information on this title: www.cambridge.org/9781107606593

First published 2012

Printed in the United States of America

A catalog record for this publication is available from the British Library.

Library of Congress Cataloging in Publication Data
Day, Stephen W., 1961–
Regionalism and rebellion in Yemen : a troubled national union / Stephen W. Day.
  p. cm. – (Cambridge Middle East studies ; 37)
Includes bibliographical references and index.
ISBN 978-1-107-02215-7 (hardback) – ISBN 978-1-107-60659-3 (paperback)
1. Regionalism – Yemen (Republic)   2. Government, Resistance to – Yemen (Republic)   3. Yemen
(Republic) – Politics and government – 21st century.
4. Yemen (Republic) – Politics and government – 20th century.   5. Yemen (Republic) –Strategic
aspects.   l. Title.
JQ 1842.A38R433   2012
953.305'3–dc23   2011039452

ISBN 978-1-107-02215-7 Hardback
ISBN 978-1-107-60659-3 Paperback

The photograph on the cover depicts the aftermath of a tragic scene in the city of Taiz on May 29, 2011, when Yemen's republican guard and central security forces stormed "Freedom Square," where peaceful protesters had camped for months as a rallying point for demonstrations against President Salih's regime. The invading troops fired live ammunition, including heavy anti-aircraft weapons and RPGs, on unarmed citizens, many of whom had taken shelter in tents that provided shelter whenever they slept in shifts outdoors. During the attack, at least four protesters died, some burned alive inside the tents, including disabled youth unable to flee without their wheelchairs and crutches. Many more people were left with serious injuries. According to the photographer, Wael al-Absi, before capturing this image on his camera, he and others had tried to dissuade the troops from attacking, pleading that all Yemenis are brothers and sisters. But the troops apparently acted under strict orders to carry out their murderous assault. After the injured were rescued, and the corpses of martyrs retrieved, Wael al-Absi snapped this photo of a man using a blanket to extinguish flames engulfing one of many tents that were intentionally ignited by soldiers. The anonymous man struggles as he fans the fire, while seeking to put out the flames. Credit: Wael al-Absi, and Aleshteraki.net newspaper.

In memory of the late professor
Othman Said Qasim al-Mikhlafi,
whose dedication to democratic principles and
resistance against government corruption and dysfunction
inspired the research contained in this book.

May Othman's children and grandchildren
always know the continued value of his work,
and one day realize the promise of his vision
for a Yemen governed in each province and district
for the sake of social justice.

Contents

Tables

Maps and Photos

Preface

I first submitted the bulk of this book's manuscript to Cambridge University Press in October 2010. At the time, I wrote urgently to the senior Middle East editor in New York City, Marigold Acland, predicting the collapse of Yemen's government. "Do I have a manuscript for you!" is a parody of my words, yet it captures the thrust of my message. At the time, I had a working title, *Yemen Unraveling*. Marigold was patient with my enthusiasm, two months before a Tunisian youth named Muhammad Bouazizi set himself on fire in Sidi Bouzid, unleashing dramatic mass street protests in Tunis and later Cairo, Egypt. By the end of January 2011, it was clear that the entire Arab world was witnessing a remarkable historical event. The following month, large street rallies commenced in Yemen, and by April it was obvious that the government of Yemen would not long endure.

Over the summer of 2011 Marigold presented a contract for publication. I was busy following every development in Yemen, as well as in other Arab countries caught in the "Arab spring," including Libya, Bahrain, and Syria. By then, the politics of Tunisia and Egypt had receded into the background, and these other Arab states, including Yemen, drew more media attention. It was fortunate, while the process of editing my manuscript got under way, I had an opportunity to add new content that could account for the dramatic developments across 2011. Some frustration came from the fact that the Yemeni president was more determined to hold on to power than either Ben Ali of Tunisia or Husni Mubarak of Egypt. Anyone who has written current political history for later publication in print can appreciate the uncertainty under which I worked on the book's conclusion.

When Yemeni President Ali Abdallah Salih was injured in a bombing at his palace in June 2011, and then evacuated for treatment in Saudi Arabia,

I sweated over a decision to change all of my references to his political leadership to past tense. After Salih miraculously recovered from his injuries and returned to Yemen in September, appearing as the zombie foe of the "Arab spring," I worried that the past tense phrases may need to be switched back to present tense. It was an enormous relief on November 23, 2011, when Salih finally signed the Gulf Cooperation Council agreement to transfer his executive powers and resign all but his ceremonial title as president. This came one week before the final deadline that I had agreed to meet. Thus the timing of political events on the ground cooperated surprisingly well with production of this book.

Given the legacy of Yemeni politics, both old and recent, it is possible that after the book enters the printing process developments on the ground may alter the meaning of this narrative. Of course, this is the nature of working on current political themes, although the case of Yemen in 2011 may be more extreme. Yemen's politics is constantly perplexing because the land is a quixotic place, and its people are more prone than others to open contestation and rapid reversals of position. Nonetheless, I hope this book effectively explains the broader background to the remarkable events of 2011 in Yemen, while providing a complete account of what took place during the year. What the year 2012 holds for Yemen is entirely another matter.

In the choice of titles for the book, I resisted using the word "revolution." Recent events in Yemen have certainly been revolutionary, not least in social terms. But the determination of whether or not their political effects amount to a revolution remains for scholars and analysts in the years to come. It is my hope that the new year and years to come bring a fulfillment of all the promises Yemeni unification held in 1990, so the people of this country can enjoy peace, prosperity, and a much brighter future. The continued failure of Yemeni politics will bring much darker times for its people, and people of the entire region.

This is my first book on Yemen. It results from seventeen years of research, which accumulated in boxes and files since the start of my doctoral dissertation at Georgetown University in 1995. I lived and studied in Yemen between 1995 and 1997, and then briefly traveled back for more research in 1998 and 2002. My last trip was a limited one in the late summer of 2005. Thus it has been a few years since I set foot in the country. I still manage to keep an active understanding of developments through contacts with friends inside Yemen, as well as the miracles of computerized telecommunication, the Internet, Arabic news Web sites and weblogs, and more recently Twitter.

It is remarkable how much a Yemen researcher can accomplish today sitting in central Florida, with a computer, compared to when I first started my studies in the early 1990s. However, I would trade this technology, and what it can do in the hands of a researcher, for a month of travels inside Yemen. There is no substitute for living in the country, following events in person, and bearing witness. I look forward to returning soon. There is already a *plus ça change* sense about the Arab uprisings of 2011. The most ardent street protesters in Cairo, Egypt, bitterly protested its transitional elections in late November, reoccupying Maidan al-Tahrir and calling for the military tribunal's immediate abolition. A deep suspicion exists in the Arab world that current political transitions are stage-managed so that little change actually takes place, belying most media reports. As Galal Amer wrote from Cairo on November 24, 2011: "We're making a big fuss about wallpaper without really changing the apartment, like the man who owns a donkey and wants to pretend it's a mighty camel." If there can be genuine revolutionary change in the Arab world, then the hardest work begins after the transition, when democratic vigilance is needed most.

A word is needed about the book's translation and transliteration of Arabic. I sought consistency by using a reverse apostrophe ['] for *'ayn*; and an accent grave [`] for *hamza*. All other essential diacritical marks are missing. Thus, although the distinction between Arabic letters, *daal* (d) and *dhal* (dh), is obvious, other similar Arabic letters with no equivalent in the Latin alphabet are not indicated. For the sake of simplicity, I use common English spelling of words such as Yemen, Ottoman, and al-Qaeda. Whenever the English spelling of proper nouns and names with *'ayn* has been popularized, I abandon the diacritical marks. For instance, Abdallah and Abd al-Aziz, as well as names of better known cities, such as Sanaa, Aden, and Taiz. Lesser known cities and places, such as al-Dali' and Yafi', appear with diacritical marks. In order to keep the text more accessible to readers who are unfamiliar with Arabic, I provide English translations of all Arabic titles that appear in footnotes. Throughout the book I translate *muhafatha* as "province," not governorate, even though the latter is common in books about Yemen's local administrative units. When referring to individual Yemenis, I first give their full names, but thereafter use their customary first names. For example, the late Shaykh Abdallah bin Husayn al-Ahmar appears more frequently as Shaykh Abdallah. The exceptions are individuals better known by their last names, such as the ousted President Salih.

Acknowledgments

It is impossible to count the people who assisted the research in this book. There are literally hundreds in Yemen and the United States. I should begin by thanking professors at Georgetown University who served as mentors when I began my doctoral dissertation on Yemen in the middle 1990s. In particular, the late distinguished and beloved professor Dr. Hanna Batatu, who always insisted on the value of examining politics in its fullest social, economic, cultural, and historical dimensions. No element in this process is insignificant for the sake of sound political analysis, thus requiring patience and a good supply of ink pens. Dr. Michael C. Hudson offered much appreciated advice and counsel over the years. Georgetown University's Center for Contemporary Arab Studies made possible my Ph.D. studies through a generous graduate fellowship. I will always be thankful for this first-rate institution in Washington, DC.

Two of my research trips to Yemen were made possible by fellowships from the American Institute for Yemeni Studies. Dr. Maria de Jesus Ellis and Dr. Christopher Edens, as well as others who served on the staff of the AIYS residence in Sanaa, provided great help over the years. Inside Yemen, I owe special thanks to the late Professor Othman al-Mikhlafi who served as my primary advisor. Without his expertise about Yemen's government administration, a willingness to make introductions to individuals inside and outside of government, and the generosity with which he shared his own time, my research would never have started or finished the same way. In countless *qat* sessions with Othman, who had earlier traveled to Europe and throughout the Middle East where he found causes for joy greater than what was so distasteful about Yemeni politics during the late 1990s and early 2000s, he refused any hint of *joie de vivre* beyond what the bitter taste of *qat* could provide. In his words, "I will not celebrate until the dictator Ali Abdallah Salih is removed from power." It is tragic that he did not live to see this day. Had he lived until 2011, he would have fiercely supported the youthful street protesters in Sanaa, Taiz, Aden, and other cities, urging them to keep standing up for their dignity and human rights, even after Salih resigned.

Also in Yemen my research benefited from assistance by a number of people at universities in Sanaa, Taiz, and Aden; the Yemeni Center for Research and Studies, the National Institute of Administrative Sciences, the Ministry of Local Administration and Ministry of Civil Service in Sanaa; and staff at provincial offices throughout the country. Most noteworthy are Dr. Abduh Ali Othman, Dr. Muhammad Husayn Shamsan, the late Dr. Abd al-Aziz al-Tarmoum, Dr. Abd al-Aziz al-Maqaleh, Dr. Muhammad al-Mutawakkel, Dr. Ahmad Ali Sultan, Dr. Abd al-Aziz al-Baghdadi, and Dr. Muhammad Ahmed al-Mikhlafi, founder of the Yemeni Observatory for Human Rights and now minister of legal affairs in Yemen's transitional government. I benefited from many long conversations with the brave, always insightful independent journalists of Yemen, including Hisham Bashraheel, his brother Tamam, son Bashar, and their *al-Ayyam* staff throughout the country; the late Dr. Abd al-Aziz al-Sakkaf, founder of the *Yemen Times*, whose daughter Nadia now carries on his proud legacy; and the late Omar al-Jawwi and his colleagues at *al-Tagammu'a*.

I must mention individuals whose kindness in Yemen never failed, not least the late Mahfouz al-Shamakh, Najeeb Shamiri, Sadiq Amin Abu Ras, Abd al-Malik al-'Ulafi, Abdallah Ghanem, Amin Qasim, Hassan Ba Zara'a, and Othman Abd al-Jabar; the fine poets Ahmad al-'Awadi and Said al-Shadadi, the late poet Muhammad Haitham, Abd al-Nasser al-Mude'a, Muhammad and Khaled al-Iryani, Abd al-Qaddus al-Bishari, and the young Ahmad Sharaf al-Din; my YCRS students Thaira Sha'alan, Aisha Dammaj, as well as Altaf, Akram, Qaid, Abd al-Karim, Abd al-Kafi, and many others, including the late Abd al-Rahman al-Amiri who was indispensable for my learning Yemeni dialects; from Taiz Abd al-Kader al-Guneid, Omar Itzak, Izzedine Said Ahmed, and Shawki Ahmad Hayel Said; from Aden Badr Naji Muhammad, Khaled Abd al-Wahed Numan, Badr Ba Sunaid, Abdallah Ibrahim, Hasan Hubaishi, Abdallah Abadan, Wahbi Uqba, Raqiyya Hamaidan, Salih Ba Surra, Aishe al-Douh, Muhammad Said Muqbil, and Farouq Bin Shamlan; from Hadramaut Saad al-Din Talib, Abd al-Rahman Bukair, Husayn Jailani, Mahmoud Ben Dahdah, Ahmad Ba Raoud, Awadh Bahrak, Abd al-Rahman al-Saqqaf, Salih Ba Qais, Muhsin al-Amoudi, Alawi Bin Sumait, and Salah al-Baiti.

I want to acknowledge the critical role played by the Middle East editor at the New York City office of Cambridge University Press, Marigold Acland. I thank her for encouraging the inclusion of my research in the Cambridge Middle East Studies series. At Cambridge, I also want to thank Joy Mizan for her assistance; Mark Fox and Joe LeMonnier for their work on the book's maps and photographs; and Laura Lawrie in Sedona, Arizona, for her project management and copyediting. I appreciate Wael al-Absi's artistry and bravery as a photographer in Taiz, Yemen, and his agreement to let me use his photo on the cover of this book. Thanks also to the publishers and photographers of *Yemen Times*, *al-Ayyam*, and *al-Masdar* for allowing me to include a few of their photos on inside pages. Any errors and omissions are my own.

Parts of this book's manuscript first appeared in other forms as articles in academic journals and online publications. I especially thank Michael Dunn, editor of the *Middle East Journal* in Washington, DC, who first published my essay on Yemen's southern al-Hirak in the summer of 2008. Much of this essay, "Updating Yemeni National Unity: Could Lingering Regional Divisions Bring Down the Regime?" appears in Chapter 8. John Calabrese, editor of the Middle East Institute's online publication, *Viewpoints*, published my essay about the cancellation of Yemen's 2009 parliamentary election. Anne Joyce, editor of *Middle East Policy*, published my earlier 2007 article comparing and contrasting the politics of regionalism inside Yemen and Iraq. I am grateful to the late, dearly missed, Christopher Boucek of the Carnegie Foundation, who thought of including my analysis of al-Hirak in the 2010 book *Yemen on the Brink*, which he coedited with Dr. Marina Ottaway. Finally, I am appreciative of the excellent work done by Dr. Bassam Haddad and others on the staff of *Jadaliyya*'s Web site, who provided the best continuous coverage of the Arab revolutions in 2011. Thank you for being willing to include three essays of mine about Yemen.

I want to acknowledge other colleagues who have helped shape my thinking about Yemeni politics, whether on conference panels or in personal exchanges. In particular, Dr. Sheila Carapico, whose decades of research has gained well-deserving acclaim and have greatly influenced my view of Yemen; and Dr. Bob Burrowes, who likewise blazed an early path down which all other American researchers walk whenever they enter into the study of Yemen. I also want to thank Dr. Abdu

Sharif, Dr. Muhammad Zabarah, Tarek al-Wazir and the Yemeni Heritage and Research Center, Dr. Renaud Detalle, Dr. Lisa Wedeen, and the new generation of Yemen researchers, April Longley, Gregory Johnsen, Sarah Phillips, Laurent Bonnefoy, and Alistair Harris.

Finally, I want to thank Bernadette, for being the one who never let my complaints prevent me from completing this work. You gave much needed inspiration to reopen my work on Yemen and to compile it for the benefit of others.

Abbreviations

ACC   Arab Cooperation Council, short-lived international organization sponsored by Iraqi president Saddam Husayn in the late 1980s

AQAP   Al-Qaeda on the Arabian Peninsula, branch of the international organization formed in Yemen with support of Saudi members in 2009

FLOSY   Front for the Liberation of South Yemen, anticolonial organization based in urban areas of Aden with Egyptian sponsorship in the late 1960s

GCC   Gulf Cooperation Council, international organization formed among the oil-rich states of the Arabian peninsula in the 1990s

GPC   General People's Congress, ruling party of the former north Yemen, YAR, founded in 1982 by Ali Abdallah Salih, who led it into unity with south Yemen

JMP   Joint Meeting Parties, coalition of the main Yemeni opposition parties, including Islamists and socialists, formed in the early 2000s

NDF   National Democratic Front, Marxist opposition group in western midland and coastal regions of YAR during the late 1970s and early 1980s, supported by PDRY

NF   National Front, first south Yemeni ruling coalition after independence in 1967, derived from the NLF

NLF   National Liberation Front, broad-based anticolonial organization operating in rural areas of south Yemen in the 1960s, including many Marxists

PDRY   People's Democratic Republic of Yemen, former south Yemen
        ruled by Marxist leadership of YSP in alliance with the
        Soviet Union, 1969–90
SEC   Supreme Elections Commission, government agency in united
        Yemen responsible for voter registration and vote
        counting; later SCER
YAR   Yemen Arab Republic, former north Yemen ruled by
        republican leaders who overthrew the last Zaydi imam,
        1962–90
YSP   Yemeni Socialist Party, Marxist ruling party of the former
        south Yemen, PDRY, that entered national unity with the
        GPC

Chronology of Modern Yemeni History

1839	British Empire begins colonization of Aden in southern Yemen
1872	Ottoman Empire begins second occupation of Sanaa in northern Yemen
1904	British and Ottoman Empires demarcate north-south border in Yemen
1918	Ottoman Empire withdraws from north Yemen; Imam Yahya Hamid al-Din restores Zaydi monarchal rule in north Yemen
1948	Imam Yahya overthrown and executed; brief constitutional monarchy under al-Wazir family until Yahya's son, Ahmad, restores authority of Hamid al-Din family
1950s	Free Yemeni activities in north Yemen; trade union activism in Aden
1962	Imam Ahmad dies natural death, and his son briefly claims to rule before being overthrown on September 26; start of north Yemen civil war, 1962–70, with Egypt backing republicans and Saudi Arabia backing Imam and royalists
1963	Beginning of south Yemeni revolution against British colonial rule on October 14
1967	South Yemeni independence on November 30 after British withdrawal
1970	North Yemen reconciliation between republicans and royalists, leading to informal "republican pact," which governs YAR
1972	First north-south Yemeni border war
1975	South Yemeni ruling party formed, leading to YSP in 1978

1977   North Yemeni president Ibrahim al-Hamdi assassinated

1978   Ali Abdallah Salih becomes president of north Yemen after
       al-Hamdi's successor, Ahmad al-Ghashmi, is assassinated
       by south Yemeni bomber

1979   Second north-south Yemeni border war

1982   North Yemeni ruling party, GPC, founded by President Salih

1984   First oil strike on northern side of border in central interior
       region

1986   Intra-regime war in Aden on January 13 leads to thousands of
       deaths; President Ali Nasir Muhammad flees into exile,
       while Ali Salem al-Bid becomes south Yemeni head of state

1989   National unity talks in November between presidents Salih and
       al-Bid in Aden

1990   Unification of north and south Yemen, forming Republic of
       Yemen on May 22

1993   First parliamentary election on April 27; no party wins
       majority, leading to political stalemate and conflict

1994   "Document of Pledge and Accord" signed in Amman, Jordan,
       in February; April–July civil war won by northern army

1997   Second parliamentary election on April 27; GPC wins landslide
       victory

1999   President Salih wins first direct presidential election with
       97 percent of vote

2000   USS *Cole* naval destroyer bombed in Aden harbor, October 12

2001   First local council elections in February; post-9/11 formation of
       Public Forum for Sons of Southern and Eastern Provinces
       in December 2001–January 2002

2004   First al-Huthi war in Sa'da; martyrdom of founder of al-Huthi
       "believing youth"

2006   Second, more competitive presidential election in September;
       Salih wins 77 percent of vote

2007   Southern peaceful protest movement "al-Hirak" formed after
       sit-ins by retired military officers in Aden

2009   Al-Qaeda on the Arabian Peninsula (AQAP) declared in
       January; fourth parliamentary elections in April canceled
       after boycott by JMP opposition coalition; army launches
       "Operation Scorched Earth" in sixth and most deadly
       al-Huthi war north of Sanaa

2010   Army launches war in southern provinces; United States and
        Britain hold emergency late January meeting in London to
        coordinate security policies on Yemen after AQAP
        attempted to bomb a jetliner in the United States in
        previous December

2011   Millions of Yemeni citizens join mass protest activities that
        brought down the Tunisian president in January and
        Egyptian president Mubarak in February, calling for the
        resignation of President Salih; Yemeni president evacuated
        to Saudi Arabia after being struck by bombing on June 3;
        Salih signs GCC-negotiated transfer of power deal and
        resigns as executive head of state, November 23

Glossary of Names of Key Political Figures

Regional origin in parentheses; underlining indicates the most common usage of names and titles.

Abd al-Aziz Abd al-Ghani (west midlands): GPC official, founder of YAR central bank, and key representative of midland Shafi'i business interests, 1970s–80s; prime minister, 1994–97; deceased August 2011

Abd al-Karim al-Iryani (highlands): GPC official and strategist, traditional Zaydi ruling class; foreign minister, 1990–98; prime minister, 1998–2001; key negotiator with GCC in 2011 crisis

Abd al-Rabo Mansour al-Hadi (mid-southern): Key partisan of Ali Nasir Muhammad, exiled from south in 1986; vice president of Yemen, 1994–2011; replaced Salih as head of state in November 2011

Abdallah bin Husayn al-Ahmar (highlands): Paramount Shaykh of Hashid Tribe, head of Islamic Islah party; speaker of Yemeni parliament, 1993–2007; deceased December 2007

Abd al-Majid al-Zindani (highlands): Religious Shaykh, fundamentalist cleric and advisor to young Bin Laden in Saudi Arabia; leader of Islamic Islah party, member first presidential council, 1990–93

Ahmad Ali Abdallah Salih (highlands): President Salih's son; head of Republican Guards, 2000s

Ali Abdallah Salih (highlands): President of Yemen; founder of GPC northern ruling party, 1982–2011

Ali Muhsin al-Ahmar (highlands): General, distant relative of President Salih, and military strongman of the regime, 1978–2011; defected from Salih with command of first artillery brigade in March 2011

Ali Nasir Muhammad (mid-southern): Former president of PDRY;
   living in exile since 1986 war in Aden; supporter of southern *al-Hirak*
Ali Salem al-Bid (eastern): Vice president of united Yemen and head of
   YSP, 1990–94; replaced Ali Nasir as southern head of state, 1986–90;
   led southern secession, living in exile since 1994 civil war
Faisal Ben Shamlan (eastern): Independent oil minister, 1994; JMP
   presidential candidate, 2006; deceased
Fareg Ben Ghanem (eastern): Independent technocrat; brief prime
   minister, 1997–98
Haider al-Attas (eastern): YSP official, prime minister of Yemen,
   1990–1994; living in exile since 1994 war; supporter of southern
   al-Hirak
Hasan Ba Awm (eastern): YSP official, secessionist; radical supporter of
   al-Hirak southern movement
Hasan Makki (west coast): GPC official, acting prime minister until
   assassin targets him at start of 1994 war
Jarallah Omar (west midlands): YSP official in old north Yemen, active
   with NDF in 1980s; instrumental in starting 2000s JMP coalition
   with Islah leader Shaykh Abdallah al-Ahmar; assassinated 2002
Sadeq al-Ahmar (highlands): Paramount Hashid Shaykh, 2007–11;
   attacked by President Salih, May 2011; afterward active in calls to
   remove Salih
Tareq al-Fadli (mid-southern): Shaykh, former sultan's son, exiled from
   PDRY until 1990; Islamist with Bin Laden and Afghan *mujahideen* in
   1980s; GPC member, 1994–2009; late supporter of al-Hirak
Yahya Muhammad Abdallah Salih (highlands): President Salih's
   nephew; head of central security, 2000s
Yahya al-Mutawakkel (highlands): GPC leader, traditional Zaydi ruling
   class; interior minister, 1993–95, resigned after pushing
   reconciliation with southern police in 1994; died suspiciously in 2003
Yasin Said Numan (southwestern): YSP official, moderate proponent of
   JMP coalition in 2000s; first speaker of parliament in united Yemen,
   1990–93; brief exile after 1994; active in calls to remove Salih in 2011

Introduction

In early 2011, popular uprisings swept through North Africa and the Middle East. In one country after another, beginning with Tunisia and Egypt, and quickly spreading to Yemen, Libya, Bahrain, and Syria, Arab citizens took to the streets calling for the downfall of old autocratic regimes. On January 14, 2011, Tunisian President Zayn al-Abidine Ben Ali was the first Arab leader to fall. He fled his country in a panicked flight to Saudi Arabia after nearly a month of demonstrations by citizens angered by rampant corruption and injustice. The next month, Egyptian President Husni Mubarak became the second autocratic leader to fall on February 11. His departure came after protesters, young and old, male and female, camped for three continuous weeks in central Cairo's *Maydan al-Tahrir* (Liberation Square).

Under a global spotlight created by satellite television broadcasters from every region of the world, participants in Egypt's momentous January 25 revolution chanted many of the same political slogans previously heard on Tunisian streets. These calls for change, mixed with songs of revolution, soon echoed across major cities of the region. Just five weeks earlier, it seemed impossible to have a peaceful exchange of state power in a region of the world long resistant to the spirit of democracy. Now, amazingly, it seemed not only possible but likely to happen in a handful of countries. Nowhere was this more true than Yemen located at the southern tip of the Arabian peninsula. Yet there was an important difference about the Tunisian and Egyptian effects when the waves of change crashed onto Yemen's shores.

During the first quarter of 2011, Yemen was the only country of the Arab world where the pending collapse of government did not come as a surprise. Long before the first signs of protest rippled through Tunisia in December 2010, and Cairo's citizens began occupying *Maydan al-Tahrir* the next month, Yemeni President Ali Abdallah Salih had faced widespread rebellion in his country. During the previous four years, major cities in Yemen, especially in southern and eastern parts of the country, experienced large street protests on a weekly basis. This fact is important for making sense of recent transformational events in Yemen. Unlike the uprisings in Tunisia and Egypt, Libya and Syria, as well as other Arab countries caught up in the "democratic spring of 2011," the downfall of Yemen's regime was widely anticipated, both inside and outside the country.

Before 2011, there were earlier protests in Egypt, especially during the formation of the April 6 movement in 2008, when badly exploited factory workers organized in a city of the Nile delta. For more than a decade, Palestinians had also protested and fought Israel's military occupation of their lands in East Jerusalem, Gaza, and the West Bank. Iraq had been embroiled in political turmoil since March 2003, following the American-led invasion to topple Saddam Hussein. And throughout 2005 and 2006, the Lebanese capital Beirut experienced dueling protests after the assassination of Prime Minister Rafiq al-Hariri. In fact, Lebanon's government, led by Hariri's son Saad, collapsed two days before Ben Ali's flight from Tunisia. Thus, the political environment in the Arab world was certainly unsettled before the spring of 2011. Public discontents boiled beneath the surface of Tunisia, Syria, and many other countries. Nonetheless, at the start of 2011, few could have predicted Ben Ali's rapid fall from power in Tunisia, and the removal of Mubarak in Egypt, let alone the approaching challenges to Muamar al-Gaddhafi's rule in Libya and Bashar al-Asad in Syria.

The same cannot be said of Yemen, since it was regularly described in media reports as a failing state. Not only was President Ali Abdallah Salih's regime expected to collapse at any moment, but there were genuine concerns the entire Yemeni nation-state might disintegrate along the lines of nearby Somalia across the Gulf of Aden. Beginning in 2004, President Salih's military and security forces confronted a rebellion by religiously inspired Zaydi tribesmen who supported a martyred leader named Hussayn ibn Badr al-Din al-Huthi. The "Huthi rebellion" centered around the old Zaydi capital in Sa'da, a famous mud-brick walled city near Yemen's northwestern border with Saudi Arabia. In successive years, the Yemeni army fought a series of six wars with Huthi fighters who attracted larger numbers of followers. The increased support for the Huthi rebellion was primarily due to rising public discontent with the regime's clumsy use of heavy artillery and air raids, resulting in hundreds, if not thousands of civilian casualties. By the last round of warfare in 2009, there were hundreds of thousands of internal refugees fleeing battles that had reached the outskirts of Sanaa the previous year.

More than one hundred miles south of Sanaa, separate groups of citizens started peaceful protests in 2007, calling for equality of rights with Yemenis in the north. These daily protests, known as the southern "peace movement" (*al-haraka al-salmiyya*, later shortened to *al-Hirak*), started among a group of former military officers who had been forced to retire in the late 1990s. These officers initially rallied to demand the restoration of their jobs and increased pension payments. But they soon attracted support from aggrieved citizens throughout provinces of the former People's Democratic Republic of Yemen (PDRY), a state that existed in the southern half of Yemen prior to national unification on May 22, 1990. After a brief civil war in the summer of 1994, during which President Salih's northern forces defeated the former PDRY army, many citizens of the south complained of political and economic discrimination while living under "northern military occupation." As Salih brutally cracked down on peaceful protesters in 2008, this radicalized the southern cause. Amidst escalating violence in 2009, supporters of the protest movement began to wave the former PDRY flag, calling for secession from the north just as southern leaders had done in 1994.

Adding to the unrest and instability generated by the al-Huthi rebellion in the north, and calls for secession in the south, there was a series of terrorist attacks in Yemen sponsored by a local branch of al-Qaeda. In January 2009, the Yemeni branch of al-Qaeda merged with exiled Saudi supporters of the international terrorist organization to form al-Qaeda on the Arabian Peninsula (AQAP). By 2010, this Yemeni-based network of terrorists was widely considered the most active and dangerous regional branch of Osama Bin Laden's al-Qaeda. Between 2006 and 2007, its agents carried out small operations against oil pipelines, security personnel, and foreign tourists in Yemen. Then in September 2008, the group carried out a bold assault on the heavily guarded American embassy in Sanaa. This assault involved two vehicles loaded with explosives, and at least five men armed with rocket-propelled grenades and machine guns. More than a dozen people were killed outside the embassy, including a Yemeni-American citizen and her newlywed husband. In the following year, associates and supporters of AQAP were linked to U.S. Army Major Nidal Malik Hasan's shooting of thirteen American personnel in Fort Hood, Texas, as well as a plot to detonate a bomb on board an American passenger airplane over Detroit, Michigan, on Christmas Day 2009.

During this time, American officials feared that President Salih's regime was so badly weakened by its confrontation with Huthi rebels and southern secessionists that Yemen had become a safe haven for al-Qaeda. From the moment President Barack Obama entered the White House in January 2009, he placed the country near the top of world trouble spots. He even mentioned Yemen's dangers in his inaugural address on the steps of the U.S. Capitol Building. During the spring and summer of President Obama's first year in office, top military and counterterrorism advisors paid repeated visits to Yemen, demanding closer cooperation from President Salih in the fight against al-Qaeda. Fearing that Salih's regime was on the verge of collapse, the Obama administration also announced an emergency aid package during the late summer of 2009. Then, before the incident in the skies above Detroit, Michigan, the American president attempted to confront the threat of AQAP by launching two separate missile strikes in southern regions of the country. The Christmas Day incident by Umar Abd al-Mutallab, a Nigerian-born student who trained in Yemen, raised even greater international security concerns.

On January 27, 2010, Yemen was the focus of an emergency meeting in London, England, arranged by Prime Minister Gordon Brown on the eve of a previously planned international conference on Afghanistan. U.S. Secretary of State Hillary Clinton and British Foreign Minister David Miliband met with the prime minister and foreign minister of Yemen to launch a "Friends of Yemen" group. This group was intended to help stabilize the country by funneling additional financial aid to the regime in Sanaa. One year before the uprisings in Tunisia and Egypt, participants in the London meeting worried that political and economic dysfunction was spreading in Yemen, making it ever more dependent on outside support and assistance. Given the tsunami of rebellions and protests during the previous seven years, the wave of Arab uprisings in 2011 hardly triggered an alert in Yemen. Quite unexpectedly, it raised hopes that Yemen's many problems might be constructively resolved, if given proper direction under a new national leadership.

In other words, the immediate impact of events in Tunisia and Egypt was not that they sparked calls for political change, as happened in Bahrain, Libya, Syria, and elsewhere in the Arab world. Such calls had existed for years in Yemen, accompanied by open rebellion in large sections of the country. Instead, the impact of Tunisia and Egypt was how they initially helped unite what had previously been disparate sources of opposition in Yemen, while pacifying voices calling for violence. President Salih's regime was certainly in no less jeopardy due to the demonstration effects of Tunisia and Egypt. But at least the voices of opposition in the country no longer called for armed conflict and the dissolution of Yemeni national unity. Most supporters of the southern movement briefly stopped waving the flag of the former PDRY. South Yemenis embraced the slogans heard on the streets of Tunis and Cairo, joining other Yemenis in northern provinces to chant *al-sha'ab yurid isqat al-nitham* ("the people want the downfall of the regime") and *Irhal!* ("Leave!"). Likewise, supporters of the Huthi rebellion joined street protesters to overthrow Salih by peaceful means.

In short, the influence of shared perceptions of what happened in Tunisia and Egypt had a positive effect on Yemen. Much like the 1952 Egyptian revolution, and its follow-on effect in the Yemeni revolutions of the 1960s, the 2011 events in Cairo served as a rallying point for the Yemeni people. Whereas it had appeared in 2009 and 2010 that Yemen was spinning out of control, perhaps splintering into several fragmented states, there seemed a genuine chance for Yemenis in all parts of the country to reformulate their national union on mutually beneficial terms. It did not help matters when the uprising in Libya turned violent in late February and early March 2011. It also did not help when, in late March, King Hamad of Bahrain invited GCC forces from neighboring Saudi Arabia to stamp out the popular uprising in his island state. The change of momentum from the more inspiring and hopeful events in Tunisia and Egypt on the one hand, to the more cynical events in Libya and Bahrain on the other hand, led Salih to conclude mistakenly that he, too, might be able to repress protesters in the streets, and survive as Yemen's ruler.

Once it became clear in May 2011 that there was no alternative to President Salih's stepping down, and putting in place plans for a political transition to a new government, there certainly remained questions about the durability of Yemen's national union. Given developments in preceding years, Yemeni unity and peace were by no means guaranteed. The possibility that Libya's popular uprising could cause the political division of its territory, especially after American and NATO military intervention in the summer raised the same possibility in Yemen. For centuries, the territory of Yemen had been ruled by multiple authorities prior to its modern unification in 1990. This unification was a highly troubled process, and ever since there have been concerns about the health of Yemeni unity.

This book recounts the politics of Yemeni unity by highlighting the regionally fragmented character of the country. I have long considered Yemen's multiple regional divisions to be the most important factor explaining its twists and turns, ups and downs, over the past two decades. These divisions are the main reason why it is mistaken to read Yemeni participation in the 2011 Arab "democratic spring" as a simple follow-on effect of what happened in Tunisia and Egypt. Given that Yemeni protesters rallied around a common national cause, after experiencing separate regional rebellions for several years, the country's multiple internal divisions were certainly a formative element of its politics. And they will continue to be one of the most important factors determining the future direction of Yemeni statehood.

It is possible to analyze the politics of Yemen in terms other than these. For example, one might focus on the misrule of President Salih, and the corruption surrounding his regime, as important causes behind the country's recent political crisis. Or one could focus on the mounting problems of poverty and underdevelopment in this poorest of Arab countries; or perhaps the spread of conservative Islamist sentiments, and the disruptive effects of terrorist attacks by Yemeni al-Qaeda. Other writers have adopted these approaches. But when it comes to explaining Yemen's internal political dynamics, I find that these approaches are less fruitful than an analysis of the country's multiple regional divisions. I am not convinced that President Salih and his family are alone to blame for the country's failures. This is because the regionally configured structure of power inside Yemen will outlive Salih's rule, and likely continue to plague the country's political and economic development. I also think that the problem of al-Qaeda in Yemen is exaggerated since its activities are minor compared to other major political, social, cultural, and economic forces.

Following the dramatic changes in 2011, there is no question that political reform and economic development are urgent matters in Yemen. Ending the networks of corruption, reducing the influence of al-Qaeda, and alleviating shocking levels of poverty, malnutrition, and illiteracy, must all be part of the country's future agenda. Each of these points is addressed in sections of this book. But the book's main purpose is to understand the politics of a population regionally fragmented along multiple lines, quite unlike the north-south division formerly associated with the country. Yemen's multiple regional divisions played an important role in its unification. They shaped the negotiation of national unity leading up to the official ceremony on May 22, 1990. Then in 1993, they fomented conflicts resulting in civil war in 1994; in the late 1990s, they temporarily helped President Salih consolidate his power over the country; and finally during the 2000s, they greatly contributed to Yemen's near failure as a nation-state.

The significance of these multiple regional divisions was generally overlooked by writers who analyzed the newly unified Yemen in the 1990s. After the achievement of national unification, it was understandable that writers describing the country's politics at the end of the millennium would downplay divisions inside the country. National unity had long been a cherished aim of both governments in north and south Yemen, and the new unionist leadership wanted to stress solidarity among its people. But the fact is that Yemeni unity was plagued by internal divisions from 1990 onward. After the brief civil war in 1994, leading Western scholars disagreed on whether northern or southern leaders were ultimately responsible for the breakdown in unity. Unsurprisingly, their scholarly positions matched their previous areas of specialization on one or the other side of the old border. The American political scientist Robert Burrowes and British anthropologist Paul Dresch, both highly respected scholars of north Yemen, accepted the arguments of north Yemenis who blamed the civil war on the southern leadership of the Yemeni Socialist Party (YSP).[1] Meanwhile, the best known scholar of south Yemen, the late British political scientist Fred Halliday, accepted the arguments of southern YSP officials who blamed the civil war on President Salih, his northern ruling party, and Islamist coalition partners.[2]

I began my field research in Yemen one year after the new union's 1994 civil war. Unlike the previous generation of scholars who tended to focus their field research on one side of the old border, I was fortunate to travel freely in northern and southern regions of the country. This allowed me to formulate my views of Yemen without bias toward one side of a long-standing political contest. What immediately impressed me about the country, as I travelled from one end of its remarkable landscape to the other, was the multiple regional divisions among its people. I found these divisions to be far more significant than the relatively superficial north-south boundary drawn by the British and Ottoman empires in the early 1900s, decades before the middle-twentieth-century Cold War. As I discovered, Yemen's multiple divisions are the key to understanding its politics. Yet the earlier generation of scholars had, for a variety of reasons, downplayed their significance.

[1] Burrowes, 1995(a) and 1995(b); and Dresch, 2000.
[2] Halliday, 1995.

My purpose in unravelling the regional dynamics of Yemen's domestic politics is to offer new perspective on the troubles of its unification in the 1990s, while also analyzing developments in the 2000s, culminating in the events of 2011, which are not found in earlier political studies. Conventional wisdom in the 1990s presumed that Yemen was truly one nation, and that its people represented a unified national body. During my first visit in 1995, I was struck by the opposite: namely, what makes people from different regions distinct from one another, as opposed to the same. One of the most significant aspects of Yemen's multiple regional divisions is how they inform political, social, and cultural viewpoints among the population in varied and complex ways. To speak of one common Yemeni viewpoint is to misunderstand the citizens of this fascinating, enigmatic land.

The land of Yemen and its people are barely comprehensible for two reasons. First, the country's convoluted three millennia-long history holds great relevance in the lives of its citizens. This history is a keystone for anyone wanting to make sense of what happens inside the country today. Second, the country's multiple internal divisions create competing interpretations of Yemeni history, both ancient and contemporary. Thus, today one must attempt to make sense of events based on multiple competing narratives. It is fair to say that the majority of Yemenis lack a good, general understanding of their own country. Instead, they have a particular understanding defined by the location from which they speak, and from which their ancestors lived. If Yemenis have difficulty grasping the wider political meanings of their country, then the task for outsiders is hardly any easier.

Few American, Canadian, and British citizens travel to Yemen. The majority who visit rarely make the effort to go beyond the capital Sanaa and its immediate surroundings, while perhaps visiting Aden or the city of Taiz located between Sanaa and Aden. The city of Sanaa creates a strong first impression because of its majestic appearance on a broad plain between two mountain peaks more than a mile high. It is relatively easy to tour the capital, and visit towns and villages in the surrounding valleys and mountains of the Yemeni highlands. But in order to comprehend Yemen's more complex realities, it is necessary to venture far from Sanaa and meet people from regions along the coasts, in the central desert, and inside a fascinating canyon in the eastern province of Hadramaut. It helps to read local histories about these regions, but most of these histories are only available in Arabic.

PHOTO 1. Sanaa's "Old City" framed by Mount Nugum

One of the best contemporary English-language writers on Yemen is the British author Tim Mackintosh-Smith who spent decades, beginning in the 1980s, gaining familiarity with the land and its people. In 1997, Mackintosh-Smith published his first book *Yemen: Travels in Dictionary Land*.[3] He modeled his work after the chronicles of the 10th century Yemeni historian, al-Hasan ibn Ahmed al-Hamdani, as well as the medieval travelogues of Ibn al-Mujawar. The original subtitle of Mackintosh-Smith's work is taken from a passage of a book written by the late blind poet, Abdullah al-Baradduni, entitled "The Popular Literary Arts of Yemen."

Poetry and literature are central to Yemeni culture. The poet's pen is often the most influential factor in defining social and political realities. Al-Baradduni lived through both revolutions in north and south Yemen during the 1960s, and the national unity process in the 1990s. He passed away in 1999, and now is remembered as one of the country's greatest poets, writers, and political commentators. Mackintosh-Smith opens his book with a quote from al-Baradduni's work:

Our land is the dictionary of our people – this land of far horizons where the graves of our ancestors sleep, this earth downtrodden by processions of sons and sons of sons.

---

[3] Mackintosh-Smith, 1997.

If Yemen's landscape is the dictionary that gives meaning to its people, then it is nearly impossible to define a single identity for Yemenis. The country's topography defies the imagination of anyone envisioning a plain desert landscape.

Along Yemen's western coast, there is a rugged, nearly impassable chain of mountains rising above twelve thousand feet. These breathtakingly beautiful mountains capture ample rains pouring into the country from storms off the Red Sea to the west and the Arabian Sea to the southeast. On rare occasions, they even collect snow during winter months. As a result, Yemen has abundant agriculture in its western mountains and valleys. Ancient terraced farmland rests on top of lava flows, which are capable of producing three crops per year. In the southwest, there are tropical forests where a breed of leopard unique to Arabia once roamed. There are vast desert sands in the central interior region. Its eastern edge forms the mouth of Hadramaut's canyon system. Each of these regions has unique characteristics which, over the centuries, preserved political and cultural diversity inside the country.

Early in Tim Mackintosh-Smith's book, he explains some early advice he received about the use of a specific dictionary for classical Arabic. The spoken dialect in Yemen is close to the classical language used during the

PHOTO 2. Mountain stream in al-Udayn, Ibb region of leopard

lifetime of Islam's prophet. A teacher once recommended that Mackintosh-Smith purchase a dictionary, in which he would find "every Arabic word means itself, its opposite or a camel." Inside Yemen, the same oppositional and quizzical meanings apply to the character of the country's politics and culture, where local trivia about camels and other oddities often make more sense. When the ancient Romans marked Yemen on their maps, they called it "Arabia Felix," or Happy Arabia. In the Roman mind, Yemen stood in contrast to the harsh desert parts of the Arabian peninsula to the north and east. Today, life in most areas of Yemen is harsher and angrier than the oil-rich desert lands of Saudi Arabia, Kuwait, the United Arab Emirates, and Qatar. But it is hardly devoid of happiness. Increasingly, the pleasures of life in Yemen are mixed with deep frustrations.

Yemen's political culture was not always associated with religious extremism. Before the era of al-Qaeda, the violence of militant groups in Lebanon and Egypt, during the 1970s and 1980s, was virtually unknown in Yemen. If foreigners were kidnapped in Yemen, they were rarely held for a long, isolated captivity. A kidnapping meant great adventure entangled in relatively tame quarrels between tribes and the government in Sanaa. The kidnappers typically ransomed foreign captives for public works projects, such as a water well or a new school building for their town or village. This is the traditional means of conducting politics in Yemen. As soon as the politicians in Sanaa pledged to provide government assistance, the foreign hostages would be released. During a short captivity, the foreigners usually enjoyed a great experience with the best food and local entertainment available. This tradition continued until the late 1990s.

On one research trip to the country in the late 1990s, I learned about a group of French tourists held captive by local tribesmen. Upon the release of seven or eight tourists, the Yemeni government sponsored a farewell ceremony at Sanaa's airport. On local television news, reporters interviewed the French citizens before they boarded their aircraft. One young woman in her late twenties looked directly into the camera, with a blushed glow on her face, as she recalled moments from their captivity. She recounted the group's excitement when the kidnappers feted and cared for them in a remote village, treating them like visiting royalty. Each day they ate fresh lamb with fruits and vegetables. In the evening, they listened to live music performed by men with drums and lutes. Before she turned to enter the door of the plane, the young woman nearly squealed with delight: "The kidnapping experience was our best time in the country. We highly recommend for tourists coming to Yemen: Try to get kidnapped!"

This was the typical reaction of foreign travelers to Yemen before the 2000s. There was nothing exceptional about it, since this was Arabia Felix, an enigmatic country with puzzling customs and means to resolve political conflict. The standard approach to settling a dispute in Yemen is, for lack of a better parallel in Western culture, close to the stories told by Mark Twain in his classic novel *Tom Sawyer*. On this topic, Harvard anthropologist Steven Caton produced the best descriptive material in a book entitled *Yemen Chronicle: An Anthropology of War and Mediation*.[4] Yemenis approach political disputes much like tradesmen in a marketplace who haggle over prices before reaching a suitable compromise. If one resorts to anger and violence too quickly, then it is a matter of losing honor and respect between disputants. Disputants tend to pursue clever, confounding means to attain their goals. The more clever and confounding the means, the greater one's reputation as a person of influence.

Yemenis are prone to disputation and argument. Once in 1997, when NASA successfully landed the Pathfinder vehicle on Mars, using remote control to operate a small rover called Sojourner to explore the Martian surface, three men in Sanaa filed a court action against the U.S. government. The men claimed that their ancestors first established rightful ownership of Mars more than three thousand years ago. Since then, the red planet had been in the possession of their tribe. According to a CNN report, the legal charge filed in Sanaa stated "Sojourner and Pathfinder, which are owned by the United States government, landed on Mars and began exploring it without informing us or seeking our approval."[5] The court papers demanded that United States "refrain from disclosing any information pertaining to Mars' atmosphere, surface or gravity before receiving approval from (us), or until a verdict is reached." By resorting to action in the courts, not violent warfare against America, the disputants showed great honor. The response from NASA officials was good-humored, so the Yemeni tribesmen felt no need to declare *jihad* and resort to arms! They had at least made known to U.S. authorities the prestige of their ancestors' territorial claim.

By custom, Yemenis admire artful compromise in politics. They are not customarily prone to fanaticism and extremism. For this reason, it is worth studying Yemeni history, culture, and politics, in order to know how best

---

[4] Caton, 2005. Steven Caton tells the preceding story of the French tourists, as well as the following story about Yemeni tribes contesting NASA's right to explore the surface of Mars during the Pathfinder mission in 1997.

[5] "3 Yemenis Sue NASA for Trespassing on Mars," *CNN*, July 24, 1997.

to deal with pressing problems in the country. What one learns is unexpected. During the last six odd decades, there has been an intense political struggle between at least four contestants for power in different regions of the country: the traditionalist (or tribalist), the Islamist, the Arabist, and the socialist. The character of this political struggle varied across time, and in different regions of the country, as the configuration of contestants altered from year to year, and place to place. For decades, Yemenis have engaged in complex pluralist politics shaped significantly by their regional identifications. This book seeks to explain political and ideological variations between contestants from different regions of the country, in order to account for the land's current predicament. The reason why Yemen risked state failure in the late 2000s, and the possible unravelling of its national unity, has more to do with its inherent complexity and unruliness than anything else.

While my own travels to Yemen have been shorter than scholars such as Tim Mackintosh-Smith, and anthropologists such as Harvard University's Steven Caton or Oxford University's Paul Dresch, their works focus primarily on just one region of the country. This is the Yemeni highland region, known as the homeland of two dominant tribal federations, called Hashid and Bakil, which are the target of research by Dresch and Caton. During my few trips to the country, I ventured outside the highlands to become familiar with all regions of the country. In fact, I made an effort to spend equivalent amounts of time in the north and south, east and west, in order to avoid forming a bias toward any particular interpretation of Yemeni culture and politics. I sought to understand the diversity of Yemen's political, social, and cultural life. In this book, I do not identify a singular Yemen. Instead I highlight the plurality of Yemeni characters and identities in seven different regions. These seven regions, and the distinctions between them, are defined more precisely in Chapter 1.

The book's general approach fits within a framework of research about nation-building processes, analyzing the roles played by political elites and institutions, political economy and culture, in defining the nation-state. The book explains the achievements and pitfalls of Yemeni unity by examining the development of its national institutions, both before and after unification in 1990, while also investigating the distribution of various political and economic resources, as well as the actions of politicians from different regions. The significance of political economy and resource distribution is their crucial role in the definition and perpetuation of regional divisions among Yemen's population. Anthropologists have long considered resource competition to be one of the primary causes of group identities, since these identities are always constructed on a social basis. In the middle twentieth century, the Norwegian-American anthropologist Fredrik Barth showed that increased competition over economic resources heightens sentiments of intragroup solidarity, while sharpening intergroup distinctions expressed along cultural lines through language, art, dress, and other customs.[6]

To follow Yemeni politics before and after 1990, especially concerning the formation of national versus regional identities in the country, it is essential to track the contest over key resources, such as state revenues and appointments to high political office, which give politicians and their associates access to state revenues. The book traces the distribution of various resources among political elites from different regions of the country. It is hypothesized that the balance vs. imbalance of resource distribution is what strengthens, respectively, national vs. regional identities among the population. The more imbalance is perceived in the distribution of resources, the more likely regional identities will be strengthened in opposition to a common Yemeni national identity.

In this study of Yemen's national union, I accept the definition of national identity used by Benedict Anderson in his pathbreaking 1993 book, *Imagined Communities: Reflections on the Origin and Spread of Nationalism.*[7] Namely, the national union of the Yemeni people is only an imagined social construct. Its preservation in the face of multiple regional divisions depends on the skillful management of competition over economic and political resources. As long as Yemen's political elites fail to temper this competition, working toward a fair and equitable distribution of resources, then the ability of its people to imagine a common national identity will falter. In other words, Yemen's national union is not a given, natural state to which the country's population returned in 1990. It is rather an ongoing social and political project which requires proper management and guidance to encourage the necessary loyalties and commitments on the part of the population. Without effective management and guidance, the country's population is more likely to revert to its past fragmented state, as groups of people in different regions find themselves in sharper competition.

In light of the mass uprisings inside Yemen in 2011, it is critical to consider the impact of the population's demand to remove a leader who failed to properly manage and guide the country. In her 2008 book,

[6] Barth, 1969.
[7] Anderson, 1993.

Peripheral Visions: Publics, Power, and Performance in Yemen, Lisa Wedeen wrote about the unifying effect of public resentments toward the failing government.[8] While the population had become frustrated and even despondent over official corruption and ineptitude, rebelling against the national leadership, such widespread criticism of the government could possibly build new political solidarities because, Wedeen hypothesized, nearly everyone shared the same hardship. There is typically a fear that the breakdown of public order in places like Yemen, combined with a loss of public trust, will lead to state failure, potential social anarchy, and a spiraling humanitarian crisis. Wedeen's exploration of Yemen's vibrant civil society, and active networks of nongovernment actors, hints at reasons for hope about the country's ability to find a peaceful, democratic solution to its current impasse.

Beginning in the early 1990s, when Somalia, the former Yugoslavia, and other countries like Afghanistan, Sierra Leone, Liberia, Haiti, Rwanda, and Zaire, became synonymous with "state failure," scholars compiled a vast literature on this topic. A decade later, when al-Qaeda terrorists struck New York and Washington, some began to associate the problem of "state failure" with the rise of international terrorism, pointing to Afghanistan and Somalia as prime examples.[9] In the wake of 9/11, the failure of state systems was considered by some a barometer for the spread of terrorism, domestically and internationally. This certainly became true of most American analyses of Yemen after 2009, when the failure of the Yemeni state was widely equated with al-Qaeda's rise. As a result, U.S. government policy was driven by a desire to prop up the Yemeni state under President Salih's leadership. This led to serious drawbacks in 2011, when masses of protesters took to the streets demanding Salih's removal from office.

The easy association between "state failure" and the threat of al-Qaeda is especially problematic in a country like Yemen, where foreign advisors might advocate an aggressive policy to shore up a failing state and confront the problem of terrorism. As witnessed in Iraq after 2003, an aggressive American military intervention is likely to incite terrorism, while undermining the stability of a state. It is important to bear in mind one of the central findings of the book *Dying to Win*, Robert Pape's seminal 2005 terrorism study.[10] Pape analyzed the growing phenomenon of suicide

---

[8] Wedeen, 2008; pp. 62–69.
[9] Rotberg, 2003; and Hoffman, 2006.
[10] Pape, 2005.

terrorism by investigating multiple cases around the world. His data clearly showed a correlation between foreign military interventions and occupations on the one hand, and the desperate decision by individuals to adopt terrorist methods, in their most radical form, on the other hand. This holds cautionary lessons for statesmen contemplating large scale foreign intervention, especially Western intervention, in a country like Yemen. Afterwards, the country would certainly become less stable and more prone to terrorism.

I remain hopeful about the peaceful, democratic aspirations of the Yemeni people, similar to Lisa Wedeen, and another American scholar who writes more extensively about Yemeni civil society, Sheila Carapico.[11] Unlike Wedeen and Carapico's focus on Yemen's informal democratic politics (what Wedeen refers to as "quotidian practices of deliberation"), my work places equal emphasis on the country's formal and informal politics. My research findings suggest that if Yemen is truly to overcome its current difficulties, then it must drastically improve the functioning of its formal democratic institutions. Perhaps it must revise them entirely along the lines of federal democracy where a coalition of rulers share powers distributed among different regional groups. Yemenis share many things in common – things that make them unique in the Arab world, especially concerning their informal politics, customs, and practices. Their "pride of place" next to Saudis and Emiratis, Sudanese and Egyptians, is a strength that should be utilized for the purpose of building stronger national solidarity. But this is unlikely to happen if there is a return to the same flawed formal politics of the past.

The book's main thesis is that the government of united Yemen became an illegitimate form of internal control exercised by President Ali Abdallah Salih and his closest associates from the northwest highland region surrounding the capital Sanaa. President Salih maintained power by forming patron-client relationships with various groups in other regions of the country. But these relationships were exploitive, and generally unhelpful to Yemen's national development, because the president and his associates preferred to play games of divide-and-rule with regional clients. Instead of investing in healthy mutual alliances to grow the national economy, and bring more benefits to the general population, Salih and his ruling group contributed to an enormous waste of resources in the country.

---

[11] Carapico, 1998.

As I finish this Introduction in the summer of 2011, more than a month after President Salih's medical evacuation from Yemen when he and several members of his inner circle were severely injured in a bombing, it is impossible to grasp the full meaning of the country's ongoing political transformation. What is the likelihood of complete state failure and the end of Yemen national unity, on the one hand, versus a political rebirth and renewal of national solidarity, on the other hand? One cannot approach any short term meaning of events in 2011, let alone predict their long-term implications, without first comprehending the significance of Yemen's multiple regional divisions. This is what the book aims to accomplish by proposing a new framework for understanding the first two decades of Yemeni national unity, and suggesting where the union might head in the future. The first six chapters of the book are based primarily on my doctoral dissertation research at Georgetown University in 2001. I conducted this research in two phases: first, over two years in 1995–1997; and second, on a shorter trip of three months in late 1998. After completing my doctoral degree, I made two brief trips to Yemen in the summers of 2002 and 2005.

My earliest research looked at the relationship between the central government in Sanaa and its local administrative branches at provincial and district levels around the country. The centerpiece of this research was a survey of local administrators holding more than twenty government posts in each province of the country between 1985 and 1997.[12] Thus the timeframe of the survey overlapped the country's unification in 1990. In designing this survey, I was interested in discovering any patterns in the appointment of local government officials before and after unification, in order to identify if Yemenis from one or more regions of the country were overrepresented in public administration at local and provincial levels. As part of my doctoral research, I also conducted hundreds of interviews with local and provincial officials, while collecting government reports about financial and other data. In total, I visited eleven of Yemen's then eighteen local administrative units, and gained assistance from Yemen's ministry of local administration to contact officers in the remaining seven units. During follow-up research trips in 2002 and 2005, I focused on broader political developments in the country, especially the stronger political opposition and, in the mid-2000s, popular rebellions spreading across the country. By late 2007 and early 2008, it was clear that the Yemeni government had entered a full-blown national crisis.

---

[12] The survey methodology is described in more detail in the Appendix of the book.

To fully understand Yemeni politics, it is essential to consider four factors beyond the country's multiple regional divisions: first, the history of the Yemeni people, and the traditional make-up of their cultures and societies; second, the power structure of President Ali Abdullah Salih's regime, especially the dominant status of his northwest highland group, and the system of patronage that he employed; third, the flawed process of uniting Yemen's northern and southern halves in the 1990s; and fourth, the policies of the Yemeni government during the 2000s, especially their political economy, halting steps toward decentralization, and the regime's record on human rights. These four factors are addressed sequentially in the book, with the first two appearing in Chapters 1 through 3. Chapter 1 presents a brief historical summary of Yemen from ancient to modern times, including the twin revolutions in the 1960s that led to the formation of two rival independent republics. Chapter 2 compares and contrasts the political, economic, and cultural makeup of these postrevolutionary regimes during the 1970s and 1980s. Chapter 3 offers further analysis of President Salih's rule, especially concerning the influence of his Hashid tribe. After unification in 1990, members of Hashid dominated politics in the entire country. Thus, before discussing Yemen's national unity, it is necessary to understand the function of this tribal group.

The next set of three chapters deals with the politics of national unity in the new Republic of Yemen's first decade. Chapter 4 analyzes the troubled unification process in 1990 and the years that followed, including the first national parliamentary election in 1993. Chapter 5 analyzes the causes and immediate consequences of the country's brief civil war in 1994, exactly one year after the first multiparty election. This era is key for understanding the multiple regional dynamics currently at work among the population. Chapter 6 then examines the period in the late 1990s when President Salih claimed to stabilize the country's politics, and consolidate his rule of the united territory.

The final set of three chapters concerns developments during the decade of the 2000s. Chapter 7 covers events in Yemen before and after the 9/11 attacks on America, including al-Qaeda's bombing of the USS *Cole* in Aden harbor in October 2000. Once President Salih aligned himself with the Bush administration in the fall of 2001, voices of popular rebellion arose inside the country, especially around the time of the U.S. invasion of Iraq in 2003. Chapter 8 explains the dangerous regional fragmentation of Yemen in the middle 2000s, when the central government began losing control of territory, and Yemeni al-Qaeda became more active. Chapter 9 analyzes critical domestic issues in the late 2000s, leading to the end of

President Salih's rule in 2011. The book's Conclusion makes a final statement on the role of Yemeni regionalism in the popular rebellion that brought down Salih's regime, while speculating on what the future might hold for the Yemeni people.

My hope in writing this book is that it may be used not only by readers interested in modern Yemen, and the rebellions of 2011, as an academic subject in the fields of Middle East comparative history and politics but also by readers interested in American or Western foreign policy in this critically important region of the world. Too often, foreign policies in the Middle East are designed and implemented without a sound understanding of domestic politics in the region. This was particularly true of the era associated with America's "war on terrorism," first conceived by the George W. Bush administration, and later adopted under different terminology by Barack Obama's administration. Similar to the policies of the U.S. government in Iraq, as well as the Afghan-Pakistan region, American decision makers have been too quick to apply military means against perceived threats in Yemen, mainly by using cruise missiles and drone-fired missiles. This frequently led to civilian casualties that aggravated conditions on the ground, while provoking anti-American sentiments among the population.

The national unification of Yemen brought hope to the vast majority of its citizens. In 1990, most Yemenis looked forward to a brighter future in a new, larger republic founded on pluralist democratic principles with constitutional guarantees of human rights and civil liberties. Two decades later, the country's national union had imploded under the pressure of its rival parts. On May 22, 2010, Yemen observed the twentieth anniversary of its national unity at a time of widespread civil unrest. In the preceding year, more than half of its provinces had witnessed organized violence against the government. At the 2010 anniversary ceremony, President Ali Abdallah Salih praised the benefits of unity, while putting his best spin on events of the last year. "Unity has restored the dignity, strength, and pride of the Yemeni people," he stated, "closing down forever separation and division."[13] In reality, Yemenis were more divided than ever. The divisions and violence in the country were as bad as, if not worse than, the period leading to its civil war in 1994.

In 1991, just one year after the unification of north and south Yemen, a local historian named Abdallah Ahmad Mahairez wrote a cautionary

---

[13] "President Calls for Carrying Out National Dialogue," *26 September Net*, Sanaa, Yemen, May 21, 2010.

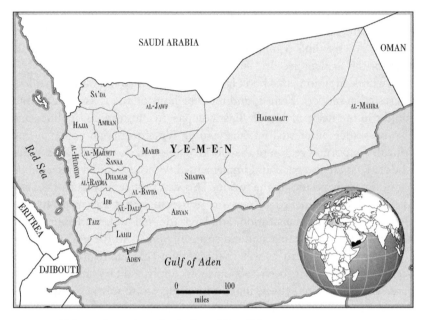

MAP 1. Cities and provinces in the Republic of Yemen, 2011

essay on interpreting political events in the lives of his countrymen. He published the article in one of the new publications that sprang up in a more pluralist environment in the early 1990s, using the title "Can a Generation Write Its Own Modern History?"[14] Mahairez's question was primarily intended for his colleagues, historians and scholars, who previously wrote about events in both halves of the formerly divided country. He recounted numerous instances in Yemeni history, when political, social, and cultural events were recorded from the perspective of one ruling group's short-term interests. After the ruler's fall from power, the same events would be recast in a different light to serve the succeeding ruler's interests.

Abdallah Mahairez intended to show that Yemen had never had a unitary history that could be portrayed from one perspective alone. In an indirect way, he was urging his fellow citizens to think carefully about the way future momentous events would be portrayed by particular ruling interests. He had the foresight to understand that, in the approaching years, there would be contests for power, creating winners and losers in

[14] Mahairez, 1991.

Yemen. Later, after 1994, national unionists from eastern and southwestern regions of the country were recast as "secessionist" villains. Meanwhile, some conservative tribal and religious elements from northwestern highland areas, who actually opposed national unification in 1990 and lobbied against the unity constitution, were relabeled "patriots" and saviors of the national union. From the beginning, Mahairez tried to alert his readers to the ways that united Yemen's history would be interpreted during the late twentieth and early twenty-first centuries.

In this land that British author Tim Mackintosh-Smith calls "Dictionary Land," where everything can mean itself, its opposite, or some unrelated local trivia, Mahairez deeply understood the whimsical nature of political realities in Yemen. This is a land with a long history of rising and falling dynasties, all of which associated their own temporary rule with the destiny of the nation. Each ruling dynasty interpreted Yemeni history through a narrow lens, based on a particular orientation to its regional location in the country. During some eras, one dynasty might have briefly expanded beyond a single region. But Yemen always reverted back to its fragmented form with rival leaders possessing rival interpretations of politics and history. Could President Salih's rule be any different from the past? Was Salih's 2010 conception of Yemeni unity, "closing down forever separation and division," an accurate description of events across the preceding twenty years? Was his vision a fair portrayal of what the future held for this spectacular land on the Arabian peninsula?

In reality, after 1990, President Salih never exercised complete governing authority in the country. The 1994 civil war fractured the nation, and afterward the president and members of his family sought control over southern and eastern provinces by military means. Local residents of these provinces objected to the presence of northern military and security troops. This generated various forms of popular resistance in the 2000s, which undermined the authority of the regime in Sanaa. Even inside the boundaries of the former north Yemen, President Salih's authority was challenged in areas of the highland mountains populated by Hashid and Bakil tribes. The political realities of Yemen mean this land is, and always has been, difficult to unite under a common ruling system acceptable to all members of society. Across the span of three thousand years, the territory of Yemen has more often been fragmented into separate regions, each with its own ruling authority.

I

Understanding the Regional Divisions of Yemen

In 1990 the Yemeni people achieved national unification when leaders from the north and south agreed to merge, creating the Republic of Yemen. The negotiation of Yemeni unity in 1989 coincided with German unification at the end of the Cold War. Contrary to common thinking at the time, Yemen's original territorial division was never part of Cold War politics. Unlike the twentieth-century political divide in Germany, as well as Korea and Vietnam, Yemen's division preceded the superpower rivalries of the late 1940s and early 1950s. In fact, regional divisions on the southwest corner of the Arabian peninsula extend centuries back in time. Across history, territorial unity in Yemen is the exception rather than the rule.

Yemen's north-south boundary line was drawn by cartographers and surveyors sent from the imperial capitals of London and Istanbul in the first decade of the twentieth century.[1] Yet neither the British nor the Ottoman Empire exercised uniform power on its side of the border. This was true both before and after the early 1900s. It was also true during earlier centuries when Yemeni rulers governed prior to the arrival of British and Ottoman forces. There is a long legacy of divided rule in Yemen, since multiple authorities exercised power in small regions of the country separated by vast mountains, canyons, and desert sands. In the nineteenth and early twentieth centuries, the British signed treaties with more than twenty separate sultans and emirs who ruled areas of varying size in the south. The country's rugged terrain, especially in the northwest mountains, gives Yemen a reputation as a difficult place to govern. Similar

[1] According to some reports, the border was first drawn between 1902 and 1904. Gause, 1987; p. 58. But the border was not adopted until 1914, when it was formally ratified as a treaty. Nagi, 1984; p. 256.

to the people of Afghanistan, Yemenis speak of their homeland as the "graveyard of empires."

Yemen's modern north-south division did not become mired in Cold War politics until the late 1960s. It was only at this time that the Soviet Union developed a sphere of influence in south Yemen, following the British withdrawal in late 1967. Meanwhile Saudi Arabia and its western allies sought to maintain a sphere of influence in the north. East-West superpower rivalries did help prolong the north-south division. Once the Cold War ended, the leaders of north and south Yemen sought to overcome their differences by making a transition to pluralist democratic rule. But the experiment with free and open multiparty elections failed in the early 1990s, resulting in civil war, social and economic underdevelopment, and escalating conflict.

To make sense of conditions on the ground in Yemen today, it is crucial to understand the combustible dynamics of unification in the early 1990s. Much of the country's current unrest and radicalism can be traced back to this period of time. But before considering the troubles of national unity in the 1990s, it is necessary to grasp the political, social, cultural, and economic significance of divisions in earlier history. Prior to 1990, Yemen never had a unified national culture. Stretching back more than three thousand years, there has rarely been unified rule in Yemen. This is a traditional Arab tribal land, where ruling systems were defined by separate lineage groups exercising control over different regions of the country. It was only after modern transportation and communication became available in the 1950s and 1960s that one could speak of the emergence of a national consciousness. Before the modern era, Yemenis were largely cut off from each other because of the land's unusual topography.

In pre-Islamic times, there were at least two rival civilizations in southern Arabia, and sometimes as many as four: one at the interior desert's western edge in Marib; a second in the northwestern mountains near Sanaa and Dhamar; a third close to the western Red Sea coast; and a fourth near the eastern canyon system of Hadramaut. Across more than fifteen centuries overlapping the start of our common era, a string of Yemeni civilizations known as *Saba* (in common English usage, "Sheba"), *Ma'in* (whose people are known as the "Minaeans") *Qataban, Raybun, Thamud, Himyar,* and *Hadramaut* existed. The wealth generated by *Saba, Ma'in, Himyar,* and *Hadramaut* from gold, frankincense, myrrh, and spices was legendary in ancient civilizations of Egypt, Israel, Greece, Persia, Ethiopia, and Rome between 1000 B.C.E.

and 500 C.E. Tales of the Queen of Sheba and her romance with King Solomon are included in the Hebraic record and Christian Old Testament.[2]

During the third century C.E., the Christians of Axum invaded western Yemen from African territory in today's Ethiopia, spreading their religion and expanding trade. During Axum's rule, churches were built including one in the mountains at Sanaa. Many Yemenis adopted Christianity until a local *Himyari* nobleman named Yusuf Dhu Nuwas, a convert to Judaism, fought the Axumites, and expelled them around 518 C.E.[3] Afterward Judaism became the state religion of Yemen, and more locals became Jews until Islam's arrival in the seventh century C.E. At this time, the majority of the population accepted the new monotheistic faith, since it was revealed in their native Arabic. A minority of Jews continued living in the country until the twentieth century. Today only a few Jews remain after mass migrations to Israel in 1949 and 1950.

Before the rise of Islam, the Sassanid empire of Persia briefly established a presence in Yemen. But the Yemeni people remained firmly in the Arab tradition, including its Jewish population. Among the ancient kingdoms of Yemen, there were constant rivalries among local rulers who sought to absorb the lands and markets of their neighbors. Sometimes two or more kingdoms formed an alliance to fight another in battle. They occasionally managed to unify territory, as *Himyari* leaders did briefly by controlling the Red Sea and Gulf of Aden coastlines. But local monarchs were inevitably forced to retreat because of the difficulty holding such rough terrain for more than a few decades.

The geography of Yemen is not like the land of other great Middle Eastern states famous for extended government stability, such as the Nile River valley that was governed by a long succession of pharaohs, or the lowlands of the ancient Sumerians and Babylonians, or even the high plateau of the ancient Persians. In ancient Egypt and Iraq, there were fertile plains around lengthy river systems that created an environment capable of

---

[2] According to local legends about the Queen of Sheba, there was more than a love relationship between the ruler of *Saba* and King Solomon in Jerusalem, because the two monarchies established trade relations. There is considerable archeological evidence that the queen played the dominant role in relationship to King Solomon because her realm was larger and wealthier. Clapp, 2002. If there are historical bases to the biblical legend, then the Queen of Sheba was clearly the one with the means to benefit from international trade, not Solomon who ruled a relatively small, inconsequential hilltop kingdom in the north.

[3] Muller, 1988; p. 52. After the Roman destruction of the second temple in Jerusalem in the late first century C.E., many Jews fled to Arabia, reaching as far south as Yemen. Thus Judaism was familiar to south Arabians before the time of Yusuf Dhu Nuwas.

sustaining large-scale centralized dynastic rule for centuries. This was decidedly not the case in Yemen. Throughout Yemeni history, its diverse terrain made it possible for small ruling groups to remain relatively isolated in different regions of the country, where group members developed distinct cultural traits. This was especially true of groups inhabiting the highlands in the northwest around today's capital, Sanaa. This area was largely cut off from the Red Sea coast to the west, and other lands to the east, by mountains. Prior to local advances in transportation in the middle twentieth century, the trip from Sanaa to the western coast meant an arduous ten-day journey by camel, traveling up and down dangerous mountain passes and ravines. Today the Yemeni national airline makes the same 130-mile trip in barely thirty minutes, essentially an airport takeoff, descent from the mountains, and landing at sea level.

The mild temperatures in Sanaa's mountains above ten thousand feet high (thirty-three hundred meters) are a stark contrast to the intense heat and humidity that suffocate the Red Sea and Gulf of Aden coasts to the west and south, respectively. The people of Yemen's coastal regions were always more open to the outside world than people of the highlands. In the midland mountains south of Sanaa around the cities of Taiz, Ibb, and al-Bayda, one finds the most fertile farmland in Yemen. The tropical green valleys of this midland region stand in complete contrast to the country's lifeless interior desert, which extends northward into the great *al-Rub al-Khali* (the vast "Empty Quarter" of Saudi Arabia). Moving east from Sanaa in the highlands, the land descends sharply to a desert floor at approximately three thousand feet above sea level. It is here that the ancient civilization of the Queen of Sheba built the great Marib dam to control seasonal rain-fed streams tumbling down mountain valleys in the highlands.

The people of Sheba used the Marib dam to create irrigated agriculture three thousand years ago. They famously made the edge of the Yemeni desert bloom with beautiful gardens until the dam burst centuries later. According to a local legend, a large mouse burrowed under the Marib dam, loosening its foundation and causing the dam to collapse in the late sixth century C.E., near the birth date of Islam's prophet, Muhammad. Both the gardens of Marib and the destruction of its dam are mentioned in the holy *Quran*. Muhammad referred to Marib as the center of an early higher civilization that was more advanced than the bedouin tribal regions around Mecca.

Yemen's interior desert lies west of the country's center line, so there are hundreds of miles of sand east of Marib, separating today's densely

PHOTO 3. Ancient Marib dam at the edge of interior desert

populated highland and western midland regions from the country's sparsely populated eastern half. The northern part of the central desert is relatively flat with hard bedrock near the surface. This makes travel easier at the edge of *al-Rub al-Khali* in Saudi Arabia, so cars and trucks passing through the desert typically turn slightly north to a point marked by a mountain called *al-'Abr*, located just inside the unmarked boundary. South of these flat desert sands, the terrain is shaped by sand dunes cresting more than ten meters high like giant waves on the ocean. These are the *Ramlat al-Sabatayn*, where walking or riding a camel, not to mention driving an automobile, is far more difficult. Yemen's eastern half is marked by yet another geographic feature that helps explain why its population existed separately for so many centuries. This is Hadramaut.

Wadi Hadramaut ("Hadramaut Valley") is the fertile green valley that exists inside a marvelous multicolored canyon system. The canyon runs east to west for 150 miles with several long branches stretching to the north and south.[4] The width of the main canyon varies between a quarter mile and twenty miles. Hadramaut once served as the center of ancient frankincense

---

[4] This part of Yemen is the birthplace of the late al-Qaeda leader Osama Bin Laden's father, Muhammad, who was born in the first decade of the twentieth century in Wadi Du'an, a southern branch of Hadramaut's main canyon. In the middle 1920s, Muhammad emigrated to Jiddah, Saudi Arabia, in search of work. He would become a multimillionaire building contractor and trusted advisor to King Abd al-Aziz. Coll, 2008; pp. 24–27. Osama

trading routes to Egypt and Syria, and then onto Europe. Four major cities are located along the length of the main canyon floor. One of these cities, Shibbam, is a protected world heritage site by the United Nations. This one-square-mile walled city with streets too narrow for automobile traffic is surrounded on two sides by sheer rock cliffs rising more than one thousand feet high. Above the canyon walls, which rise more than two thousand feet in the west near Yemen's interior desert, there is an arid plateau of sandstone and igneous rock called the *jawl*. The *jawl* stretches for one hundred miles in all directions with no observable life forms.

The branches of Hadramaut's main canyon originate in shallow ruts worn into the face of the *jawl* by seasonal rains and flash flooding. Its surface has an undulating, almost lunar appearance. This gives the landscape an ominous quality that no doubt protected Wadi Hadramaut from invaders. Foreign armies arriving at the southern coast had to march inland for days without access to water. Then, if they reached the edge of the canyon's sheer cliffs, they would die of thirst unless they knew hidden access points to reach the green valley floor. North of Wadi Hadramaut are the sands of *al-Rub al-Khali*. To the east, there is a good access point through Wadi al-Masila, where the canyon narrows and drops below a hundred feet. But it is far simpler to leave Wadi Hadramaut by this route than to find entryway without a guide.

The main access to the west of Wadi Hadramaut is easy to navigate because the mouth of the main canyon gapes open more than forty miles wide. But to reach this point one must first traverse the wave-like sands of *Ramlat al-Sabatayn*. The Arabic word Hadramaut means "the presence of death." Thus Wadi Hadramaut carries a meaning similar to California's "Death Valley." Yet the valley floor of Hadramaut's canyon has abundant agriculture and palm tree oases. Camels and goats graze in grass lands, and the air is filled with the sound of birds. This rich environment is possible because ground water exists barely ten meters down. The only thing life-forbidding about Wadi Hadramaut is the long trek in. For outsiders, the journey was always associated with great danger. This served the monopoly interests of ancient traders in frankincense who gladly encouraged frightful rumors to scare off potential invaders. Greeks and Romans consumed much of the frankincense shipped from Hadramaut by camel caravans. Once upon a time, Europeans believed fantastic tales about the highly prized frankincense growing in a land of fire-breathing dragons that could fly![5]

was born three decades later in Riyadh, Saudi Arabia to Alia Ghanem, one of Muhammad's younger wives from Syria. Coll, p. 74.

[5] Mackintosh-Smith, 1997; p. 37.

PHOTO 4. Saiyun, Hadramaut palace of former Sultan

In the ancient world, as well as the early Muslim world, Yemen's varie-gated geography left distinct local communities in place. Each community had its own unique interests, outlooks, and customs, which were upheld for centuries by multiple ruling lineages in southwest Arabia. More than any-thing else, the communities of this naturally beautiful land were character-ized by cultural and political diversity. Before unification in 1990, Yemen was never united in a national sense by the will of the people. The land was only united when a ruling dynasty in one region had the ability to forcibly extend its authority over people in other regions. When this occurred the unifying authority maintained a superficial presence in other regions, and usually for brief periods of time. Perhaps the only time a local ruler truly unified the land of Yemen, from the Red Sea to Hadramaut, was during the Qasimi dynasty of Zaydi imams in the mid-seventeenth century. Yet after a few decades, the imam's forces were thrown out of areas in the south and east due to popular rejection of the Zaydi government.[6]

REGIONALISM IN THE ISLAMIC ERA

By tradition, the name "Yemen" was adopted by people inside the country only during the Islamic era. The word itself is a geographic reference

[6] Stookey, 1978; pp. 146–147.

expressed from the vantage point of someone living in Mecca to the north. "*Al-Yaman*" is the way Islam's prophet Muhammad referred to the land on the "right side" of Mecca, when facing the holy city from the Red Sea coast in the west. The land of *al-Sham* (the traditional name for Greater Syria) is located north of Mecca, while *al-Yaman* is the land in the south. Muhammad spoke of the Yemeni people accepting the message of Islam earlier than the bedouin tribes of Mecca. He referred to Yemenis as a forthright, honest, and respectable people. Famous *hadith*, or sayings of the prophet passed down by his associates and later recorded by Islamic scholars such as Muhammad al-Bukhari in the ninth century C.E., record Muhammad saying "Faith is Yemeni, Wisdom is Yemeni." (In 2011, youthful protesters in Sanaa formed their "Change Square" around the base of an obelisk recording this saying.) Today this remains a source of great pride in the country.

The prophet Muhammad's trust in Yemen helped rally people of south Arabian lands behind a new common mission, but there continued to exist divisions inside the country. During the time of Muhammad and his early successors who ruled the caliphate in al-Medina, Yemen was divided into three geographic regions: 'Asir in the northwest, which included the south-western part of modern Saudi Arabia as well as the mountain highlands around Sanaa; al-Janad in the southwest, which included lands between Aden on the coast and the green valleys of Taiz and Ibb; and finally, the vast eastern region of Hadramaut. Each of these regions evolved in different ways during the Islamic era, adopting variations of Islamic customs and traditions in later centuries.

Early Muslim historians record Yemenis forming a large contingent of the Islamic armies during the middle and late seventh century C.E. So it is clear that the Yemeni people migrated in large numbers outside their homeland, helping to populate newly acquired lands of a rapidly expanding Islamic empire. For example, they helped spread the new faith to Egypt and the rest of north Africa, eventually reaching the straits of Gibraltar and southern Spain by the middle eighth century C.E. Yemenis from the eastern Hadramaut region were among the first to spread Islam to Malaysia and Indonesia in the twelfth and thirteenth centuries C.E. Today one can still find Hadrami family names among prominent Muslims of southeast Asia.

Across the centuries, the main division among Muslims inside Yemen is the distinction between Zaydis in the northwest mountain highlands (centered around the first Zaydi capital at Sa'da north of Sanaa, near the Yemeni-Saudi border), and Shafi'is in every other region of the country, but especially the western coast, midlands around Taiz, and southern coast stretching from Aden to Hadramaut. The people of Hadramaut and neighboring areas follow their own Sufi *Alawi* leaders, who are descendants of Ahmad bin Isa al-Muhajir ("the emigrant," d. 924 C.E.), a sixth generation grandson of the prophet Muhammad through the Shia imam, Jafar al-Sadiq. Under the Abbasid caliphate in the late ninth century C.E., al-Muhajir fled renewed persecution of the prophet's family in Iraq, traveling from Basra to Mecca, before eventually settling in Wadi Hadramaut. His tomb between the cities of Tarim and Saiy'un is an important pilgrimage site for Hadramis living in or visiting the great canyon.

The association between Hadramis and *Alawi* customs makes them distinct from Shafi'i in the southern and western parts of Yemen. Yet most Hadramis claim to be part of the Sunni branch of Islam, like Shafi'is, and unlike the Zaydis who are part of the Shia branch. The Zaydi-Shafi'i distinction is Yemen's version of the larger divide within Islam between followers of Shia and Sunni doctrine. For centuries, this sectarian split inside Yemen, which reflects one of the country's long-standing regional divides separating the northwest mountains, on the one hand, from the midland and coastal regions, on the other hand, presented a barrier to joint action among the population. Throughout the last millennium, it shaped Islamic identities in the country, but never as severely as the original Shia-Sunni division in Iraq and Syria.

Shafi'ism preceded Zaydism in Yemen. It is one of the four classical *madhahib*, or legal schools of Sunni Islam, which evolved in the late eighth and early ninth centuries C.E. It is named after the legal scholar Muhammad bin Idris al-Shafi'i (d. 820) who was born in Gaza, studied in al-Medina, and worked in Baghdad, Yemen, and Egypt. Al-Shafi'i was appointed to serve as the judge in Najran, located in Yemen's 'Asir region, during the time of the Abbassid caliph Harun al-Rashid, whose reign is associated with the founding of Baghdad's famous library, the "House of Wisdom," and great Arabic works of literature like *A Thousand and One Nights*. Shafi'ism represents a moderate approach to *shari'a*, Islamic law, based on rational discourse about the religion's moral principles, and the importance of contextualizing the law's application to human behavior. Today it has influence in many parts of the Muslim world, but especially Yemen, Egypt, parts of Somalia, Malaysia, and Indonesia.

Zaydism is a minority branch of Shia Islam. In the modern Muslim world, it is unique to Yemen. Zaydism arrived in the country during the late ninth century C.E., first settling in Yemen's northwest highlands near the modern border with Saudi Arabia. Zaydism did not generate a significant political division with Yemen's Shafi'i population until three centuries later.[7] Beginning in the twelfth century, Zaydism and Shafi'ism defined two distinct ruling systems in highland and midland/coastal regions, respectively. When the north-south border was drawn in the early twentieth century, there were practically no Zaydis living in the southern half of Yemen, while the northern population was nearly evenly divided between Zaydis and Shafi'is. Northern Shafi'i formed a majority along the Red Sea coast and midland region closest to British areas in the south, while a large Zaydi minority (35–40 percent) lived inside the highland mountains.

Yemen's Zaydi population is sometimes referred to as "Fiver" Shia, named after the succession struggle during the generation of the fifth Shia imam in the early eighth century C.E. This succession struggle occurred in Iraq long before the Hadrami al-Muhajir, descendant of the sixth imam Jafar al-Sadiq, fled Basra. Zayd ibn Ali ibn Husayn, whose followers assert should have been the rightful fifth imam, was the younger brother of Jafar al-Sadiq's martyred father, Muhammad al-Baqir (d. 733 C.E.). Zaydis are not like today's "Twelver" Shia in Iraq, Iran, and Lebanon, who take their name from a belief in the mystical disappearance of the twelfth imam. "Twelvers" have a conflicted relationship with Sunni Muslims because of the martyrdom of Imam Ali's son, Husayn, the grandson of Muhammad, at Karbala, Iraq in the year 680 C.E.. The more populous line of "Twelver" Shia disputed the claim of Zaydis, concerning who was supposed to be the fifth imam. Thus Zaydis were marginalized in northern Arab lands. Nearly two centuries later, when Zayd's followers arrived in Yemen, they came to south Arabia with none of the overt anti-Sunni hostility of "Twelver" Shia in the north.

The first Zaydi arrived in Yemen in 893 C.E., shortly before the arrival of al-Muhajir, the Hadrami. This founder of Zaydism in Yemen was known as al-Hadi ilal-Haqq, but his full name was Yahya bin Husayn bin al-Qasim al-Rassi (d. 911 C.E.). Like al-Muhajir, he was a member of the *sada* class or those who claim direct descent from the prophet Muhammad. Al-Hadi was a religious cleric and judge invited to Yemen from al-Medina to arbitrate a tribal dispute near the northwestern city of Sa'da. After resolving this dispute in the highland region, al-Hadi persuaded the local tribesmen to follow Zaydi customs. The sect slowly spread across the mountainous highlands as the tribes of Hashid and Bakil accepted the authority of a long succession of Zaydi imams. Zaydism was never adopted by the country's majority Shafi'i population, but later Zaydi imams

---

[7] Stookey, 1978; pp. 124–125.

PHOTO 5. Sa'da mosque of al-Hadi, first Zaydi imam of Yemen

were eventually able to expand beyond the highlands to rule over Shafi'i communities.

The religious practices of Zaydis and Shafi'is are both defined as moderate within the larger Shia and Sunni traditions. As a result, intercommunal relations witnessed less tension than those in northern Arab lands. Zaydi clergy sought to conform their customs with those of the Shafi'is, as a way of creating more peaceful relations inside the country. This was especially true of a reformist Zaydi cleric, named Muhammad al-Shawkani, who sought social and cultural reconciliation with Shafi'is during the late eighteenth and early nineteenth centuries.[8] In a sense, Zaydi-Shafi'i politics were less a matter of religious sectarianism than they were a reflection of the age-old division between highland and midland/coastal regions of Yemen.

Just as *Saba* and *Ma'in*, *Himyar* and *Qataban* were divided by the country's rugged terrain in pre-Islamic times, the division between Zaydi and Shafi'i was likewise a matter of regional geography. In other words, the arrival of Zaydism in Yemen roughly a century after the spread of Shafi'i legal principles did not dramatically alter the country's prevailing divisions. Likewise, it is important to note that the end of the Zaydi imamate a full one thousand years later in 1962 did not eliminate the political relevance of regional divisions inside the country. Indeed, the division between highland and midland/coastal regions, and the question of who rules over the northern and southern halves, remained politically relevant even after Yemen's unification in 1990.

What prevented a union of Zaydi and Shafi'i Muslims earlier in Yemeni history, in addition to geography, was the Zaydi doctrine that a member of the *sada*, or descendants of Muhammad, must serve as ruler. This is the source of the original dispute between Sunni and Shia Muslims in and around Iraq, since the Shia believed that only a descendant of the prophet Muhammad should lead the Muslim community as imam. The traditional Sunni practice was that a *caliph* or selected "successor" should lead the Muslim community, depending not on his lineage as a blood relative of Muhammad, but rather his personal leadership qualities as recognized by a council of elders.

The question of who ruled Yemen created problems because Zaydis in the highland region would never accept a midland, southern, or coastal Shafi'i as a capable leader of the country. Even today, nearly fifty years after the last Zaydi imam was overthrown, one can still hear Shafi'is complain of President Ali Abdallah Salih ruling like a Zaydi imam, who presumed to pass power to his son. President Salih was not a member of the *sada*, yet his later years in office reminded many Yemenis of the Zaydi highland tradition of passing power from father to son. The Shafi'is

[8] Haykel, 2003.

interpreted Saleh's inclination to pass authority to his son, Ahmad, as derivative of Zaydi rule. They long complained that Zaydi highland tribesmen like Salih would not allow a Shafi'i to become president. Indeed for more than forty years, only individuals from a Zaydi background served as president of governments in Sanaa, even though they were a minority and the Zaydi imamate ended in 1962.

When Zaydi imams and their tribal armies first sought, after the tenth century C.E., to extend their rule beyond the highland region, it troubled Yemen's Shafi'i Muslims. The Zaydi claim to legitimacy based on direct descent from the prophet Muhammad conflicted with Shafi'i views of political legitimacy, just as Shia claims of an inherited right to rule northern Arab lands conflicted with northern Sunni views. But in Yemen's context, the political contest between Zaydis and Shafi'is was never dramatically different from political contests between highland and midland/coastal rulers throughout Yemeni history. In short, the contest was not purely an Islamic sectarian issue. It also involved traditional tribal and regional claims to authority based on old divisions inside the country. The most significant factor in Yemen's Islamic political history is not religious sectarianism, but rather regional tribalism defined by the country's remarkable geography.

Beginning in the eleventh and twelfth centuries C.E., Zaydi imams in the resource-poor highland region sought control of tax revenues in wealthier markets and agricultural areas of Tihama along the Red Sea, and Taiz and Ibb in the lowlands, much like the Himyari kings wanted to seize the territory and markets of their neighbors. This was true as late as the twentieth century, when Zaydi imam Yahya Hamid al-Din sought to expand the territory under his control after a brief second Ottoman occupation of the northwest highlands from 1872 to 1918.[9] When the Ottomans were defeated in the first World War, and forced to withdraw from Arab lands, Imam Yahya advanced with tribal armies of Hashid and Bakil into western midland and coastal regions. In Tihama along the Red Sea coast, local members of the once powerful Zaraniq tribe south of the port city al-Hudayda were nearly wiped out by highland tribal forces.[10]

---

[9] Stookey, 1978; pp. 194–195.
[10] Interview with a member of the Yemeni parliament from al-Hudayda, October 9, 1996. There exists extensive documentary evidence of these events, but its full details have never been recorded. Othman Sayf al-Mikhlafi, a former Shafi'i officer in north Yemen's first intelligence agency, has many of these documents in a personal library. He claims that Yemen's official histories do not focus on these events because many highland Zaydis refuse to accept that resistance to the imams began outside the highlands region.

Those who remained were put in chains, and sent on a long death march to the imam's mountain prisons.

When Imam Yahya's troops reached Taiz in 1919, they faced a popular uprising. Local Shafi'i leaders organized a public conference during the same year to demand their right to maintain self-government.[11] Imam Yahya did not forcefully subjugate the people of Taiz as his tribal armies did to Tihamis on the west coast, but he and his sons eventually gained as much control of the western midlands. Under Yahya's rule, any extra tax funds raised in midland and coastal regions were used to subsidize his tribal armies. This relieved the Zaydi imam of domestic pressure at home from rebellious shaykhs of Hashid and Bakil inside the highlands. One financial history of north Yemen concludes that the Zaydi imam "was quite literally engaged in pauperizing his (Shafi'i) subjects on behalf of (Zaydi tribal) mercenaries."[12] Over the decades, Shafi'i communities chafed under the imam's excessive taxation policy, and local demands for self-government never diminished. During the 1950s, leaders of a political opposition movement in Taiz published a widely circulated pamphlet entitled *The Demands of Our People*.[13] Among their demands was local self-rule because they refused to continue living under the rule of religious and tribal Zaydi groups in the highlands.

Shafi'i Muslims typically pushed back whenever Zaydi forces descended from the northwest highland mountains. The Rasulid dynasty of Taiz established one of the great Islamic states in Yemen between the thirteenth and fifteenth centuries C.E., when they resisted the initial advance of Zaydism outside the highlands. Rasulid leaders extended their power and influence across a wider territory than any earlier states in Yemen's Islamic history. The same thing happened during the first Ottoman occupation of Yemen because imperial Sunni rule in Istanbul aided Shafi'i communities, while driving the Zaydis back to remote, defensible mountain towns. North Yemenis have a knack for building their homes on the most inaccessible mountain cliffs. One example is the town of Kokaban close to Sanaa in al-Mahwit province. Some towns in higher elevations of the highlands resemble sites in Tibet, so high they feel like the top of the

[11] Al-Mujahid, 1997; pp. 203–204. The people of the Shafi'i midlands later demanded that more tax revenues be used for local development, instead of being sent to the imam's treasury in Sanaa. There was a clear regional element to these tax revolts. Later there were also reports that Shafi'is around al-Rayma, overlooking the Tihama coast, pushed for regional autonomy in the 1930s. Swagman, 1988, p. 129.

[12] Chaudhry, 1997; p. 109.

[13] Douglass, 1987; p. 215.

PHOTO 6. Kokaban cliff top town, al-Mahwit province

world. The town of Shahara further to the north is built on a narrow rocky peak that can only be reached by crossing a stone-arched footbridge spanning a vertiginous chasm. The latter site served as the last place of refuge for Zaydi imams whenever they felt threatened.

When the Qasimi dynasty of Zaydism expanded its control to Aden and Hadramaut after the seventeenth century, this brought an end to large-scale Shafi'i religious rule. Afterward Yemeni politics was dominated by Zaydism until the 1960s, when Arab nationalist and socialist ideologies became the main currency of local politics. The Qasimi hold on Aden and Hadramaut weakened after several decades, as various tribal leaders began to assert themselves in the south. Then in the late nineteenth century, the British Empire negotiated separate "protection" treaties with these south Yemeni tribes after first seizing possession of Aden in 1838.[14] The British subsidized and armed local tribal leaders, providing them "traditional" titles as emirs and sultans who served imperial interests. Britain's primary interest was India, so it only defended a small colony in Aden because its port offered a secure coaling station halfway between Suez and Bombay. Under British rule, Aden and Hadramaut were the only two exceptions to tribal rule in the south. From an early stage, tribalism ceased to exist in Aden colony, and in Hadramaut, the British assisted the sultans of

[14] Lackner, 1985; pp. 14–18. Gavin, 1975; pp. 297–301 and 312–317.

al-Qu'ayti and al-Kathiri to develop improved government administration and the rule of state law in the twentieth century.[15]

DIVISIONS IN THE MIDDLE TWENTIETH CENTURY

In 1948, Imam Yahya Hamid al-Din was overthrown in Sanaa and killed by military forces loyal to a rival Zaydi *sada* family, al-Wazir. Abdallah al-Wazir briefly served as the new imam in what was intended to be a constitutional monarchy. But in short time, he too was deposed and executed by tribesmen loyal to Imam Yahya's son Ahmad. The main problem with Abdallah al-Wazir leading the drive for political change was that, as a Zaydi imam, he did not represent the north's majority Shafi'i population. Later in the 1950s, Shafi'i opposition leaders in Taiz, who published *The Demands of Our People*, sought to end the Zaydi imamate in its entirety. Their group, called the "Free Yemenis," was led by Ahmad Numan, his sons, and a few Zaydi supporters like Muhammad al-Zubayri. In order to succeed, they had to find a way to surmount the north's regional sectarian division. Their solution was to build social solidarities around the idea of unity among the descendants of an ancient south Arabian ancestor, *Qahtan*, who in local lore is believed to be the great grandson of the prophet Noah.[16]

The idea of a brotherhood among "the sons of *Qahtan*" served three critical purposes. First, it ushered in Arab nationalist ideologies, ending Islamic rule in Yemen. Second, it effectively marginalized the Zaydi imam's family, as well as the aristocracy, by driving a wedge between them and adherents of Zaydism among two large highland tribal federations, Hashid and Bakil. The Zaydi aristocracy claims descent from northern Arabs around Iraq, known classically as the descendants of *Adnan*. But the tribesmen of Hashid and Bakil are southern Arabs, descendants of *Qahtan*. From the time of Imam al-Hadi ila'l-Haqq in the late ninth century C.E., Hashid and Bakil accepted the Zaydi imams as *sada* religious elites worthy of leading the nation. But in the middle twentieth century, the era of the *sada* was finished. Third, rhetoric about the "sons of *Qahtan*" united Hashid and Bakil tribesmen with the larger Shafi'i population outside the highlands. "Free Yemeni" leaders in Taiz, and other midland and

---

[15] Interview with Faruq Ben Shamlan, director of south Yemen's local government affairs in the late 1980s, and an administrator in the Hadrami bedouin army of Wadi Hadramaut in the 1950s and 1960s; January 4, 1997.

[16] Douglas, 1987; p. 35 ff.

coastal regions, knew they depended upon support from Hashid and Bakil because these tribes had long served as two pillars holding up the Zaydi imamate. After overthrowing a Zaydi leader, there was always a risk that highland tribes would rally behind a new imam as happened in 1948. By addressing the sons of *Qahtan,* Shafi'i opposition leaders could appeal to Zaydi tribesmen over the heads of their own shaykhs.

Beginning in the 1950s, many nationalists in both halves of Yemen adopted a unionist stance toward each other. Northern residents near the border had long emigrated south to work in the British-run port at Aden where the pay was higher. Some served as leaders in Aden's growing labor union movement, protesting discriminatory colonial policies like the denial of Arab voting rights in municipal elections. Just as north Yemenis joined southern political causes, many southerners also joined northerners to oppose the Zaydi imamate. In the late 1950s, when Gamal Abd al-Nasser was at the peak of his power in Cairo, the call for Arab solidarity was so popular that in 1958 even Imam Ahmad joined Egypt and Syria in their short-lived United Arab Republic. Imam Ahmad advocated a literal interpretation of "Yemen" as all lands south of Mecca beneath an imaginary line stretching from the Red Sea to the Persian Gulf. This conjured up the idea of a "Greater Yemen" that included not only south Yemen, but the United Arab Emirates, Oman, and large sections of Saudi Arabia.[17] Nonetheless, his claim to broader territory was only of sentimental value without practical foundation.

Inside south Yemen, Britain never attempted to create a unified governing structure until the end of the colonial era, nearly two decades after World War II. Since local rulers in the south were fiercely independent of each other, British officials considered a federalist model to be the best option. In February 1959, the Federation of South Arabian Emirates was announced.[18] From the beginning, this federal project was doomed for two main reasons: first, south Yemen's sultans and emirs had little experience with joint rule, and even less desire to cooperate with each other; and second, the plan was unpopular with a broader public that regarded it with deep suspicion as a creation of the colonial power.[19] The eastern protectorates of Hadramaut had always remained separate from British-ruled Aden and its western protectorates. So the two Hadrami sultans had little incentive to join the new federation. Likewise the leaders of Upper Yafi',

---

[17] Al-Waysi, 1962; pp. 19–21. Nagi, 1984; p. 242.
[18] Gavin, 1975; p. 340.
[19] Lackner, 1985; pp. 19–24.

some parts of Lahij, and other areas north and east of Aden rejected the federal plan.[20] Even among those local leaders who joined the federation, it was difficult to reach agreement on who would head the new government.[21] British officials eventually settled on a rotating presidency, much like the initial American attempt to establish a transitional Iraqi governing council in Baghdad during late 2003. But the plan never got off the ground.

Beginning in late 1963, the British government faced an armed rebellion when south Yemenis launched guerrilla warfare to gain their independence. The rebellion was sparked by events on October 14, 1963, when British security forces shot and killed seven Radfani men in a small lowland mountain town called al-Habilayn, just north of Aden. Yet it was also inspired by the revolution on the northern side of the Yemeni border on September 26, 1962, when the last Zaydi imam (son of the deceased Imam Ahmad who died of natural causes) was driven from office and forced to flee Sanaa. Until today, each anniversary of these two dates is celebrated as the start of Yemen's national independence struggle. The fighting in the north dragged on six more years as Egypt supported the new republican army, while Saudi Arabia, Britain, and the United States financed and armed highland tribal militia loyal to the fallen imam. Meanwhile in south Yemen, the campaign of hit-and-run violence, including bombings and assassinations inside crowded urban neighborhoods of Aden, lasted just four years until the British lowered the Union Jack flag on November 29, 1967.

The chaotic end of British rule partially indicates how the multiple regional divisions in the southern half of the country differed from the main northern division between Zaydis in the highlands and Shafi'is in midland and coastal regions. In the north, the fight was waged primarily to drive out loyalists of the Zaydi imamate who controlled the highest points in Yemen's mountains. In the south, there was never a history of one regional group dominating all other groups, so the fight was waged by many local rebels eager to oust a foreign imperial power. The closest equivalent in south Yemen to Zaydi domination of the north was the role played by Yafi' tribesmen in Hadramaut, where they were brought as mercenary soldiers in the sixteenth century.[22] Again in the nineteenth century, Yafi' tribal soldiers were used by al-Qu'ayti sultans to expand their base of power in Hadramaut. Al-Qu'ayti rulers trace their roots to

[20] In the 1950s, leaders of Yafi' set up a free constitution of their own. Carapico, 1998; p. 95.
[21] Gavin, 1975; pp. 340–343. Lackner, 1985; p. 20.
[22] Gavin, 1975; p. 161.

upper Yafi' north-east of Aden. But they arrived in Hadramaut from India where they had established a family fortune commanding military troops for local princes in Hyderabad.[23] Since Hadramis were the first to spread Islam to southeast Asia, their primary orientation was directed across the Indian Ocean toward India and Indonesia. For this reason, the role of Yafi' tribes in south Yemen was never internally hegemonic like the role of highland Zaydi imams and tribes in north Yemen.

The people of southern and eastern Yemen simply never had the experience of Yemenis in the north, where highland Zaydis dominated large regions of the country for centuries. South Yemenis generally did not seek control over one another. In fact, it was a Zaydi imam from the north who made the last bid for broad control over south Yemen. In 1912, before the Ottoman empire collapsed, Imam Yahya tried to renew centuries-old Qasimi claims to Aden from the seventeenth century. He sent letters across British and Ottoman lines to local tribal leaders in the south, appealing for Yemeni unity and calling them to fight the British.[24] In the book *Aden Under British Rule*, R. J. Gavin concludes that Imam Yahya's expansionist policy ironically resulted in a stronger British protectorate system, "and with it a nexus of interests involved in South Arabian or South Yemeni separatism."[25] Most southerners refused to associate with northern Zaydism. When Imam Yahya's son Ahmad dabbled in pan-Arab politics in the 1950s, his appeal to south Yemenis was no greater than his father's appeal before World War I.

When residents of Aden later began to organize against British rule, some opposition groups like the South Arabian League refused to be called "Yemeni" due to the word's negative association with the Zaydi imamate.[26] This shows that a common Yemeni identity was not inherent to southern society in the twentieth century. Some people in the eastern British protectorate maintained a purely Hadrami identity that was distinct from every other part of Yemen, both north and south. In a brief

---

[23] Gavin, 1975; pp. 158–160. Al-Batati, 1989.

[24] Gavin, 1975; p. 240 ff.

[25] Ibid; p. 275.

[26] Interview with the Adeni director of the South Arabian League, February 1, 1997. As one of Yemen's oldest political parties, it is interesting to trace the evolution of the League's name. In the 1960s, the League changed its name to the League of the Sons of South Yemen, due to the rise of Yemeni nationalism following the northern republican revolution in 1962. Then after the unification of Yemen in 1990, it changed its name once again to the League of the Sons of Yemen, keeping in step with changing times. During a civil war in 1994, the head of the League, Abd al-Rahman al-Jifri, joined the short-lived secessionist government in Aden before fleeing into exile.

history of unionist ideas in Yemen, written in the early 1980s, Sultan Nagi summarized a political debate published during the late 1940s in the northern "Free Yemeni" movement's Aden-based newspaper, *Fatat al-Jazira*.[27] The debate involved a citizen of Hadramaut who disagreed with the Yemeni nationalist views of the newspaper's editor. Nagi quotes the newspaper stating that this Hadrami went so far "as to ask the Free Yemenis to go back home if they wanted to continue talking about their Yemenism ... Hadhramis today have their own nationality."

The Arab nationalism of the 1950s, and Yemen's twin revolutions in the 1960s, did more than anything else to spread unionist sentiments among people living in both halves of the country. Suddenly, after the overthrow of the Zaydi imamate in the north and the ouster of the British in the south, a populist spirit of Yemeni nationalism spread throughout the land. Unfortunately, once the new republican governments were established on a more solid foundation, the northern Yemeni Arab Republic (YAR) and the southern People's Democratic Republic of Yemen (PDRY) drifted apart due to rival social and economic policies. The differences between the YAR and PDRY, and their contrasting internal dynamics, deserve in depth analysis in the next chapter. Subjects covered in Chapter 2 are particularly important for setting the stage of the troubled unification of rival Yemeni regimes in 1990. But it is important to note that people on both sides of the old border aspired to form a united state largely because of unionist propaganda throughout the 1970s and 1980s.

After the Zaydi imamate was overthrown in 1962, the idea of unity among "the sons of *Qahtan*," both north and south Yemenis, became official propaganda of the YAR state in its capital, Sanaa. The myth of *Qahtan* had a strong influence on postrevolutionary ideology because it not only helped dissolve sectarian tensions on the northern side of the border, but it also cultivated a common public identity among citizens. It was primarily on this basis that the great writers and poets of north Yemen, like the late poet Abdallah al-Baradduni and the dean of Sanaa University, Abd al-Aziz al-Maqaleh, built their populist tales of Yemenis united by revolution.[28] For many years, northern intellectuals read poetry of *Qahtan*

---

[27] Nagi, 1984; p. 247.
[28] Al-Baradoni, 1992. Dr. Abd al-Aziz al-Maqaleh writes frequently in the north Yemeni daily newspaper, "*al-Thawra*." The north's unionist mythology also strongly influenced the works of Western scholars. In his insightful history of the "Free Yemeni" movement, J. Leigh Douglas chose to focus on Yemeni solidarity. Especially at the beginning of Douglas's book, he downplayed the regional nature of Zaydi/Shafi'i differences, choosing to make reference only in footnotes rather than in the text of his book.

at anniversary celebrations of the September 1962 revolution, while a succession of military rulers tied to the highland tribal shaykhs of Hashid and Bakil sat and applauded. After the British were expelled from Aden and the rest of south Yemen in 1967, the southern PDRY government used similar rhetoric. Thus the myth of *Qahtan* served the agendas of both states, while keeping alive the possibility of broader national unity. The difference in the south is that its Arab nationalist ideology became strongly mixed with Marxist socialism, and southern officials sought to eliminate traditional religious and tribal influences from society.

Two decades later in November 1989, when north and south Yemeni leaders met in Aden to sign a preliminary unification agreement, they referred to national unity as "the destiny of our people." Amid rising public expectations, since citizens anticipated better economic opportunities in a united country, the two heads of state met a second time in April 1990 to confirm the procedures of unity. This second meeting was held in Sanaa, and it resulted in a signed agreement declaring Yemen's unity "is based on the eternal revolutions of September 1962 and October 1963, arising from nationalist, Islamic, and common human origins."[29] The latter phrasing was an implicit reference to *Qahtan*. Yemenis on both sides of the border certainly understood the reference, since two generations of schoolchildren had been brought up on the mythology of *Qahtan*.

Educators in the YAR and PDRY used the myth of *Qahtan* to develop a common historical narrative of their people, glorifying Yemeni unity from ancient to modern times. Long stretches of history, both Islamic and pre-Islamic, were idealized as periods when south Arabians lived together in a single community. This narrative influenced not only schoolchildren but their parents and other members of society. For three decades, it motivated Yemenis to work toward the day when they could erase the north-south border. During the run up to unification on May 22, 1990, national unity held a sacred quality in the minds of most citizens. The average person on the street would have rejected any suggestion that regional differences ever existed among the Yemeni people. This was particularly true of well-educated citizens in urban areas whose self-knowledge was filled with unionist ideas about Yemenis living together as one family.

In the final months leading to the day of mass celebration for Yemeni unity, most people in the north and south believed that they already formed one nation. There were some groups on each side of the border that were sworn enemies of the other side; and there were politically

[29] *Al-Thawra* newspaper (in Arabic), April 1990, Sanaa, Yemen; p. 1.

influential individuals on both sides who opposed the steps taken to create a unified state. Nonetheless, belief in national unity, especially the idea of a common Yemeni people, was pervasive among the population. The old north-south boundary line never held social or cultural significance for Yemenis. It never served their interests. The only reason the line was drawn was because the British and Ottoman governments realized Yemen's strategic importance at the gateway of the Red Sea, and they wanted to protect larger interests elsewhere. Yet while the north-south division clearly needed to be erased, there was no basis for the illusory notion that one people, the sons of *Qahtan*, ever lived in unison on a single territory.

DEFINING YEMEN'S MULTIPLE REGIONAL DIVISIONS

At the time of Yemen's national unification in 1990, its population showed significant diversity beyond the late Cold War ideological differences between northern and southern political elites, one tribal, Arab conservative and the other Marxist socialist. In social terms, the population's diversity was due to a combination of ethnic, cultural, linguistic, and to a lesser extent, religious differences. Among the Yemeni people, there is no ethnic division as sharp as the Catholic-Protestant division of Ireland, or the Greek-Turkish division of Cyprus. Nothing compares to the deep sectarian divisions in Arab countries like Lebanon, Syria, and Iraq. But Yemen's population is filled with lesser ethnic distinctions that correspond to identifiable regions of the country.

Yemenis typically identify themselves and others by these regional distinctions, often using one's regional birthplace as a surname. For example, al-Hamdani and al-Arhabi are common names of people from districts north of Sanaa, while al-Mikhlafi and al-Sharjabi are common names of people from districts of Taiz province. One may readily assume that the former come from Zaydi families speaking with accents and dialects common to the northwest highlands region, while the latter come from Shafi'i families speaking with accents and dialects common to the western midlands. Hadrami surnames are the most distinct in Yemen, often beginning with "Bin" like Bin Laden and Bin Shamlan, or "Ba" like Ba Mattraf and Ba Shamakh. The Hadrami dialect from the east is easy to distinguish, as is the Tihama dialect on the western coast. Tihamis do not use the standard "al-" for the definitive, rather "am-."

Most Yemenis are Arabs, yet there are also significant African influences in Tihama; Somali and Indian influences in Aden and the south; East African, Malay, and Indonesian influences in Hadramaut; and Turkish and Persian influences in Sanaa and other parts of the northwest. While Arabic is the main language, the multiple dialects spoken inside Yemen are distinct enough that citizens from one side of the country have some difficulty understanding citizens from the opposite side. These dialects clearly distinguish a person's regional background. In the eastern-most province of al-Mahra along the sparsely populated border with Oman, as well as the island of Soqatra roughly half way to Somalia, locals speak al-Mahri language which derives from ancient south Arabian. This language is largely incomprehensible to Arabic speakers in other parts of the country. In western Yemen, some citizens of African descent form a distinct underclass called the *Akhdam*. They make up the country's lowest class employed in street cleaning and trash removal, much like the "untouchable" caste of India.

Since national unification, it is necessary to refer to some regions of the country in different terms than those used before 1990. For instance, north Yemenis previously described Marib province as an "eastern" region because it is located east of Sanaa. But in united Yemen, it no longer makes sense to call Marib "eastern." Marib is now a central interior province because most of the former southern PDRY territory lies east of Marib. Hadramaut and al-Mahra are now properly called the eastern region of Yemen. Yet another example of altered regional terminology is the basic north-south distinction in the country. Sanaa is actually a northwest city, while Aden is in the southwest, since both capital cities are located near the western edge of the country. Old habits die hard, so references to the former "north/south" division are likely to persist. For the sake of this book's political analysis, north and south will only apply to preunity definitions of the land. Postunity Yemen will be described in terms of seven regions (Map 2).

These seven regions are: (1) northwest highlands; (2) west coast; (3) western midlands; (4) southwest lowlands; (5) mid-southern; (6) central interior; and (7) eastern. Identification of these regions is neither meant to imply that people living inside them are distinct, homogeneous subnational groups, nor that they automatically share common political interests. Within the seven regions, there are important sub-divisions which are frequently the source of political tension and conflict. For instance, the northwest highlands are divided between the tribes of Hashid and Bakil, some of which regularly clash with each other in territorial feuds. Yemen's seven regions are based on loose social structures, inside which regional group bonds are weak compared to other social bonds like tribal and clan affiliations. Tribes and clans create the most powerful group bonds inside

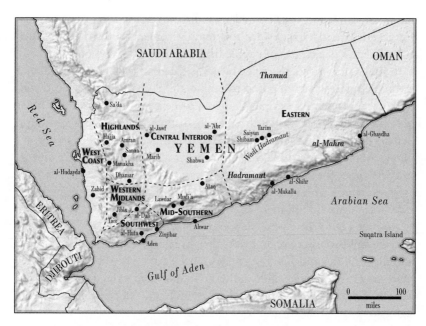

M A P 2. Seven geographic regions of Yemen's population

Yemen.[30] Perhaps the single strongest regional bond is among the Hadrami people of the eastern region, who have a fairly strong regional identity separate from other Yemenis. Nonetheless, all seven regions are important for political analysis of Yemeni unity.

For the sake of drawing relevant conclusions about Yemeni politics since 1990, it is essential to make regional distinctions among the population. For example, without understanding the dynamic between Yemen's seven regional groups, it would be impossible to make sense of the country's 1994 civil war and its aftermath. In addition, it is vital to comprehend the differences among the seven regions, in order to analyze variations in voting patterns during Yemen's first two national elections in 1993 and 1997. The regional divisions are also vital for identifying the general relationship between strong and weak groups in Yemeni society, and examining the role of various regional representatives in government. Finally, they are critical to understanding the slow unraveling of President Salih's regime in 2011. After 1990, Salih ruled a territory that

[30] It is the exception for tribal and clan affiliations to overlap regional divisions in Yemen. Yet some Hashid and Bakil tribes overlap the boundary between the northwest highlands and central interior region.

had nearly tripled in size. To understand the troubles he had maintaining power, it is essential to consider how his government represented, or failed to represent, the interests of people from all regions of the country.

In some of Yemen's seven regions, it is true that common political and economic interests, as opposed to ethnic and cultural traits, help distinguish local residents from people living in neighboring regions. In other cases, the local population is more easily distinguished by ethnic, cultural factors. In short, the overall significance of political-economic factors and ethnic-cultural factors varies from one region to another. At the time of unity in 1990, the region best defined by political interests was the midsouthern region of Abyan and Shabwa provinces, where two generations of political leaders, and their associates and clients, had been exiled from the former PDRY between 1969 and 1986. In 1990, the political elites from this mid-southern region were the strongest rivals of southern leader Ali Salem al-Bid and his Yemeni Socialist Party. Thus it is particularly interesting to distinguish mid-southerners after 1990, even though many of them do not differ in cultural or ethnic terms from Yemenis in neighboring regions.

The voting patterns of mid-southerners also hold great interest after 1990. Yet this does not mean that all mid-southern citizens are the same, or think alike. The northwest highland region is another area where political factors are key, since elites from this region form the traditional ruling group in Sanaa. Yet there are also important cultural markers that distinguish people in the highland region from residents of neighboring regions. For instance, their spoken dialect and Zaydi sectarian identity clearly distinguish the highlands people from those living in neighboring regions.

The populations of the remaining five regions are linked to observable ethnic cultural markers. One of the most obvious markers in Yemen is the regional dress styles of women, since there is great variety in the style and colors of material that women use to veil themselves in the Islamic tradition. Men also have different regional dress styles, especially the material used in turbans and the *futa*, a long wrap worn around the waist. But the strongest regional identifier among Yemeni men is their spoken dialect. It is important to bear in mind that cultural markers are not fixed and inflexible. There is considerable cultural mixing at the boundaries between Yemen's seven regional groups. And of course, cultural markers do not automatically determine an individual's political views or loyalties, since politics obviously shift from one person to another across boundaries of time and space. What follows is a simple summary of the defining characteristics of Yemen's seven regional groups.

1. The "northwest highland" region is centered around the flat mountain plain of Sanaa, including most of the areas in the provinces of Hajja, Sa'da, al-Mahwit, Dhamar and Amran (the latter of which was part of Sanaa province until the late 1990s), as well as the northern edge of Ibb province located above the high Samara mountain pass. This region is bounded by steep mountain descents to the south, east, and west, and the Saudi Arabian border in the north. For shorthand purposes, the region may be called the "highlands" because no other area of Yemen reaches the same high elevations and relatively cool day time temperatures. Its residents come almost entirely from Zaydi-Shia backgrounds except for migrant families in larger cities, particularly the capital Sanaa. This is the Zaydi heartland, but it is also home to approximately one hundred thousand Ismaili Shia living in the Haraz mountains at the western edge of the highlands around the city of Manakha. Highlands people have a very distinct dialect of Arabic, usually spoken with an exaggerated nasal tone and playful sing-song qualities. They are also distinguished by very strong, unbroken tribal customs, since the area is home to Yemen's two most powerful tribal federations, Hashid and Bakil. These tribesmen share old martial traditions, wearing the customary curved dagger in their belts with rifles slung over their shoulders. This is a resource poor region with chronic water shortages, and only modest agriculture except for large scale production of the highly popular and profitable *qat* bush or small tree. On a daily basis, the majority of Yemenis meet with friends in afternoon social gatherings, where they discuss current events and tell jokes while "chewing" the plant's tender juicy leaves and buds (in Arabic *khazan*, literally "storing" wads of chewed *qat* in the cheeks). *Qat* contains a drug stimulant comparable to very strong coffee, but it is nonaddictive and carries no risk of physical impairment or overdose. The plant thrives at high elevations, so the highland region is famous for *maqil al-qat*, or "qat talk" sessions.

2. The "west coast" is the Tihama region of Yemen. This is essentially the Red Sea province of al-Hudayda, but it also includes the mountain slopes at the western edge of these provinces: Hajja, al-Mahwit, al-Rayma (which was part of Sanaa province through the 1990s), Dhamar, Ibb, and Taiz. The people of this region are almost entirely Shafi'i. A high percentage of the population in Tihama is influenced by African descent, customs, and traditions, since their territory lies directly across from Eritrea, once part of Ethiopia and the ancient

PHOTO 7. Qat session, Kokaban, al-Mahwit province

Christian kingdom of Axum that invaded and occupied Yemen's west coast in the pre-Islamic era. The people of Tihama once had a vibrant tribal culture, but it was weakened during the rule of the last Zaydi imams. The people on the west coast also have a distinct dialect, using "am-" to denote the definitive "the." The west coast region has substantial agricultural resources, particularly around Zabid where the waters of Wadi al-ʿUdayn tumble down from the mountains of Ibb province. In the middle ages, Zabid was a famous center of Shafiʿi learning in the Islamic world. The west coast region has a bustling fishing and trade industry, especially around its main port in the city of al-Hudayda. Inside the region, there are also a few Shafiʿi-owned factories producing fruit juices and other basic foods.

3. The "western midlands" are the mountains and valleys east of Tihama, south of the highlands, and north of the low mountains bordering the port city of Aden. This area of Yemen receives the highest average annual rainfall in the country. Its soil is very fertile, and the area is known as Yemen's "green land." In the former YAR, this region was sometimes called the "middle regions" (*al-minataq al-wusta*), and other times the "southern uplands" or lowlands. But since unification with the PDRY, it is better to refer to the "western

midlands," or just "midlands" for shorthand purposes. There are large mountains in this region, such as the massive Jabal al-Sabr towering over the city of Taiz, but the region lacks the wide mountain plain of the highlands. It generally has a moderate climate between the cool windswept highlands and the sweltering western and southern coasts, but Taiz turns very hot in the summer. The region contains the large city of Taiz and the old towns of Ibb, Jibla, and al-Janad, where Yemen's oldest mosque was built in the sixth Islamic year during the prophet's time. It also includes western al-Bayda province around the city of Rada'a. Like the west coast, this region is predominantly Shafi'i-Sunni. However, the people of the western midlands do not share the strong tribal traditions of highlanders and west coast Tihamis, primarily because of different land settlement patterns in this strong agricultural region. The region's main tribe is al-Maddhaj. The dialect and other customs of people in this region are closer to the residents of Aden than either the highlands or Tihama. In fact, the boundaries of the western midlands can be extended across the former north/south borderline to include some areas of Lahij province, particularly around the town al-Muqatira. In the late 1990s, the government in Sanaa combined parts of Taiz and Lahij provinces to form the new province of al-Dali', in order to erase the old border division. The western midlands have substantial agricultural production, as well as the greatest industrial activity in Yemen with many Shafi'i-owned factories that produce food and fruit juice items, plastic, paper, soap, and other household goods. Yemen's most successful merchant class and educated technocrats come from this region of the country.

4. The "southwest lowlands" region is the area running along Yemen's southern coast around the port city Aden. The Gulf of Aden is a narrow body of water separating the Arabian peninsula from the Horn of Africa. Aden is a remarkable city built around a large volcanic mountain. One of its districts is called "Crater" because it is built inside the mouth of the dormant volcano. Since the province of Aden has a history as a large cosmopolitan urban center, it stands in sharp contrast to surrounding rural tribal areas in Lahij, al-Dali', and parts of Abyan province. Aden remains the most liberal and tolerant place inside the country, yet nearby villages and towns are socially conservative like the rest of the country. Regardless, the city of Aden serves as the main regional center for all residents in the southwestern region, including the population of Abyan's

provincial capital Zinjibar and the lower Yafi' areas around the town of Ja'ar. The majority of Aden's population comes from these surrounding areas, as well as the Shafi'i areas across the old northern border in the western midlands.[31] The people in the southwest region around Aden are all Shafi'i-Sunni who share a common dialect of Arabic. There was previously a strong tribal tradition among people in rural areas outside Aden, but their tribal ties were weakened during the two decades of Marxist socialist rule in the 1970s and 1980s. Since the late 1990s, there has been a revival of tribal allegiances in the southwest region, as well as other parts of the former PDRY state. Thus unification with north Yemen brought a return to old local customs, partly encouraged by President Salih in Sanaa. There is good fishing off the coast of the southwest region. Agriculture in the region is poor due to bad soil quality and scarce water sources. Near the cities of al-Hawta, Lahij and Ja'ar, Abyan, there are irrigation systems built around flood plains that carry seasonal rainwater from mountains to the north. Farms in these areas do provide better agricultural production than neighboring sites. Historically speaking, Aden had a large industrial base, but many of its state-run factories were shut down in the 1990s due to implementation of IMF-mandated economic reforms. The city still has one of the best natural harbors in the world, and recent expansion and modernization of its port facilities offer great potential for future development as a hub for sea trade and transportation.

5. The "mid-southern" region is centered around the mountains of eastern and central Abyan, southeastern al-Bayda, and southwestern and central Shabwa provinces. It stretches across the former north/south borderline, and encompasses areas of Bayhan, al-Awadhil, al-Awaliq, and Ahwar on the southern coast. This area is Shafi'i-Sunni like the southwest region, but it neither shares a close association with Aden nor the same customs and traditions. Many people of

---

[31] There are few pure Adenis. When Britain first entered, it was just a collection of small fishing villages. The first British census in 1839 counted only 1,297 people. By 1856, Aden's population was more than twenty thousand, but a majority were British, other Europeans, Indians, and Somalis. By 1901, the city's population reached forty-three thousand; and in 1946, it surpassed eighty thousand. Around this time, Aden became an important world shipping center, and it attracted more migrants from Taiz and Hadramaut. By the 1970s, Aden's population rose above four hundred thousand, and the vast majority traced their family roots to other regions of Yemen. Unpublished report from the Office of Statistics; Aden, Yemen, 1996.

this region retained their tribal traditions and loyalties, despite the influence of Marxist socialism in the former PDRY. Throughout the PDRY's history as an independent south Yemeni republic, citizens of the mid-southern region were more often marginalized, and forcibly removed, from political leadership than any other people. This began with attacks against prominent individuals from western Shabwa and eastern Abyan in the late 1960s, and continued through a major political breakdown in January 1986 that forced President Ali Nasir Muhammad and his close associates from north central Abyan to flee into exile.[32] The common experience of political marginalization and exile is one of the main factors binding the mid-southern people together. Martial customs are prevalent in this region, particularly in western Shabwa province and the area of Bayhan. The archeological site at the deserted ancient town of Shabwa is actually not part of the mid-southern region. The same is true of the nearby oil fields that are more correctly included in the "central interior" region described next. During the middle twentieth century before south Yemen's independence, the deserted town and oil fields were part of the al-Qu'ayti sultan's realm in Hadramaut. But the new leaders who came to power in the late 1960s detached the deserted town from Hadrami territory, and adopted Shabwa as the namesake of a new province in the 1970s, hoping to create a new regional identity among the mid-southern people. Generally speaking, the mid-southern region is a resource-poor area, except for some agricultural production and plentiful fishing along the coast.

6. The "central interior" or "desert interior" region is located east of the highlands, west of Wadi Hadramaut, north of the mid-southern area, and south of the great Arabian desert in Saudi Arabia known as *al-Rub al-Khali*, the famous "Empty Quarter." This region contains the ancient lands of the Queen of Sheba. It forms part of Yemen's long border with Saudi Arabia, which is not properly demarcated because of shifting desert sands. The area is sparsely populated, and stretches across the country's former north/south borderline. From the northern territory of the former YAR, it includes Marib and al-Jawf provinces, as well as a small

---

[32] An intra-regime conflict in January 1986 pitted many of Ali Nasir Muhammad's most loyal mid-southern supporters from Abyan and Shabwa provinces (Ali Nasir's hometown is Mudi'a in the old Dathina area of Abyan) against his political opponents who came largely from the southwestern region of Lahij, especially Radfan and al-Dali'. These events are discussed in greater detail in Chapter 2.

northeastern part of al-Bayda province, while it includes the northern half of Shabwa province and western sections of Hadramaut province from the former PDRY. This is Yemen's desert region, where bedouin tribes once migrated between oases with camel and goat herds. Herding activity still takes place in the desert, but local tribes now use land rover vehicles and camp in settled locations for longer periods of time. The people of this region speak a dialect that is closer to classical Arabic than any other region of the country. They are also distinguished by very strong tribal identities and martial customs. The men commonly wear curved daggers and carry firearms like the powerful highland tribes. Although its residents are a mixture of Shafi'i and Zaydi, their kinship ties are far stronger than any internal sectarian differences. The region contains some of Yemen's best oil resources, especially at the Hunt Oil Company's production field in Marib, and new oil and natural gas fields discovered in northwestern Shabwa province.

7. The "eastern" region consists of all territory east of Yemen's desert interior and mid-southern region along the coast. Thus it encompasses the area of Thamud on the border of Saudi Arabia, Wadi Hadramaut and the Hadrami coastline, including the south-eastern corner of Shabwa province, as well as the province of al-Mahra on Yemen's far eastern border with Oman. Due to the unique language spoken by al-Mahri people, it might make sense to define al-Mahra and the island of Soqatra as a separate eighth region of Yemen. However, al-Mahra and Soqatra are so remote and sparsely populated that it makes little sense, for the purposes of political analysis in this book, to distinguish them from the territory of Hadramaut. Culturally and geographically speaking, al-Mahra and Soqatra form Yemen's eighth region, but their people have practically no influence on the greater national politics of Yemen. In the governing structure of the former PDRY state, al-Mahra and Soqatra were administered from neighboring Hadramaut and the capital Aden, respectively. After unity, both land masses were closely tied to governing bodies in Hadramaut, so it hardly makes sense to analyze al-Mahri politics in isolation. The residents of Hadramaut, both inside the wadi and along the coast, are the one people of Yemen who represent a relatively strong and cohesive sub-national group. They have far more influence in the national economy and politics than the people of al-Mahra and Soqatra. The people of Hadramaut clearly identify themselves as Hadramis, who are distinct from all

other Yemenis, due to their unique culture, traditions, dialect, and history. Like the people of Aden and the southwest region, they are mainly Shafi'i (although with Alawi traditions) who gradually lost their tribal customs under the British protectorate system, and especially later during Marxist rule. During the late 1990s, tribalism was revived in Hadramaut due to the policies of President Salih in Sanaa. Throughout most of Yemen's history, Hadramis operated a relatively autonomous trading zone between the coastline and a chain of cities in Wadi Hadhamaut. Its businessmen have long been famous for their trading and financial investment activities throughout the Arabian peninsula and beyond to India, southeast Asia, and the east coast of Africa. Hadhamaut has rich natural resources, including oil and gold. The most productive oil field in the entire country is located in Wadi al-Masila, near the province's border with al-Mahra. The Hadrami coast has good fishing and a few factories, and the interior wadi has substantial agriculture with excellent ground water sources. Al-Mahra has good agriculture with a misty humid climate, and both it and Soqatra have excellent fishing. Soqotra Island is best known for its rare animal and plant species, and powerful winds that blow half of the year, forcing many locals to retreat from the seafront to live in mountain caves.

Based on these seven regional groups, it is possible to make a rough estimate of the national population's distribution across the land of Yemen in Table 1.1. The newly united Republic of Yemen released its first census in 1994, the year of civil war. Although the accuracy of this census was questioned by officials involved in the compilation of data in Sanaa, it remains the best population count after unification. In 1996, a top deputy in the Yemeni ministry of planning's central statistical organization explained that the census results inside the provinces of the northwest highlands were inflated, in order to strengthen the highland group's political weight in future parliaments. Thus if there is any error in the numbers of Table 1.1, it amounts to an overestimation of the size of the highland population.

According to the 1994 census, Yemen's total population was more than 15,750,000, including roughly one million residents in the capital Sanaa. Residents of the capital come from all regions of the country. There is a particularly strong mix of families that migrated from the western midlands and west coast regions. Since it is not possible to know their relative balance with local highland families living in the capital, the 1994 census

TABLE 1.1. *Population Distribution among Yemen's Seven Regional Groups, 1994*

1) Northwest Highlands	3,914,927 (24.9%)
2) West Coast/Tihama	3,038,769 (19.3%)
3) Western Midlands	4,329,761 (27.5%)
4) Southwest/Aden	1,258,742 (8.0%)
5) Mid-Southern	682,926 (4.3%)
6) Central Interior	631,677 (4.0%)
7) Eastern/Hadramaut	1,001,707 (6.4%)

count of one million people in the capital city has been excluded from Table 1.1. For this reason, the numbers listed in the table do not add up to the country's total population of 15.75 million.

Based on the 1994 census figures, the northwest highland group represented a relatively large minority in Yemen. Its 3.9 million residents represented close to 25 percent of the total. This means that the percentage of Yemeni citizens from a Zaydi religious background may be considered slightly higher, 30–35 percent, because a large number of Zaydis live within the Sanaa capital zone and smaller numbers live outside the highland region. The country's largest regional group is in the western midlands around the cities of Taiz and Ibb. The population of the west coast group is third, slightly smaller than the highlands. These three regional groups formed the bulk of united Yemen's population in the early 1990s, roughly 78 percent if one includes the population of the capital city. The remaining five regions hold very small minority populations.

The provinces of Hadramaut and al-Mahra in the eastern region are vast in size, making up nearly half of Yemen's land mass, but their populations are just over 6 percent of the total. The southwest region around Aden holds a slightly larger percentage of the country's population. Yet the city of Aden holds considerably more significance as a political and economic center, since its seaport played a critically important role in Yemeni history throughout the twentieth century. During British colonial rule, the port and its surrounding industrial zones were a magnet for labor migration between the 1940s and 1960s. This was especially true of Yemen's largest regional group in the western midlands. Many midland residents migrated to Aden to find better paying jobs around the port facilities.

Any person who sees the remarkable landscape of Yemen for the first time, whether it is Wadi Hadramaut's breathtaking canyon in the east or the towering mountains of the west, and the vast desert of the central interior, can understand how regionalism among the Yemeni people persisted for so many centuries. Until today it is common for Yemenis to marry within their regional, cultural, and tribal groups. Thus group divisions are fairly static, even in the twenty-first century. Tribal membership in Yemen's highland mountains differs from tribal membership in the midland, coastal, and eastern regions. Throughout the north-south division in the twentieth century, there developed different inter-regional dynamics among groups in each half of the country. The important point is to understand how these different dynamics persisted after the country's revolutionary era in the 1960s. Chapter 2 explains the different regional dynamics inside the YAR and PDRY republics, and how these dynamics shaped and defined two very different regimes that united in May 1990.

2

Two Revolutions, Two Republics

Yemen's revolutions commenced slightly more than one year apart: September 1962 in the north, and October 1963 in the south. In both cases, the process of securing a new republican form of government extended through the late 1960s. The simultaneity of these revolutionary processes fostered greater national solidarities. Unionist sentiments rose on both sides of the border, as citizens in all regions felt pride in overturning their traditional rulers, and fighting to end British colonialism. As a result of these revolutionary activities, Yemenis also won a place of honor in the Arab world and among Third World countries. The experience was similar to what Egyptians went through after their national revolution in 1952, and what Algerians experienced following their long war for independence between 1954 and 1962.

Expectations of northern and southern unity soared in the mid-1960s when a prominent south Yemeni nationalist, Qahtan al-Shaabi (who eventually became the first president of independent south Yemen in 1967), was appointed cabinet minister in charge of the northern government's unity affairs. Before the old border could be erased, however, each side faced the daunting task of unifying its own half of the country. Multiple regional divisions continued to shape northern and southern politics. Prior to independence in the south, the main political division was between two rival nationalist movements. The Front for the Liberation of South Yemen (FLOSY) was centered in Aden and backed by the government of Egypt.[1] The National Liberation Front (NLF), a name later shortened to the National Front, was larger and more powerful

[1] Halliday, 1974; pp. 207–213.

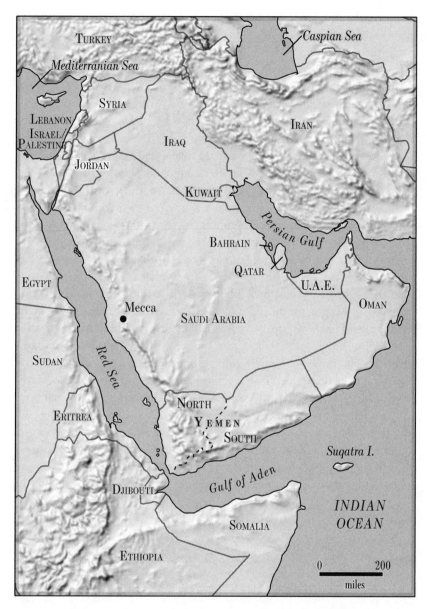

MAP 3. Yemen's north-south division on the Arabian peninsula until 1990

with broad rural support among tribes in Aden's hinterland, as well as migrants from north Yemen's Shafi'i areas in the western midlands.

On the eve of independence, the NLF clashed with FLOSY in an outer district of Aden, called Shaykh Othman.[2] The NLF quickly gained the upper hand before the British departure. Under the leadership of Qahtan al-Shaabi, the new National Front government turned its attention to pockets of opposition east of Aden. Tribal shaykhs of al-Aulaqi in the midsouthern region (belonging to the same tribe of Anwar al-Aulaqi, the Yemeni American cleric who was linked to al-Qaeda attacks in the United States in 2009) previously held the top command posts in the British-run federal army. There was an early clash between soldiers under the command of al-Aulaqi officers, and representatives of the new national army who primarily came from neighboring areas of Abyan to the west. This clash came to be known as the "al-Sa'idi events," named after a town in al-Aulaqi territory.[3] By 1970, prominent families from al-Aulaqi had fled into exile in the north, leaving a rift in the middle of the southern republic as citizens of what later became Shabwa province were largely cut from power. Only the citizens of al-Mahra, the most distant and least developed area in the eastern region, would be more poorly represented in government in Aden.

In the spring of 1968, there was a similar military clash in Hadramaut when the Hadrami Bedouin Legion (HBL, another force trained by the British) refused orders sent by the central government.[4] The HBL formerly served al-Qu'ayti sultans, and its members did not merge with the national army until the early 1970s. Hadramaut was critically important to the new regime in Aden because it, and its eastern neighbor al-Mahra, represented roughly two-thirds of the south's total land mass. Hadramaut also formed most of the long undefined border with Saudi Arabia. In addition, it was believed to contain large sources of gold and oil.[5] Various governments in

---

[2] Ibid, p. 220.

[3] Interview with Othman Abd al-Jabbar, a former cabinet minister in many southern governments; October 22, 1998 in his home in Sanaa. Also refer to Lackner, 1985; p. 68.

[4] Interview with Faisal al-Attas, one of the leaders of the "popular revolutionary committees" in Hadramaut during the 1960s; June 29, 1996, in al-Attas's home in Sanaa. These events occurred after President Qahtan al-Shaabi dismissed many leftists from the government and ruling party in March 1968. Al-Attas claims that the central authorities in Aden suspected the Hadramis of conspiring to become independent with the help of Saudi Arabia. Fred Halliday reports that the Aden regime considered the Hadrami activists to be "secessionists," even though Hadramaut was not previously united with other parts of south Yemen. Halliday, 1974; p. 235.

[5] The British first discovered oil in Hadramaut in the 1950s, but at the time the deposits were too small to warrant investment in the extraction process. Halliday, 1974; p. 165. After

Aden tried to split Hadramaut in half, dividing it between the coast and the interior valley, Wadi Hadramaut, in order to make the province easier to control.[6] But Hadramis inside and outside the regime successfully resisted all attempts to divide their land.

In the early years of independence, the southern government faced the Herculean task of uniting lands that previously consisted of more than twenty separate sultanates, emirates, and shaykhdoms. Its primary agenda was to create a uniform system of laws capable of integrating all regions. Political boundaries in the south previously corresponded with territories ruled by the various local leaders who had much earlier signed treaties with the British. The new government judged the danger of these internal divisions to be so severe that it substituted a numbering system for the names of its provinces and districts.[7] This was done to prevent regionally based opposition movements from using traditional place names and identities to generate antigovernment sentiment. Officials also redrew some boundary lines to cut through territory of large tribes like Yafi', which became divided between province Number Two (later known as Lahij) and province Number Three (later known as Abyan).[8]

In some of the new south Yemeni regime's earliest legislation, it banned the carrying of arms, and took the extraordinary measure of weakening tribal allegiances by making revenge killings punishable in state courts.[9] These crucial steps to establish state authority, and develop a society based on the rule of law, were never considered possible in north Yemen, where tribalism remained a strong component of government policy through the

unification in 1990 the largest reserves of new oil in the Republic of Yemen were found in Hadramaut. This was one of the factors contributing to political tensions leading to the 1994 civil war. Today it is still a source of tension between many Hadramis and the central government in Sanaa.

[6] Soon after independence, the desert areas around ancient Shabwa and coastal region of al-Wahidi were broken off Hadramaut's western edge to form part of the new province of Shabwa. But most of the former sultanate lands of al-Qu'ayti (along the coast to Shibbam in the wadi) and al-Kathiri (inside the wadi at Saiyun and Tarim) remained intact.

[7] Lackner, 1985; p. 54. According to Lackner, the provincial and district numbering system remained until 1980, when the regime introduced new regional names that would not "revive tribalism"; p. 111. The first regime also discouraged the use of regional surnames and traditional titles of respect, such as "Shaykh." A later radical regime abandoned general use of "Mister," or "Sir," for the more egalitarian title of "Brother."

[8] In particular, the borders between provinces Number Two and Number Three, as well as provinces Number Three and Number Four (Shabwa) cut across lands of the strongest tribes of Yafi' and Aulaqi, respectively.

[9] Lackner, 1985; pp. 110–111. The first law against revenge killings is in a supplement to the southern PDRY's *al-Jarida al-Rasmiyya* (*Official Gazette*, in Arabic), #33, July 18, 1968. A second law, #22 of 1969, set the penalty for revenge killing at 10,000 dinar, twenty years in jail, or capital punishment.

1980s. Tribal feuds and killings remained common in the north even after unification with south Yemen, and they are still a problem today. Some northern highland shaykhs of Hashid and Bakil operate their own prisons, independent of the state's criminal justice system, just as they did under the former rule of Zaydi imams. The supreme authority of state law was never established in north Yemen's highland region.

In June 1969, a radical contingent of south Yemen's National Front drove President al-Shaabi from office in Aden, bringing to power a group of younger men who initiated policies to reform government in line with Marxist ideology. This "correction" movement introduced the ideological component of socialism into Yemen's modern politics. The younger politicians who took power in Aden renamed the country, the People's Democratic Republic of Yemen (PDRY), and began appropriating private property, nationalizing broad sectors of the southern economy, and establishing state-run corporations in the fields of trade, banking, and insurance. During the previous year, President al-Shaabi had formed a central planning board in Aden. The new leaders quickly extended branches of this board to all provinces of the country. By 1974 they were able to prepare the PDRY's first five-year plan for all southern provinces and districts. This level of public administration was something the northern government in Sanaa failed to accomplish because its leadership was never as unified, and it lacked the necessary discipline to enforce regular state policies.

POLITICS OF NORTH AND SOUTH YEMEN

The dynamics of early political development in north Yemen were completely different from those in the south. Whereas the southern PDRY sought to eliminate tribalism and alter its territory's old regional divisions, the north's provincial and local district boundaries barely changed. Under the old order of the Zaydi imamate, internal boundaries were drawn to serve the imam's interests in the highlands. Previously under Ottoman rule in the late nineteenth and early twentieth centuries, the north had been divided into three provinces: Sanaa in the highlands, Tihama on the west coast, and al-Janad in the midlands.[10] When Imam Yahya seized power in the late 1910s, he created a new province in the Zaydi heartland at Sa'da,

---

[10] A-Hamdani, 1990; pp. 124 and 132. During the late era of Ottoman rule, the Zaydi imamate existed only in areas around Sa'da, and 'Asir in today's Saudi Arabia. Areas in the central interior desert were beyond the control of the government.

and later cut off part of Sanaa province to form Hajja in the northwest. Within these highland regions, the boundaries between districts (the administrative sub-unit beneath provinces) matched the tribal divisions of Hashid and Bakil. Outside the highlands, Imam Yahya implemented a different policy.

In the Shafi'i regions of the country, Imam Yahya separated many of Taiz's agriculturally rich subdistricts and attached them to Zaydi regions north of Samara mountain pass to form the new province of Ibb. He also cut the more agriculturally rich parts of the western coastal mountains, such as Wusabayn and al-Rayma, and attached them to Sanaa province.[11] Later, al-Bayda province was formed south-east of Sanaa. In this way, administrative divisions in Shafi'i coastal and midland areas served the interests of Zaydi highland groups. In the 1940s Imam Yahya appointed three sons to govern the high-taxation provinces of Ibb, Taiz, and al-Hudayda. Each of these governor-princes grew wealthy taxing the people.[12] Additional political appointments in Shafi'i districts were used to reward tribal shaykhs from the highlands. In the five decades prior to the 1962 revolution, numerous tribal and nontribal Zaydis moved south to Ibb and Taiz, and west to coastal regions of Tihama, where they became prominent landholders.

Following the 1962 revolution, there were a few changes made to the former imamate's provincial boundaries. For example, the new province of al-Mahwit (possessing one of the main centers of Zaydi religious authority in the cliff top town of Kokaban) was carved out of western Sanaa province. The province of Dhamar was formed from areas in southern Sanaa province and northern al-Bayda. Dhamar's capital was an old Zaydi religious training center. Later Marib and al-Jawf provinces were created from the "eastern area," or the desert interior region. It is important to note that all of these changes by the new republican government affected the Zaydi highland region of the country. The administrative boundaries in Shafi'i areas essentially remained the same. Instead of being attached to al-Hudayda and Ibb, which are closer in location, al-Rayma in southwest Sanaa and Wusabayn in southwest Dhamar continued to be oddly appended to the Zaydi highlands.

---

[11] Ibid, pp. 124 and 132. Additional information was obtained during an interview with Abd al-Malik al-Ulafi, a former deputy in Sanaa's local administration during the imamate and republican eras; July 22, 1996 in Sanaa.

[12] Stookey, 1978; p. 194.

The continuation of these administrative boundaries inside lowland regions showed the persistence of the highland group's control from Sanaa. The tribal structure of local districts in the highlands remained the same.[13] Moreover, the most prominent highland shaykhs controlled important provincial posts. The Bakil shaykh of Nihm, Sinan Abu Luhum, became the influential governor of al-Hudayda province. The Hashid shaykh Mujahid Abu Shawarib played a dominant role as governor of Hajja province.[14] Inside the northern republic, the boundaries of its local districts and provinces remained as they were under the imams. There was no attempt to break up the strength of the highland tribes, or reduce the political control of groups from the northwest highland region. Indeed, throughout the history of the northern Yemen Arab Republic (YAR), the dominance of the highland regional group remained the most significant political factor.

The first full cabinet of the YAR in September 1968 was almost perfectly balanced between highland and midland/coastal members, as seen in Table 2.1. But within a year the balance shifted, giving the highland group a two-thirds advantage, while midland/coastal officials were relegated to the least influential ministerial posts.[15] Because the north's revolutionary movement was waged against an internal Islamic autocrat, rather than a foreign power, northern regional groups had different objectives. People from Shafi'i areas were the strongest supporters of the new republican order. Meanwhile, tribal and nontribal groups in the highlands were more cautious. Instead of being united like the south against a foreign enemy, the north's revolutionary struggle attracted foreign powers to opposing sides of the conflict. Saudi Arabia aided the imam's royalist cause with British and American assistance, while Gamal Abd al-Nasser's Egypt aided the republicans with Soviet support.[16] As a result,

---

[13] As a result of the complex nature of the boundaries between dozens of tribes from Hashid and Bakil, many subdistricts in the northwest highlands assume strange forms. In some cases, one subdistrict may exist in two distinct areas separated by great distances because the two areas are controlled by one tribe. Thus, one shaykh may administer two distinct areas under one district's name. Interview with officials in the Ministry of Local Administration, Sanaa; April 7, 1996.

[14] In the early 1970s, Abu Shawarib personally redrew the boundaries of Hajja to include two subdistricts of Sanaa that were part of his own tribal group. Interview with a deputy official in the ministry of local administration; July 15, 1996.

[15] Stookey, 1978; p. 234. Stookey reports that the rapid imbalance of power in the YAR led one of the few remaining Shafi'i members of the north Yemeni government to open secret talks with the British in the south, in order to establish a separate Shafi'i state around Taiz with close economic ties to Aden.

[16] Badeeb, 1986; pp. 33 ff. and 51 ff. Halliday, 1974; pp. 101–118.

TABLE 2.1. *Regional Distribution of Early Ministerial Posts in the Northern YAR[a]*

Date	Zaydi	Shafi'i
9/68	9	8
3/69	10	9
9/69	11	5
2/70	9	6
5/71	10	5
8/71	8	3
3/74	10	9
6/74	11	10
1/75	13	8
12/78	10	6
1/80	13	7
10/80	16	8

[a] Peterson, 1982; p. 127. It is important to note that while John Peterson distinguished in his data table between Zaydi and Shafi'i officials, this distinction roughly corresponds with the regional division between officials from the northwest highlands and others from regions in the western midlands, and along the west coast.

the population was divided, and the north was drawn into a long civil war between 1962 and 1970.

Following the start of revolution on September 26, 1962, the property of the imam's family was seized, but unlike the south there was no radical upheaval in the social and economic order. The primary axis defining postrevolutionary politics in north Yemen was still the regional distinction between Zaydi highland and Shafi'i midland/coastal interests, just as it defined the politics of the north's Free Yemeni movement in the 1940s and 1950s. By contrast, the main axis of postrevolutionary politics in south Yemen was social and economic, not regional. The south's revolution broke old tribal loyalties that bound citizens to their sultans and emirs. This radical change was driven by the greater influence of socialist ideas in southern politics. Socialism provided a unifying link between middle and lower classes in different southern regions, uniting groups from Lahij and Abyan in the west to Hadramaut and al-Mahra in the east.

Unlike the government cabinets of north Yemen, which after the spring of 1969 were consistently controlled by a two-thirds regional majority from the northwest highlands, Table 2.2 reveals that early government cabinets in Aden were routinely balanced among ministers from Aden and

TABLE 2.2. *Regional Distribution of Early Ministerial Posts in the Southern PDRY*[a]

	Southwestern		Mid-Southern		Eastern	Cross Border
Date	Aden	Lahij	Abyan	Shabwa	Hadramaut	North Yemen
4/69	2	4	2	1	3	1
6/69	3	1	2	1	3	1
8/71	4	1	2	1	1	3
5/73	5	2	2	0	2	4

[a] The data in this table was created by taking the names of south Yemeni ministers from the PDRY's *al-Jarida al-Rasmiyya* ("*Official Gazette*"). Then the regional background of each minister was determined in interviews with knowledgeable former southern government officials.

Lahij in the southwest region, Abyan in the midsouthern region, and Hadramaut in the eastern region. Citizens of Aden and Hadramaut were generally better educated and more professionally trained than people from other areas. Adenis and Hadramis complemented each other in the southern government because they represented opposite ends of the country. There were also professionally trained citizens from north Yemen, mainly migrants from Taiz in the western midlands, who regularly held ministry posts in Aden. Thus, the southern government was truly cross-regional, unlike the northern government.[17] In 1971 and 1973, there were as many north Yemeni cabinet ministers in Aden as ministers from Lahij and Abyan combined. Socialist technocrats from Aden consistently held the most cabinet posts, but they were never more than one-third of the total.

The only time when there was similar regional parity on north Yemeni cabinets in Sanaa was during the few months before and after the coup that brought populist leader Ibrahim al-Hamdi to power in June 1974. Al-Hamdi was an Arab nationalist figure comparable to Gamal Abd al-Nasser in Egypt, whom al-Hamdi greatly admired. Yet by January 1975, the two-thirds majority from the highland region returned to the northern cabinet, and it would remain until unification with south Yemen in 1990. One of the last north Yemeni cabinets in 1987 consisted of eighteen government ministers from Sanaa and the northwest highland region,

---

[17] It is true that some southern emigres, like Abdallah al-Asnaj and Muhammad Ba Sindwa, served on government cabinets in north Yemen. But they never played the influential role that north Yemenis played in the southern PDRY. Al-Asnaj and Ba Sindwa were former members of FLOSY during the 1960s.

and only seven ministers from the western midlands and west coast regions.[18] There was never a reliable census taken in north Yemen, but it was widely assumed that citizens in the midland and coastal regions formed a 55–60 percent majority. Taiz was the single most populous province in the country, yet it lacked sufficient representation.

After the revolutions in the 1960s, each new republic faced different regional dynamics partly because of different revolutionary goals on opposite sides of the border. Whereas southern citizens rallied behind a common agenda to oust a foreign occupier, the northern population was divided by the removal of the last Zaydi imam. But the main reason for different regional dynamics in north and south Yemen is the contrast between their political economies, specifically the different distribution of economic resources in each half of the country. South Yemen's most valuable economic resources were concentrated in its capital city. This allowed the new regime a relatively free hand to centralize power in Aden. Across the border, the YAR's most valuable resources were disbursed outside the capital Sanaa.

The highland plateau around Sanaa has few resources. Even water is scarce. There are no rivers or lakes near Sanaa, and subterranean aquifers are difficult to reach. As a consequence, there is only modest agricultural production in the area. The highland region's most valuable product is the *qat* plant, but its production requires large amounts of water. Due to the absence of other exploitable resources, political elites in the highland region have always sought control over the western midland areas of Taiz, Ibb, and al-Bayda, and the western coastal province of al-Hudayda, where agricultural production is far greater. As discussed in the previous chapter, the quest to control outlying resources defined the expansion of the Zaydi imamate, especially after the seventeenth century.

When revolution came to north Yemen in September 1962, one of the first things that happened in western midand communities was the formation of local cooperative associations, financed by money previously paid to the Zaydi imam's tax collectors. Taking full advantage of the imamate's overthrow, local Shafi'i leaders began managing their own municipal and rural affairs, first in Taiz, and later in the Tihama along the west coast.[19] This was a bold first step toward democratic self-rule. By

---

[18] Cited in German, *Arabishe Republik Jemen: Politik*, Munzinger-Archiv./IH-Landeraktuel, Heft 12–13/88; pp. 1–2.

[19] Interview with Dr. Abduh Ali Othman, one of the leading activists in the north Yemeni cooperative movement; November 1, 1995 in his office at Sanaa University. Also refer to al-Harbi, 1989; and Piepenburg, 1992; p. 56.

keeping local taxes at home, many towns and villages in the western midland and coastal regions were able to initiate much needed public work projects, building roads, digging water wells, organizing markets, and starting new schools. Businessmen and merchants in these areas encouraged the process because the development of better infrastructure strengthened the economy. Economic elites from regions outside the highlands quickly became the leading businessmen in postrevolutionary north Yemen. This was especially true after traders fled the southern PDRY, when Aden's socialist regime nationalized properties.[20] In the north, many highland merchants went bankrupt when business was disrupted by civil war during the 1960s.[21] The main fighting took place in the highland mountains north of Sanaa.

When the war wound down in the late 1960s, and a reconciliation was reached with Zaydi royalists in 1970, the political compromise resulted in a cross-regional governing pact. Lowland elites would maintain dominance over economic affairs, while traditional highland tribal elites would maintain political and military control in Sanaa. In her book, *The Price of Wealth*, Kiren Chaudhry describes north Yemen's "republican pact" leading to a policy of noninterference between the state and merchant class.[22] There was never a formal power sharing agreement signed by representatives of regional groups. But different regional interests became weakly balanced in support of the new republican system. In effect, informal power-sharing allowed highland elites to maintain political hegemony, while business elites from the western midland and coastal regions ran the economy.

By the mid-1970s there was an unwritten rule in north Yemen that the president and head of state would come from the highland region, while the prime minister in charge of ministry affairs would be a midland figure, usually from Taiz. After 1975, Abd al-Aziz Abd al-Ghani was the primary person representing midland economic interests. He was born in Taiz with close connections to the midland region's leading businessmen, later serving as founding chairman of north Yemen's central bank. Between 1975 and 1990, he served as prime minister of north Yemen for all but two and a half years.[23] The only other prime minister was Dr. Abd al-Karim al-Iryani

---

[20] Chaudhry, 1997; p. 230.
[21] Ibid, pp. 128–129. Chaudhry's survey of Sanaa's main shopping district (outside the old city's suq) showed that, even in the late 1980s, roughly 80 percent of the city's merchants were Shafi'i, whose families came from midland/coastal regions of the country; p. 213.
[22] Ibid, pp. 125 and 136.
[23] Ibid, p. 127.

from a prominent family of judges in the highland border region of Ibb, south of Sanaa. Dr. al-Iryani is sometimes described as a "Shadi" because his family historically played a compromise role between Shafiʻi and Zaydi. The senior Abd al-Rahman al-Iryani served as head of state after the postwar reconciliation.

President Abd al-Rahman al-Iryani was deposed during a 1974 military coup that brought to power the popular Arab nationalist, Ibrahim al-Hamdi, who was the son of a Zaydi *qadi* or judge from the Hashid tribal region of al-Hamdan northwest of Sanaa. Before his rise to power, al-Hamdi served as director and champion of north Yemen's local cooperative movement, which became known in the 1970s as the Confederation of Yemeni Development Associations (CYDA).[24] The larger significance of al-Hamdi's rise to power through the CYDA organization is what it says about the lingering need to build public consensus across regional lines. Before the bloodless coup in 1974, al-Iryani's government faced mounting criticism that it was weak and dysfunctional. The compromise at the heart of the north's "republican pact" had created at least the possibility of stable government by agreement among elites. But there was no broader public consensus behind the pact.

Because President al-Iryani proved to be an ineffective leader with no real influence over the highland tribes, and no real appeal within non-tribal western midland and coastal regions, there existed a political void for a dynamic populist like al-Hamdi to step forward. As a military man from the highlands, President al-Hamdi appealed to many tribesmen of Hashid and Bakil. Yet as head of the CYDA, he also had popularity in midland and coastal regions. In short, al-Hamdi was a leader with potential to develop effective political hegemony based on public consent in different geographic regions. Through the CYDA, al-Hamdi sought to accomplish two goals. First, he wanted to expand the CYDA's public representation by extending its model of cooperative development into highland areas, where it was underrepresented among the tribes of Hashid and Bakil. Second, he wanted to use the organizational structure of the CYDA as a tool of state-building by holding democratic elections. He also enlisted the support of local cooperative leaders in raising taxes, allowing them to keep 50 percent of all revenues to finance local development projects.[25]

[24] Under al-Hamdi's leadership, the number of cooperatives multiplied from forty in 1973 to sixty-five in 1974, and then 130 during his first full year as head of state. Lutz, 1992; pp. 44–46 and 52.

[25] Ibid, pp. 45–46. Lutz notes that, by associating itself with the local cooperative movement, al-Hamdi's regime succeeded in "raising the (country's) tax morale considerably."

In 1976, al-Hamdi's administration arranged north Yemen's first nationwide elections, culminating in a large conference of the CYDA. The delegates who attended the national conference were the top vote recipients at provincial and district levels. Al-Hamdi hoped to cement his popularity by promoting the candidacy of his closest supporters for seats on the CYDA's higher council. However, the results of the conference's internal election disappointed the president. Delegates voted primarily against his nominees, supporting instead a group of "young, conscious, and sincere" socialist activists from Taiz.[26] The conference took on the feel of a national parliament with delegates debating national issues in ways that "showed the people were not willing to follow (al-Hamdi) blindly."[27] This challenge to al-Hamdi's leadership of the CYDA reflected continuing regional tensions over north Yemen's "republican pact."

In October 1977, President al-Hamdi was assassinated in bizarre circumstances. He was shot at close range with his brother, who was a close political associate. Their corpses were found near the corpses of two French women caught in a conspiracy to kill the president.[28] The intention of the assassins was to make it look like the president died in a scandalous lovers' quarrel with his brother, but everyone knew the assassination was arranged by al-Hamdi's rivals among the shaykhs of Hashid and Bakil. Among business elites in Taiz and other nonhighland regions, there was concern that highland tribal shaykhs would seize control via the military. Indeed, al-Hamdi was replaced by one of his deputies, Ahmad al-Ghashmi, who was a Hashid tribal-military figure.[29] When al-Ghashmi was killed eight months later, a young highland army officer, named Ali Abdallah Salih, stepped from relative obscurity to become the next president.[30] Salih was unable to focus on domestic matters because the northern government was dragged into a brief border war with south Yemen in early 1979, followed by a longer counterinsurgency campaign in the early 1980s against southern-backed Marxist guerrilla fighters in the midland region.

[26] Al-Audi, 1975; p. 119. Cited in Lutz, 1992; p. 52.

[27] Lutz, p. 52.

[28] Peterson, 1982; p. 121, footnote 35.

[29] In early 1978, a highland army officer close to al-Hamdi, Major Mujahid al-Kuhhali, was forced from his military post in Amran. Al-Kuhhali was from the Bakil tribe, and Amran is a key Hashid town near Sanaa. Al-Kuhhali's removal indicated intertribal rivalry inside the highland region, where the top Hashid shayhs had been marginalized by al-Hamdi. Burrowes, 1987; p. 90.

[30] Al-Ghashmi was killed in June 1978, when a messenger from south Yemeni president Salem Rubaya Ali delivered a concealed bomb to al-Ghashmi's office. Ibid, p. 92.

The young and inexperienced President Salih did not turn his attention to domestic political matters until 1982. When the occasion arrived, Salih borrowed from Ibrahim al-Hamdi's original plan to build state institutions via the CYDA.[31] Just as President al-Hamdi arranged a voting congress of the CYDA in the mid-1970s, Salih used the organization to hold the first General People's Congress (GPC), which later became the ruling party of north Yemen. Salih did not make al-Hamdi's mistake of allowing CYDA activists to vote in a closed election. At the GPC's founding conference in Sanaa during the summer of 1982, leaders of the old cooperative movement attended among more than six hundred delegates. On this occasion the activists who voted in the majority in 1976 were outnumbered by highland tribal groups, and religious conservatives from the midland region who supported a new anti-Marxist Islamic front. This Islamic front was established during the president's counter-insurgency campaign in the early 1980s.

In effect, President Salih stacked the GPC's founding conference with delegates who ensured the regime's chosen candidates would head the new political umbrella organization. Three years later in 1985, Salih's government passed a new law transforming the former cooperatives into local elected councils.[32] This appeared to be a natural political evolution of the CYDA, but the regime used the legislation to co-opt leaders of the old "self-rule" movement in lowland regions. In theory, the head of each council represented the interests of local voters, while in practice the two top officials of each local council became paid employees of the central government. The new law also repealed each council's share of local tax revenues, requiring 100 percent of taxes be sent to the central bank in Sanaa. As a result, local councils became dependent on credits from the central government to carry out local development projects.

During President Salih's first decade in office, he strengthened state institutions by converting the CYDA into a branch office of a central government ministry. By statute, the newly elected councils were allowed to serve only a consultative role with provincial governors and local deputies, all of whom were appointed by the central government. The vast majority of governors and deputies were originally from Sanaa and

---

[31] Ibid, p. 111.
[32] Piepenburg, 1992; p. 58 ff. Piepenburg concluded that the effect of the new law "turned out to be detrimental, if not fatal, to the spirit of self-help and private initiative"; p. 60. He added: "In a move which might be considered brilliant by political strategists, all elected representatives of the (local councils) automatically became members of the General People's Congress"; p. 61.

the northwest highlands.[33] The regime effectively shut down independent political and economic activities around the country, silencing the strongest expression of democracy since the 1962 revolution. Like the Zaydi imams of old, President Salih operated from his base in Sanaa, while drawing revenues from high production regions to the south and west. The tax burden was hardly felt in the highlands, where new businessmen connected to the regime, and the shaykhs of Hashid and Bakil, regularly escaped paying taxes.

According to the YAR government's records for 1985 and 1989, state revenues drawn from taxing citizens in the western midlands increased from a rate 43 percent higher than revenues from citizens in the highland region to a rate 115 percent higher. (Refer to Table 2.3.) In short, the average citizen in Taiz, Ibb, and al-Bayda contributed more than twice what citizens contributed on the highland plateau around Sanaa. This increase occurred at a time when highland tribal shaykhs began taking business away from traditional merchants of the midland region, so they clearly should have paid equal or higher taxes. Citizens along the west coast in al-Hudayda province paid the largest amounts to the state, a full 110 percent higher than people of the highland region in 1985, and 435 percent higher in 1989. During the 1990s, a top official at Sanaa's central tax authority explained that his staff would never dare to enforce taxes on businesses owned by highland tribal shaykhs with military connections to the regime.[34] He gave only one reason: fear of physical retribution, since past staff members who tried to collect taxes from shaykhs of Hashid and Bakil were physically assaulted and threatened with death.

Since the era of the Zaydi imams, people living outside the highland region have complained that their share of the tax burden is unfair. Under President Salih, there remained a solid basis for this complaint.[35] The

---

[33] This is the conclusion of a survey of local administrative personnel in Yemen conducted by the author between 1996 and 1998. The results of this research appear in the Tables 2.5–2.7 of this chapter. See the Appendix for a description of the methodology used in the local administrative survey.

[34] Interview with a top official at Sanaa's central tax authority, summer 1996.

[35] In her political economy study of north Yemen, Kiren Chaudhry described northern state institutions in "predatory" terms, where highland officials exploited groups from outlying regions. Chaudhry, 1997; p. 207. This recalls her description of the former Zaydi imam's policy in the 1930s and 1940s, when the imam's Shafi'i subjects were "pauperized" in order to pay his tribal "mercenaries" in the highlands. Chaudhry claimed that government expenditures in the former YAR's state institutions were regionally divided: the ministry of interior's department of tribal affairs served interests in the highland and central interior regions, while the ministry of social affairs, youth, and labor served interests in the western

TABLE 2.3. *Regional Government Revenues (per capita) in the Northern YAR, 1985 and 1989*

	Personal Taxes	Consumer Taxes	Service Fees	Total Current Revenues (without customs)
1985				
Highlands	51.8	5.3	8.3	130.4
Western Midlands	58.3	20.1	14.6	187.1
West Coast	108.7	88.6	18.8	274.0
Central Interior	25.4	5.1	8.7	55.8
1989				
Highlands	71.5	38.1	15.7	165.6
Western Midlands	119.7	43.4	25.8	349.6
West Coast	200.8	161.8	29.7	883.7
Central Interior	118.1	30.4	22.5	218.1

discovery of oil in Marib in 1984, and the start of production shortly thereafter, funneled even more revenues to the state. This soon became yet another example of highland elites exploiting the resources of an outlying regional group, in this case rebellious tribes in the central interior desert. Before the end of the decade, Marib's tribal shaykhs intensified their opposition to the regime in Sanaa by obstructing work on the oil fields. But President Salih's power was enhanced by extra revenues from oil, and the northern capital grew even more wealthy.

A TALE OF TWO CAPITALS

It is worth considering the different political and economic developments in Yemen's two capital cities: Aden in the southern People's Democratic Republic of Yemen (PDRY), and Sanaa in the northern Yemen Arab Republic (YAR). The contrast between Aden and Sanaa at the beginning of the revolutionary era in the 1960s, and later on the eve of unification in 1990, offers a tell-tale sign of the different social and economic forces at

midlands and west coast; p. 209. The YAR's tribal affairs were linked to northern military and security forces, and these expenditures made up more than half of the YAR's total state budget. Carapico, 1998; p. 39. Thus, highland tribal groups benefited more from state funds, while contributing less to state coffers.

work in each half of the country. Before southern independence on November 30, 1967, the level of economic development in Aden dwarfed the rest of the south. For much of the 1940s and 1950s, Aden had been the second busiest port in the world, behind only New York City.[36] The revolutionaries from Aden's hinterland, who fought the British between October 1963 and November 1967, looked forward to gaining control of vast revenues from the city's free port.

After coming to power in 1967, the new regime imposed customs duties and tariffs in Aden, since it would depend on these revenues for national development.[37] Unfortunately, trading activities at the port dropped precipitously after June 1967, when Israel closed the Suez canal by bombing a ship passing through Egyptian territory. Large shipments were diverted from Aden and the Red Sea to the southern route around the cape of Africa until 1975. When Dubai in the Persian Gulf replaced Aden as a port of call, the new southern regime failed to benefit as expected from local economic resources. Aden still contained an industrial zone, including an oil refinery on its northern harbor. It also had large neighborhoods with a well-organized educational system through post-secondary levels. In fact, before the oil boom in the 1970s transformed the capitals of Saudi Arabia, Kuwait, the UAE, Bahrain, and Qatar, Aden was the largest and most cosmopolitan city on the Arab peninsula. It once was a destination of choice for Arab students seeking a better education. This contrasted with the northern capital, Sanaa.

At the start of north Yemen's revolution on September 26, 1962, Sanaa was a small, traditional walled city with several thousand people packed inside a few square miles. Under the Zaydi imamate, it was customary to lock the city gates at dusk and unlock them at dawn, in order to protect against nighttime marauders and bandits. Security outside the city walls could not be guaranteed. Even Imam Ahmad chose not to live in Sanaa after his father's murder in 1948, moving the national capital to the safer environment of Taiz instead. Following Imam Ahmad's death by natural

---

[36] "Port Development Strategy," an unpublished report of the Aden Port Authority, 1996; p. 1. While the PDRY had a long coastline, its interior was rocky and desert terrain. One study estimated that less than 1 percent of southern lands was suitable for cultivation. Lackner, 1985; p. 170. As a result, the PDRY never developed large-scale agricultural production capable of sustaining a large population like the northern YAR.

[37] Before southern independence, "more than sixty per cent of all revenue had come from British aid." Halliday, 1974; p. 250. The British withdrew without promising any further aid, so the new government was forced to depend on revenues from the port and other national sources.

causes in the late summer of 1962, the national capital returned to Sanaa. When Imam Ahmad's son was overthrown one week later, thousands of people migrated from surrounding areas to build homes in new neighborhoods outside the old city's wall. Large stones from the old wall were used as the foundations of many new homes. But the structures of these homes were constructed with cheap cinder blocks. This broke the pattern of using traditional materials in the design of Sanaa's homes: specially baked red bricks, finished with a white gypsum paste around windows and upper parapets. The urban sprawl around Sanaa eventually stretched fifteen miles wide between the famous mountain peaks of Jabal al-Nugum in the east and Jabal al-'Asr in the west.

By the time of national unity in 1990, Sanaa's population had grown exponentially. Although the YAR started from a comparatively weak position with little central government control of its territory, north Yemen's economic growth outpaced the PDRY. As President Salih centralized revenues drawn from outside the highland mountains, and began receiving large sums of hard currency from the sale of Marib's oil, Sanaa experienced a second building boom with construction on nearly every flat plot of land. In the late 1980s, city streets became congested with traffic. Several main thoroughfares were transformed into bustling commercial zones. This was no longer a third or fourth ranked urban center behind Aden, Taiz, and al-Hudayda. At the end of the decade, Sanaa had surpassed Aden with nearly one million people. By contrast, Aden looked like a dilapidated reminder of its former self, stripped bare by power struggles over dwindling resources in the southern capital.

In January 1986, Aden was literally torn apart during intraregime warfare between rival factions of the Yemeni Socialist Party (YSP). The fighting started on January 13, when President Ali Nasir Muhammad's personal security launched an astonishing attack inside a YSP politburo meeting.[38] President Ali Nasir is originally from the mid-southern town of Mudi'a in Abyan province. The politburo officials who were killed in the fighting mainly came from southwestern districts of Radfan and al-Dali' in Lahij province. In the end, military commanders from Radfan and al-Dali', including the commander of one tank unit, fought their way into the

---

[38] Four key members of the politburo were assassinated: the former minister of defense Ali Antar; the acting defense minister Salih Muslih Qasim; the former secretary general of the YSP Abd al-Fattah Ismail; and Ali Shai Hadi. The future secretary general of the YSP and vice president of united Yemen, Ali Salem al-Bid, was the only individual who survived the assassination attempt. According to supporters of Ali Nasir Muhammad, the attack was a preemptive strike against rivals who had plotted a similar move.

PHOTO 8. Aden's outer beach with shipwreck in breaking waves

seaside capital, and overturned Ali Nasir. The president and his associates were forced to flee. What followed was a period of revenge killings against city residents from Abyan province, who were accused of supporting the exiled president. Thousands died, and tens of thousands fled the country, mainly citizens from Abyan and neighboring Shabwa province in the mid-southern region.[39] Most of these political refugees settled in north Yemen.

During the course of the fighting in January 1986, Aden was bombarded from land, sea, and air. Many buildings in the city still bear the pocked marks of tank and mortar shells. On the city's outer beach, south of the massive volcanic mountain *Shamsan*, a large section of a naval vessel washed ashore after the vessel was ripped in half by an airstrike. Today it rests in shallow water like the carcass of a giant whale beached at high tide. The rusting heap of steel symbolizes the fate of the entire city since its postwar economic boom in the late 1940s and 1950s. Immediately after the violence ended, Fred Halliday, the late British scholar of Yemeni politics, described the warring political factions as "tribal" in nature.[40] A few years later he wrote more precisely: "these links were not tribal in a straightforward sense but encompassed regional groupings broader than the traditional tribe."[41] The political rupture in January 1986 caused a deeper split in the center of the country, where Shabwa province (home to the once powerful Aulaqi tribe) had been cut from power in the late 1960s.

[39] Halliday, 1990; p. 47. Any resident of Aden who was born in the mid-southern region was targeted in the violence, even writers and artists, regardless of whether or not they were active associates of the former president.

[40] Halliday, 1986; p. 39.

[41] Halliday, 1990; p. 47.

Now Abyan was added to neighboring Shabwa, creating a huge rift in the country's mid-southern region.

Some YSP officials from Abyan remained in government, such as Muhammad Haydar Masdus. But thereafter, the cabinet in Aden was balanced between political and military elites from Lahij and al-Dali' in the southwestern corner of the country, and Hadramaut in the east. The PDRY president, and secretary general of the YSP, who replaced Ali Nasser was Ali Salem al-Bid, a long-serving Hadrami in political and military posts who survived the politburo shootings on January 13. From a relatively early stage in the PDRY's history, the government had successfully eradicated revenge killings and the destructive cycles of tribal warfare in rural areas. After 1967, it discouraged regional identities among the population, inhibiting citizens from thinking of themselves as Hadrami or Radfani, Yafi' or Aulaqi. Until 1986, politicians sought balance and collegiality within the central bureaucracy by appointing representatives of outer regions to serve together in the same offices (Table 2.4). Since the south kept many British administrative practices, including a strong financial "audit and control" system, its bureaucracy maintained a fair degree of professionalism that made it nearly impossible to exert overt personal influence over government spending. There was little room for nepotism or favoritism because the regime disallowed political fiefdoms that might cause the kind of factional conflict seen in 1986.

For all of these reasons, PDRY state institutions represented different regional groups in the south fairly well through the early 1980s. Three things changed before January 1986: first, a growing financial crisis forced reforms in the political and economic system, particularly in 1985 when new Soviet leader Mikhail Gorbachev pushed a reform agenda in Moscow; second, the southern regime's continued entanglement in north Yemeni politics fed growing factionalism and jealousies in society; and third, rivalries surfaced and hardened between the regime's different military and security units.[42] After the truce in the northern guerrilla war in 1982, Aden was forced to absorb Marxist militias that refused to reconcile with Salih's regime in Sanaa.[43] This primarily concerned military commanders from al-Radfan and al-Dali' in the southwest region because their homes were closer to the battlefronts in

---

[42] Fred Halliday also explained the January 1986 violence based on three factors dividing the regime: the alliance with the Soviet Union and East Bloc countries; support for insurgent groups in north Yemen; and socialist ideology in the state's economic policies. Halliday, 1990; 47 ff.

[43] Ibid, p. 130.

the north.[44] They were also on friendlier terms with northern Marxist guerrillas than citizens from other regions of south Yemen, who preferred that north Yemenis work to resolve their conflicts across the border and allow the southern state to serve the interests of its own citizens. President Ali Nasir took the latter position. He also favored innovative reforms in government to decentralize power, and encourage entrepreneurial behavior, as a way to simulate economic growth.

One of President Ali Nasir's closest associates from his home region was Muhammad Ali Ahmed, the influential governor of Abyan province. From the governor's office east of Aden, Muhammad Ali took advantage of the central government's new decentralization policy to develop his own line of imports in Abyan's seaside capital, Zinjibar.[45] Word quickly circulated in Aden that the governor's office was equipped with "first world" technologies, including fax machines and color printers. At the time, many central ministries lacked this type of equipment, and the close ties between Abyan's governor and President Ali Nasir fueled accusations of favoritism and corruption. Southwestern groups in Lahij complained. They also resisted further reform measures, demanding that the YSP maintain its socialist principles.

The chief Marxist ideologue in the YSP, Abd al-Fattah Ismail, originally came from the midland province of Taiz. Abd al-Fattah migrated to Aden in the 1950s, and soon became active in the city's labor movement and the NLF's liberation struggle. During the late 1970s, he briefly became head of state, but was later exiled to Moscow because of his rigid ideological views.[46] After Abd al-Fattah's return to Aden in the early 1980s, he

---

[44] Former YSP secretary-general Abd al-Fattah Ismail was south Yemen's main proponent of the policy to support Marxist groups in north Yemen's midland region. But he had strong support among military commanders from Lahij province. Ismail saw this policy as the best strategy to weaken the regime in Sanaa, and he used his leadership role in the ruling party "to cultivate the insurgent bodies in North Yemen as offshoots of the party he governed." Kostiner, *South Yemen's Revolutionary Strategy*, 1990; p. 65. Fred Halliday documents how the formation of the two main northern insurgent groups, the National Democratic Front and "Howshi," or the Party of Popular Yemeni Unity, coincided with different stages of political party development in south Yemen. Halliday, 1990; pp. 122–127.

[45] Interview with former south Yemeni officials in Aden during 1996 and 1997.

[46] Halliday, 1990; pp. 128–129. The radical orientation of Abd al-Fattah Ismail had long prevented the PDRY from developing the kind of beneficial relations which many southerners desired with Arab Gulf countries. In 1976, Ismail used his influence in the central party to rally opposition against a significant five-year $400 million aid package from Saudi Arabia, an amount representing "almost double the total planned PDRY investment for that period." Kostiner, 1990; pp. 67–68. Fred Halliday and Joseph Kostiner both

TABLE 2.4. *Regional Distribution of Ministerial Posts in the Southern PDRY, 1985–86*[a]

| | Southwestern | | Mid-Southern | | Eastern | Cross Border |
Date	Aden	Lahij	Abyan	Shabwa	Hadramaut	North Yemen
2/85	6	6	4	1	7	3
2/86	3	6	0	0	5	4

[a] This data was gathered in a similar way to the data in Table 2.2.

began agitating on behalf of the northern Marxist movement, pressing military commanders in al-Radfan and al-Dali' to assert their power and influence. Amidst growing economic and political strains, these commanders started to concentrate more military power in their own hands, while weeding out officers from other regions whose loyalties they questioned. Likewise, President Ali Nasir and his closest associates began maneuvering to strengthen their hold on power, before plotting against their rivals in the YSP politburo.

Twice before in south Yemeni history, there had been a forced removal of the head of state: first, in 1969, when President Qahtan al-Shaabi of Lahij was removed during the Marxist "correction" movement; and second, in 1978, when President Salem Rubaya Ali from Zinjibar, Abyan was removed and executed. The upheaval in 1986 created far greater problems for the PDRY's political system. On previous occasions, there had always been a way to repair the internal political damage, and produce renewed balance in the central government. But in 1986, the southern republic was knocked completely off balance by the scale of killing that took place in Aden. Afterward, the rupture inside the regime was not limited to a few individuals in top leadership posts, as happened in 1969 and 1978. It impacted all levels of government administration in Abyan and Shabwa of the mid-southern region.

In February 1986, the new cabinet formed by Ali Salem al-Bid included six ministers from Lahij, five from Hadramaut, three from Aden, and four ministers from northern Yemen. There were no ministers from Abyan and Shabwa provinces. Even more indicative of the January 1986 violence's impact on the people of Abyan and Shabwa is the change in their local

showed that, throughout the years of the Arab oil boom in the mid-1970s, many southern political elites realized the need to moderate the PDRY's revolutionary character, in order to foster better economic ties with wealthy, conservative Arab Gulf countries. But Abd al-Fattah opposed this moderation.

TABLE 2.5. *Percentage of Native Officials in Southern PDRY's Ten Major Provincial Posts*[a]

	1985	1986	1987	1988	1989	1990
SOUTHWEST REGION						
Aden	43	29	29	29	29	43
Lahij	100	86	86	86	86	86
MID-SOUTHERN REGION						
Abyan	100	50	50	50	50	50
Shabwa	100	63	63	63	63	63
EASTERN REGION						
Hadramaut	100	90	90	90	90	90
Wadi Hadramaut	100	100	100	100	100	100
al-Mahra	43	43	43	43	43	43

[a] The data in Table 2.5 and the remaining tables of this chapter were collected from the author's local administrative survey, which is described in the Appendix. The odd percentages in some of the "ten major" posts are due to the fact that some local administrative posts did not exist in every province. For example, Shabwa did not have a customs office. In addition, the survey results were incomplete in some provinces. Although the survey covered only one year prior to south Yemen's political violence in 1986, a former ministry official in the PDRY's local administrative service confirmed that the percentages from 1985 reflect the percentages during the previous ten to fifteen years. In short, the PDRY typically had 100 percent native representation in its provincial administrative staff.

administrative personnel (Table 2.5). In the history of the southern PDRY, local administrative bodies were generally staffed by citizens native to the provinces in which they served. For example, after "al-Sa'idi events" in the late 1960s, Shabwa province's staff continued to come from native residents in the province. In 1985, the ten major administrative posts in Abyan and Shabwa (including governor, deputy governor, directors of public and political security, chief prosecutor, and the directors of finance, banking, taxation, customs, and audit and control) were all staffed by native residents. After January 1986, the percentage of native officials in Shabwa dropped to 67 percent, when a governor from Hadramaut and two security directors from Lahij were appointed to serve in the province. Abyan province dropped from 100 percent native staff in 1985 to just 50 percent after 1986. Abyan received a new public security director from Hadramaut and a political security director from Lahij, as well as three finance and banking directors from other provinces.

The post-1986 change in local administrative staff was unprecedented in the history of south Yemen, where the central government generally trusted citizens to run their own local affairs. Aden was the main

TABLE 2.6. *Percentage of Native Officials in Northern YAR's Ten Major Provincial Posts*

	1985	1986	1987	1988	1989	1990
HIGHLAND REGION						
Sanaa City	86	86	86	86	86	86
Sanaa	86	86	86	86	86	86
Hajja	38	38	25	13	13	13
al-Mahwit	0	0	0	0	0	0
Sa'da	0	0	0	0	0	0
WEST COAST REGION						
al-Hudayda	10	10	10	10	10	10
WESTERN MIDLAND REGION						
Taiz	30	30	30	30	30	30
al-Bayda	30	30	30	30	30	30
Ibb	13	13	13	13	13	13
CENTRAL INTERIOR REGION						
Marib	0	0	0	0	0	0

exception, since its residents came from all provinces of the south as well as areas of north Yemen. Thus, Aden's provincial staff reflected great regional diversity. Al-Mahra also had a low percentage of native staff, since it was the most remote and least developed province in the southern half of the country. There were few qualified candidates in al-Mahra to staff its administrative offices because the population of this far eastern region had the lowest educational standards in the PDRY. Officials in Aden always struggled to find local Mahris interested in bureaucratic work.

The key point is that local government practices in the southern PDRY were unlike practices in north Yemen, which had a long legacy of political elites from the northwest highland region dominating provinces in midland and coastal regions. For the sake of comparison, Table 2.6 reveals the native representation inside the same ten major administrative posts of the northern YAR's provinces. Between 1985 and 1990, it is clear that most north Yemeni provinces had very low or no native representation. Only Sanaa province and the northern highland capital zone had a high percentage of native officers serving in the ten major administrative posts. Indeed, the percentage of native representation in each of the remaining northern provinces was lower than the percentage of native representation in Abyan and Shabwa after the southern PDRY erupted in violence in 1986. This offers another strong indication of the different regional dynamics at work in north and south Yemen. North Yemen commonly had the type of regional marginalization of whole segments of the population only found in the PDRY's mid-southern region, first at a minimal level in Shabwa after 1969, and later extended more broadly to Abyan and Shabwa provinces in 1986.

Before January 1986, the only province in the southern PDRY that had government administrators appointed from outside the local population was al-Mahra. Unlike the northern YAR, there was practically no experience of individuals from one or more regions dominating the provincial administration of another region. But after 1986, the central government in Aden was wary of allowing mid-southern citizens to run their own provincial affairs. It is particularly telling that, from 1986 to 1990, the directors of political security in Abyan and Shabwa came from Lahij. In north and south Yemen, "political security" is a domestic spy agency like the *mukhabbarat* of other Arab states. It provides regular surveillance reports to the regime, and occasionally uses coercion against domestic political opponents. In January 1986, members of all security branches in Lahij resisted President Ali Nasir's grab for power after murdering top party officials, and then sought revenge against average citizens from Abyan and Shabwa. The fact that Lahij political security officers remained in Abyan and Shabwa, four years after 1986, is a clear sign that the southern PDRY had lost some of its noteworthy regional balance just prior to uniting with north Yemen in 1990.

MIRROR OPPOSITES

During the run up to national unity in the late 1980s, the governments of north and south Yemen were heading in opposite directions. The north Yemeni state was expanding with new sources of revenue, and a policy of centralization in Sanaa. The south Yemeni state was contracting with fewer sources of revenue, and a fractured central government. After centralizing power in Aden during the late 1960s and 1970s, the government of the PDRY began experimenting with decentralization in the early and middle 1980s. The opposite was true in the northern YAR, where the cooperative movement created decentralization during the 1960s and early 1970s, only to be reversed once officials in Sanaa created stronger state institutions through the CYDA.

The mirror reflection of politics in north and south Yemen, evident by the two capitals' contrasting conditions in the late 1980s, is best explained by the different regional group dynamics on each side of the former border, as well as the two states' different distribution of economic resources.

These differences fundamentally shaped and defined the two ruling parties that united north and south Yemen in 1990. Beginning in the first decade after southern independence, the Yemeni Socialist Party (YSP) evolved from the National Liberation Front. The successor National Front organization served as an important instrument for recruiting political leaders from different regions of the country.[47] In 1975, it formally united with two small parties, one communist and the other Arab nationalist, to form the Unified Political Organization of the National Front. Three years later, this political umbrella organization changed its name to the Yemeni Socialist Party.

In less than eight years, southern Marxist leaders had built a centralized one-party ruling system. This one-party system was crucial for maintaining cross-regional balance in PDRY government. The balance in ministerial cabinets in Aden, and the strong native representation in local provincial offices, were a direct reflection of the YSP's own balanced representation across the country. But in 1986, this regional balance collapsed in intra-regime warfare. Across the border in the YAR, the General People's Congress (GPC) was created relatively late in the northern republic's third decade. At the time of its formation in 1982, there were doubts about the GPC's capability of serving as a nationwide political party. Indeed it did not prove its viability as an effective ruling party until two years before unification with south Yemen, when it held popular elections for a national "consultative council" in July 1988. This council ratified the presidency of Ali Abdallah Salih, giving legitimacy to a northern president for the first time since 1970.

For nearly twenty years, north Yemen was governed by military rule without a fixed constitutional government. The extent to which the GPC's political development was slower than the southern YSP is largely because the northern half of Yemen remained more regionally divided during its early republican history. The myth about the "sons of Qahtan" helped reduce lingering sectarian divisions between Zaydi and Shafi'i citizens, and the "republican pact" of 1970 ended the north's long civil war. But the political system remained unsettled until the middle 1980s. It was only at this time, following the discovery of oil and the southern regime's political meltdown in 1986, that President Salih appeared to gain a firmer grip on power in Sanaa than his national rivals in the port city of Aden.

---

[47] Some scholars concluded that the ruling party in the south played an important assimilation role in the PDRY with an extensive recruitment program in all regions of the country. Ismail, 1986; pp. 35–36 and 54–60. Lackner, 1985; pp. 206–207.

TABLE 2.7. *Percentage of Highland Officials among Northern YAR's Top Four Provincial Posts*

	1985	1986	1987	1988	1989	1990
HIGHLAND REGION						
Sanaa City	100	100	100	100	100	100
Sanaa	100	100	100	100	100	100
Hajja	100	100	75	100	100	100
al-Mahwit	75	75	100	100	100	100
Sa'da	100	100	100	100	100	100
WEST COAST REGION						
al-Hudayda	75	50	50	50	50	50
WESTERN MIDLAND REGION						
Taiz	75	75	75	75	75	75
al-Bayda	50	50	50	50	50	50
Ibb	75	75	75	75	75	75
CENTRAL INTERIOR REGION						
Marib	75	75	25	75	75	75

The greatest political contrast between north and south Yemen is the legacy of regional domination by highland tribal elites in the north. This was never an element of south Yemeni politics. After 1986, military and security leaders from the southwest region may have asserted dominance over residents in the midsouthern region. But actors from the southwest region hardly controlled state institutions in Aden as highland elites controlled northern state institutions. Top YSP officials from Hadramaut and Aden, and even areas of north Yemen, continued to play influential roles in Aden, limiting the power of security and military officers from Lahij. By contrast, the northern presidency, military, and security forces were controlled by highland political elites three decades after the last Zaydi imam. Highland elites also maintained a regular two-thirds majority control of cabinet ministries in the YAR.

The full extent of the highland group's domination in the north is indicated in Table 2.7. Northern highland officials consistently held fifty percent or more of the "top four" provincial posts (governor, deputy governor, and directors of public and political security) in every northern province during the late 1980s. The only exception was the central interior province of Marib in one year, 1987. This shows that the government in Sanaa tended to appoint people from the highlands region to govern outlying provinces, rather than allow native born officials to run their own provincial affairs. Between 1985 and 1990, three of the "top four" provincial posts in the critically important western midland provinces of Taiz and Ibb, and the central interior province of Marib, were held by highland officials. Indeed, the vast majority of northern governors and deputy governors came from Sanaa and the highland region.

Inside the highland region, the central government maintained native representation in the "top four" and "ten major" administrative posts in Sanaa province and the capital zone. Thus it was permissible for citizens of Sanaa to govern their own affairs, but not the people of Taiz, Ibb, al-Hudayda, and Marib. In other highland provinces, Hajja, Sa'da, and al-Mahwit, the government did not appoint native officials, except on a few occasions in Hajja. However, there was nearly 100% highland representation in the "top four" and "ten major" administrative posts of all three provinces. Citizens from western midland and coastal regions never served as governors or security directors in highland provinces. The reality of north Yemeni politics in the late 1980s is that the political umbrella of President Salih's GPC provided institutional cover for prevailing highland group interests. Myths about unity among the "sons of Qahtan" meant people in lowland and coastal regions were free to imagine a common brotherhood with their highland neighbors, whereas highland political elites and tribal shaykhs were free to continue ruling outlying regions of the country, in order to exploit their greater resources.

Before the northern YAR began to generate oil revenues, it faced an economic crisis in the early and middle 1980s, similar to the one in south Yemen. In 1981, the international price of oil dropped, and remittances from migrant workers in Saudi Arabia decreased. During these years, the regime in Sanaa implemented an economic restructuring program, ostensibly to reduce its trade imbalance. It instituted a restrictive import licensing policy, which largely closed down the country's private sector, channeling up to 60 percent of all imports into state-run corporations.[48] In Kiren Chaudhry's 1997 book, *The Price of Wealth*, she suggests that President Salih was able to impose severe economic measures with virtual "impunity" because the interests of Shafi'i businessmen from Taiz and al-Hudayda were detached from real political power.[49] The effect, Chaudhry states, was "deeply divisive" because it favored members of the highland regional group who controlled political and military

---

[48] Kiren Chaudhry, 1997; pp. 270 and 276.
[49] Ibid, pp. 284–288. In other words, President Salih was able to carry out his economic reforms precisely because of the country's regional divisions.

institutions.[50] During the same time, it was hardly a coincidence that powerful new groups of highland traders, often the top shaykhs of Hashid and Bakil, cornered import markets for basic food and construction materials, while serving as local agents for foreign car companies and other international corporations doing business in the Middle East.

After north Yemen's economic reform program in the early 1980s, its trade imbalance remained. What changed was that import businesses became dominated by highland elites with tribal and military connections. The transformation in the north's political economy was profound. Kiren Chaudhry concludes that it signaled the end of the north's old cross-regional pact of "non-interference" between political and economic forces.[51] The "republican pact" was still observed by politicians from Taiz and other lowland regions. Abd al-Aziz Abd al-Ghani continued serving as northern prime minister until unification with south Yemen in 1990. Other midland and coastal elites continued to hold their one-third share of cabinet seats. The largest Shafi'i businessmen continued to operate at a profit, most notably the Hayil Said Anam group which manufactures basic consumer goods in Taiz. But the first rumblings of discontent could be heard as small and mid-size traders in western midland and coastal regions were increasingly cut from business deals.

North Yemen's informal power sharing arrangement, adopted in 1970, came undone at precisely the moment the YAR prepared to enter a formal power sharing arrangement with PDRY government officials. This is important to bear in mind when analyzing Yemen's unification process in the 1990s because it signaled false intentions by northern highland elites to compromise their political power. When north and south Yemen agreed to form one state for "one people" and "one nation," there were two very different regimes entering the unity process together. In late 1989, President Ali Abdallah Salih travelled to Aden to meet Ali Salem al-Bid at a time when military and tribal elites from the highland region had gained nearly complete control in Sanaa. Meanwhile al-Bid's southern regime was busy trying to mend a massive rupture in his ruling party, just three years earlier. The southern regime continued to be balanced between representatives of the eastern region in Hadramaut, and the southwestern region in Lahij. But it maintained this balance across a chasm in the mid-southern provinces of Abyan and Shabwa.

[50] Ibid, p. 292.
[51] Ibid, p. 291.

During the late 1980s, the most influential representatives of mid-southern interests lived as political exiles in north Yemen, where President Salih played host to them in Sanaa. This placed al-Bid's regime in Aden in a noticeably weaker position. Not only was the southern government in a deep political and economic crisis at home, but its internal party rivals had taken up residence across the border. During unity negotiations in 1989, President Salih could rely on advice and support from former President Ali Nasser and his partisans, the latter of whom would later play influential political roles. In short, the southern YSP leadership in Aden was in a risky position because northern President Salih held most of the political cards at a time when Marxist socialism was in retreat around the world. This had an enormous impact on how Yemen's unification played out in the early 1990s, which is the topic of Chapter 4. But it is first necessary to examine the character of President Salih's highland ruling group in more detail.

3

Salih Family Rules and the Sanhan Tribe

In the highland mountains encircling Sanaa, the tribesmen of Hashid and Bakil set themselves above other tribal and nontribal people of the country. They are very proud of a local culture that is deeply conservative, paternalist, and militarized. This is the part of Yemen where it is frequently said that guns outnumber people. On average, each adult male possesses three or four firearms: common handguns, rifles and machine guns, and even heavier fire power like rocket-propelled grenade launchers (RPGs) and in rare cases, heavy artillery. In the early 2000s, Sanaa's capital zone began to enforce a gun ban. This required all entrants to deposit their weapons at special registration centers, where they could be retrieved upon exiting the city. Outside the capital, most men remained well armed. It is common to see local tribesmen carrying AK-47s, while wearing the traditional curved dagger known as *jambiyya*. Guns and *jambiyya* are found in other regions of Yemen, but in the northwest highland mountains they are omnipresent.

The custom of carrying guns feeds a sense of superiority among highland tribesmen, especially the tribal shaykhs of Hashid and Bakil who feel they are more powerful and capable of ruling the country than Yemenis living at lower elevations. People in lower lying regions acknowledge this sense of superiority among highland tribes, yet it is greatly resented. The word for the highlands, *al-jabali*, is closely associated with power and dominance in Yemen. Highland culture is best described by a local phrase used to express a type of *machismo* among men. *Ahmar al-'ayn*, meaning "red of the eye," describes a man of great daring and boldness, who surpasses his rivals in courage. It may also apply to a man who goes beyond bravery to recklessly aggressive behavior. As leader of Yemen, and a member of Hashid, President Ali Abdallah Salih long fashioned himself as the quintessential red-eye man.

PHOTO 9. President Salih poster image

On every government building across the country, there were posters of Salih. Owners of private shops and restaurants typically hung one of a variety of presidential photos, showing the man in different roles. When President Salih first came to power in his early thirties, he appeared in photos as a military officer with bushy hair, mustache and reflective aviator sunglasses. In more recent times, the carefully scripted poster image depicted a balding man in an Italian-cut suit with the same requisite mustache, but no sunglasses. In most posters, Salih's eyes squinted slightly with focused determination, conveying strength and confidence. During his long reign, Salih played many roles in the minds of average citizens. It was the poster image of Salih the tribesman, *ahmar al-'ayn*, that best captured the persona of the man.

Ali Abdallah Salih was born on March 21, 1946. In his youth, he attained only a basic level of education. His Arabic speaking skills continued to reflect this fact in adulthood, as he was known for crude speech habits. The president's father, named Abdallah Salih, died when Ali was a young boy. Ali's mother remarried to her deceased husband's brother, Muhammad Salih. This paternal uncle became young Ali's stepfather and mentor.[1] The family lived in a small village

---

[1] This story of President Ali Abdallah Salih's upbringing is common knowledge in Yemen.

twenty miles southeast of Sanaa, called Bayt al-Ahmar. Bayt al-Ahmar sits on a barren, dusty, relatively nondescript plain with none of the natural markers that are common features of the Yemeni landscape. Crows circle overhead, and a few stray dogs roam the outskirts of the village. What set Bayt al-Ahmar apart was the large number of palatial villas at its core. These multilevel stone buildings decorated on the exterior with slabs of local marble, limestone, and volcanic basalt mutely colored red, green, beige, white, brown, purple, and black are the symbol of the country's *nouveau riche*.

Yemen has its share of palaces and wealthy elite, but the concentration of wealth in Bayt al-Ahmar was always out of place. The appearance of so many palatial villas towering over the village recalls the artificial grandeur of casino hotels built along a remote highway in the dust fields of Nevada. Each villa sits enclosed behind a high perimeter wall with large iron gates. Plainclothes security men with sunglasses, mustaches, but no beard, guard all roads leading to the village located inside the administrative district of Sanhan. Sanhan district is adjacent to the national capital, and it forms part of the larger province of Sanaa which surrounds the capital zone on all sides.

President Salih's family is from a clan of the Sanhan tribe, which itself is part of the larger highland tribal federation of Hashid. Since the revolution that overthrew Yemen's last Zaydi imam in September 1962, Hashid has managed to hold the most powerful government and military posts in the country. Although smaller in number than Bakil, Hashid maintains its dominance by being more cohesive and active as a group. Prior to north Yemen's revolution, the leading shaykhs of Hashid and Bakil could either make or break the rule of an imam. During transitions of power, they often cast the deciding vote in councils of elderly men. But Sanhan's shaykhs were rarely influential inside these higher councils.

Among all the tribes of Hashid, Sanhan is a weak subtribe. The last imam to rule Yemen for an extended time, Ahmad ibn Yahya Hamid al-Din, spoke disparagingly of Sanhan tribesmen, describing them as mere "grunts" at the lowest level of his army. Compared to the powerful and more troublesome tribes to the north and east of Sanaa, the Sanhan tribe was virtually a nonactor in Yemeni politics. When the revolution came in 1962, no one would have ever predicted that a simple tribesman from Sanhan could rise to power during the next decade. On the eve of President Ali Abdallah Salih's ascendance in the summer of 1978, at the young age of thirty-two, few Yemenis knew his name. Even fewer would have predicted his continued rule three decades later.

THE MAN FROM SANHAN

There are three key points that help explain President Salih's rise to power, and his longevity in office. First, it is important to consider that his two predecessors were assassinated less than nine months apart. Both were military officers like Salih, although more distinguished in rank and reputation. After their assassinations, there was great fear of dying a violent death in the presidential palace. As a consequence, few men of power and influence were prepared to step forward as possible successors. Ali Abdallah Salih became president of north Yemen partly because no one else dared to take the job.

Second, it is important to understand that President Salih's family clan, and related clans inside Sanhan, provided a protective shield guaranteeing his survival in office. Since his widowed mother remarried a paternal uncle, the president had many half brothers and sisters, in addition to a full brother named Muhammad Abdallah Salih. There were also many uncles, and male cousins and nephews. Soon after becoming president, Salih built a wall of power around himself by appointing the men of this extended family to top military and security posts. The president's full brother became commander of the national security force, called "central security," while a half-brother named Ali Salih was appointed army commander in Sanhan district, where he could defend the family's interest.[2] The strongman behind the president, General Ali Muhsin al-Ahmar, was from a different clan, but still a member of Sanhan tribe. Ali Muhsin, as he is commonly known in Yemen, became commander of Yemen's first artillery brigade in the primary tribal lands of Hashid and Bakil, north of Sanaa. This made his job crucial for keeping the president in office.

Third, it is essential to comprehend the president's position relative to the "republican pact" that united influential highland figures with economic elites from western midland and coastal regions. During the 1970s, Salih served as a junior military officer in the midland province of Taiz. Before 1978, he befriended many of the leading Shafi'i businessmen who supported the "Free Yemenis" in the 1950s, and backed the republican alliance with Egypt in the 1960s. It was partly due to these connections that Salih was prepared to step forward as president in July 1978.

By many accounts, Ali Abdallah Salih was a courageous young soldier, and a business-minded officer. Before the 1962 revolution, he volunteered as a teenager in Imam Ahmad's army like many other young men from

---

[2] Dresch, 2000; p. 149.

Sanhan.[3] Once the revolution commenced, he joined the republican cause. According to Salih's official biography, he was twenty-one when he fought in the famous "Seventy Days" battle in Sanaa at the end of 1967. This battle witnessed a long siege after royalist forces moved artillery within range of the capital, following Egypt's withdrawal to confront Israel in the summer of 1967. Nearly every member of north Yemen's republican elite claimed to have fought in the "Seventy Days" battle. Since national memories of this battle came to define patriotism in the infant republic, it was important for a politician's reputation to be known as someone who helped rescue the city. Yet at the time, many highland tribesmen had divided loyalties. If Salih played any role in defending the city, it was only a minor one.

At the end of the northern civil war in 1970, the future president wanted to become commander of a tank brigade, in order to burnish his credentials as an *ahmar al-ayn* soldier. For this to be possible, he needed entry into the army officer's training school in Sanaa. Before qualifying for the school, he had to find a financial guarantor. Since Salih came from a weak tribal background on the south side of Sanaa, there were no wealthy businessmen in his village to provide the necessary endorsement. He sought and received help from an exiled southern businessman, named Mahfouz Shamakh, whose family emigrated to live in the north during the 1960s. Members of the Shamakh family are successful traders and business agents throughout Yemen, who originally come from Shibam in Wadi Hadramaut. During Salih's military training and his early career as an officer, Shamakh and other Shafi'i businessmen served as counselors to the young man.

After graduation, Salih's first post was a military base along the main road between Taiz and Mocha, a port town on the Red Sea. This road was famous for smuggling alcohol imported from Africa, unloaded at docks in Mocha, and then transported to Taiz and northward into the mountains. Mocha became famous during the sixteenth and seventeenth centuries as the point of origin for the coffee trade in Europe. But in the 1970s, Mocha bustled with black market whiskey. Yemenis consumed larger quantities of alcohol after the imam's religious order collapsed in 1962. Salih and the soldiers under his command operated a roadside checkpoint, where they inspected cars and trucks for smuggled goods. Like the port officials in Mocha, Salih turned a blind eye as long as the whiskey smugglers paid

---

[3] This information is from President Salih's official biography on his government website. Retrieved October 2010.

sufficient bribes. According to local legends, Yemen's future president prospered in this work, while developing important friendships with merchants in Taiz.

Under the Rasulid dynasty between the thirteenth and fifteenth centuries, Taiz became the greatest Shafi'i political, commercial, and agricultural center. The city briefly became the seat of political authority a second time under Imam Ahmad in the late 1940s and 1950s. It was unusual for a Zaydi imam to rule from the midland region because the imams traditionally built their capitals in Sanaa, Shahara, and Sa'da in the highland mountains. Under Imam Ahmad's rule, Taiz experienced a commercial boom. Many city merchants secretly supported leaders of the Free Yemenis who relocated to Aden in the late 1950s. The extra trade allowed Taiz merchants to provide more financial support to the underground liberation movement. Following Imam Ahmad's death in 1962, Shafi'i businessmen hoped to advance their earning power in a new republican system. But the city returned to its sleepy provincial status, when the new government relocated the capital to Sanaa.

During the years of northern civil war in the 1960s, Taiz and al-Hudayda provided the real strength behind the republican cause. Among the Shafi'i population of the western midlands, Egyptian officers found eager recruits who had the motivation and education to train with new artillery and commando divisions. One of the heroes of the "Seventy Days" battle was the Egyptian-trained commander of paratroops Abd al-Raqib Abd al-Wahhab, a Shafi'i from Taiz who led reinforcements to Sanaa and kept open supply lines to prevent the capital from falling to the royalist army.[4] Zaydis who joined the republican side, including top shaykhs of Hahsid and Bakil, perceived Shafi'i officers like Abd al-Raqib as a threat to continued highland control of the country. Abd al-Raqib was eventually betrayed and murdered by highland figures who sought reconciliation with Zaydi royalist forces in 1968.

Between 1967 and 1970, there was a three or four-man "republican council" that headed the northern government.[5] Two Shafi'i from Taiz sat on the first council in 1967: Ahmad Numan, cofounder of the Free Yemenis; and Shaykh Muhammad Ali Othman, a quasi-tribal leader of al-Maddhaj. After two weeks, Numan resigned for political reasons in late November 1967. He was replaced by the Zaydi general Hasan al-Amri, who came from a prominent family in Sanaa city. General al-Amri became

[4] Halliday, 1974; pp. 122–124.
[5] Al-Zhahiri, 1996; pp. 156–159.

the main enforcer of highland interests in the new government. Ahmad Numan was later invited back to lead a new government in 1971. But he was quickly driven from office by highland tribal shaykhs who voted "no confidence" on a key advisory council. Thereafter, the government in Sanaa remained in the hands of highland presidents, first Abd al-Rahman al-Iryani, then Ibrahim al-Hamdi and Ahmad al-Ghashmi, before Ali Abdallah Salih came to power. The latter two presidents both came from a Hashid tribal background.

Before al-Ghashmi's assassination in the summer of 1978, Salih was able to join social gatherings of Taiz's most prominent businessmen once he was promoted as army commander of the western midland region. Yemenis have a custom of socializing in large groups after lunch, when they chew the leaves of the mild stimulant *qat*. These *qat*-sessions often last several hours into the early evening. This is a time of friendly banter and joke telling. Salih was known as a spirited participant in *qat*-sessions. Many Yemenis described him as a clever, although crude interlocutor with a sharp wit and strong memory. His lack of education was not a shortcoming in Yemen, where people admire the skills of verbal storytelling. By joining Taiz's *qat*-sessions, Salih advanced his personal status among the city's merchants.

After al-Ghashmi's assassination in Sanaa, the topic of discussion at Taiz's *qat*-sessions turned to the selection of the next president. The merchants of Taiz pondered how they might influence the selection process.[6] Meanwhile, in Sanaa, vice president Abd al-Karim al-Arashe acted as transitional head of state. Al-Arashe was neither a military man, nor a tribal shaykh. He was a *qadi* trained in the Zaydi legal tradition, who came from a prominent family in Sanaa city. Members of al-Arashe's family feared for his life if he remained president, so they dissuaded him from seeking a permanent role as leader of the nation. When the first rumors circulated that al-Arashe had withdrawn his name as president, civic and business leaders in Taiz came up with the implausible idea of asking Ali Abdallah Salih to volunteer for the job. During a private meeting in a house located near the central *suq* of Taiz, a group of businessmen met Salih to discuss their proposal. They promised to fully support the new president with all of their financial resources.

Given the atmosphere in Sanaa, the political transition became an awkward waiting game. Political insiders in the capital anticipated the

---

[6] This information comes from interviews the author conducted at a traditional Friday *qat*-session, hosted by some of Taiz's most influential business families in 1996.

arrival of some poor man willing to put his neck on the line. When Salih accepted the plan of Taiz's merchants, the group of businessmen immediately chartered an aircraft to fly him to Sanaa before anyone else dared to take the job. Given Salih's rapid rise from his role as a junior military officer, serving checkpoint duty on Yemen's whiskey road, to the presidential palace in Sanaa, it is clear Taiz's merchants helped behind the scenes to elevate the young man's career. Coming from a tribal background in the highland region, and relying on support from Shafiʻi businessmen in the western midlands, President Salih could bridge north Yemen's main regional divide.

Just as the Free Yemenis struggled to unite the "sons of Qahtan" in the 1950s, and Yemeni republicans in 1970 sought to reconcile separate regional interests in a post-civil war "republican pact," what emerged from the 1978 meeting at a private house in Taiz was an improvised version of the same cross-regional bridge. For Salih the man, it was purely an *ahmar al-ayn* moment. Once he reached Sanaa, all he needed were nerves of steel, and the good fortune not to stand in the way of an assassin's bullet. Many Yemenis liked to joke about Salih's rare public appearances during his first year as president. He looked nervous in newsreel shown on television. His eyes darted from side to side, as if he expected an assassin to leap forward at any moment. During the 1990s, Yemenis could afford to laugh about these old television images because Salih survived so long as president. But in the late 1970s, most north Yemenis did not think the president would survive more than a few months, let alone a year. In the end, he stayed far longer than anyone anticipated, "outliving his welcome" according to the merchants of Taiz.

A SIMPLE TRIBESMAN AS PRESIDENT

Given the tumultuous events in north Yemen one year before Salih's rise to power, it appeared that the president set sail in the eye of a hurricane. Fair skies appeared over head, but there were rough seas all around. As it turned out, the risks during Salih's early years in the presidential palace were not as great as many suspected. Individuals of greater power and influence, especially among the leading shaykhs of Hashid and Bakil, did not perceive the young president as a threat because he came from Sanhan. Ali Abdallah Salih is short in stature, a Napoleon Bonaparte figure barely over five feet tall (1.52 meters). His origin from Sanhan made him appear even shorter in the imagination of highland tribal shaykhs, who believed Salih could be easily manipulated. The neighboring tribe of Khawlan is one

of the largest tribes in the Bakil federation. Khawlani tribesmen far outnumber Sanhanis, so they felt confident about gaining influence over the
new president. Likewise, Hashid tribesmen north of Sanaa were content
because Sanhan sits low among their ranks.

While the diminutive military officer from Sanhan was relatively
unknown, most people of influence were willing to accept his rise to the
helm of state. Taiz's merchants and traders wanted someone prepared to
conduct business with them, someone who could help expand their economic interests. They saw the new president as a convenient pawn. The
shaykhs of Hashid and Bakil saw the same thing. The unanswered question of Salih's presidency concerned the strength of the 1970 "republican
pact," and the balance of interests behind him. Would President Salih
move further in support of businessmen in western midland and coastal
regions, or would he primarily support the highland tribes?

The most powerful actor in the early years of Salih's presidency was the
paramount shaykh of Hashid, the late Shaykh Abdallah bin Husayn
al-Ahmar. (This surname should not be confused with members of
President Salih's family, some of whom use the same name drawn from
the Sanhan village, Bayt al-Ahmar.) For decades, Shaykh Abdallah was a
cagey politician in Sanaa, until his death in late December 2007. He served
as speaker of north Yemen's semi-elected parliament, or constituent assembly (*al-majlis al-tasisi*), and after 1994 as speaker of united Yemen's elected
parliament (*majlis al-nuwab*). Although Yemen's parliament is a weak
institution, the speaker's post gave Shaykh Abdallah considerable sway
over public opinion and important matters of the day. The shaykh's traditional family home is in al-Khamr district of Amran province, deep in
Hashid tribal territory north of Sanaa. But he also built a large family
compound on the capital's north side, in order to maintain a presence in
city and state politics. His Sanaa home in a neighborhood called Hasaba
sits diametrically opposite the presidential palace on the city's south side at
60 Meters Road. Thus, in political and geographic space, the house of
Hashid's paramount shaykh existed as a counterweight to Salih's palace.

As tribal leader of the Hashid federation, Shaykh Abdallah commanded
authority over seven subtribes with several thousand men under arms.
Many of these Hashid subtribes are heavily armed with tanks and full
artillery, which they operate independently of the state's military. There
are times in Sanaa when these tribesmen descend on the capital to blockade
main roads by force of arms. Thus, Hashid can cause considerable chaos
for the national government. When Shaykh Abdallah lost power in Sanaa
during President al-Hamdi's rule in the mid-1970s, he withdrew to his

tribal homeland more than a hundred miles to the north. After al-Hamdi's assassination in 1977, Hashid's paramount shaykh returned to the national capital. The Hashid sub-tribe closest to President al-Hamdi, and his successor Ahmad al-Ghashmi, is called Hamdan. The Hamdan tribe also remained close to President Salih in the late 1970s and 1980s. Both Hamdan and the president's Sanhan tribe were subordinate to Shaykh Abdallah. Nonetheless, the interests of Hashid did not always coincide with the president and the national army.

In July 1978, Shaykh Abdallah could have pressured the new and inexperienced president, if he wanted to remove the young man from office. He did not take this initiative due to widespread fears of political instability. As a consequence, President Salih had time to build his personal defenses, appointing family members to key military and security posts. Salih and his extended family in Sanhan accumulated power in ways that al-Hamdi and al-Ghashmi never tried in the past. Yet Shaykh Abdallah's own power grew at the same time. The relationship between tribe and state has always been a complex matter in Yemen. Before unification in 1990, it was often misdiagnosed. Hashid and Bakil were typically described as obstacles to President Salih's regime.[7] Yet the leading highland tribal shaykhs were simultaneously part of the ruling elite. They were also increasingly part of the northern business establishment. Much to the dismay of merchants in Taiz and other outlying regions, the shaykhs of Hashid and Bakil began competing in the fields of construction, contracting, and trade. In reality, President Salih more often tipped his hand in favor of the highland shaykhs.

On the one hand, political observers depicted highland tribal shaykhs as rivals of President Salih, obstructing his government's policies and hindering the rule of law. This was often used as an excuse for why the YAR remained a weak state. On the other hand, observers acknowledged the great role that tribal shaykhs played in north Yemen's political and commercial affairs. There developed a tendency to describe the shaykhs who gained a foothold in state business as pseudotribal because they had grown increasingly "out of touch" with tribal traditions and customs. This was particularly true of western political analysts relying on the research of British anthropologist Paul Dresch.[8] Dresch defends the purity of tribal

---

[7] Dunbar, 1992.

[8] Dresch, 1989. Paul Dresch also coauthored an important 1995 article with Bernard Haykel entitled "Stereotypes and Political Styles: Islamists and Tribesfolk in Yemen" in the *International Journal of Middle East Studies*.

identity in Yemen. So within his anthropological framework, the tribesmen who play official roles in state politics or business no longer qualify as
"tribal." Yet there is an important difference on this topic when making a
political analysis versus an anthropological analysis.

In the field of anthropology, Paul Dresch presents the views of common
tribesmen whom he interviews in the lands of Hashid and Bakil. Many of
these tribesmen frequently express criticism of their shaykhs who move to
the "city-world" of Sanaa, and engage in dialogues about state policy.
According to Dresch, these shaykhs in the capital district of Sanaa "belong
to the tribal system only nominally."[9] In the effort to maintain a clear
definition of "tribe," Dresch inevitably depicts the shaykhs of Hashid and
Bakil who engage in state politics, such as the late Shaykh al-Abdallah or
President Salih's tribal allies, as separating themselves from Yemen's real
tribal culture. But this creates a problematic distinction between tribe and
state in Yemen, since the highland tribes had effectively captured influential arms of the state by the late 1980s.[10] Under President Salih's later rule,
tribal culture was no longer separate from the culture of the government.
In fact, it came to define the government's culture.

This is the greater significance of state-tribe relations in the northern
YAR before national unification in 1990. After the 1962 revolution, Zaydi
sectarian principles could no longer justify the political dominance of
highland elites. But the tribalism of Hashid and Bakil, operating in the
name of "the sons of Qahtan," became an easy substitute. A famous saying
from the prerevolutionary era implied that the Zaydi imam was only one
leg of the table supporting the traditional ruling system. The tribal shaykhs
of Hashid and Bakil represented the table's other legs. Although highland
shaykhs did not run all government offices in the YAR, they profoundly
shaped northern political culture just as they had in the imamate era. The

---

[9] Dresch, 1995(b); pp. 33, 42, and 55. A good example of anthropological versus political
distinctions is when Dresch makes the dubious claim that there was "no tribal factor" in
the 1994 civil war. He makes this claim only by discounting the "tribal authenticity" of
leading Hashid and Bakil figures who directed northern military forces.

[10] The idea of the highland tribes capturing control of the state is the thesis of a number of
important Yemeni and Arab social scientists and philosophers, such as Dr. Abu Bakr
al-Saqqaf and Bashir al-Bakr. It is widely assumed that the Yemeni political philosopher
al-Saqqaf authored the 1988 book *al-Jumhuriyya bayn al-Sultana wa al-Qabila fi
al-Yaman al-Shamali* (*The Mixed Tribal-Sultanate Republic of North Yemen*) under the
pseudonym Muhammad Abd al-Salam. Bashir al-Bakr wrote a critical 1995 study of
Yemen's early unity years, entitled *Harb al-Yaman: al-Qabila Tantasar 'ala al-Watan*
(*Yemen's War: The Tribe Triumphs over the Nation*). Al-Bakr argues persuasively that
the northern highland tribes captured the unified Republic of Yemen during the country's
1994 civil war.

relationship between Zaydi imams and the shaykhs of Hashid and Bakil was frequently contentious. Tribal shaykhs criticized the imam, and occasionally rose in rebellion. In this sense, little changed in the north Yemeni republic where the shaykhs of Hashid and Bakil criticized and rebelled just as often, even though a Hashid tribesman from Sanhan became president in 1978.

Throughout Zaydi history, the religious aristocracy in Sanaa and Sa'da, Shahara and Kokaban, was inextricably bound to the highland tribes. The ruling class developed a unique *modus operandi* for dealing with tribal shaykhs. When highland tribal shaykhs had grievances against an imam, they might challenge the ruler in Sanaa by coercive means until their grievances were addressed. But the imam rarely responded by attacking the highland tribes, in order to subordinate them to state authority. Instead, the imam used divide and rule tactics. When this failed, the imam co-opted the shaykhs with lucrative tax farming opportunities in outlying regions of the country.[11] The same relationship between state and tribe existed under President Salih. It was unthinkable for Salih to attack the highland tribes, or attempt to subordinate them to state authority. Although the land of Hashid and Bakil remained beyond state control, tribal shaykhs had their hands buried in the state's treasury. They benefited from considerable government largesse, either by tax farming in midland/coastal regions or by listing the names of their tribesmen multiple times as salaried members of the national armed forces.

The state-tribe relationship in the northern YAR created an unstructured political system, which often appeared chaotic whenever highland shaykhs acted coercively toward state leaders. But the relationship ultimately served the mutual interests of tribal and political elites from the highland region. As long as highland elites respected the status quo, and showed a degree of tolerance toward each other, they prospered by dominating and exploiting outlying regions of the country. There were inherent contradictions in this political system, which became apparent after 1990 when President Salih assumed leadership of both halves of the country. After unification, and particularly after a brief civil war in 1994, south Yemenis felt the full impact of the northern system's highland tribal culture. As a result, many of them began to retreat from the idea of sharing a national identity with citizens on the other side of the old borderline.

One of the significant differences between the northern YAR and southern PDRY was that the YAR operated a "tribal affairs" office in each

[11] Al-Hibshi, 1991.

province. By contrast, in the late 1960s and early 1970s, the PDRY
eliminated nearly all vestiges of southern tribalism. Northern "tribal
affairs" were run through the ministries of interior and local administration by the top shaykhs of Hashid and Bakil. The directors of provincial
offices in western midland and coastal regions were typically shaykhs from
the highland region.[12] In effect, the local tribal shaykhs of Shafi'i regions,
many of whom no longer practiced tribal customs, were under the political
control of highland tribes. Thus the Zaraniq tribe along the western Red
Sea coast, and al-Maddhaj in the western midlands, served as mere extensions of the highland power structure. The main reason Hashid and Bakil
shaykhs came to al-Hudayda, Taiz, and Ibb was to exploit tax farming
opportunities, just like the practice of earlier generations under the Zaydi
imams. The tribes of the central interior region in Marib and al-Jawf
provinces maintained greater autonomy until the discovery of oil in the
middle-1980s. At this time, the regime in Sanaa began to interfere more
often in their affairs.

In the middle 1990s, one highland director of tribal affairs in Zabid of
al-Hudayda province developed a particularly bad reputation. Local residents along the west coast described the man as a chauvinist who behaved
in such condescending ways that his actions drew comparisons to the
treatment of the Zaraniq tribe after Imam Yahya's tribal soldiers invaded
in the 1920s.[13] The spoken dialect of the highland region has a peculiar
tone, called *lughat al-nakheet*, which is characterized by a degree of
derision and condescension. It is a sharp and biting tone of voice, which
has a sing-song quality when it is used in mischievous or deceitful ways.
Lughat al-nakheet establishes a false air of superiority on the part of the
speaker, and it is strongly associated with Yemen's highland culture.
Yemenis in lowland regions often mimic this distinct highland tone of
voice, using humor to express their dislike of unequal regional relations
inside the country.

People of the western midlands tell a particular joke about a highland
tribal soldier in the 1920s, who traveled down the Samara mountain pass
with Imam Yahya's army to collect taxes from town residents in Ibb.[14] The

---

[12] The author's local administrative survey between 1985 and 1996 revealed that, prior to
national unity, the directors of tribal affairs in al-Hudayda, Taiz and Ibb provinces came
from highland regions around Sanaa. Al-Bayda was the only exception in the western
midland region.

[13] Interview with local residents of Zabid in spring 1996.

[14] This joke was told to the author on more than a few occasions by different people in Ibb
and Taiz.

soldier carried a "horizontal rifle" which would not fit through the doorway of the homes of poor peasant farmers. Before entering, the soldier labored to turn his rifle to a vertical position, which required peasant farmers to pay an additional tax surcharge! This joke is told with greatest effect using *lughat al-nakheet*. Many generations of lowland residents experienced coercion and exploitation at the hands of gun-toting highland tribesmen. Most Yemenis in outlying regions realize that not all highland residents are coercive and exploitive in the same way. It is understood that the stereotype does not apply to poor residents of highland villages and towns, many of whom experience similar coercion and exploitation at the hands of highland military and security officials. But the stereotype generally applies to highland political elites, especially President Salih who was perceived as someone who gained power and wealth by deceptive means.

During the 1980s when Ali Abdallah Salih built the General People's Congress by coopting the local CYDA cooperative movement, and forming new local councils subservient to the central bureaucracy, members of Taiz's municipal council held a meeting with the president to discuss their needs and aspirations.[15] Many of these council members had been activists in the early cooperative movement, devoting themselves to economic progress in their home region. When they met the president in the early 1980s, they appealed to him for greater autonomy, explaining that it was important to keep more revenues in the province in order to pay for local development projects. These city officials recall that Salih belittled their concerns, addressing them with the same condescending *lughat al-nakheet* tone used by highland tribesmen. Salih used this language of derision with great ease to establish an air of supremacy based on his regional group's dominance. He indicated to the group in Taiz that real government power would remain in the hands of central government officials in Sanaa.

Throughout Salih's rule of north Yemen, he governed with the mind-set of a tribesman, acting as guardian of the old status quo where nontribal elites from midland and coastal regions must accommodate themselves to the highland tribes. When one considers the history of the northern YAR from its post–civil war reconciliation in 1970 to the unification with south Yemen in 1990, it is reasonable to conclude that the highland power structure had been gradually rebuilt with a "republican" veneer. The roles played by Ali Abdallah Salih as president, and Shaykh Abdallah as

---

[15] Interview with three longtime government employees in the office of Taiz's elected provincial council, July 2002.

speaker of the parliament, may not have reflected pure tribal customs and traditions. But representatives of the highland tribes clearly held greater power as a result. This is why it was misleading in political analysis to rely on Paul Dresch's anthropological studies of tribal practices. Dresch's ethnographic conclusion that President Salih and Shaykh al-Ahmar did not govern north Yemen "by tribal custom" did not reflect the dynamics of power in north Yemen. The key point about political development under Salih's leadership in the late 1970s and 1980s is that government and business in north Yemen became increasingly dominated by the tribal shaykhs of Hashid and Bakil.

The primary difference between the former Zaydi imamate, on the one hand, and the northern republican government in the 1980s, on the other hand, is arguably that the top shaykhs of Hashid and Bakil gained a more direct role running state affairs. Formerly, under the Zaydi imams, the shaykhs of Hashid and Bakil represented other legs of the table. But inside the YAR, highland tribal elites became the dominant political and military authorities in all regions of the country. The power of the state was essentially the power of President Salih's Hashid tribe. Differences existed between the president's family, and the family of Hashid's paramount shaykh, Abdallah bin Husayn al-Ahmar. There were also regular conflicts among tribes of Hashid and Bakil. But this was also true under the Zaydi imams. These contradictions are inherent to the highland region's political culture.

MIXING RELIGION AND POLITICS

In January 1979, when a border war erupted between north and south Yemen, the southern army seized a few towns and villages on the northern side of the border. The troops of young president Ali Abdallah Salih fought back, and before the end of March 1979 negotiators arranged a cessation of hostilities with restoration of the old borderline. But there remained a guerrilla war in the midland provinces of Taiz, Ibb, and al-Bayda, where northern Marxists received support from the southern Yemeni Socialist Party (YSP). The story of President Salih's conflict with northern Marxists, the National Democratic Front (NDF) and Howshi, is crucial to understanding state politics during his early years in office. The antiguerrilla campaign rallied support for his administration among western midland business interests as well as highland tribal interests, while at the same time fostering a new Islamic trend inside the country.

In 1979, Saudi Arabia and the U.S. administration of President Jimmy Carter rushed financial and military support to north Yemen to bolster Salih's new regime. Saudi and American officials viewed events in Yemen with the same alarm they felt when the Soviet military intervened in Afghanistan later in the year. From the beginning of the Cold War in the late 1940s and early 1950s, American officials perceived Islam as a bulwark against the spread of Soviet influence in the Middle East and South Asia. But the Carter and Reagan administrations advanced this idea further by providing direct financial assistance to Islamic fundamentalist groups acting in coordination with Saudi Arabia.[16] In Afghanistan, the United States and Saudi Arabia shared funding on a fifty-fifty basis. But in Yemen, the Saudis invested more heavily on their own because of Yemen's closer proximity to Saudi territory.

Beginning in 1979, the Saudi government poured Islamic assistance into north Yemen, spreading Sunni orthodox ideas known as *Wahhabism.* Historically, Yemenis rejected al-Wahhabi doctrine. They resisted Saudis proselytizing their faith because it threatened to spread sectarian interpretations of Islam that could ignite conflicts between Zaydi and Shafi'i. Wahhabism originated in Arabia during the last half of the 18th century, as a puritanical movement. Its founder, Muhammad ibn Abd al-Wahhab, formed a partnership with the top shaykh of al-Saud tribe to expand their common rule of the Arabian peninsula. This tribal-clerical state went through three periods of expansion and decline in the eighteenth, nineteenth, and twentieth centuries.[17] Generations of Yemenis grew accustomed to the ebb and flow of Islamic puritanism across the northern frontier. Saudi customs never suited Yemenis because they traditionally practiced moderate forms of Islam. What changed in the 1970s and 1980s is that millions of Yemenis migrated to Saudi Arabia to find work in its high-wage oil economy. While living inside the country, they naturally fell under the influence of al-Wahhabi doctrine. Thus Wahhabism was not only exported to Yemen by Saudi government and religious officials. It was also imported by Yemeni migrant workers, returning home on vacation or at the end of their job contracts.

Saudi officials funneled money and materials not only to the Yemeni government, but also to key tribal shaykhs. Indeed, most Saudi Arabian influence south of the border came through unofficial channels. President Salih adapted to this wave of conservative, religious influence by

[16] Cooley, 1999; pp. 81–82, 107–126. Coll, 2004; pp. 260–279, 397–415.
[17] Safran, 1985; pp. 9–56.

organizing an Islamic front in the western midland provinces to assist his campaign against Marxist guerrillas. The regime treated NDF and Howshi fighters as foreign-inspired insurgents, and referred to its own policy as a counterinsurgency campaign. This campaign eased President Salih's adjustment in office after 1978 because highland tribal shaykhs and midland business elites became united in a common Islamic cause financed largely with Saudi Arabian funds. Big industrialists in Taiz like the Hayil Said Anam group stood with the president. They actively supported the Islamization of north Yemen, as did hundreds of southern economic elites who fled Marxist rule in the previous decade. Small scale merchants and shop owners typically went along with the Islamist trend. A few influential, mid-sized businessmen remained true to the liberal ideas of the Free Yemenis in the 1950s.

The member of President Salih's inner circle who took the lead using Saudi support to develop an Islamic front was General Ali Muhsin al-Ahmar. Ali Muhsin cultivated ties to fundamentalist clerics and religious militants who later supported Osama Bin Laden's al-Qaeda organization in the 1990s. Foremost among these clerics was Abd al-Majid al-Zindani, a Yemeni highland figure who spent time in Saudi Arabia during the 1970s and 1980s. Al-Zindani is known as a political chameleon and opportunist. Before the 1962 revolution, he was a fervent Zaydi royalist. Residents of Sanaa recall him as a young man who dutifully carried an umbrella to shield the imam from the sun. After the republican revolution in the 1960s, al-Zindani adopted Sunni fundamentalist views based on al-Wahhabi doctrine during his long exile in Saudi Arabia. In the late 1970s and early 1980s, he was a spiritual advisor to Osama Bin Laden at the start of the anti-Soviet jihad in Afghanistan.

The bulk of activists in Yemen's Islamic Front were supporters of older Muslim Brotherhood groups in Taiz and Ibb. The Muslim Brotherhood originated in Egypt during the late 1920s, and soon formed branches in other Arab countries. Its followers in Yemen grew slowly between the 1940s and 1960s, mainly in Red Sea coastal towns and western midland areas. By the 1970s and 1980s, the organization became increasingly influential at the community level, running charities, schools, and health clinics. Although the anti-Marxist Islamic Front was conceived and organized by individuals in the Zaydi highland region, its base was among Shafi'i in midland and coastal regions. By coordinating internal security policies with Muslim Brotherhood leaders in the late 1970s and early 1980s, Salih limited the spread of Marxist ideas coming from south Yemen. But the regime also used highly repressive measures inside the western midland

and coastal regions, leading to many instances of disappearance and torture. The highland political security commander in the region, Muhammad al-Yadumi, was responsible for the worst human rights abuses. In the late 2000s, he became chairman of Yemen's largest Islamic party, *Islah*.

In 1982, when guerrilla fighters agreed to lay down their arms, Salih's advisors worked out a plan to build on the president's political momentum by binding together various political trends that had seemed threatening just three years earlier. This was the origin of the General People's Congress (GPC). The GPC brought together nationalists of all stripes, including pan-Arabists from Nasserist groups and local branches of the Ba'th party, as well as socialists, traditional tribal shaykhs, and members of the Islamic Front. It created a new institutional structure on which Salih could stand as he sought greater political legitimacy in north Yemen. Eight years later, the GPC also became the vehicle that he steered toward national unity with south Yemen.

After national unification in 1990, smaller factions within the GPC split to form independent political parties in the new Republic of Yemen's early experiment with pluralism. This weakened President Salih at a time when the GPC competed for popular support with the Yemeni Socialist Party (YSP), the ruling party of the former PDRY. In the unified state, north Yemeni socialists tended to support the YSP. Two northern Ba'th parties, and two Nasserite parties, took additional votes away from the GPC. Members of the Islamic Front formed the independent *Islah* (Reform) party, which was led by highland tribal and religious elites like Hashid's paramount shaykh Abdallah bin Husayn al-Ahmar, and the fundamentalist cleric Abd al-Majid al-Zindani, who returned from Saudi Arabia to establish an Islamic university in Sanaa. At this time, Muhammad al-Yadumi was third in line in the Islah party's hierarchy.

Due to partisan fragmentation after 1990, it was difficult to judge the strength of President Salih's hold on power in a new pluralist environment. North Yemenis outnumbered south Yemenis more than four-to-one. But what percentage of north Yemenis were loyal supporters of the GPC? Would the Islah party split the northern vote, thus allowing southern socialists to gain a surprise victory in the first national poll? On the one hand, the majority of north Yemenis lived in midland and coastal regions, and it was possible that this population would split its vote between Islah and the YSP. On the other hand, the presence of so many prominent highland tribal, religious, and military figures within the Islah party, including associates of General Ali Muhsin al-Ahmar and other members of Salih's inner circle, raised questions about Islah's independence. Was Islah just the Islamic wing of President Salih's regime? And would a vote for Islah amount to a vote for Salih himself?

Before national unification, President Salih clearly used the GPC to establish greater stability in north Yemen. The highland tribes of Hashid and Bakil were no less rebellious than in the past. They still caused minor conflicts on occasion. But northern state institutions had grown stronger partly due to the discovery of oil in 1984 near the border with south Yemen. This further helped strengthen President Salih's hand in negotiations with the PDRY, since southern leaders were eager to cooperate in joint oil exploration. In a real sense, petroleum lubricated the process of national unity. It made a considerable difference for President Salih's standing in the north. It also helped that south Yemen no longer posed a military threat after the YSP's internal war in January 1986. On the whole, domestic and international conditions looked hospitable for President Salih, allowing him to feel relatively secure compared to his early years in office.

It is difficult to mistake the causal link between the discovery of oil in Yemen and a stronger President Salih. But new sources of wealth also created problems for his regime. Oil spread greed inside the president's inner circle, among family members as well as his tribal and military associates. Following unification, it would also generate greater political tensions. In particular, it fed opposition in south Yemen where the largest new discoveries of oil were made in the early 1990s. As greater revenues from oil started flowing through the ministry of finance in Sanaa, members of Salih's family realized riches beyond their wildest dreams. Yet the president needed to share these revenues with a larger network of associates inside a more complex, pluralist government. As the following chapters show, the contradictions within this system exploded in civil war four years after unification.

After the civil war in 1994, President Salih, members of his family, and other tribal elites in the highland region were able to double, even triple their personal wealth in a very short time. Yemeni unification proved highly profitable for a small group in Sanaa. But it was disastrous for the vast majority in the country. Throughout the country, north and south, east and west, the middle class was destroyed when its standard of living was cut in half or worse. Spokesmen for President Salih often said that his rule improved the lives of south Yemenis, who previously struggled to get ahead in a heavily centralized, low-growth socialist economy. Yet poverty spread rapidly in Aden, when the average salary dropped from an estimated U.S. $661 in 1990 to below U.S. $300 in 1997. Yemenis in all regions of the country experienced similar declines in personal income, but for political reasons it mattered most in territories of the former PDRY because southern citizens soon learned that their lands contained the greatest petroleum reserves in the country. Increasingly they felt that their regional resources were being exploited in the interests of northern military and tribal elites in the northwest mountain highlands.

United Yemen's single largest oil discovery came in 1992 in the eastern region of Hadramaut province, where Canadian Occidental operated inside an area called Wadi al-Masila. President Salih later made an effort to stimulate economic development in the province, and improve the area's infrastructure. The airport in Wadi Hadramaut was renovated after 1994. New schools were also founded, and roads were improved with a layer of fresh asphalt. This generated early good will among people living inside the canyon far from the coast. But political relations remained strained around the seaside capital, al-Mukalla, where the majority of Hadramaut's population lives. During the early 2000s, a major advance was made in al-Mukalla when a sea inlet was constructed to relieve an awful sewage problem in the middle of a city with more than 150,000 residents. The quality of city life improved, but the general population continued living in poverty conditions.

More than a decade after Yemeni unification, it was estimated that oil receipts made up as much as 75 percent of all government revenues.[18] More than half of total revenues was spent on the presidential office, and state military and security forces that generally funneled money into the hands of citizens from the highland region. During the 2000s, the annual value of Yemen's oil receipts varied widely between U.S. $6 and $14 billion, depending on domestic production levels and international prices for a barrel of crude. There is no way to know what percentage of oil receipts were skimmed off the top before being added to Yemeni government accounts. But it is widely believed that President Salih and his extended family raked in billions of dollars.

Government revenues from oil and other resources were badly needed for economic development and social welfare in an impoverished country like Yemen. Yet large sums of money were squandered between 1990 and 2010. President Salih owned a half dozen or more palaces, in addition to his sprawling official residence in Sanaa and his family's compound of villas in Sanhan. The Salih family was known neither for its frugality, nor

[18] World Bank website, "Country Brief: Yemen." Retrieved 2009.

its solidarity with masses of poor people who needed guidance, support, and wise long-term planning from state officials. The president liked to flaunt the fact that he governed by corrupt and immoral means, posing with shadowy associates and practically daring others to hold him accountable. Wikileaks released an October 2007 U.S. diplomatic report that depicted Salih inviting an arms smuggler and gun runner to attend an intergovernment meeting in Sanaa with American officials, where he teased the officials about his own failure to apprehend men the United States wanted to detain at Guantanamo Bay, Cuba.[19]

In the late 1990s and early 2000s, President Salih built an enormous mosque in Sanaa at great cost. This ornate white stone building now dominates the capital's skyline. It appears like a flash of brilliance amidst the city's standard light brown color. During its lengthy construction, many domestic critics complained about the building project's financial and religious excess. It is estimated the entire project cost tens of millions of U.S. dollars, which the president claimed came from his rather deep pockets. This beautiful towering structure, called "Salih Mosque," is capable of holding forty thousand worshippers. Once it was completed, its attractive dome and minarets were best viewed from Salih's nearby palatial residence, where the structure could be admired against the background of Sanaa's legendary old city. Like a king or imam, or perhaps a Mughal emperor, the simple tribesman from Sanhan had marked the city with his architectural Taj Mahal.

---

[19] Wikileaks, "Townsend-Saleh Meeting Provides Opening," #07SANAA1989, October 30, 2007.

4

Unity in Name Only

When the united Republic of Yemen was formed on May 22, 1990, it was an historic achievement in an ancient, divided land. The cameras flashed before Ali Abdallah Salih and Ali Salem al-Bid, as they stood together with dozens of other officials and dignitaries from both sides of the border. In the individual faces of the photographs taken that day, one can see the great sense of national pride in united Yemen. Standing together were Yemenis representing nearly every region of the country, the highlands and the midlands, Aden and Lahij in the southwest and Hadramaut in the east. One can easily distinguish the Zaydi judge, posing in a long robe and turban, from one of Aden's socialist technocrats in a collarless business suit. The highland tribesman, standing with a curved dagger sheathed in his belt, contrasts with the lone southern woman who attended the event without an Islamic head scarf. North and south Yemenis appeared in front of the cameras as one people united without divisions.

There was a time after Yemen's unification when copies of this official "Unity Day" photograph hung in nearly every government office around the country. It made a powerful symbol of national unity, showing northern and southern political leaders together as one. The photograph represented the hope and promise that brought the two political regimes together. Unfortunately, this was just a ceremonial display of unity. In the following months, political disputes quickly ended what little sense of trust the two regimes had for each other, exposing their worst motives, and leading the country onto a path of more conflict and warfare. More than twenty years later, one never sees the old unity photograph because it has come to symbolize something very different – a mixture of betrayal and false expectations.

PHOTO 10. Yemeni Unity photograph, May 22, 1990

Before the end of 1990, conflicts arose in practically every ministry of the unity government. Cabinet ministers were nearly evenly divided between north and south in an effort to balance their share of power until the first elections, originally scheduled for November 1992. As Table 4.1 shows, there were twenty ministers from the north, and nineteen from the south. Each minister was paired with a deputy from the other side of the border, in order to encourage cooperative relations. The greater task was to merge two very different political and administrative systems into one governing structure. The original idea was that northern GPC and southern YSP officials would determine the "best administrative practices" from the two former governments, and then devise a new set of regulations based on this vague standard.[1] The "best administrative practices" were supposed to be determined before unification, but three years later the issue remained unsettled.

There was also supposed to be a public referendum on a national constitution that was first drafted in the early 1980s.[2] But the two sides rushed into unity without the referendum. Disagreements inevitably arose. Since there was no mechanism to decide whether northern or southern practices were better, critical decisions were postponed until after the

[1] Interview with a departmental director at Yemen's ministry of local administration, March 1996.
[2] The Arabic text of this draft constitution appears in a book by Khalid Muhammad al-Qasim, 1987.

TABLE 4.1. *The Republic of Yemen's First Cabinet, 1990*

Name	Cabinet Post	Regional Origin
Southerners		
1) Haider al-Attas	Prime Minister	East/Hadramaut
2) Salih Aubayd Ahmad	Deputy Prime Minister	Southwest/ al-Dali'
3) Muhammad Masdus	Deputy Prime Minister	Mid-south/Abyan
4) Abd al-Aziz al-Dali	Minister of State for Foreign Affairs	East/Hadramaut
5) Rashed Muhammad Thabit	Min. of State for Parliamentary Affairs	Aden/West-Midlands
6) Salih Ben Husaynoun	Min. of Oil & Resources	East/Hadramaut
7) Haitham Qasim Taher	Min. of Defense	Southwest/Radfan
8) Fareg Ben Ghanem	Min. of Planning	East/Hadramaut
9) Fadhl Muhsin Abdallah	Min. of Supply & Trade	Southwest/Yafi'
10) Muhammad Said Abdullah	Min. of Local Administration	Aden/West-Midlands
11) Abd al-Wasi Salam	Min. of Justice	Aden/West-Midlands
12) Muhammad Ahmad Jarhum	Min. of Information	Southwest/Yafi'
13) Salih Abdullah Mithena	Min. of Transportation	Southwest/ al-Dali'
14) Abd al-Quwi Mithena	Min. of Housing	Southwest/ al-Dali'
15) Salih Munasser al-Sailee	Min. of Emigrant Affairs	East/Hadramaut
16) Salem Muhammad Jibran	Min. of Fishing	East/Hadramaut
17) Mahmud al-Arasi	Min. of Tourism	Aden
18) Abd al-Rahman Theiban	Min. of Labor	Mid-south/ Shabwa
19) Ahmad Salem al-Qadi	Min. of Higher Education	Southwest/ Zinjibar
Northerners		
20) Hasan Makki	Vice Prime Minister	West coast/ Tihama
21) Mujahid Abu Shawarib	Deputy Prime Minister	Highland/Sanaa
22) Yahya Husayn al-Arashe	Minister of State for Cabinet Affairs	Highland/Sanaa
23) Muhsin al-Hamdani	Min. of State for General Affairs	Highland/Sanaa
24) Abd al-Kareem al-Iryani	Min. of Foreign Affairs	Highland/Ibb
25) Alawi al-Salami	Min. of Finance	West Midlands/ Bayda
26) Ghaleb al-Qamsh	Min. of Interior	Highland/Sanaa

TABLE 4.1. *(cont.)*

Name	Cabinet Post	Regional Origin
27) Muhammad al-Wajeeh	Min. of Civil Service	Highland/Dhamar
28) Ismail al-Wazir	Min. of Legal Affairs	Highland/Sanaa
29) Muhammad al-Jaefi	Min. of Education	Highland/Sanaa
30) Muhammad Ali Muqbil	Min. of Health	West Midlands/Taiz
31) Sadeq Amin Abu Ras	Min. of Agriculture	Highland/Ibb
32) Abdullah al-Korshami	Min. of Construction	Highland/Sanaa
33) Abd al-Wahhab Mahmoud	Min. of Water & Electricity	West Midlands/Taiz
34) Muhammad al-Attar	Min. of Industry	Djibouti
35) Ahmad Muhammad al-Ansi	Min. of Communication	Highland/Dhamar
36) Muhsin Muhammad al-Ulafi	Min. of Religious Affairs	Highland/Sanaa
37) Ahmad Muhammad Luqman	Min. of Welfare/Insurance	West coast/Tihama
38) Hassan Ahmad al-Lauzi	Min. of Culture	Highland/Sanaa
39) Muhammad al-Kabab	Min. of Youth & Sports	West Midlands/Taiz

country's first election. The public referendum on Yemen's unity constitution was eventually held in 1991, passing with 98 percent of the votes. Islamists in the new Islah party, led by Hashid's tribal shaykh Abdallah bin Husayn al-Ahmar, boycotted the vote because they opposed unity with southern socialists. Radicals in Islah denounced socialists as infidels.

By early 1991, the trust between leaders of the GPC and YSP was broken. Northern ministers started working at cross purposes with their southern colleagues who occupied separate floors or wings of the same ministry buildings. The result was political infighting and stalemate. In the second year of unity the power-sharing arrangement became purely a matter of gamesmanship. Political turf battles were fought at central and local administrative levels.[3] This only magnified the country's worsening economic problems, after hundreds of thousands of migrant workers in Saudi Arabia and other oil-rich Gulf countries were forced to return home

---

[3] Michael Hudson argues that the two Yemens "qualified as an 'amalgamated' system." They achieved a formal political merger, but the two sides were never truly integrated. Hudson, 1995; pp. 20–21.

before the 1991 Gulf War. During the spring of 1991, there were strikes and demonstrations in Aden, where many basic food prices had jumped an incredible 400 percent in one year.[4]

In Sanaa, certain government ministries were forced to make early decisions about their administrative standards. This was particularly true of the ministry of finance, since it was responsible for receiving state revenues and disbursing state expenditures. The salaries of all government employees were dependent upon the finance ministry in Sanaa, so it was forced to operate with or without an agreement on standards. The northern minister in charge of financial affairs was a close confidant of President Salih. He decided to use the old YAR's financial practices, and eliminate all financial and accounting institutions of the old PDRY. This was a critical decision because it virtually guaranteed northern control over the government. The justification involved a bit of huckstering by GPC officials who used arguments about capitalism triumphing over communism to rationalize their take over of south Yemen's financial institutions.

The problem with the GPC's financial takeover is that the financial and accounting institutions of the former PDRY were not drawn from communist practices of the Soviet Union and East bloc countries. In fact, the PDRY maintained the financial administrative system established by Britain during the colonial era.[5] This system included a strong preaudit and postaudit of all government payouts that guaranteed public funds were disbursed in a responsible way. In the search for the "best administrative practices," the south's financial system should have served as a model to reform north Yemeni institutions, which were based on Ottoman and Egyptian practices. During the 1970s, East German advisors were invited by the PDRY's Marxist leaders to consult about Aden's financial, banking and accounting institutions. Instead of recommending that the PDRY tear down "the last remnants of British colonialism," the East Germans praised the existing financial practices in Aden as better than their own.[6]

Ironically, north Yemeni president Ali Abdallah Salih eliminated "the last remnants" of Western capitalism in Aden after the first year of national unity, perpetrating what Soviet and East German advisors refused to do. This was not a post–Cold War advancement of Yemen's government

---

[4] Joseph Kostiner provides a more detailed description of the country's political breakdown, 1996; pp. 36–39.
[5] Interview with Dr. Abdul-Aziz al-Tarmoum, a former top official in the PDRY's ministry of finance; July 14, 1996.
[6] Interview with Wahbi Uqba, a former top official in the PDRY's ministry of finance; August 12, 1996.

administration. It only advanced the political hegemony of highland groups who waited nearly a century to gain control of revenues drawn from Aden and other areas in the southwest region.[7] Within a year Yemen's minister of finance began appointing deputies to serve in provincial and district offices across southern provinces. In nearly all cases, these were northern highland officials who moved south, and worked to ensure that all state revenues flowed to Sanaa.[8] More than anything else, this elevated political tensions because it challenged southern autonomy and pride of self-rule.

Before the end of 1991, Yemen's political environment turned violent when the first of many assassinations occurred against southern politicians. The first did not target officials of the YSP, but rather Omar al-Jawi, the outspoken leader of a small populist party. Before unification al-Jawi was an exiled southerner living in north Yemen. He led north Yemen's writers and journalists syndicate, and was typically unafraid of expressing criticism of the government. After unity he became more critical of northern politicians, especially the increasingly militant Islamic rhetoric of tribal and religious elites in the highland region. Al-Jawi survived the attempted assassination in December 1991, but his deputy Hussayn al-Huraybi was killed in the attack. In 1992, there were nearly one hundred assassinations or attempted assassinations of southern politicians, mainly members of the YSP party.[9] According to a senior YSP official, the northern attorney general's office had the names of highland tribesmen who were implicated in a few of the assassination attempts.[10] But President Salih was unwilling to bring criminal charges against the men.

While the YSP blamed the political violence on tribal soldiers serving in northern military and security forces, GPC officials blamed it on south Yemeni exiles who had scores to settle from 1986, and further back in the 1960s. Much of the focus rested on the former *mujahideen* who fought the

[7] In the 1920s, after the collapse of the Ottoman empire in World War I, Imam Yahya's tribal armies desired to push toward Aden once they took control of Taiz. Refer to the *zamil* passages after footnote 39 of Chapter 5.

[8] The author's field survey of changes in local administrative personnel showed that most northern and southern personnel continued to serve in their same local positions, during the first three years of unity. This was true in roughly 90 percent of the cases. But by the end of the first year of unity, there were new northern directors of finance in Lahij, customs in Hadramaut, taxation in Hadramaut and Shabwa, and the central bank branches in Lahij and Abyan. The biggest changes were in Aden, where new northern directors were appointed to the offices of finance, customs, taxation, and the central bank.

[9] During 1992, there were bombings outside the homes of southern prime minister Haidar al-Attas and presidential council member Salem Salih Muhammad. *Middle East Economic Digest* discussed these incidents in its cover story on August 28, 1992; pp. 2–4.

[10] Interview at YSP offices in Sanaa; October 1998.

Soviets in Afghanistan, and then returned to Yemen to carry out jihad against the Soviet's old allies in the YSP party. Two southern *mujahideen*, Jamal al-Nahdi and Tareq al-Fadli, the latter a son of the former sultan of al-Fadli territory east of Aden, were strongly implicated in the bombing of two hotels in Aden in late 1992. Al-Fadli was briefly detained on this charge, but later released. It was impossible to establish clear responsibility for most of the violence because, since the 1980s, northern military commanders and tribal shaykhs had funded and supported the *mujahideen* involved in Yemen's Islamic front.

General Ali Muhsin al-Ahmar had the closest relationship with the Islamic front and *mujahideen* fighters. But there were a number of other highland elites involved in the same work. Financial support came from Saudi Arabia, and was funneled through leading tribal shaykhs of Hashid and Bakil in the Yemeni army. There was a chain of relations between commanders of military and security forces, highland tribal shaykhs, Islamic activists from Zaydi and Shafi'i regions, and ardent anti-communists among the southern exiles who came to Sanaa in the late 1960s. The forces aligned against the YSP were much like the network of state, military, tribal and religious interests in Pakistan that used Saudi money to fight the Soviet-backed Afghan leaders in Kabul. Anyone from President Salih and General Ali Muhsin to Tareq al-Fadli and Jamal al-Nahdi may have been involved in the string of assassinations in the early 1990s. As southern distrust of the northern regime increased, many YSP leaders left Sanaa and returned back to Aden. Vice president al-Bid withdrew from Sanaa three times, beginning in the fall of 1992. On the last occasion in late 1993, he declared that he would never return to the northern capital.[11]

A BUNGLED POLITICAL TRANSITION

From the beginning of 1990, there were good reasons to question the motives of northern and southern political elites to unite Yemen. Most observers point to the 1984 discovery of oil, near the shifting desert borderline, as the real catalyst for Yemeni unity.[12] Politicians in both halves of the country realized that they would need to cooperate in joint exploration and extraction activities, in order to fully benefit from oil-financed development. Otherwise, they might return to the border wars of

---

[11] *Al-Ayyam* newspaper (in Arabic), Aden, Yemen, October 20, 1993; p. 1.
[12] Dunbar, 1992; pp. 464, 465, and 469.

the 1970s. The intraregime fighting in Aden in January 1986 had presented a temporary setback for unity talks. When discussions revived later in the decade, both sides appeared to be in a rush to make unification happen. Ali Salem al-Bid was in such a hurry that he proceeded without full support of the YSP politburo.[13]

Many YSP officials were wary of uniting with north Yemen, especially party members from Radfan and al-Dali' in the southwest region. They were more familiar with north Yemen's rough tribal politics, due to their involvement with the Marxist guerrilla movement in the early 1980s.[14] Ali Salem al-Bid, the secretary general of the YSP, was from Hadramaut. He represented a different regional perspective that was not as hostile toward the northern regime. When al-Bid met President Salih in Aden in late November 1989, he acted largely on his own to propose full unification with the northern YAR.

President Salih travelled to Aden in 1989 with a delegation of senior GPC advisors. They were prepared to discuss a slow merger between the two governments beginning with military and foreign affairs.[15] What came out of the November 1989 meeting was a surprising agreement to pursue national unification based on a transitional sharing of power within a system founded on pluralist democratic principles. GPC officials preferred to merge with the YSP and form a large governing party. But YSP officials insisted on keeping their party's independence, in order to compete for the vote of citizens in national and local elections.[16] While the YSP

---

[13] Interviews with two YSP officials in their homes in Sanaa, Yemen; October and November 1998.

[14] The director of state security in south Yemen, Said Salih Salem of Lahij province, was so opposed to unity with the northern regime that he allegedly refused to hold a government post in Sanaa, and was instead appointed as the first postunity governor in Aden.

[15] Interview with former prime minister Abd al-Karim al-Iryani, who was a member of the northern delegation to Aden in November 1989, at his home in Sanaa; November 15, 1998. According to Dr. al-Iryani, the idea of merging defense and foreign affairs was first proposed by the northern YAR in the summer of 1989.

[16] The best source of information on how the south Yemeni regime influenced the unity talks is a three-part series by Dr. Muhammad Ahmad Ali in the Yemeni Socialist Party's weekly newspaper, *Al-Thawri* (in Arabic), January 23, 30, and February 13, 1997, #1458–1460, "The Requirements and Dangers of Political Pluralism"; p. 5 in all editions. A senior YSP official claims that, prior to unification, south Yemeni leader Ali Salem al-Bid's greatest concern was to avoid the mistake made by the Syrians in the late 1950s, when they united with Gamal Abd al-Nasser's Egypt under a short-lived one-party state. Interview with Othman Abd al-Jabbar, a member of the YSP's Central Committee and a former minister in the PDRY; October 22, 1998.

accepted a temporary sharing of power with the GPC, its primary motive was a competitive one to contest the GPC in national elections.

The leader of south Yemen understood that the YSP could not expect to hold the upper-hand during the political transition to elections. The southern population was less than one-fourth of the northern population. But in a new pluralist system with free democratic elections, al-Bid expected the YSP to win a large share of the popular vote among northern citizens who never supported the GPC. Northern leaders were not enthusiastic about democratic pluralism, since the GPC was a relatively new and largely untested party.[17] Yet Salih anticipated gaining political leverage over the YSP during the transitional phase, relying on strategic partners among southern exile groups, and supporters of the north's Islamic front, to undercut the YSP. In the end, the GPC's main motive was to absorb the south within the larger northern system, while marginalizing southern socialists as a dying relic of the Cold War.

There was one other factor shaping President Salih's motive to unite with south Yemen. South Yemen's foreign alliances with the Soviet Union and East bloc countries were crumbling, while north Yemen had a strong Arab ally in Saddam Husayn. The previous year Iraq's leader formed the Arab Cooperation Council (ACC) with Jordan, Egypt, and north Yemen, as a counterweight to Saudi Arabia's Gulf Cooperation Council (GCC). At the end of Iraq's long war with Iran in the 1980s, speculation grew that Saddam would seek regional hegemony through the ACC. President Salih apparently rushed into unity with south Yemen because the Iraqi leader had promised to bankroll the process as a counterweight to Saudi Arabia.[18] Beyond a doubt, Iraq's Ba'th party strongly supported Yemeni unity, while the Saudi monarchy actively opposed it. As Saddam Husayn thought ahead to his invasion of Kuwait in August 1990, he likely encouraged Salih to speed up the unity process in order to pose a greater threat on Saudi Arabia's southern border. Indeed, President Salih hastily requested

---

[17] When Ali Abdallah Salih signed the Yemeni unity agreement at the end of November 1989, political pluralism was outlawed by the north Yemeni constitution as a form of treason against the state. According to Sheila Carapico, before unification, Salih "denounced pluralism and cited the (YAR's) military as an example of a democratic institution." Carapico, 1998; op. cit., p. 52. Salih would remain uneasy about democratic politics in united Yemen. Throughout the negotiations leading to unification in May 1990, his regime continually tried to get the southern leadership to merge the YSP and the GPC into a joint political organization.

[18] During many personal interviews with southern officials who participated at lower levels in the unity negotiations, they often claimed to have heard stories that Saddam was "bankrolling" the north's unification with the south.

in the spring of 1990 that the date of Yemeni unity be moved up six months to May, instead of November 1990.[19]

As long as Salih could rely on Iraq's leader, he had confidence in controlling the process of unification. Once Saddam Husayn was defeated in early 1991, Salih appeared vulnerable to pressure by YSP officials. It is also true that flaws in the GPC-YSP power sharing arrangement created a "structural logic for conflict."[20] This was particularly true of the early concentration of financial power in Sanaa, as well as plans to hold competitive elections. This combination is a recipe for social unrest in any regionally divided country, let alone one that had recently formed two rival states, because it meant a winner-take-all contest for control of national resources. Flaws in the arrangement, and the lack of preparation by GPC and YSP officials, were quickly exposed by the economic and diplomatic crisis that followed Iraq's invasion of Kuwait. The GPC and YSP stood together during the crisis, and continued sharing power on a nearly equal basis. But they remained mutually suspicious with conflicting motives and interests.

The GPC held a slight one vote majority on the first cabinet, while the first prime minister, Haidar al-Attas, was a southern YSP technocrat from Hadramaut. Real power was vested in a five member presidential council that operated behind the scenes. This council gave the GPC another one vote majority. Ali Abdallah Salih served as president on the council, along with Abdul-Aziz Abdul-Ghani, the former prime minister from Taiz who long represented lowland Shafi'i business interests in Sanaa, and Abdul-Karim al-Arashe, the elderly *qadi* who had turned down the opportunity to become president of the YAR in 1978. On the southern side, Ali Salem al-Bid served on the presidential council with Salem Salih Muhammad, a YSP official from Yafi' of Lahij province in the southwest region.

What is noteworthy about the power sharing arrangement is how membership on the presidential council, as well as the first cabinet,

---

[19] Robert Burrowes, 1992; p. 56. It must be considered very unlikely that President Salih was ever privy to Saddam Husayn's ultimate designs on Kuwait. After the Iraqi invasion on August 2, 1990, the ensuing crisis placed great strain on the new united Yemeni state, so it is hardly conceivable that Salih would have agreed to participate in the plot to invade Kuwait.

[20] In an essay entitled, "Bipolarity, Rational Calculation, and the War in Yemen," Michael Hudson asked if the "structure and configuration of power" in post-unity Yemen could explain the country's violent turn toward war. Hudson, 1995; pp. 19–20. Hudson concluded that the "logic" of structural factors meant the two former regimes would behave in "mutually threatening" ways that ultimately resulted in open conflict; p. 31.

reflected pre-unity regional divisions in each half of the country. President Salih and Qadi al-Arashe held the Zaydi highland group's traditional two-thirds majority over Abd al-Aziz's one-third representation of Shafiʻi lowland and coastal regions. Meanwhile on the southern side, the regional backgrounds of al-Bid and Salim Salih Muhammad reflected the post-1986 division of power between Hadramaut and Lahij inside the former PDRY. Nearly the same proportion of seats existed on the first cabinet, as seen in Table 4.1. Thirteen of the GPC's twenty cabinet ministers (65 percent) came from the highland region, while seven ministers came from lowland and coastal regions (35 percent). Again on the southern side, seven of the YSP's nineteen cabinet ministers (37 percent) came from Lahij and Aden's hinterland in the southwest region, six came from Hadramaut (32 percent), three were northern migrants living in Aden (16 percent), and one each were native of Aden, Abyan, and Shabwa provinces. In short, the same pre-unity pattern of northern and southern regionalism persisted after unification.

YEMEN'S 1993 PARLIAMENTARY ELECTION

The date of Yemen's first national election was postponed in the fall of 1992, when Vice President al-Bid first withdrew from Sanaa due to a string of assassinations. It took long negotiations to convince al-Bid and other colleagues to end their boycott in Aden. The emerging pattern was for GPC leaders to pressure the YSP into creating one unified political party. President Salih and his advisors argued this would create the best conditions for political campaigning. Early in 1992 YSP representatives discussed the possibility of a party merger, and talks were ongoing throughout the year.[21] But the YSP's politburo believed northern officials sought to guarantee their continued majority control of the government. Thus the YSP stuck to its original preference for a pluralist competition in single-member electoral districts. The plan to hold direct winner-take-all elections without proportional representation, and no postelection pact beyond vague promises to form a national unity coalition, fed a sense of competition that magnified social and political divisions.

---

[21] Interview with former prime minister Abd al-Karim al-Iryani; June 14, 1996. Various YSP officials say their leadership never seriously considered a political merger with the GPC. Rather they joined the talks to gain greater insight into GPC electoral strategy.

The elections were eventually rescheduled for April 1993. Once the campaigning started, the level of competition was high. More than twenty registered political parties, and three thousand candidates, vied for just 301 seats in parliament.[22] This meant ten candidates on average competed for each seat in parliament. As a result, the election was hardly a direct face-off between the GPC and the YSP. The two ruling parties did not field candidates in all 301 constituencies: the GPC fielded a total of 275 and the YSP only fielded 210.[23] The stiffest competition frequently came from third party candidates, or the nearly two thousand independent candidates, some of whom had strong local name recognition.[24]

The final tally of votes showed that the GPC won the largest bloc of seats in the new parliament, but not a majority. It won a total of 122 seats, or 41 percent of the 301 total seats in parliament. This was more than twice the fifty-six seats (19 percent) won by candidates of the YSP. The big surprise was that the highland-based Islamic party, Islah, garnered more seats than the YSP, taking a total of sixty-three seats (21 percent). The remaining sixty seats went to independent candidates who won a total of forty-eight seats (16 percent), and candidates of the smaller third parties (four of these parties combined to win twelve seats or less than 4 percent of the total). The most significant outcome was the way the voting mirrored the country's regional divisions. One political observer noted that the elections proved "Yemen's political divide was along geographical rather than ideological lines."[25] A closer inspection reveals regional differences beyond the old north-south division.

Table 4.2 provides a complete regional breakdown of the three main parties' winning candidates in each of Yemen's then eighteen provinces. Most of the GPC's winning candidates came from provinces in the former north (119 seats out of its total 122). It won only three seats from the south, and most of its victories, north and south, were by narrow margins.

---

[22] Both males and females were permitted to vote and run as candidates in the Yemeni elections. But there were only a few female candidates in the main cities, and only 15 percent of women (478,000) registered to vote, while 2.2 million, or 72 percent of men registered. Al-Mansoub, 1995; p. 32.

[23] Ibid, p. 117. The YSP could not possibly match the strength of the GPC in the north. Across the border the competition was more balanced. Yet the GPC still fielded more candidates in southern districts than the YSP. Refer to Table 4.2.

[24] Yemen did not have a mature party system. Only seven or eight parties could be considered national political organizations. The largest third party, Islah, fielded 189 candidates, while the Ba'th party had 159 candidates; the Nasser Unionists, 89; and the old League of the Sons of Yemen, 88. Al-Mansoub, 1995; p. 117.

[25] Brian Whitaker, 1997; p. 23.

TABLE 4.2. *Winning Candidates in Yemen's 1993 Parliamentary Elections[a]*

Region/Province	(Number of fielded candidates in parentheses)				
	GPC	YSP	Islah	Others	Total
a) North					
Highlands:					
Sanaa City	11 (16)	0 (16)	6 (12)	1	18
Sanaa	21 (33)	1 (17)	5 (23)	9	36
Dhamar	11 (21)	1 (20)	7 (18)	2	21
Al-Mahwit	5 (8)	0 (6)	0 (5)	3	8
Hajja	15 (22)	0 (20)	3 (17)	5	23
Sa'da	5 (8)	0 (7)	1 (4)	3	9
West Coast:					
Al-Hudayda	22 (31)	1 (11)	6 (20)	5	34
Western Midlands:					
Taiz	8 (39)	6 (30)	18 (30)	11	43
Al-Bayda	2 (9)	3 (9)	2 (4)	3	10
Ibb	17 (38)	2 (27)	13 (26)	6	38
Central Interior:					
Al-Jawf	1 (2)	0 (2)	1 (2)	0	2
Marib	1 (3)	1 (2)	1 (1)	0	3
SUB-TOTALS	119 (230)	15 (169)	63 (162)	48	245
b) South					
Southwest:					
Aden	0 (7)	8 (8)	0 (5)	3	11
Lahij	0 (7)	8 (8)	0 (2)	4	12
Mid-southern:					
Abyan	1 (8)	7 (8)	0 (3)	0	8
Shabwa	1 (6)	5 (6)	0 (3)	0	6
Eastern:					
Hadramaut	1 (15)	11 (11)	0 (14)	5	17
Al-Mahra	0 (2)	2 (2)	0 (0)	0	2
SUB-TOTALS	3 (45)	41 (43)	0 (27)	12	56
TOTALS	122 (275)	56(212)	63 (189)	60	301

The column marked "others" includes the winning independent candidates as well as the winning candidates of the smaller third parties, such as the Ba'th and Nasserite parties.
[a] The figures in this table are calculated from information in Abd al-Aziz Sultan al-Mansoub's 1995 book, pp. 90 and 117. There is not a perfect correspondence between the eighteen provinces and the seven regional divisions in the left column. This is an unavoidable problem in presenting this data, but it still effectively reveals the regional dimensions of the electoral results.

Meanwhile the YSP won most of its seats in the provinces of the former south (forty-one seats out of its total fifty-six), and still gained a relatively large number (fifteen) in the north. More importantly in the south, YSP candidates swept to victory by large margins. In fact, the YSP lost only two southern electoral races in which it competed, one each in the mid-southern provinces of Abyan and Shabwa.[26] In Hadramaut, the YSP did not contest the single seat won by the GPC.

The only places the GPC truly performed well were in the highlands (winning 63 percent of its contests) and in the west coast province of al-Hudayda (winning 71 percent of its contests).[27] In other regions of the former north the GPC performed poorly, especially in the most populous western midlands (winning only 31 percent of its contests). The southern socialist party actually fared better than the GPC in al-Bayda, and it nearly matched the number of seats won by the GPC in Taiz. The YSP did match the GPC's output in Marib, where each party claimed one seat. In short, the YSP performed very well in the southern half of the country. But the GPC could not follow suit in the north. The GPC's primary strength was limited to the highlands and the western coast.

The difference between the GPC's performance in the north and the YSP's in the south appears even greater when looking at official results at the local electorate level.[28] Not only did the YSP win more than 75 percent of all southern seats in parliament, but its candidates generally won in a landslide. In Aden, Lahij, and al-Mahra the average winning YSP candidate's percentage of the total vote was 60 percent, 80 percent, and 62 percent, respectively. The winning percentage of YSP candidates dropped off in Hadramaut, where seven of the YSP's eleven winning candidates polled a majority of the vote, but the remaining four squeaked to victory with pluralities of 40–49 percent of the vote. The YSP's poorest performance came in the mid-southern provinces, where barely half of its winning candidates in Abyan polled above a 50 percent majority, and two stumbled to victory with pluralities of less than 33 percent. In Shabwa, the YSP's

---

[26] This was true because of the lingering effects of the January 1986 fighting, in Abyan and Shabwa and the local opposition to the YSP by partisans of Ali Nasir Muhammad.

[27] The GPC's strong electoral performance in al-Hudayda was largely an indication of its patronage system run through the province's largely Shafi'i business class. Since the mid-1980s, these big traders were increasingly coerced to support the President's party through his military and tribal patrons in the highlands. Interview with a group of prominent merchants in al-Hudayda; November 1996.

[28] The following information is from the official, yet unpublished vote tally of Yemen's Supreme Election Committee.

candidates fared even worse. Nonetheless, the party still rode to victory across the south in a much stronger fashion than the GPC did in the north.

President Salih's ruling party failed to sweep the vote in a single northern province. The GPC performed most poorly in the western midland provinces of Taiz and al-Bayda, where only three of its ten winning candidates polled a majority of the vote. Both of the GPC's victories in al-Bayda came with 40 percent pluralities, and two of its winning candidates in Taiz barely squeaked by with 25 percent of the vote. Its experience in the central interior provinces of Marib and al-Jawf was similar. The GPC performed better in other northern provinces, but they still failed to win majority support. In Sanaa city and Sanaa province, less than half of the GPC's victors won with clear majorities. In Sa'da, Hajja, and al-Mahwit, this was true in less than 40 percent of its victories. In Ibb less than a quarter took a majority of the vote, and in Dhamar, only one of the GPC's eleven winning candidates polled a majority. Even in al-Hudayda, only nine of the GPC's twenty-two winning candidates polled majorities.

In summary, the GPC's electoral showing in the north was not nearly as convincing as the YSP's showing in the south. This cannot be attributed to the GPC facing more competition in the north because southern constituencies saw just as many candidates. The former southern capital of Aden had the single highest candidates-per-constituency ratio (25:1), yet the YSP won more than 70 percent of the available seats by large landslide margins.[29] The YSP held remarkable popular support in the south, while the GPC failed to prove its popular appeal in any northern provinces. The GPC came out on top, as the party with the most seats in parliament, primarily because there were nearly five times as many northern seats available. Yet the GPC barely won twice the number of seats of the YSP. The YSP counted on a poor showing by the GPC, in order to pull a surprise on election day. But it did not count on the strong performance of the religious third party, Islah. This party provided the great surprise of Yemen's 1993 election.

Islah was the only opposition party to run large numbers of candidates throughout the country, both in the former north and south. Table 4.2 shows that Islah failed to win a single seat in southern provinces, where all twenty-seven of its candidates lost. Contrary to expectations, Islah

---

[29] Among the other southern provinces, Abyan had nearly thirteen candidates per constituency, while Shabwa and Hadramaut each had ten. In the north, al-Jawf had the highest candidates-per-constituency rate with seventeen, followed by Sanaa city with sixteen. Most of the north's other provinces ranged between nine and twelve candidates per constituency. Al-Mansoub, 1995; p. 117.

performed poorly in the highlands region, where it won only 28 percent of its contests. Its greatest success came in the western midlands, where Salih's regime built the Islamic front in the 1980s. Islah picked up more than half of its sixty-three seats in this region. Local polling results showed that Islah won its races by the smallest of margins, especially in Taiz where only two of its eighteen victories came with clear majorities. In short, Islah barely managed to scrape out victories in the western midlands because the votes tended to be distributed among a few front-running candidates.[30]

The significance of Islah's surprise performance in the western midland region is that it prevented the YSP from winning more northern parliamentary seats. If the socialists were going to match the GPC's performance, then they needed to win more votes in the populous provinces of Taiz and Ibb. But Islah outperformed both the GPC and YSP in these provinces. Islah was partly able to play the role of spoiler because, in the western midland and western coastal regions, it coordinated some electoral contests with the GPC.[31] This coordination between the GPC and Islah became far more overt once the electoral results were made public.

POSTELECTION DEVELOPMENTS

Despite the GPC's failure to win a majority in the new parliament, President Salih interpreted the electoral results as a popular mandate to control the government. He stuck to an informal agreement with the YSP to form a new coalition government. But his GPC allied with Islah to form a three-way coalition, in order to weaken the southern socialists. GPC officials wanted to keep possession of three of the five seats on the presidential council, leaving one seat each for the YSP and Islah. But the YSP insisted on balanced power sharing with the GPC in a 2:2:1 arrangement that would leave Islah holding the odd seat. Dispute over this critical matter led to political stalemate, and delayed the formation of a national government. The problem for the GPC was that, while the 1993 electoral results made them kingmakers in a new government, the regional pattern

---

[30] This was generally true of Islah candidates throughout the country. Only eight of its sixty-three winning candidates gained a majority of the vote. Eleven won with less than 33 percent of the vote, while another thirty candidates won less than 40 percent of the vote.

[31] Since President Salih's regime used the Islamic Front, during the late 1970s and early 1980s, to help defeat the southern-backed Marxist guerrillas in the western midland region, GPC officials were well aware that Islah could help defeat YSP candidates in the same region. The GPC swung some midland districts in favor of Islah, while Islah agreed to do the same for the GPC along the west coast.

of the voting left them weak kingmakers. The YSP could still claim to represent the southern half of the country

South Yemeni politicians used the postelection stalemate to press additional demands, including the devolution of government powers to regions outside the highlands. The YSP argued that its landslide victory in southern provinces entitled it to regional self-rule in the south. One top party official, Salem Salih Muhammad, raised the possibility of amending the unity constitution to create a federal form of government.[32] By September 1993, the YSP's politburo packaged its demands into an 18-point plan to reform the government.[33] Politburo members vowed not to participate in a second coalition government until action was taken to meet their demands. From the beginning of unity, YSP ministers wanted to push government reforms in several fields. But they were obstructed by northern GPC officials. Southern socialist leaders gradually realized that their interests were not served by centralized government in Sanaa, and that a devolution of power was necessary to maintain their interests as one of the original partners in national unity. Yet President Salih never intended to give up central government control. He accused YSP leaders of being unwilling to accept their electoral loss, and acted as if the GPC received nationwide support from all citizens. This was a mistaken interpretation of the role elections play in democracy, especially the first election in a divided country like Yemen.

After Yemen's troubled transition to its first national election, the two ruling parties were destined to reach a crisis point where one side sought more control and the other side resisted. The YSP had badly miscalculated the effects of a pluralist competition for political power. Before unification, its leadership was aware of the potential risks. In an interview at the beginning of unity, southern prime minister Haidar al-Attas suggested that the YSP could deal with any problems by "extend(ing) the discipline or 'nidham' of the South to the anarchy or 'fawda' of the North."[34] However, al-Attas and other southern leaders did not anticipate how their early policy initiatives would be obstructed, nor how they would come under repeated violent attacks.

South Yemeni leaders did not expect to exercise full control over the government. They entered unity with a vision of long-term political change. Their best hope for survival depended on the country's new

---

[32] Former prime minister Abd al-Karim al-Iryani says that when Salem Salih raised the issue in the fall of 1993, he called YSP prime minister Haidar al-Attas to tell him that it was too late for a federalist option. Interview at Dr. al-Iryani's home in Sanaa; June 14, 1996.

[33] Carapico, 1998; pp. 174–176.

[34] Hudson, 1995; p. 18.

pluralist system reforming the existing government. This is a critically important point. While southerners had a long-term view of unity, the northern regime focused on a short-term agenda to maintain the status quo and assert political control through a process of bureaucratic centralization.[35] Once a unified state was established, and the first national election carried out, President Salih expected to continue exercising the same power and influence. Unity was seen as a singular event that did not require great adjustments on his part. When YSP leaders began talking about revising unity on a federal basis, Salih and northern elites in the GPC and Islah parties started to accuse southern politicians of plotting to secede from the union.[36] This elevated political tensions because it amounted to accusations of treason against the nation.

The idea that the YSP lost the 1993 election, and then plotted to secede under the pretense of devolving government power, suffused early analyses of Yemen's unity troubles.[37] But this is historically inaccurate. The YSP's demand for a devolution of government power began before the 1993 election, so it is wrong to see it as a response to the party's poor electoral showing.[38] In fact, before the election, the YSP campaigned on a platform of giving local governments "total powers ... (with) financial and administrative independence."[39] To find the origin of Yemen's unity troubles, it is necessary to look at the first year when the northern minister of finance sought to centralize all government revenues in the capital. By the second year, southern officials resisted this process of centralization when they rejected the treatment of Aden as one of many provinces, and insisted that staff in Aden hold the rank of deputy ministers.[40] Then in late 1992 and 1993, the YSP's appointed governor in Aden withheld local revenues as a

---

[35] Kostiner, 1996; pp. 108–109. Joseph Kostiner suggests that south Yemeni leaders saw unity "as an initial step in a complex process of state and social development," while northern leaders focused on "the achievement of Yemeni unity in itself as the most significant goal."

[36] Hudson, 1995; p. 28.

[37] Burrowes, 1995(b); pp. 9–10 and 20.

[38] Brian Whitaker speculates that Vice President al-Bid's first withdrawal from Sanaa in 1992 signified the real beginning of the secession crisis. Whitaker, 1997; p. 24. According to Whitaker, once al-Bid withdrew in 1992, "the YSP began to use the threat of separation in the hope of extracting concessions from Saleh."

[39] Al-Bishari, 1993; p. 103. Islah's campaign platform referred simply to the need to minimize government centralization (p. 83), and the GPC's platform talked in vague terms of giving local authorities "the necessary powers ... to supervise and monitor" local affairs (p. 62).

[40] Interview with Othman Kamarani, the preunity elected governor of Aden, at his home in Aden; February 1, 1997.

matter of policy, distributing the funds to pay for local development projects.[41]

At the beginning of unification, local government matters were divided into two areas, each handled by a joint north-south committee. The first committee dealt with drafting a new law of local administration. The second committee dealt with redrawing provincial boundaries. Both regimes were committed to creating new boundaries in order to increase administrative efficiency and eliminate any remnants of the old north/south border line. The first minister of local administration was a southerner originally from the western midlands, named Muhammad Said Abdallah, best known by his nickname Muhsin, who was the tough-minded former director of southern state security. He was clearly chosen by the YSP to serve as a strong representative of the party's interests in this crucial area of state policy.

The northern regime also appointed political heavyweights to the two local administrative committees: Abdul-Karim al-Arashe, who sat beside President Salih on the presidential council; and Shaykh Abdallah bin Husayn al-Ahmar, the Hashid tribe's paramount shaykh. The involvement of these two men in the joint committees is testament to the serious nature of the work. It is particularly significant that Shaykh Abdallah was involved in redrawing boundaries. As president of the Islah party, Hashid's shaykh was supposedly in opposition to President Salih's regime. Yet Salih gave Shaykh Abdallah the authority to represent northern interests on this committee. After unification, there was little doubt that Shaykh Abdallah would serve the northern regime in a significant capacity because he represents one of the tribal bases of the highland group's dominance of Yemen.

The committee charged with drafting the new law on local administration completed its work in less than a year. Law #52 was passed by the joint parliament on April 25, 1991, combining aspects of former northern and southern local administrative practices. The boundaries committee did not find similar success. Its work touched on highly sensitive issues for highland tribal leaders, so Shaykh Abdallah obstructed Muhsin's plans at the ministry. One of the biggest conflicts arose when the minister discovered that many local district managers in the north were army officers loyal

---

[41] This appointed governor was Said Salih Salem, the former head of southern security who replaced Othman Kamarani, mentioned in the previous footnote. Finance Ministry officials in Sanaa accused Salem of embezzling government funds, and this added to northern suspicions about southern intentions to secede.

to the top shaykhs of Hashid and Bakil.[42] In 1992, he developed a plan to replace these army officers with the ministry's many idle civil servants. These personnel changes were advanced in the spirit of administrative reform, and it was Muhsin's prerogative to make them. However, President Salih intervened to cancel the plan after being pressured by Shaykh Abdallah and other highland shaykhs.[43]

The northern regime clearly intended to resist any government reforms that undercut highland power. Certain members of the highland group, particularly inside the northern army and tribes, refused any YSP reforms. This contrasts with the early administrative changes implemented by the northern minister of finance, which first created tensions in 1991. Then in 1992, when southern officials resisted northern financial control, YSP leaders faced assassination and other coercive political pressure. The reaction of southern leaders to the early string of assassinations is what forced a six-month postponement of the 1993 elections. There is no doubt that southern leaders had turned against the unity government before these elections.

PRELUDE TO CIVIL WAR

When leaders of the GPC and YSP reached a political stalemate in 1993, an independent national dialogue committee began negotiating between the two sides during the fall.[44] In early 1994, this committee drafted a "document of pledge and accord" to avert the collapse of national unity. The document derived largely from the YSP's original 18-point list of demands, which represented a comprehensive political plan to repair the shortcomings of Yemen's hasty unification. Its most important feature was arguably a plan to devolve political power to local government bodies after direct elections for provincial governors and district managers.[45] This plan did

---

[42] Interview with a well-informed northern ministry official; March 1997. According to this official, highland army officers used local administrative funds to pay the leading Hashid shaykhs. Approximately twenty-five such officers were loyal to Shaykh Abdallah, and another ten to fifteen officers were loyal to Mujahid Abu Shawarib.

[43] This conflict was similar to the power struggle in the former YAR, during the mid-1970s, when President al-Hamdi attempted to restrict the power and influence of the top highland tribal shaykhs.

[44] Carapico, 1998; pp. 176–182. By the middle of November 1993, there was evidence that both sides were openly preparing for warfare, and a war at this time was barely averted by U.S. intervention. Al-Madhagi, 1996; p. 157.

[45] Ahmad al-Bishari, the late editor of the Sanaa-based political journal *al-Thawabit*, referred to the DPA's plan for "local government" as the document's "principal element." Al-Bishari, 1996; p. ii. This book does not reprint the DPA. But an analysis of the DPA

not represent the desires of the YSP alone. It resulted from a genuine dialogue among a broad cross-section of north and south Yemenis led by prominent social figures who were deeply concerned about the future. The plan also had international supporters. Jordan's King Hussayn agreed to host an international signing ceremony in Amman on February 20, 1994, with President Salih, Vice President al-Bid, and Shaykh Abdallah in attendance.

Yemen's "document of pledge and accord" was the first and final attempt at a constructive solution to Yemen's unity problems. Unification in 1990 was clearly ill-conceived and inadequate. A better plan was required, especially to resolve the problem of central-local government relations, and members of a burgeoning civil society came close with the document. However, their timing was off by two or three years. Coming at such a late stage, the deal was virtually impossible to implement. When President Salih signed the document, he reportedly had a wry smile on his face, and no intent to abide by its terms.[46] In his view, this was yet one more concession that he was forced to make to a small, "ideologically outdated" Marxist party. When Shaykh Abdallah signed, he reportedly added a clause denying his written consent to any devolution of local government power.[47] Al-Bid signed the document, but most observers interpreted his body language as expressing deep doubt. Afterward, he did not return directly to Yemen.

The late Fred Halliday described the document signed in Amman, Jordan as "a document of divorce."[48] It certainly functioned this way because skirmishes broke out the next day between northern and southern army brigades. Full-scale civil war began two months later. North Yemeni officials claimed that the civil war resulted from Ali Salem al-Bid's plot to secede. They pointed to the 1992 discovery of a major oil field in the eastern region of Hadramaut as the start of the plot.[49] According to this

is provided by Dr. Rashad al-Aleemi on pp. 311–319. The document was originally published in Arabic on January 18, 1994, by the "national dialogue" committee. It appeared in several of Yemen's newspapers, and was reprinted in English by the *Yemen Times*, Volume IV, #4, January 23–29, 1994.

[46] After civil war in 1994 Salih reportedly referred to the DPA as *Watheeqat al-Ahr wa al-Nifaq* or the "Document of Prostitution and Hypocrisy," a crude play on the Arabic words for Document of Pledge and Accord, *Watheeqat al-Ahd wa al-Itifaq.*

[47] Al-Bishari, 1996; p. iii, footnote 2.

[48] Halliday's statement was made during a BBC interview in London after the DPA was signed on February 20, 1994. Al-Bishari, 1996; p. iii, footnote 4.

[49] During Vice President al-Bid's absence from Sanaa in 1992, he sat for an extended period of time in the Hadrami capital, al-Mukalla, near the new oil fields and close to his own ancestral home. The oil fields in Hadramaut came on line three months after the April 1993 elections. *Yemen Times*, July 28, 1993; p.1.

argument, since al-Bid is Hadrami, he was tempted by oil riches to betray national unity. The possibility of Hadramaut's small population carrying out autonomous development with its own oil financing, similar to Dubai or Qatar, may realistically have been a better option for the YSP leader. The idea of a southern plot to secede is also linked to theories of a foreign conspiracy against Yemen, usually involving Saudi Arabia.[50] There is evidence that Saudi Arabia and other states provided assistance to southern YSP leaders during the 1994 civil war.[51] But the primary source of Yemen's unity troubles existed inside the country, not outside, due to deadly political disputes between north and south Yemeni leaders.

One well-informed western observer of Yemen's 1994 civil war claimed that the idea of a secessionist plot was improbable because "it is doubtful whether the YSP had a single, clear strategy–mainly because it could not agree on one."[52] YSP leaders were divided over political strategy from the start of unification in 1990. Again on the eve of civil war in 1994, they were divided and indecisive. After the fighting started, the YSP politburo voted on "unity vs. secession" in early May 1994. The result was eleven in favor of unity, only six in favor of secession, and one abstention.[53] This apparently remained true until the formal declaration of secession on May 21, 1994, more than three weeks after the war commenced.

---

[50] According to Michael Hudson, "northern officials claim that the plot to undo Yemeni unity was hatched in Geneva in 1992 at a meeting between a senior YSP leader and a high-ranking Saudi foreign policy 'trouble-shooter'." Hudson, 1995; p. 27.

[51] Katz, 1995; pp. 82–85.

[52] Whitaker, 1997; p. 23. Brian Whitaker provides a more complete analysis of the later secession on pp. 25–26.

[53] Warburton, 1995; p. 44, footnote 18.

5

The Spoils of Civil War

In the summer of 1994, Yemen experienced full-scale warfare across its territory, although the fighting on eastern fronts was limited. Military aircraft, short- and medium-range missiles, tanks, and other heavy artillery were all employed in the fighting. Populations, north and south, were mobilized against each other, as politicians spread propaganda about the opposing side. Religious rhetoric in the north portrayed the war as a jihad against infidel socialists.[1] General estimates of those killed ranged between five thousand and seven thousand, including soldiers and civilians.[2] Financial estimates of the war's costs ran anywhere from U.S. $2 billion to $8 billion.[3]

Aden faced the worst aspects of the war. The northern military laid siege to the city for more than a month, cutting off water supplies and food provisions to a population of nearly one million in sweltering summer heat. Other areas of the south did not experience the same hardships. Large parts of Lahij and Abyan were overrun during the war's early phase in May 1994. Hadramaut held out until the end. But unlike Aden, the cities of Hadramaut fell without a real fight.[4] Thus they did not experience the

---

[1] See a sermon given by Shaykh al-Zindani, one of five members of Yemen's presidential council in 1994; *Yemen Times*, Vol. IV, No. 24, June 20, 1994; p. 1. The editor described al-Zindani as mastering "the art of holding a large public in a trance-like situation." Reprinted in *Yemen Update*, No. 35, Summer/Fall 1994; p. 11.

[2] Hudson, 1995; p. 21.

[3] Halliday, 1995; p. 133. The government in Sanaa claimed the war's costs were at the upper end of this scale. If true, this would be roughly equivalent to the country's annual GDP. Nonneman, 1997; p. 99.

[4] There was one brief battle outside al-Mukalla where al-Bid's Hadrami commander, and former minister of oil, Salih Ben Husaynoun, was killed. Al-Bakr, 1995; pp. 110–111. He died in a mysterious ambush while in the company of Muhammad Said Abdallah, the minister of local administration. The fact that the latter was tied to the "Unity" brigade,

same loss of life. As many as one thousand people died in Aden, especially during the last three weeks of war when many civilians were killed by northern artillery barrages. Residents of Crater district later recalled burying dozens of corpses each morning in late June and early July. The numbers killed in outer districts, like Shaykh Othman and Khormaksar, were higher.[5]

After unification in 1990, the merger of the two regimes' military forces was critically important. The YSP held the defense ministry post, but northern leaders had no intention of allowing southerners to gain military control.[6] As a result, the two militaries never merged under a unified command. Instead, they carried out a symbolic exchange of troops, sending a few brigades from both armies to new camps across the old border line. Southern troops deployed deep inside the northern highlands in Dhamar and Sanaa provinces, while northern troops camped in Abyan and Aden.[7] These exchanges took place without serious incident. But the north violated the spirit of the unity agreement when it deployed two brigades, one from the military police and another from central security forces, inside the former southern capital. The YSP registered its complaint over this issue because all troops were supposed to be kept outside major cities. But in the early spirit of unity, southern leaders did not want the issue to escalate into a major crisis.[8]

The major conflicts during the early years of unity took place inside the ministry of defense in Sanaa. The southern minister had heated arguments with his northern counterparts over the military's command structure and the ministry's lack of financial accountability. The southern minister discovered that northern commanders had a habit of using defense funds to support irregular tribal forces in the highlands. He engaged in ongoing disputes with President Salih's family members who held top command posts in the northern army.[9] These disputes preceded the campaign of

---

which failed to defend Hadramaut, and that he escaped the ambush without injury, made some Hadramis suspicious.

[5] The morning after Vice President al-Bid declared a separate southern state, a northern missile struck a mosque in Shaykh Othman, killing several worshipers. As northern forces moved closer to Aden, citizens in outer districts crowded into Crater for protection. Personal interview in Aden; December 1996.

[6] A joint north/south military committee met in Taiz for forty days, before unity, without reaching an agreement. Interview with Dr. Muhammad Said Muqbil, a former director of economic affairs in the southern military and member of Yemen's parliament; December 23, 1996.

[7] Warburton, 1995; p. 24.

[8] Interview with a former southern military official; May 1997.

[9] Interview with a former southern military official; April 1997.

political assassinations in 1992. One example was a southern initiative to merge irregular fighters of the old NDF into Yemen's army. President Salih refused even though many irregular tribal forces existed on the state payroll. Later President Salih turned the tables by providing separate funding to members of the NDF, encouraging them to start their own newspaper.[10] Through such maneuvering, President Salih effectively sowed the seeds of discord inside the YSP while also denying it the opportunity to win public support across the northern border, especially in the western midlands. Such gamesmanship, combined with the utter failure to build a single unified military command, aggravated political differences in all fields of government.

The record of events at the beginning of Yemen's civil war in April 1994 clearly shows that northern military commanders pursued an aggressive strategy against the southern army. The fighting started on April 27 in the northern provinces of Sanaa and Dhamar, where northern troops had camped adjacent to two southern brigades since 1991. At the camp near Amran in Sanaa province, southern commanders tried to bring Bakil tribal militias into their compound as a protection force. They hoped that northern Hashid shaykhs would prevent any military actions that could spark an intertribal war. However, the northern troops denied the Bakil tribesmen access to the southern camp. Soon afterward southern troops became pinned down by northern artillery barrages from strategic high ground surrounding the camp. During intense, close range shelling, hundreds of southern soldiers were massacred.[11] Similar fighting occurred in Dhamar. By the end of the war's first week on May 4, the remnants of the southern brigades at Amran retreated under the protection of Bakil tribesmen. Once northern commanders secured Sanaa and Dhamar from ground attack by southern troops, they advanced toward Aden and Hadramaut.

The local director of the American Institute for Yemeni Studies in Sanaa, David Warburton, published the most reliable analysis of Yemen's war. Warburton concluded that southern military commanders

---

[10] Interview with a former NDF activist in the western midlands and a former southern defense official; March 1997. During the mid-1980s, NDF politics created divisions between YSP officials from southwestern and mid-southern regions, leading to the 1986 fighting in Aden. After 1990, Salih skillfully exploited the old NDF to redivide the YSP.

[11] Warburton, 1995; p. 43, footnote 9. The death toll in this one battle was greater than the death toll in Yemen's two border wars in the 1970s.

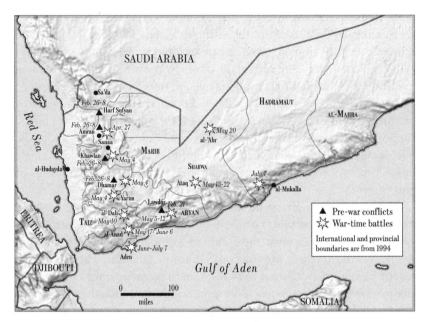

MAP 4. Battlefronts in Yemen's 1994 civil war, April–July[12]

never pursued an aggressive strategy against the northern army.[13] According to Warburton, who was in Yemen at the time of the fighting, southern YSP leaders adopted a defensive posture throughout the war. Operating with a bunker mentality in Aden, southern commanders began lobbing Scud missiles in an attempt to hit the northern capital. Following one Scud strike on May 11, which hit an outer residential neighborhood of Sanaa and killed two dozen civilians, President Salih ordered YSP leaders to leave the country or be executed.[14] The formal announcement of southern secession came ten days later on May 21.

Evidence from the battlefield clearly showed that the northern side was the military aggressor in 1994. According to Warburton, "the primary goal of the southern military defense was to win international political support (for an independent state)," not to defeat the northern army on the

[12] This map is based on David Warburton's article "The Conventional War in Yemen" in the Spring 1995 issue of *The Arab Studies Journal*.

[13] Ibid, pp. 42–43.

[14] *Yemen Update*, No. 35, Summer/Fall 1994; p. 5. In the prior week, Shaykh Abdallah bin Husayn al-Ahmar initiated a call in parliament to dismiss Ali Salem al-Bid from the presidential council; p. 4.

battlefield.[15] Meanwhile, the northern army rushed to defeat southern forces as quickly as possible, in order to prevent outside intervention. In early June 1994, President Salih announced a series of unilateral ceasefires to alleviate growing pressure from the UN Security Council, where foreign diplomats in New York called for an end to fighting.[16] Members of the Security Council never recognized the new independent state of south Yemen. This led northern forces to break ceasefire arrangements, and continue their offensive. Southern Islamic groups, and former Arab-Afghan mujahideen, participated in the northern army's siege of Aden along with leaders of the exiled Ali Nasir group. Thus northern troops did not fight alone.

Under the pressures of war, the division between YSP leaders in Lahij and Hadramaut provinces ultimately worked to the advantage of President Salih in Sanaa. During the north's march toward Aden, Salih's commanders bought the passivity of many groups in Lahij who distrusted Ali Salem al-Bid and other Hadrami officials.[17] A rift formed among YSP leaders. In June 1994, al-Bid and other Hadrami officials advocated a strategic retreat from Aden to al-Mukalla and Wadi Hadramaut, where southern military forces might better defend themselves, while politicians continued searching for international recognition of the new southern state. But senior commanders from Lahij accused the Hadramis of planning to establish an independent Hadrami state, and in the process sacrifice Aden to the northern army.[18] Thus, changes of treason and secession existed in the north and south.

In the end, Ali Salim al-Bid was defeated by tribal military forces from the northwest highland region, not the internal divisions among south Yemenis. The partisans of former southern president Ali Nasir Muhammad did not uniformly support the northern war effort. From his exile in Syria, Ali Nasir took a publicly neutral stance on the war.[19] His closest political associate, Muhammad Ali Ahmad, the former governor of Abyan, actually rejoined

---

[15] Warburton, 1995; pp. 42–43.

[16] Ibid, pp. 36–37. The UN Security Council passed two resolutions in June 1994, UNSC Resolutions Nos. 924 and 931, calling for an end to the fighting in Yemen and peaceful resolution of all political disputes.

[17] Interview with independent newspaper publisher Omar al-Jawi in Sanaa, July 28, 1996. The publisher of the *Yemen Times*, Abd al-Aziz al-Saqqaf, also claimed that northern commanders were able to buy the support (or at least neutrality) of many southerners, including soldiers in some army brigades. *Yemen Times*, Volume IV, No. 27, July 11–17, 1994; p. 8; reprinted in *Yemen Update*, No. 35, Summer/Fall 1994.

[18] Interview with former prime minister Haidar al-Attas in December 2002.

[19] Halliday, 1995; p. 139, footnote 1.

the YSP central committee in 1993, and was then promoted to the YSP politburo shortly before the war started. In early April 1994, the Ali Nasir group's fifth brigade left its highland military base at Harf Sufyan, and retreated to the south under the command of Abdallah Shaleel. Shaleel and the fifth brigade fought against northern troops. The northern victory required long and costly siege warfare by ground forces sent from the mountains of Sanaa. The fighting lasted until July 7, 1994, when southern leaders fled into exile.

POSTWAR POLITICAL CONDITIONS

President Salih realized that military aggression against the south risked creating permanent resentment among broad cross-sections of the southern population. Thus he understood the need to continue power sharing with southerners. During the civil war, he appointed a few south Yemenis to fill cabinet vacancies left by YSP ministers. A respected non-partisan southern technocrat, Faisal Ben Shamlan, was named to the top post in the oil ministry.[20] One of the leaders of the Ali Nasir group, Abd al-Rabo Mansour Hadi, was asked to become the new minister of defense. Another Ali Nasir partisan, Ahmad Musaid Husayn, was named minister of transportation.[21] Both of these men are originally from the mid-southern region. Their appointments were superficial in nature, since northern officials primarily directed ministry affairs during wartime.

President Salih's main purpose was to show that he intended to include south Yemenis in his postwar government. In the short term, this possibly encouraged the defection of southern soldiers on the battlefield. In the long term, Salih's alliance with the Ali Nasir group would be crucial for recreating a balance of power in government. After the war, it was announced that Abd al-Rabo would replace al-Bid as vice president. By switching one southern vice president for another, President Salih hoped to create the impression that Yemeni unity remained intact. But Salih was mainly interested in the appearance of power sharing, not genuine representation of southern interests in government. Other postwar changes made clear the president intended to secure his own hold on power. On September 29, 1994, the constitution was amended to strengthen his personal authority

---

[20] Ben Shamlan had previously directed the southern oil refinery in Aden before and after unification.
[21] Before the January 1986 conflict in Aden, Abd al-Rabo Mansour Hadi had been Ali Nasir's chief of military staff, and Ahmad Musaid Husayn directed the PDRY's state security.

by abolishing the five-member presidential council.[22] This gave Salih full powers including the right to rule by decree. Nearly half of the original 131 constitutional articles were redrafted, virtually eliminating the last remnants of the former south Yemeni government, while adopting the northern system in full.[23]

In October 1994, President Salih agreed to form a coalition government with the Islah party in a minority role. When he selected a new prime minister, Salih tapped the experienced hand of Abd al-Aziz Abd al-Ghani, the trusted GPC insider who held the prime minister's post for more than a decade in the former YAR. His return signified the return of the north's old balance of power between highland tribal interests and western midland/ coastal business interests. Meanwhile, south Yemenis experienced a sharp decline in representation from 1990 when they held nearly half of all cabinet posts. Table 5.1 shows that only eight southern cabinet ministers were appointed after the war, seven by the GPC and one by Islah.

Among northern ministers in 1994, a majority (eleven out of nineteen) came from the highland region. The eight ministers from lowland Shafi'i regions (including the minister of industry who immigrated to Yemen from Djibouti) now equaled the total number of southern ministers. In effect, south Yemenis were reduced to the minority status held by lowland Shafi'i in the former YAR. Four southern ministers appointed in 1994 were native Hadramis of the eastern region, but they were largely dissociated from the former southern regime. The minister of oil, Faisal Ben Shamlan, was an independent technocrat. The ministers of information and fisheries lived in north Yemen for many years prior to unification.[24] The minister of planning had been jailed in Aden, prior to unification, for political reasons related to the January 1986 fighting.

The minister of legal affairs from Aden (whose family originally emigrated from the western midlands), and the three ministers from the mid-southern region were all partisans of Ali Nasir. It is noteworthy that none of the post-war ministers came from Lahij in the southwest region. Southerners from Lahij province were the chief rivals of Ali Nasir. Thus

---

[22] Carapico, 1996; p. 315. Sheila Carapico describes the amended constitution being "railroaded" through the Yemeni parliament.

[23] Hasan Abu Taleb described "deepening public resentment" in the south caused by a regime that aimed "to erase all significant identifiably separate administrative entities from the former South, and has tried to erase the heritage of the YSP in every field." Abu Taleb, 1997; p. 58.

[24] Muhammad Ba Sindwa frequently served in north Yemen governments; and Abdul-Rahman Ba Fadhl worked for decades as a businessman in Saudi Arabia.

TABLE 5.1. *The Republic of Yemen's Postwar Cabinet, 1994*

	Name	Post	Party	Regional Origin
1	Abd al-Aziz Abd al-Ghani	Prime Minister	GPC	West Midlands/ Taiz
2	Abd al-Karim al-Iryani	Foreign Affairs	GPC	Highland/Ibb
3	Husayn Arab	Interior Affairs	GPC	Mid-south/Abyan*
4	Abdul-Malek al-Siyani	Defense	GPC	Highland/Sanaa
5	Muhammad al-Junaid	Finance	GPC	West coast/ al-Hudayda
6	Faisal Ben Shamlan	Oil & Resources	Independent	East/Hadramaut*
7	Abd al-Qadr Ba Jamal	Planning	GPC	East/Hadramaut*
8	Muhammad al-Jubari	Supply & Trade	GPC	Highland/Dhamar
9	Abdallah Ghanem	Legal Affairs	GPC	Aden/Midlands*
10	Sadeq Amin Abu Ras	Civil Service	GPC	Highland/Ibb
11	Muhammad Ba Sindwa	Information	GPC	East/Hadramaut*
12	Ali Hameed Sharaf	Housing	GPC	Highland/Hajja
13	Muhammad al-Attar	Industry	GPC	Djibouti
14	Ahmad Musaed Husayn	Transportation	GPC	Mid-south/ Shabwa*
15	Ahmad Muhammad al-Ansi	Communication	GPC	Highland/Dhamar
16	Ahmad Salem al-Jabali	Agriculture	GPC	West coast/ al-Hudayda
17	Yahya al-Arashe	Culture	GPC	Highland/Sanaa
18	Muhammad al-Butani	Social Security	GPC	Mid-south/Abyan*
19	Abd al-Wahab Raweh	Youth & Sports	GPC	West Midlands/ Taiz
20	Abd al-Wahab Al-Ansi	Vice P.M.	Islah	Highland/Sanaa
21	Qadi al-Daylami	Justice	Islah	Highland/Dhamar
22	Abdallah al-Qubati	Education	Islah	West Midlands/ Taiz
23	Najeeb Ghanem	Health	Islah	West Midlands/ Taiz
24	Muhammad Dammaj	Local Admin.	Islah	Highland/Sanaa
25	Abd al-Rahman Ba Fadhl	Fisheries	Islah	East/Hadramaut*
26	Abdallah Al-Aqwa	Water & Elec.	Islah	Highland/Sanaa
27	Ghaleb al-Qurashi	Islamic Affairs	Islah	West Midlands/ Taiz

* Southern ministers.

President Salih effectively exploited the regional rift in the southern population. Combined with Vice President Hadi, and the selection of another Ali Nasir partisan from Shabwa to serve as military chief of staff, President Salih relied heavily on Ali Nasir's partisans from the mid-southern region to reconstruct a degree of north-south power sharing in late 1994. Nonetheless, southern representation in government remained largely symbolic because members of the Ali Nasir group were held in check by lower-ranking ministry officials who served at the president's bidding. This was especially true of the selection of Abdallah Ali Aliwa to serve as military chief of staff in the fall of 1994. He exercised minimal authority because many of the officers ostensibly under his command were members of President Salih's family.

Before the 1994 civil war, it was widely known that Salih's family controlled the army. But its control was hidden behind a facade of nominally higher-ranked officers. After 1994, all pretenses to conceal the presidential family's monopoly of military power were abandoned. General Ali Muhsin al-Ahmar remained in charge of the "central region" around Sanaa, including the northern Tihama and central interior regions. A maternal uncle, named Muhammad Ahmad Ismail, became commander of Hadramaut and Shabwa provinces. Another maternal uncle, named Muhammad Ali Muhsin, took command of the southwest region around Aden, the western midlands, and the southern half of Tihama.[25] The final regional command in al-Mahra province was given to an Ali Nasir partisan who had a limited role to play on the remote eastern border with Oman.

After July 7, 1994, the regime in Sanaa offered a general amnesty to southern soldiers and their commanders. A list of sixteen southern leaders, including al-Bid and al-Attas, were tried in absentia for treason, and five were sentenced to death.[26] Despite the amnesty, Salih's regime disarmed all southern military and police forces. The president met his postwar pledge to retain them as state employees. But the vast majority of southern

---

[25] This information is taken from several interviews conducted in 1996 and 1997 with various members of Yemen's political opposition in the north and the south. In an appendix to the book, *Yemen's War: The Tribe Conquers the Nation*, Bashir al-Bakr provides a list of more than thirty top military commanders who are related to President Salih, or come from his tribal district of Sanhan. Al-Bakr, 1995; pp. 130–132.

[26] All sixteen of these southern officials fled the country along with thousands of others, including some northerners who joined the southern cause. The vast majority of war refugees ended up in the UAE, Oman, and Saudi Arabia. Most were eventually invited to return to Yemen without facing charges, and the five death sentences were revoked.

military and security personnel were not recalled to active duty. Instead, they sat at home collecting half-pay without benefits, while northern soldiers and policemen took control of southern lands. The minister of interior in charge of police was a well-respected former north Yemeni ambassador to the United States named Yahya al-Mutawakkel. Immediately after the civil war, he tried to retain and rearm the southern policemen.[27] He developed a postwar plan to foster mutual trust between northern and southern police officers, in order to build the institutions of a "modern" nation-state. Al-Mutawakkel claimed to have brought back 80–90 percent of the southern police force in Aden and Hadramaut during the first five months after the war. But his intention to rearm these men was obstructed by other top officials in Sanaa.

According to Dr. Mohammed al-Mutawakkel, Yahya's cousin who is a political scientist at Sanaa University, it was the president's relatives, specifically Ali Muhsin and Muhammad Abdallah Salih, who obstructed the interior ministry's plan to rearm the southern police force.[28] Shortly afterward, Yahya al-Mutawakkel resigned his ministry post, rather than continue serving without authority to carry out critical decisions affecting national development. There were two primary sources of political power after the 1994 civil war: first, the army under President Salih's family; and second, the highland tribes of Hashid and Bakil, many of which operated independent paramilitary organizations in the country. The concentration of power in the army and the highland tribes is the main reason why the postwar experience of most south Yemenis was not one of unity and inclusion, but rather exclusion and disempowerment. Some partisans of Ali Nasir benefited from their elevation to leadership positions in the government. But a majority of south Yemenis experienced humiliation under occupation by northern military forces. The prominent Yemeni political philosopher Dr. Abu Bakr al-Saqqaf, who teaches at Sanaa University, argued that south Yemenis experienced a form of "internal colonialism" after the civil war, falling under the control of northern political and military elites.

POSTWAR CHANGES AT THE PROVINCIAL LEVEL

At the beginning of unity, the only local power sharing plan involved an exchange of provincial governors similar to the exchange of troops across

---

[27] Interview with Yahya al-Mutawakkel at his home in Sanaa; July 9, 1996.
[28] Interview with Dr. Mohammed al-Mutawakkel at his home in Sanaa; July 10, 1996.

the border. The regimes agreed to exchange only an equal number of governors. The YSP was unwilling to allow a northerner to serve as governor of Aden, so this left five southern provinces in which the GPC could appoint the top official. The two sides were prohibited from appointing partisan allies from the other side of the border. This was also true in central government appointments. So the GPC could only appoint native north Yemenis to central and local government posts, while the YSP was expected to appoint native southerners. President Salih chose to send tribal and military allies from the highland region to serve as governors in the south. The only exception was the new governor of Shabwa, Dirham Numan, who is a military officer and GPC supporter from Taiz in the western midlands.

On the northern side of the border, the GPC prohibited southerners from governing five northern provinces: Sanaa, Taiz, al-Hudayda, al-Bayda, and Marib.[29] This left the YSP holding three provincial posts in the highland region, Sa'da, Hajja, and Dhamar, plus one post in the western midlands, Ibb, and al-Jawf in the central interior region. The southern governors in the north complained about frequent obstruction by their northern assistants. One transfer governor, Muhammad Ali Ba Shamakh, rarely stayed in his office in Hajja because he had virtually no decision making power.[30] Northern governors in the south also complained of similar treatment by their local staff. The transfer governor in Hadramaut, Salih al-Khawlani, was particularly vocal about his complaints. Given the political conflict and stalemate in Sanaa between 1990 and 1994, it was hardly surprising that the transfer governors remained idle on the job. In most cases, they served as mere tokens of an imaginary national union. Following the civil war, southern provincial offices witnessed sweeping changes from top to bottom. (Table 5.2) In the short term, President Salih appointed a few south Yemenis to high profile posts, in order to demonstrate his intent to work in partnership with local citizens. But he appointed a few dozen northern officials to the most sensitive security and financial posts.

Hadramaut was the only southern province to have its previous northern governor reappointed after the civil war. Salih al-Khawlani fled north in late 1993, and a Hadrami member of the YSP party served as governor through the civil war. Al-Khawlani claimed that Hadramis greeted him

---

[29] The preunity governor of al-Hudayda, Abd al-Rahman Muhammad Ali Othman, remained in his post (the only governor to do so); and a member of the Iryani clan was appointed as the new governor of Taiz.

[30] Interview with Ali al-Ahmadi who became governor of Hajja after the 1994 war; November 19, 1996.

TABLE 5.2. *Percentage of New Provincial Administrators, Postwar 1994*

	Top Four Posts	Ten Major Posts	Other Minor Posts
SOUTHWEST REGION			
Aden	100	90	71
Lahij	100	75	63
MID-SOUTHERN REGION			
Abyan	100	71	81
Shabwa	100	88	44
EASTERN REGION			
Hadramaut	100	70	73
Wadi Hadramaut	100	50	56
al-Mahra	100	70	63
HIGHLAND REGION			
Sanaa City	0	22	15
Sanaa	25	0	25
Hajja	100	50	32
al-Mahwit	50	33	22
Sa'da	75	56	16
WEST COAST REGION			
al-Hudayda	50	20	17
WESTERN MIDLAND REGION			
Taiz	50	20	9
al-Bayda	25	10	0
Ibb	75	67	18
CENTRAL INTERIOR REGION			
Marib	25	38	28

with tears of joy when he returned in late 1994. But residents of al-Mukalla and towns in Wadi Hadramaut did not recall his return in these terms.[31] Although most residents respected al-Khawlani, they regarded him as an outsider sent from Sanaa. In the five other southern provinces, President Salih appointed native governors and deputy governors, except for Lahij where a highland security official became deputy governor.

Most of the newly appointed southern staff represented President Salih's alliance with supporters of exiled southern leader Ali Nasir Muhammad, or the adult children of families who fled the PDRY during the 1960s. In Aden, Abyan, and al-Mahra provinces, the postwar

---

[31] Interview with a group of local administrators in al-Mukalla; January 1997.

governors were all Ali Nasir partisans who fled south Yemen during the intraregime fighting in January 1986. In Abyan, Ali Nasir's home province, the new governor was Ali Shaykh Omar, a former commander of the southern army. The new governor of Aden, Taha Ghanem, had previously been a popular governor in the former southern capital. Both men were well received after their homecomings. In Lahij and Shabwa, the new governors had been exiled during an earlier period of south Yemeni history. For decades, they lived in north Yemen, and became loyal supporters of leaders in the Islah and GPC parties, respectively. For this reason, they were not as well received by local citizens in the south.

Despite the appointment of a large number of native southern governors and deputy governors, they were easily overruled by northern military and security commanders who worked in the same regions. Throughout the last half of the 1990s, the top military commanders in the southwest, mid-southern, and eastern regions, all had family and tribal connections to President Salih in Sanaa. Thus the southern governors understood that real power remained in the hands of Salih's inner circle. The heavy postwar presence of northern military and security personnel, often camped inside major cities and on the periphery of other southern towns, was regarded as an extension of Salih's highland tribal group. For years, northern soldiers continued to operate roadside checkpoints between southern cities and towns. Thus local residents sensed that they were under military occupation by forces sent across the former border.

In 1995, President Salih rotated the governors of Abyan and Shabwa for political reasons. He also appointed a new deputy governor in Abyan, Muhammad Husayn Ashaal. The latter is a key southern Islamist figure who returned after unification, and sympathized with the violent attacks against the YSP in 1992 and 1993. Ashaal's father was a top commander in the former British-trained South Arabian army. His appointment to lead Abyan with the disreputable former governor of Shabwa was further evidence that President Salih had no intention of allowing Ali Nasir partisans to reestablish a power base in Abyan. In 1996, Salih also replaced the governor of al-Mahra with a loyal GPC military officer from al-Hudayda. Then in 1998, he replaced Lahij's governor with a GPC military officer from Taiz. Thus, within a few short years, there was a significant retreat from allowing southerners to serve as local governors.

Based on the local administrative survey cited in Chapter 2, concerning the regional background of officials in the "top four" and "ten major" posts of Yemen's provinces, it is possible to use the same survey to better understand political changes in the postwar south. Table 5.3 shows that

TABLE 5.3. *Percentage of Northern Officials in Southern Postwar Administration, 1994–96*[a]

	Top Four Posts (years)			Ten Major Posts (years)			Other Minor Posts (years)		
	1994	1995	1996	1994	1995	1996	1994	1995	1996
SOUTHWEST REGION									
Aden	50	50	50	50	60	70	48	45	45
Lahij	75	75	75	62	75	75	13	12	12
MID-SOUTHERN REGION									
Abyan	50	50	50	43	43	43	5	5	5
Shabwa	0	0	0	38	25	25	6	5	5
EASTERN REGION									
Hadramaut	75	75	50	40	50	50	0	0	0
Wadi Hadramaut	50	33	33	25	13	13	0	0	6
al-Mahra	0	0	50	13	13	25	11	11	11

[a] It is noteworthy that the percentage of northern administrators in Wadi Hadramaut is lower than the percentage for Hadramaut province. After the 1994 war, Salih's regime sought to win favor among citizens of the Wadi, in order to gain their approval to split Hadramaut into two provinces. The plan to split Hadramaut is discussed in Chapter 6.

after 1994 north Yemenis held 50–75 percent of the "top four" and "ten major" administrative posts in the southwest and eastern regions. These two regions formed the base of the YSP ruling group in 1990, so President Salih appeared especially eager to control local administration in the provinces of Lahij, Aden, and Hadramaut. In the mid-southern region, and in al-Mahra province of the eastern region, Salih was more willing to promote southern governors and deputies. Yet across southern provinces, northerners directed the other two "top four" posts: general security, *al-amn al-'amm*, and political security, *al-amn al-siyasi*. The only exceptions to President Salih's reliance on northern officers to command security operations in the south were a native political security director in Wadi Hadramaut, and two Ali Nasir partisans in Shabwa province. The director of Shabwa's general security was a native, while the director of political security was from neighboring Abyan. In all other southern provinces, each post-war security director came from the highland region.

Details of the data in Table 5.3 reveal a heavy concentration of government officials from the northwest highland region in the postwar south. This lends credence to the idea of "internal colonialism" in southern provinces after the 1994 civil war. In the southern provincial offices of state prosecutor, taxation, customs, and finance, President Salih consistently appointed officials from the highland region to serve in the post-war south. Several northerners in the "ten major" financial posts, and other minor administrative positions, came from nonhighland provinces, Taiz, al-Hudayda, and al-Bayda. But a clear majority came from the highland region, especially those who served in Aden and Hadramaut where economic resources are greater. More native southern officials could be found working in public service fields, such as health, labor, education, and so on. These provincial posts were less politically sensitive, since the regime in Sanaa did not focus on the provision of public services.

During the late 1990s, GPC officials frequently mocked the idea that local representation was important in southern provinces. During interviews, they typically commented that "all Yemenis are the same," and often mentioned the "importance of mixing northerners and southerners together as one nation." If a southerner suggested that local residents should be allowed to elect their own governors, or direct their own security and financial affairs, then they risked being accused of spreading secessionist ideas. This was similar to the charges brought against Ali Salem al-Bid and other southern YSP leaders in late 1993, when they advocated a federal restructuring of Yemen. President Salih and his associates in the GPC sought hegemony over the south based on narrow unionist views common to ruling circles in Sanaa. This created intolerance toward any expression of regionalism or localism.

Dr. Abu Bakr al-Saqqaf, who authored the idea of "internal colonialism" in the wake of the 1994 civil war, was one who frequently spoke out against narrow thinking in the office of the president and central government ministries. In December 1995, he was kidnapped and brutally beaten by political security officers in Sanaa. The local weekly English newspaper, *Yemen Times*, published horrifying color photos of his badly bruised and swollen face, arms, shoulders, and back, after he was struck numerous times by an electrical shock baton.[32] This was an ominous sign of what was to come in the late 1990s and 2000s.

GPC officials, and supporters of the status quo in Sanaa, offered poor apologies for the regime's human rights abuses. Apologists tended to find consolation in the fact that President Salih was not "a bad dictator" like the former Idi Amin of Uganda. Salih's security forces limited themselves

---

[32] *Yemen Times*, December 25, 1995, Volume 5, No. 51; p. 1. Al-Saqqaf's injuries were permanently disabling.

to beating dissidents, not killing them. In Sanaa, a group of cultural elites and opinion makers credited the regime's "mild" authoritarianism to its tribal roots. According to one popular theory, tribalism made the regime moderate because the president and his supporters were fearful tribal rivals could use greater violence against the regime itself, if the regime resorted to more severe authoritarian practices. The problem with this theory is that it did not apply to nontribal people, like Dr. al-Saqqaf, who could be seized on the street and beaten for expressing critical ideas. Dissident tribal shaykhs might have been protected, but not individuals lacking tribal support. Much of the southern population was vulnerable in the 1990s because tribalism had been nearly eradicated in the PDRY.

To appreciate the full significance of President Salih's political changes after the 1994 civil war, it is important to recall that local administration in the PDRY was characterized by high "native" representation. (Confer Table 2.5.) To a large extent, this remained true until 1994. The exception was the five symbolic northern governors who crossed the border in 1991, and the few appointments made by the northern minister of finance. For decades, south Yemen had a tradition of allowing local governors and office managers to serve in their own home provinces. In fact, this was a requirement of local office holders, when the YSP began holding elections during the late 1970s. These elections were rigged to favor ruling party candidates. But it was not possible for a resident of one province to run for a local government seat in another province.

The northern YAR was different because the regime in Sanaa continued the practice of Zaydi imams who appointed highland governors, security directors, and tax officials to serve in agriculturally rich provinces of the western midlands and west coast regions. When President Salih did the same after 1994 in key southern provinces, it was promoted as a policy of unification among north and south Yemenis. But the rhetoric about unity struck a sour chord for southerners who thought highland officials violated local customs. Meanwhile, highland officials continued to hold their traditional dominance in northern provinces. As Table 5.4 shows, only Hajja, Sa'da, and Taiz had slightly lower percentages of highland officials after 1994. Taiz made an interesting case because for the first time since the 1960s, it had a native governor, deputy governor, and two native security directors.

Postwar developments in Taiz were surprising because this province in the western midlands had long been the primary hegemonic concern of highland elites in the YAR. Before unification, highland officials held more

TABLE 5.4. *Percentage of Highland Officials in Northern Postwar Administration, 1994–96*

	Top Four Posts (years)			Ten Major Posts (years)			Other Minor Posts (years)		
	1994	1995	1996	1994	1995	1996	1994	1995	1996
HIGHLAND REGION									
Sanaa City	100	100	100	100	100	89	80	86	81
Sanaa	100	100	100	100	100	100	81	81	81
Hajja	75	50	50	87	75	63	84	84	89
al-Mahwit	100	100	100	89	100	100	83	78	83
Sa'da	100	75	75	100	87	87	84	84	89
WEST COAST REGION									
al-Hudayda	75	75	75	60	50	40	52	48	43
WESTERN MIDLAND REGION									
Taiz	0	25	25	20	40	40	23	18	18
al-Bayda	100	100	100	80	80	80	11	20	35
Ibb	75	75	75	67	67	67	64	64	73
CENTRAL INTERIOR REGION									
Marib	100	75	75	87	50	50	40	20	20

top administrative posts in Taiz than any other lowland or coastal province. (Confer Table 2.7.) This remained true after 1990. Following the civil war in 1994, President Salih needed to make room for local Islah supporters to serve in Taiz's government, since the GPC agreed to form a ruling coalition with the Islamist party.[33] Salih was also willing to relax his hold on Taiz in order to consolidate control over the south. Taiz no longer possessed the most lucrative resources for the central government to exploit. The resources of Aden and Hadramaut offered a greater prize after the war, and there was a rush to grab what could be taken. Many highland elites looked to profit from the old southern regime's defeat.

Before Yemen's civil war ended, when foreign governments pressed for a ceasefire in early June, Salih dispatched Abd al-Aziz Abd al-Ghani on a diplomatic mission to Cairo, Egypt. During a meeting with Egyptian president Husni Mubarak, Abd al-Aziz pledged that Sanaa would protect

---

[33] In April 1994, the citizens of Taiz held the largest anti-war protests. Many residents were sympathetic with Aden, especially YSP supporters. Islahis generally stood with Sanaa, and Taiz merchants were just as eager as highland merchants to exploit new business opportunities in the south.

PHOTO 11. Port of Aden, al-Ma'ala neighborhood in distance on left

the interests of Adenis and all south Yemenis in a united, free, and democratic country.[34] President Salih was so desperate to fend off international pressure that he promised to observe the "document of pledge and accord." Much of this document signed in February 1994, particularly its emphasis on political decentralization, was strongly opposed by President Salih and other highland elites. But diplomats at the UN considered it the best means of reaching a post-war reconciliation. Two days after Yemen's civil war ended, the acting Yemeni prime minister, Muhammad al-Attar, sent a letter to UN Secretary General Boutros Boutros Ghali spelling out the Yemeni government's "continuation of the national dialogue ... and compliance with the provisions of pledge and accord as a basis for building the modern Yemeni state."[35]

During the following months, President Salih made a number of pledges about local government, including a promise to respect southern regional rights. When prime minister Abd al-Aziz submitted his new government program to parliament on October 31, 1994, he specifically called for local elections within the coming year.[36] The program required the government to define what revenues would be kept in the hands of locally elected

---

[34] Warburton, 1995; pp. 37–38.
[35] Quoted from a copy of Mohammed al-Attar's July 9, 1994 letter to Boutros Ghali, reprinted by the exiled Yemeni opposition group, MOWJ, based in London, England.
[36] Al-Bishari, 1996; p. v, Introduction.

authorities. This created some hope that President Salih would abide by his promises to the United Nations. Salih realized the best way to win support from south Yemenis, and the international community, was to speak as a champion of political decentralization. But during the following year his actions differed from his words. In 1995, he delayed taking the necessary steps to hold local elections, and demonstrated clear intent to continue running affairs through the central government in Sanaa.

President Salih and other northern highland elites were aware of the broad popular appeal of local government outside Sanaa. Yet after the war, Salih would create a more heavily centralized system of government. All government revenues and expenditures became tightly controlled in Sanaa. In 1996 local officials in Hadramaut and other southern provinces were required to send daily accounts of local revenues to the Yemeni central bank.[37] Like the Zaydi imams of earlier centuries, elites in Salih's government depended on resources from outlying regions to remain in power. They understood that devolving power would restrict their control in Sanaa. Thus it was not in their political and economic interests to decentralize power. After Yemen's 1994 civil war, President Salih's actual plan was to transform the southern provinces to fit the more conservative tribal and religious mold of north Yemen.

TALES OF DAHBASH

The first indication of what highland tribal rule would mean for the post-war south was large-scale looting in Aden during the last weeks of July 1994. Once Aden fell, tribesmen of Hashid and Bakil descended from the highland mountains to collect whatever booty they could find.[38] Looting is customary for Yemeni tribes whenever they engage in warfare. Hashid and Bakil once looted Sanaa and northern cities in the same way. After World War I, they raided wealthy regions of Tihama and Taiz, where they seized property from local residents. Due to the former British protectorate system in the south, Hashid and Bakil tribesmen in the imam's army were unable to reach Aden in the 1920s. As Imam Yahya's army pushed close to the southern boundary, the tribal soldiers boasted in a traditional *zamil*:[39]

---

[37] Interview with local finance officials in al-Mukalla, Hadramaut; January 1997.

[38] Fred Halliday, op. cit.; p. 133. According to Halliday, the looting lasted ten days.

[39] A *zamil* is a rhythmic poem that Yemeni tribesmen chant in unison to rally around a political agenda, typically against a rival tribe.

Ya Wadi al-Hawban Tanaffas. Li Jaishena wa al-Madafe'a. Maktub lina men Allah. Naqbadh Aden wa Abyan wa Yafi'.

Translation: "O Wadi al-Hawban (a valley near Taiz) stretch out before us. For our army and our artillery. It is written from God. That we will seize Aden, Abyan, and Yafi'."

For nearly a century, Hashid and Bakil had waited to loot Aden. When the opportunity came in July 1994, they packed as much booty as they could on trucks and cars, and returned into the mountains. Residents of Aden say the line of cars and trucks caused a traffic jam on the narrow causeway crossing Aden's shallow east harbor.[40]

In the years after 1994, highland elites exploited many southern resources, such as the oil fields in Hadramaut and the port in Aden. Some of President Salih's closest political associates, including members of his own family, were directly involved in spreading the kind of postwar anarchy witnessed in Aden. Salih's family asserted "northern" privileges at Hadramaut's main oil field in Wadi al-Masila. The field's production operator, Canadian Occidental, had established its Yemeni headquarters in Aden during the early 1990s to avoid the regular bribes demanded by government officials in Sanaa. But after the civil war, President Salih ordered the company to relocate to Sanaa.[41] One of the president's maternal uncles, Muhammad Ismail, developed a bad reputation as eastern military commander in Hadramaut. Operating around oil facilities, General Ismail forced out the local tribesmen who had previously been employed as Canoxy's security guards, and renegotiated the oil company's security services for himself.

Muhammad Ismail not only profited from taking personal control of Canoxy's security. He also gave the oil company a list of northerners to replace many of the local Hadramis on its staff.[42] This angered the local population, and decreased the oil company's security because Hadramis began sabotaging the company's facilities. During security sweeps in the area, Ismail often used the hostage-taking tactics of highland tribes, seizing the family members of wanted suspects until the suspects surrendered. In

---

[40] The independent newspaper publisher, Omar al-Jawi, witnessed the post-war looting in Aden: "There was total disorder where you saw people looting and destroying everything. I have never in my life seen anything like it. I must admit that I did not see any cases of rape but, apart from that, anything else you might think of was violated." Al-Jawi, 1997; p. 86.

[41] Interview with a top Canoxy official in Sanaa, February 23, 1997.

[42] Ibid. Canoxy officials reported that the company was satisfied with its southern staff, especially the "peaceful" young people it recruited from Wadi Hadramaut. The fact that Salih's regime required the company to use northern employees after the war created great tension between the company and surrounding Hadrami communities.

one case, a village elder died of heat exhaustion after Ismail's men locked him inside a shipping container.[43] This led to more resistance by local citizens. Despite the president's post-war rhetoric about "establishing law and order" in the south, and "building modern institutions" after two decades of Marxist rule, his regime fulfilled all of the worst stereotypes about "backward" (*mutakhallif*) highland tribal culture.

For more than two decades, the Marxist PDRY empowered state law, and virtually eliminated tribalism from southern society. Yet in 1994, President Salih's family and the family of Hashid's tribal leader, Shaykh Abdallah, made it state policy to revive tribal customs in southern provinces.[44] The unsettling influence of tribalism had long been apparent in and around Sanaa. One incident at the start of the civil war foreshadowed future problems in the south. It occurred in April 1994 after President Salih met with his closest political associates to discuss the growing political crisis. By this date, Ali Salem al-Bid had been absent from Sanaa for nine months, and the last YSP prime minister, Haidar al-Attas, had been politically inactive since earlier in the year. The acting prime minister was Hasan Makki, a northern GPC official from al-Hudayda in the west coastal region.

During a meeting with President Salih after the opening battle on April 27 in Amran, Prime Minister Makki cautioned about the need to deescalate conflict with the southern military, and seek a working relationship with the YSP as a partner in unity. Makki's position clearly ran against the president's plan for an aggressive military campaign against the south. Shortly after the meeting Makki was shot and nearly killed, while riding in the streets of the capital. The driver of his car and two bodyguards died in the attack.[45] The gunmen were arrested, and quickly identified as tribesmen close to the Bakil shaykh Naji Abd al-Aziz al-Shayif.

Shaykh al-Shayif is a close associate of President Salih. He readily admitted to ordering the attack because, in his view, Hasan Makki was too sympathetic with the YSP.[46] Once the civil war ended, there were never

---

[43] Interview with members of the political opposition in al-Mukalla; January 1997. The deceased, Ali Salameen al-Garzi, died of a heart attack. This was confirmed by top Canoxy officials in Sanaa; February 23, 1997.

[44] Shortly after the 1994 war ended, Shaykh Abdallah's elder son Sadeq and Hashid tribesmen camped at the main airport in Wadi Hadramaut, where they proceeded to loot merchandise from air shipments and demand bribes from arriving and departing passengers. Some of Sadeq's men eventually provoked a fatal shooting incident with staff of the local traffic department. Interviews with several prominent civic leaders in Saiyun, Hadramaut; January 1997.

[45] *Yemen Times* newspaper article, Volume IV, No. 18, May 1–7, 1994; p. 1.

[46] Shaykh al-Shayif reportedly wrote a letter to a major Arabic newspaper claiming responsibility for the attack.

criminal charges brought against Shaykh al-Shayif, despite his admission to ordering the assassination of the country's acting prime minister.[47] The only justice served for the attack on Makki's life, and the murder of three other men, was a crude form of tribal justice when Shaykh al-Shayif arranged a bull to be slaughtered outside Makki's home. This is the traditional tribal settlement to end a blood feud in Yemen. But Makki is a nontribal man who does not accept the custom for blood feuds.

The fact that the acting prime minister of Yemen could be shot on the order of a tribal shaykh, who then makes amends by "bull sacrifice," is the strongest indication of how tribalism defines Yemen's dominant highland culture. Within western scholarship there are sensitivities about referring to north Yemen's tribal customs as politically "backward." This is especially true of western anthropologists who reject the concept of "backward" cultures on foreign lands. British anthropologist Paul Dresch and others have shown that there are many honorable aspects to Yemen's tribal customs. But these positive aspects only exist within the tribal community, not when tribal customs are used as a means of asserting larger political agendas across regional lines in Yemen, especially in southern provinces where society had already accepted the rule of state law.

As a basis for national policy in the twenty-first century, the highland region's dominant tribal culture is properly defined as "backward" because it retards the development of state institutions and the rule of law. Hasan Makki's shooting at the beginning of Yemen's civil war symbolized this backward political culture. It also signified the imbalance of power between Yemen's different regional groups. On the one hand, there are individuals like Makki from outside the highland region who serve in the civilian government. Makki was instrumental in establishing the GPC in 1982. But his political influence was marginal compared to military and tribal officials from the highland region. Non-highland officials did not have support from the powerful tribal elements in the northern army and security forces. Thus they could not oppose the regime in Sanaa. They either towed the government line, or else risked their lives as Makki did in 1994. On the other hand, highland tribesmen from Bakil could openly oppose Salih's regime, as many YSP-allied Bakil shaykhs did prior to 1994, without coming under similar attack.

Nontribal elites in the highland region, especially members of a few prominent families in Sanaa city, have an uneasy working relationship with

---

[47] In October 1994, Shaykh al-Shayif was seen walking arm-in-arm with President Salih at the reopening of the Yemeni parliament. Al-Shayif's son held a seat in the 1994 parliament from Sanaa province.

highland tribes. They frequently complain about the tribes' unruly influence, and the country's lack of law and order. But at a deeper level, they recognize that their own interests are served as long as the hegemony of the larger highland group is preserved. For this reason, nontribal highland elites, like Qadi al-Arashe and al-Iryani family members, tended to support the status quo during times of political crisis. The same was true of the Bakil shaykhs who briefly allied with the YSP on the eve of civil war. Once war erupted, they did not fight alongside the YSP because they did not want to upset the status quo. This status quo ultimately served the interests of Hashid, Bakil, and the majority of people of influence inside the highland mountains.

For political elites outside the highland mountains, their relationship to Yemen's dominant tribal culture was different in the 1990s because they lacked tribal protection. People in southern provinces, including the eastern region of Hadramaut, received a rude introduction to highland tribal culture after 1994. This covered everything from municipal budgets to traffic regulations. The latter was a common source of complaint because the northern tribesmen who descended on Aden disobeyed every driving and parking standard, often leading to accidents. Postwar complaints involved deadly serious matters. In several instances, northern military and security forces used lethal force against the southern population. In 1995 and 1996, there were a number of shootings at labor protests and strikes in Aden.[48] One year after the war, two shooting incidents occurred at athletic competitions between northern and southern teams.[49]

During the mid-1990s, south Yemenis used a slang term to describe the backward, chaotic influence of President Salih's tribal regime. The term was taken from the name of a popular television comedy series during the early years of Yemeni unity. The series, called *Hakayaat Dahbash* or "The Tales of Dahbash," was named after the show's lead character. The storyline originated in the late 1980s among a group of talented actors from Taiz who first performed comedy skits on stage in some of north Yemen's main cities. After unification, a television broadcast of the skits

---

[48] During the Ramadan holiday of 1995, one worker was shot and killed at a protest of the Adeni tourism authority. Also in 1995, when the government announced its first price increases on basic subsidized food, police used non-lethal force in the north, but they responded with firearms in the south. Three people were shot and killed in Aden.

[49] During an April 1995 soccer match at al-Hubaishi field in Crater, Aden, four people were killed and a few dozen injured. *Al-Ayyam* newspaper (in Arabic), Aden, Yemen, May 26, 1996; p. 8. A similar incident occurred at a soccer match in al-Mukalla, Hadramaut in November 1996, leaving one person seriously injured by gunshot. *Al-Ayyam*, November 3 and 6, 1996; front page of both editions.

became extraordinarily popular in both northern and southern provinces.[50] Between 1991 and the political crisis in 1993, the streets of Yemeni cities and towns were often emptied during the half-hour evening broadcasts because families were at home watching on television.

The role of Dahbash was played by the talented actor, Adam Saif, who was born and raised in the old city of Taiz. He portrays Dahbash as a mischievous, yet still likable character who constantly conspires to take advantage of his friends, neighbors, and acquaintances. He is distrustful, lazy, and without the self-discipline necessary to earn an honest living for his family. A typical television episode has Dahbash carrying out some deception or trickery to steal from his hard-working friend, Naji. In the middle of the plot, there is always a slap-stick comedy scene. But in the end, Naji or some other victim seeks revenge against Dahbash, who then delivers one final lovable wisecrack.

The "Dahbash" television series took on political significance because the lead character was played with a thick, highland accent. This accent, particularly the way Adam Saif used the condescending tone (*lughat al-nakheet*) that is so unique to the highland people, added a vital comic element to the television series. At the time of the show's first broadcast, this comic element was well appreciated by all Yemenis. But the political connotations of Dahbash's accent were not appreciated by President Salih and other highland ruling elites after 1993, when domestic opponents began using the term "Dahbash" to refer to corrupt and coercive officials from the highland region. During Yemen's mounting political crisis in 1993, southern YSP officials used "Dahbash" in reference to their northern counterparts. This became such a sensitive subject that the ministry of culture ordered Adam Saif to change Dahbash's accent to one common in Taiz, and then the ministry canceled the show after the civil war.[51]

Despite the show's cancellation, the name of the lead character continued to be part of the country's vernacular, especially in the south where it took on a broader meaning. The term "Dahbash," or "Daha`bash" in the

---

[50] The television version of *Dahbash* was first broadcast in Sanaa during Ramadan 1990 as a nightly half-hour episode for two weeks. Then it was rebroadcast on Adeni television during Ramadan 1991. Interview in Taiz with Abd al-Karim Mehdi, the actor who played Dahbash's friend Naji; May 1997.

[51] Friends of the show's actors say that Adam Saif was actually interrogated by political security agents in Sanaa. They claim the show's creators never had any political motivations. The character of Dahbash was always played with a strong highland accent, even back in the late 1980s during its stage productions. This accent was used simply because it made the show more funny for the audience. Interview in Taiz; May 1997.

plural, was used symbolically to describe the general social and political effects of northern control in the south. In effect, Dahbash stood for the culture of northern highland tribal groups. The consequences of the spread of this culture in south Yemen could be seen in many fields of government, including the administration of justice. After the civil war, many northern judges appointed to serve in the south's court system were corrupt and unprofessional. In one case, a judge from Sanaa went on vacation, and left his eleven-year-old son in charge of the courtroom.[52]

In a 1996 interview, a top southern judicial official spoke of his efforts to correct the growing problem of corruption in southern courthouses. But he was afraid to press the issue too hard, or too fast, because he feared being labeled an "anti-union secessionist" by his northern colleagues at the ministry of justice.[53] After the civil war, this was the common experience of south Yemenis who had their political loyalties constantly questioned by northerners. Provincial officials across southern provinces complained about the northern financial system being excessively slow and corrupt.[54] While the central government was diligent about collecting local taxes and other government fees, and recording them on a daily basis in accounts of the Central Bank, it was common for southern administrators to wait more than eight months for their salaries. Older southern officials, including retirees who served in the former British colony, described changes to the financial administrative system as a tragedy.[55] They made no apologies about the excesses of one-party rule in the former PDRY. As technocrats they had no loyalties to the YSP. But they insisted the former south's financial administrative standards had enormous advantages over the northern system.

According to one top retired southern finance officer, a well-respected independent figure in Aden, "corruption is the norm at the ministry of finance in Sanaa because the north lacks the independent system of audit and control, which the former south's central treasury provided."[56] The problem of corruption in Sanaa was not a matter of a few exceptional cases that spoiled an otherwise beneficent government administration. It was

---

[52] Interview with members of the Hadramaut Charitable Society in Sanaa; July 12, 1996.

[53] Interview with a top southern judge at is home in Sanaa; June 1997. This judge said nearly all the judges cited for corruption came from the highland region.

[54] Several interviews with finance and planning officials in Aden, Abyan, Hadramaut and Lahij between August 1996 and January 1997. These southern officials claimed that each government minister in Sanaa had his own discretion to disburse funds, or if he preferred to use the money for other purposes.

[55] Several interviews in 1996–97 with top-ranking financial officials from the former south.

[56] Interview with a retired finance officer at his home in Aden; August 1996.

a systemic problem, deeply rooted in the traditional dominance of the northwestern highland group. Because the highlands are a resource-poor region, political elites have historically sought to control the more valuable resources of surrounding regions. This continued to be true in united Yemen. Indeed, President Salih's drive to centralize control over southern resources was one of the main reasons Yemen descended into civil war. After the war, President Salih was able to seize complete control of these resources.

Following national unification, political elites from the northwest highland region were not the only ones guilty of government corruption. There were certainly corrupt ministers from the western midlands and the west coast.[57] After 1994, there were also a few southern ministers who participated in corruption. But highland tribal elites were the predominant authorities, and it was primarily their political culture that created an atmosphere of government corruption.

President Salih's preference was to promote ministry officials from other regions who sought personal gain, instead of the public good, because he knew that he could rely on them to maintain the status quo, and not upset the prevailing system.[58] Publicity about corrupt ministers might provide justification for their later dismissal, if President Salih ever had a political reason to get rid of them. In other words, it gave Salih leverage over other officials because he could dismiss them at will. This was the time-tested practice of many Zaydi imams in the highland region, where appointments to state office were part of the government's distributive function. Throughout the history of Sanaa, the city's rulers operated a system of patronage by granting or withholding access to public offices, and the revenues generated by these offices, among various rivals for power.

RESOURCE MANAGEMENT IN THE POSTWAR SOUTH

Following the civil war in 1994, Yemen's economy was in critical shape. The Yemeni riyal lost great value in international currency markets. It had fallen from 14:1 U.S. dollar in 1990 to 70:1 just before the war. After the war, it continued tumbling downward until it hit a low of 165:1 U.S. dollar in mid-1995. As a result, the salaries of citizens, and their savings, drastically

---

[57] After the 1994 war, Salih's minister of finance and central bank governor, both from the western midland region, were accused of corruption. Salih applied a typical "Dahbash" solution to the problem. He reappointed the finance minister as the governor of the central bank, and vice versa.

[58] Interview with Dr. Muhammad al-Mutawakkel, Sanaa University professor of political science; July 10, 1996.

shrunk in value. Inflation was above 100 percent. Unemployment climbed, and government debt soared due to the costs of war. Investment and production in the oil sector remained strong in the 1990s. But the regime had trouble attracting foreign investors to participate in industrial development at a proposed free trade zone in Aden.[59] The civil war had devastated the plan to create an industrial-based economy with tens of thousands of new jobs. Between 1991 and 1993, investors among the wealthy exiled Hadrami community raced to join economic projects and purchase land in Aden and al-Mukalla. But during the postelection crisis, these investors fled the country, and remained wary of returning after 1994.

Due to the dire nature of Yemen's economic crisis, prime minister Abd al-Aziz Abd al-Ghani was forced into talks with IMF and World Bank officials in 1995 to negotiate an emergency package of loans. These loans were coupled with a structural adjustment plan to reduce state subsidies and privatize much of the public sector.[60] IMF involvement largely focused on Yemen's monetary policy to restore value to the national currency and bring down inflation. This was a success, but Yemen's wider reform program failed to translate into substantial economic benefits because it did not touch the deeper problem of administrative corruption and inefficiency. The structural adjustment plan inevitably had other poor ramifications. The leadership of the GPC used the terms of the plan to justify selling off large state enterprises in southern provinces, especially Aden, which were previously controlled by YSP officials.[61] This policy was exclusively applied to institutions in southern provinces, not the large state-run enterprises in Sanaa such as the Military Economic Corporation, which produced some consumer goods.

Unlike northern economic elites who held capital in the form of land and business enterprises, southern citizens did not have sources of wealth beyond their government salaries because the former PDRY restricted private ownership of land and enterprises. As a result, they did not have the capability to take advantage of the mass sell off of southern properties.

---

[59] In the late 1990s, there was growing concern that President Salih was disinterested in advancing economic development in Aden. The northern director of the Aden Free Zone office, Col. Dirham Numan, shocked World Bank officials in late December 1996 when he declared that "Yemen does not need a free trade zone in Aden." President Salih later began discussing the possibility of creating a separate free trade zone on the island of Soqotra in the Gulf of Aden. Such talk made the international business community even less confident in the Aden port project.

[60] Detalle, 1997; pp. 35–43.

[61] After the 1994 war, Aden's state shipping corporation was one of the first enterprises to be auctioned off. The immediate impact was the dismissal of hundreds of local union workers. The policy of privatization hit south Yemeni workers particularly hard.

Northern economic elites, primarily from the president's highland tribal
group, benefited most from the IMF-driven privatization policies. Some
businessmen from Taiz and the western midlands, such as the Hayil Said
Anam group, also benefited. However, they typically worked in partnership with influential highland agents, who always took a percentage of the
profits. Later in the 1990s, former southern exiles began participating in
state auctions under the same terms as investors from the midland
region.[62] Wealthy Hadrami families such as Bin Mahfouz, Bin Laden,
al-Amoudi, Ba Wazir, and al-Kathiri became associated with large deals
involving land and private enterprise in Aden. Yet these Hadrami investors
did not take the risk without partners among President Salih's inner circle,
or his coalition partners under Islah's leader, Hashid shaykh Abdallah bin
Hussayn al-Ahmar.

Following the 1994 war, the families of President Salih and Shaykh
Abdallah were the centers of power in Yemen's highland tribal group.
They increasingly operated like a "business mafia" across the country,
providing protection services to independent business clients.[63] The message
sent to citizens in Aden and the rest of the south was that their economic
resources would only be developed, if it served the interests of highland elites
in Sanaa. Questions about resource management, particularly the lack of
accountability at Hadramaut's large oil field in Wadi al-Masila, led to the
1995 resignation of oil minister Faisal Ben Shamlan. His status as an
independent southern technocrat was considered a barometer of how
President Salih would share power after the war. Following Ben Shamlan's
resignation, Salih made a minor shuffle in the cabinet, which lowered the
number of southern ministers even further.[64] This sent a worse signal about
politics and resource management in the new postwar environment.

The regime in Sanaa needed to rebuild a sense of common national
identity among the population. Instead it aggravated interregional

---

[62] In 1996, a leading Hadrami businessman bid for a contract to repair oil tankers in Aden
harbor. Before the end of the year, he was roughed up near a government office in Sanaa,
and told not to try to enter this business field because the president's family and Shaykh
Abdallah's family were already involved in the work. Interview with leading members of
the Hadrami business community in Sanaa; February 1997.

[63] The late newspaper publisher, Omar al-Jawi, who served as president of a joint north/
south journalists' union prior to unification, stated that postwar business practices were
unlike anything the country had seen in the past. He described them as "mafia business
practices." Interview in al-Mukalla, Hadramaut; January 1997.

[64] After this cabinet shuffle in 1995, there were twelve ministers from the northwestern
highland region, nine from western midland and coastal regions, and only seven from
the south.

relations, north-south and east-west, by increasing the sense of competition over scarce valuable resources. Intergroup resource competition is one of the main factors that hardens group identities in opposition to outsiders. The families of President Salih, Shaykh Abdallah, and other highland elites in the GPC and Islah parties, believed that their involvement in economic enterprises in the post-war south assisted national unity, by bringing north and south Yemenis together as one people. Yet in southern and eastern regions of the country, citizens perceived their land and resources being exploited by outsiders from the north who withheld potentially greater benefits from the local population.

The best example is the postwar regime's management of private property ownership in southern provinces. In 1990, the unity government planned to restore private ownership of all southern residential and business properties that were seized under the old socialist regime's nationalization policies in the late 1960s and early 1970s. Both leaderships of the YSP and GPC agreed to this plan. Before the political crisis leading to civil war in 1994, a government commission was set up in Aden to supervise the return of all properties to their previous owners. Property rights were a matter of precise record because city officials maintained the old registry books of the former British colony.[65] Following the war in 1994, northern officials began tampering with the process of restoring private property ownership through the southern offices of land registry and housing development.[66] These offices became prized appointments for northern officials eager to profit from bribes and other forms of corruption. In Aden, President Salih appointed a particularly disreputable man from his home district of Sanhan to direct the land registry.

The Sanhan official in charge of Aden's land registry in late 1994 and 1995 was so corrupt that his office quickly became known among Adenis as the "Office of Plunder and Theft." The local officials who possessed old land registry books became so concerned about the problem, they decided to make multiple photocopies of the British-era land and housing books. Then they hid the copies at different locations around Aden to prevent northern officials from corrupting or destroying the public record.[67] One

---

[65] Interview with officials in Aden's municipal administration; April 1997.

[66] Aden's main independent newspaper, *al-Ayyam*, ran several reports on this subject. "A Malicious Campaign to Plunder and Seize Aden's Real Estate" (in Arabic), October 2, 1996; p. 1 and 4; and October 6; 1996, p. 1. Similar problems existed in al-Mukalla and Hadramaut. "Soldiers Use Force to Receive Land Deeds in Saiyun," *al-Ayyam*, November 1, 1995; p. 1; and November 22, 1995; p. 1.

[67] Interview with officials in Aden's municipal administration; April 1997.

postwar incident reinforced their pre-cautions, when a group of highland tribesmen seized property along Aden's northern harbor. The tribesmen began developing it for commercial purposes under the name of an investment group called *Munqith*, backed primarily by supporters of the Islah party.[68] The members of Munqith claimed to have a three-hundred-year-old land deed that proved their rightful ownership of the property. They were taken to court, where it was revealed that the land in dispute was actually part of a harbor reclamation project in the mid-twentieth century. The British had created the land in the 1950s, when they expanded docking facilities of Aden port. Thus Munqith's investors had forged a three-hundred-year-old land deed for property that, in the seventeenth century, would have been offshore and several meters under water.

The Munqith case created enormous publicity in Aden because it symbolized the theft and plunder by north Yemenis. It also illustrated the effects of spreading *Dahbash* culture in the post-war south. Adeni residents complained that civil society was shrinking after the 1994 war, as citizens grew cynical and careless. Around the time of the Munqith court case, a city official in Aden complained that he overheard his children referring to Dahbash when they wanted to skip their homework: *Yallah, Dahbash lak!* ("Come on, do it the way Dahbash would do it!") For northern investors in Munqith, the final court ruling in Aden was not the end of the story. In Sanaa, they registered a complaint about lost investments, and lobbied parliamentary speaker Shaykh Abdallah for government compensation. Instead of advocating that the investors be sent to jail for fraud, Shaykh Abdallah arranged a reimbursement for Munqith's investors.

The precedent for property theft in Aden was set by President Salih and members of his own family. Salih seized nearly all of the Yemen Socialist Party's property, including its financial assets and headquarters building in Aden. The seizure of YSP properties went beyond party assets to include the private homes of former party officials who fled the fighting in Aden.[69] The home of former YSP leader Ali Salem al-Bid, on the southern tip of the Aden peninsula, was taken by Shaykh Abdallah's family. President Salih's director of security in Aden seized the home of a former elected governor. Disputes about private ownership of homes and apartments in Aden

---

[68] Interview with an Adeni judge and a civil servant in Aden; December 1996.

[69] The second official appointed to direct Aden's state land and real estate office in 1996, Yahya Duayd, was an in-law relative of President Salih. He made personal threats against the publisher of *al-Ayyam* because of its continuing coverage of land and housing theft in Aden; *al-Ayyam* newspaper (in Arabic), February 5, 1997; p.1.

multiplied in the last half of the 1990s. Most residents lived in government housing, mainly properties nationalized by the YSP in the late 1960s and early 1970s. Thus the plan to restore private ownership of residences in Aden was complicated and politically explosive.

The poor management of south Yemen's land and housing, Aden's port facilities, and Hadramaut's oil fields, offers the greatest examples of how northern highland elites used political power to serve their own economic interests. But north Yemenis gained access to hundreds of other economic opportunities in the south, including everything from agriculture to retail sales and taxi services. South Yemenis felt that their markets were being overrun by merchants and laborers from the north. The new class of highland tribal businessmen, the most successful of whom operated construction and engineering companies, easily obtained contracts from central ministry officials in Sanaa to implement development projects in southern provinces. Their competitors from other regions lacked the same political connections, and typically become tied up in endless bureaucratic red tape. Highland business elites not only used inside connections to win government contracts. They also could use these connections to avoid paying taxes and customs duties.

The data in Table 5.5 reveals that, before and after Yemen's 1994 civil war, the central government in Sanaa applied a far lower "per capita" tax rate in the highland region than in lowland and southern "super" regions. In terms of the "personal taxes" in the first column of Table 5.5, between 1991 and 1997, each individual in the highlands paid roughly a fifth of what each southerner paid in provinces of the old PDRY. Meanwhile, the personal tax rate of northerners in "lowland" regions, namely western midland and western coastal provinces, was only slightly higher than the rate in the highland region in 1991. But over the next six years, people in these "lowland" provinces paid twice as many "personal taxes" as people in the highland region. It is possible that the low "personal tax" rate of highland residents reflects lower incomes among highland residents. But the second and third columns of Table 5.5 show that highland residents also paid lower consumption taxes and government service fees.

The Yemeni government consistently applied a tax rate in the highland region which was roughly 20 percent of the rate applied in other regions of the country. This is the strongest indication that Yemen's political system served the highland group's interests. Just after unification in 1991, the average person in the southern provinces contributed fourteen times more revenues to the state's coffers than a person in the highland region. This

TABLE 5.5. *Per Capita Government Revenues in Three "Super" Regions, 1991–97 (Yemeni rivals)[a]*

	Personal Taxes	Consumer Taxes	Service Fees	Total Current Revenues Excluding Customs at Ports
1991				
Highlands	73.5	6.9	11.5	110.4
Lowlands	99.3	56.9	23.3	451.3
Southern	399.4	86.6	54.6	1,581.2
1993				
Highlands	106.2	29.2	14.8	173.1
Lowlands	188.3	140.2	35.1	770.2
Southern	501.8	107.8	78.2	1,091.5
1995				
Highlands	192.9	44.2	29.0	294.5
Lowlands	344.6	224.4	60.5	1,733.1
Southern	769.2	165.2	91.4	1,653.6
1997				
Highlands	218.0	272.5	50.2	759.0
Lowlands	529.8	1,003.9	79.1	3,144.0
Southern	1,312.0	771.9	178.3	3,250.0

[a] The data in Table 5.5 is taken directly from the Yemeni government's annual Final Accounts reports. Service fees, and personal and consumer taxes, typically make up the largest share of "total current revenues" in Yemen, excluding port customs. There are other smaller sources of "current revenues" not included in this table. Thus, the numbers in the first three columns do not add up to the total in the fourth column. "Lowlands" include provinces of western midlands and coastal regions. "Southern" includes all provinces of former PDRY.

ratio gradually fell to 6:1 in 1993 and roughly 4:1 in 1997. Nonetheless, the people of the southern provinces continued to bear more of the country's tax burden. After the 1994 war, each man, woman, and child in the northern "lowland" provinces of Taiz, Ibb, al-Bayda, and Al-Hudayda contributed approximately the same amount of "total current revenues" as the southern people. Thus it was specifically the people living in the highland region who avoided carrying a fair share of the tax burden.

Across the board, people of the highland provinces contributed less to the central government's revenue base. Yet they benefited most from government largesse in the form of payouts by the central government. Yemen's official "Final Accounts" do not portray an accurate picture of the government's regional spending patterns. But international consultants working at the ministries of planning and finance in Sanaa, who had access to more precise information about state expense accounts in the middle and late 1990s, estimated that as much as half of the government's total outlays went into the highland region's tribal networks.[70] Most of these expenses were paid out to the highland tribes through the regime's various military and security services.

[70] Personal conversation at the Ministry of Planning in Sanaa; November 1996. Yemen has one of the world's highest per capita rates of military and security spending. Its "Final Accounts" books from 1997 showed that 53 percent of total current expenses went to just four institutions – the presidency, ministries of defense and interior, and political security. It is possible that this percentage is even higher because more than U.S. $670 million were not accounted for in the "Final Accounts."

6

A Regime in Control?

In the spring of 1997, President Salih felt confident enough about his grip on power that he proceeded on schedule with Yemen's second parliamentary elections, exactly four years after the first elections. Unlike the weak showing of the president's party in 1993, the GPC swept the voting in a convincing victory on April 27, 1997. According to the official results, the president's party gained 62 percent of the parliamentary seats. But unofficially, the GPC controlled up to 70 percent. From the outset the GPC did not want an overwhelming majority of parliamentary seats like the older ruling parties of Egypt, Syria, and Iraq, which often received 90 percent or more in national parliamentary elections. In Yemen, the GPC needed to prove there was still a viable opposition, in order to justify its claim to democratic rule. It also did not want the burden of responsibility that would come with a 90 percent majority.

The 1997 election was hardly a real pluralist contest. Unlike the election in 1993, the GPC controlled all public funds, the government media (which provides the only source of radio and television broadcasts in a country where more than half of the population is illiterate), and most important, the country's Supreme Elections Committee (SEC). The GPC's control of the SEC meant there was no independent supervision of Yemen's second election. This created problems from the beginning of voter registration in the summer of 1996. The problems were so severe that in the fall of 1996 every opposition party, including Islah, united in calling for a boycott unless the SEC was reformed and voter registration corrected.[1] After the GPC made a

---

[1] The first meeting between Islah, the YSP, and other opposition parties occurred on August 10, 1996. *Al-Ayyam* newspaper covered later meetings in its August 21 and 25, 1996, issues, as well as its issues throughout October, November, and December 1996. In

few concessions to split the opposition, Islah and the small Nasserite and Ba'th parties agreed to participate in the election, while the YSP and a few smaller opposition parties continued to boycott.[2]

The YSP was no longer a serious contender for political office in Yemen, since President Salih seized nearly all of the party's assets. Operation of the party newspaper, *al-Thawri* ("The Revolutionary"), was practically the party is only function in the mid-1990s. The willingness of Islah to partic- ipate in the second election was never in much doubt because its leaders had too much at stake as partners in the post-war ruling coalition. In 1997, the highland leadership of Islah, particularly its president Shaykh Abdallah bin Husayn al-Ahmar and general secretary Muhammad al-Yadumi, never intended to disrupt the status quo. They dutifully served the new regime after the civil war. In the western midland provinces of Taiz and Ibb, relations were more bitter between the GPC and Islah. But the highland leaderships of the two parties were in general accord.[3]

In late March 1997, just one month before the polls opened, the leaders of the GPC and Islah reached a campaign coordination agreement. According to local reports, President Salih and Speaker of the Parliament Shaykh Abdallah decided to close 129 of the country's 301 electoral districts to interparty competition.[4] This allowed GPC candidates to run without facing Islah opposition in eighty-four districts, while Islah

November 1996, the independent Election Monitoring Committee directed by Abdul-Aziz al-Saqqaf, the late publisher of the weekly *Yemen Times*, announced that more than one hundred thousand registration complaints had been filed; and many of these complaints came from supporters of the GPC. *Yemen Times* newspaper, November 11, 1996; p. 1. According to Abdul-Aziz al-Saqqaf, 68 percent of the complaints had been reviewed, and 18,630 of these were "deemed as legitimate and credible."

[2] In January 1997, the Higher Coordinating Committee of the Opposition Parties published a small booklet, entitled "Guarantees for Free and Fair Elections," which reprinted the letters exchanged with Salih's regime. These letters confirmed the regime acknowledged irregu- larities had occurred in the registration process.

[3] The bitter relations between the GPC and Islah in the western midlands grew out of disputes over Islah's religious training institutes. Beginning in the late 1970s, Salih encouraged these religious institutes as a way to counter the influence of the region's leftist groups. However, once the south was defeated in 1994, and the YSP was stripped of its assets, Salih no longer needed support from midland Islamists. Shortly after the war he began challenging Islah's control over the institutes. In early December 1996, there was a deadly military confronta- tion over one such institute in Ibb province. *Al-Ayyam* (in Arabic), December 4, 1996, "Armed Clashes between GPC and Islah Groups in Ibb," No. 314; p. 1. This signaled the end of the regime's Islamic alliance in the western midlands. But the highland leaders of the two ruling parties continued to find common cause.

[4] "A Coordination Agreement Between the Ruling Coalition to Be Put into Force," *al-Ayyam*, (in Arabic), March 26, 1997; p. 1. In its next issue, *al-Ayyam* reported that the pact between Islah and the GPC extended into the southern provinces as well, covering four districts in Wadi Hadramaut; March 30, 1997; p. 1. Before the day of the vote, the GPC withdrew twenty-five

candidates could run without GPC opposition in forty-five districts. In the remaining 172 districts, they were free to compete. Inside the highland region, the GPC and Islah worked in close coordination, particularly in the tribal heartland of Sanaa and Hajja.[5] According to the governor of Hajja, Ali al-Ahmadi, who was the only southern governor still serving in the north, the difference between the highland supporters of GPC and Islah was superficial "because they all come from the same tribes."[6]

GPC officials were willing to negotiate a similar campaign agreement with the socialist party, allowing the YSP to run candidates without inter-party competition, but only if the YSP dropped its boycott. Prior to the election, Muhammad al-Tayyib, a top GPC official, stated that the GPC was prepared to offer the YSP thirty to forty seats in the next parliament.[7] Al-Tayyib acknowledged that the ruling party had greater facilities to compete in parliamentary elections than the opposition parties. The GPC controlled detailed voter registration lists not available to the opposition. According to al-Tayyib, the ruling party operated a computer program that allowed complex calculations of voter identifications and voting preferences. The opposition parties only received basic electoral informa-tion on paper printout sheets. As a result, the GPC could afford to give away seats in parliament from those districts where it knew voters would likely reject the ruling party. In this way, GPC officials arranged the electoral results in advance, while creating the appearance of an openly competitive political contest.

GPC officials sought a closer electoral victory than their 70 percent landslide because they knew a close victory would be more convincing. In the end, the electoral results demonstrated the dominance of the presi-dent's ruling party. The GPC won a higher number of seats in 1997 even

of its registered candidates, and Islah pulled forty-nine. Their coordination was most obvious in Hadramaut and Aden in the southern provinces, and Sanaa and Hajja in the north.

[5] There was strong competition between the candidates of the GPC and Islah in the capital city of Sanaa, and in some electoral districts of al-Mahwit and Dhamar provinces, which are two centers of Zaydism. But in the two largest provinces, Sanaa and Hajja, Islah's leader-ship virtually capitulated to the GPC.

[6] Interview with Governor al-Ahmadi in Hajja city; November 19, 1996. In his experience, highland representatives of Islah, such as Shaykh Abdallah and his sons, "only pretend to be in opposition to President Salih and the GPC." Many south Yemenis reached the same con-clusion. This was particularly true of Hadramis who voted for Islah candidates. In the words of a leading Islah supporter in Hadramaut "after the 1997 elections there is no Islah party because the President and the Shaykh are together." Interview with anonymous; May 1997.

[7] Interview; March 19, 1997. Al-Tayyib implied that the GPC was unconcerned about the YSP because the southern population is so small. He initially said "we were willing to give the YSP 30 to 40 seats in the next parliament." Then he quickly corrected himself: "well, of course we would not give them these seats, but we could assist them in winning this many seats."

TABLE 6.1. *Winning Candidates in Yemen's 1997 Parliamentary Elections*[a]

Region/Province	GPC	Islah	Other	Independent	Total
a) North					
Highlands:					
Sanaa City	15 (15)	1 (13)	0	2	18
Sanaa	23 (32)	5 (21)	1	7	36
Dhamar	14 (17)	1 (16)	1	5	21
Al-Mahwit	8 (8)	0 (6)	0	0	8
Hajja	17 (21)	5 (12)	1	0	23
Sa'da	6 (7)	0 (2)	0	3	9
West Coast:					
Al-Hudayda	25 (30)	2 (17)	0	7	34
West Midlands:					
Taiz	19 (29)	16 (32)	3	5	43
Al-Bayda	4 (5)	2 (8)	0	4	10
Ibb	28 (30)	2 (24)	0	8	38
Central Interior:					
Al-Jawf	0 (2)	2 (2)	0	0	2
Marib	1 (2)	2 (2)	0	0	3
SUB-TOTALS	160 (198)	38 (155)	6	41	245
b) South					
Southwest:					
Aden	6 (7)	2 (5)	0	3	11
Lahij	6 (8)	2 (8)	0	4	12
Mid-southern:					
Abyan	6 (7)	1 (4)	1	0	8
Shabwa	2 (2)	1 (4)	0	3	6
Eastern:					
Hadramaut	6 (10)	8 (11)	0	3	17
Al-Mahra	1 (1)	0 (2)	0	1	2
SUB-TOTALS	27 (35)	14 (34)	1	14	56
TOTALS	187 (233)	52 (189)	7	55	301

[a] This table shows the number of winning candidates in each province. The original number of candidates sponsored by the GPC and Islah parties (before they negotiated their campaign coordination agreement) appears in parentheses. The "other" category represents the Nasserite, Ba'th, and smaller third parties which eventually joined the election campaign. The numbers in this table are based on the official election results published in the independent *al-Ayyam* newspaper on May 18, 1997; pp. 4–6, and May 21, 1997; pp. 4–5.

though it sponsored a fewer number of candidates (Table 6.1). It only had 233 candidates in 1997, as opposed to 275 candidates in 1993. The winning percentage of GPC candidates nearly doubled from 44 percent in 1993 to a remarkable 80 percent in 1997. The party's control over the electoral process was so complete that, as the votes were tabulated, party officials feared they made a mistake by winning too many seats.[8] If this happened, they would then be expected to deliver on their campaign promises to improve social and economic conditions.

Between 1990 and 1997, the GPC learned that it was convenient to have coalition partners to blame for the failure of Yemen's economy. A few days after the votes were counted, GPC officials hung a banner across one of the main streets in the capital: "Building a modern state is not the responsibility of one individual or one party, but the responsibility of us all." The street over which this banner hung is associated with the Hayil Said Anam corporation from Taiz. The Hayil Said family has a large home on the street, close to the city's main thoroughfare, al-Zubayri Street. Local residents refer to the street by the Hail Said name. The meaning of the banner's text was directed at elders of the family who had shifted their support away from the GPC to Islah. The message was clear. Despite the GPC winning the vast majority of seats in the next parliament, President Salih was already dodging responsibility for the country's poor economic and social conditions.

When President Salih came to power in 1978 backed by Taiz's merchant class, Hayil Said Street was the heart of the capital's main shopping district. After years of government neglect, it had literally become a disaster zone. Massive sections of the asphalt pavement were washed away, leaving gaping pot holes filled with sewage. Some potholes were large enough to swallow entire vehicles. Cars and buses lumbered along at a snail's pace, weaving around the largest potholes, as if the street were an obstacle course. After the GPC won a landslide victory at the polls, the public expected the president to use the GPC to champion the nation's interests. This was time for strong leadership of a party that Salih founded in 1982. Yet when the president looked for a new prime minister to head the government, he chose an independent southerner, Dr. Fareg Ben Ghanem, from outside the ruling party. Moreover, when the new parliament met for the first time on May 18, 1997, President Salih instructed his party members to vote for Islah's leader Shaykh Abdallah to remain as speaker of the parliament.

---

[8] At a post-election reception in the house of GPC secretary general Abd al-Karim al-Iryani the mood was not one of celebration, but caution and understatement. Conversations at Dr. al-Iryani's house in Sanaa; April 28, 1997.

TABLE 6.2. *The Republic of Yemen's Postelection Cabinet, 1997*

Name	Post	Party	Regional Origin
1 Fareg Ben Ghanem	Prime Minister	Independent	East/ Hadramaut*
2 Abd al-Karim al-Iryani	Deputy Prime Minister/ Foreign Affairs	GPC	Highland/Ibb
3 Ahmad Ali al-Bishari	Minister of State/ Cabinet Affairs	GPC	Highland/Ibb
4 Husayn Arab	Interior	GPC	Mid-south/ Abyan*
5 Muhammad Daif-Allah	Defense	GPC	West Midlands/ Al-Bayda
6 Alawi al-Salami	Finance	GPC	West Midlands/ Al-Bayda
7 Muhammad al-Wajeeh	Oil and Resources	GPC	Highland/ Dhamar
8 Abd al-Qadr Ba Jamal	Planning	GPC	East/ Hadramaut*
9 Abd al-Rahman Muhammad Ali	Supply and Trade	GPC	West Midlands/ Taiz
10 Abdallah Ghanem	Legal Affairs	GPC	Aden/West Midlands*
11 Mohammed al-Junaid	Civil Service	GPC	West coast/ al-Hudayda
12 Abd al-Rahman al-Akwaa	Information	GPC	Highland/Sanaa
13 Abdallah al-Dafei	Housing	GPC	Highland/Sanaa
14 Ahmad Muhammad Soufan	Industry	GPC	Highland/Sanaa
15 Abd al-Malek al-Siyyani	Transportation	GPC	Highland/Sanaa
16 Ahmad Muhammad al-Ansi	Communication	GPC	Highland/ Dhamar
17 Ahmad Salem al-Jabali	Agriculture	GPC	West coast/ al-Hudayda
18 Abd al-Malek Mansour	Culture	GPC	Highland/Sanaa
19 Muhammad al-Butani	Social Security	GPC	Mid-south/ Abyan*
20 Muhammad al-Tayyib	Labor	GPC	Highland Sanaa
21 Ismail al-Wazir	Justice	GPC	Highland/Sanaa
22 Yahya Muhammad al-Shoaibi	Education	GPC	Southwest/ Lahij*

TABLE 6.2. (*cont.*)

Name	Post	Party	Regional Origin
23 Abdallah Abd al-Wali Nasher	Health	Independent	Aden*
24 Sadeq Amin Abu Ras	Local Administration	GPC	Highland/Ibb
25 Ahmad Musaid Husayn	Fisheries	GPC	Mid-South/ Shabwa*
26 Ali Hameed Sharaf	Water and Electricity	GPC	Highland/Hajja
27 Abdallah Salih Sabaa	Emigrant Affairs	Independent	Mid-South/ Shabwa*
28 Ahmad Muhammad al-Shami	Islamic Affairs	al-Haqq	Highland/Ibb
29 Abd al-Wahab Raweh	Youth and Sports	GPC	West Midlands/ Taiz

* Southern ministers.

At the beginning of unity in 1990, Ben Ghanem served as minister of planning. He was a well-respected technocrat from Hadramaut not closely associated with the YSP. But if Salih wanted a southerner to serve as prime minister, then he could have chosen any one of a dozen members of his own party. The same was true of choosing the next parliamentary speaker. Islah barely held 17 percent of the new parliament's seats. Yet the pre-election pact between the GPC and Islah apparently stipulated that Shaykh Abdallah would retain the speaker's chair. After the GPC's landslide victory, it was strange for two individuals outside the party to take charge of key government institutions. For his part, President Salih was content to have an opposition leader in charge of parliament, so he could blame someone else for delaying reform legislation. He had other reasons for wanting Dr. Ben Ghanem as prime minister.

Dr. Ben Ghanem's appointment served at least two purposes for President Salih's regime. First, it put a clean face on his administration, creating the appearance that he was serious about reforming government and putting an end to corruption. Second, it made a strong impression that the divisions of the civil war were a thing of the past. By bringing in a prominent southerner from the original unity cabinet to replace Abd al-Aziz Abd al-Ghani, it appeared Salih wanted to recapture the country's early unionist spirit by sharing power with south Yemenis at the highest levels of government. The leader of the Ali Nasir group, Abd al-Rabo Mansour Hadi, remained vice president. Now with Ben Ghanem as prime minister, the government's power-sharing formula appeared to shift back to what existed in 1990, when southerners held the same two posts.[9]

The appearance of strong southern representation in government was short-lived because Prime Minister Ben Ghanem resigned after less than a year in office. Ben Ghanem resigned for several reasons, all relating to the fact that he had no real authority to design and implement government policy. During his short term in office, Ben Ghanem announced bold plans to increase financial transparency and reduce corruption.[10] More important, he wanted to decentralize power to locally elected provincial councils. He proposed an experimental program of local government in four or five provinces, including his home province of Hadramaut. In the PDRY, the socialist government often tested new government policies in the eastern region, where Hadramis proved capable of innovating procedures to help implement new policies. When Prime Minister Ben Ghanem resigned, it was mainly because of the lack of support he found for government decentralization. According to Ben Ghanem's assistants, the plan was opposed by President Salih and Shaykh Abdallah.[11] GPC officials preferred to blame the head shaykh of Hashid alone.

LOCAL RULE AND THE 1996 AL-MUKALLA CRISIS

One year before Dr. Fareg Ben Ghanem became prime minister, he and other southern leaders became aware that President Salih did not intend to give real local power to southern regions. This became clear around a 1996 criminal court case in al-Mukalla, Hadramaut, which led to the first mass protests since the civil war. In late March 1996, two women, one married and one single, were arrested by a northern policeman in al-Mukalla. The women claimed to have been taken to the local bureau of criminal investigations, where both say they were assaulted, and the younger single

---

[9] In the new cabinet (Table 6.2), there were fourteen ministers from the Zaydi highlands, six from northern Shafi'i regions of the west coast and western midlands, and nine from the former south. Thus, southerners held 32 percent of cabinet seats, a slight increase from their percentage following Faisal Ben Shamlan's resignation as oil minister in 1995.

[10] At the beginning of 1998, the World Bank confronted the Yemeni government with a list of 143 top officials accused of major corruption. *Bareed al-Junub* an opposition newspaper published in London, England ran an article about this story in its January 26, 1998 edition; Vol. 3, No. 144; pp. 1 and 5. Prime Minister Ben Ghanem tried to remove a number of people on the list, but he was obstructed from doing so.

[11] Interview with active and retired southern ministry officials close to Dr. Fareg Ben Ghanem; October 1998.

woman was raped, before being released later in the day.[12] The next day, the two women returned to a local police station with the married woman's husband to file charges of rape and assault. But all three were thrown in jail.

Al-Mukalla's rape case quickly gained public attention in the independent and opposition media. In mid-April, opposition members of parliament from northern and southern provinces went to al-Mukalla to investigate the case. They confirmed the rape story, and called for the women, and the one woman's husband, to be released immediately from jail. The three individuals sat in jail for nearly two months until a local judge ruled that they should be set free. The director of the criminal prosecutor's office in al-Mukalla was a northern highland official from Sanaa, named Abd al-Aziz al-Dawraani. Al-Dawraani initially refused to accept the judge's ruling, but the two women and one man were finally released on May 21, 1996. Al-Dawraani and the Attorney General's office in Sanaa handled the case very poorly.[13] They postponed bringing charges against the northern police officer, and began making accusations that the women's story was part of an elaborate conspiracy against the northern police to create another secession crisis.

When the trial was held in al-Mukalla in early June, it drew large crowds. Al-Dawraani senselessly provoked a disturbance at one hearing on June 6, 1996, when he walked from the courtroom saying "the women of Hadramaut have no morals and are prostitutes."[14] The crowd in attendance, many of them Hadrami women, stormed out of the court house in pursuit of al-Dawraani. Outside the building al-Dawraani ordered his security guards to open fire. Seven people were injured, and al-Dawraani ordered the arrest of more than fifty people among the protesters. Four days later a larger crowd of thousands gathered outside the governor's office, demanding that al-Dawraani be put on trial. These demonstrators

---

[12] *Yemen Times*, April 15, 1996, and May 6, 1996; p. 1 in both editions. Yemen's local Arabic papers covered this story in greater detail throughout April and May 1996.

[13] From the beginning al-Dawraani maintained that the two women ran a house of prostitution outside Shihr approximately fifty miles east of al-Mukalla. The women said they had come to al-Mukalla for a doctor's appointment; and they had a receipt from their doctor as proof. Defenders of the two women accused the police officers of lying about the women being prostitutes, a lie which even if true did not excuse the way the women were arrested, and later assaulted in police custody. Interview with a group of local administrators in al-Mukalla, January 1997.

[14] "Interior Minister Forms a Committee of Inquiry into the Charges of Slander against (Hadramaut's) Women," *al-Ayyam* (in Arabic), June 9, 1996, No. 263; p. 1. The veracity of this reporting was confirmed in interviews with local administrative officials in al-Mukalla.

were again fired upon by northern security forces who stood on top of the nearby central bank branch. Seven more people were injured, two of whom were in critical condition, and had to be evacuated outside the country for treatment. As the protesters scattered, northern security troops chased them into crowded residential areas of the city. Young and old citizens erected street barricades to slow the police pursuit. In the end, more than 140 people were arrested.[15]

These were the worst disturbances in the south since the 1994 war. They signified a widespread feeling of anger and frustration throughout the southern provinces.[16] Immediately after the second shooting incident, President Salih sent the southern interior minister Husayn Arab, along with the attorney general and a deputy director of political security (both from the highland region), to investigate the violence in al-Mukalla. When this government delegation from Sanaa met with the province's executive board, a few native Hadrami board members were brave enough to

PHOTO 12. Al-Mukalla, coastal capital of Hadramaut

---

[15] *Al-Ayyam* newspaper (in Arabic), June 12, 1996, No. 264; pp. 1 and 4.
[16] Civic leaders in al-Mukalla say that the people demonstrated in such large numbers not because of the original rape case, but because of their general frustration with northern domination. This domination had gravely affected the rights of women in south Yemen. Thus the accusations of rape had a broader political significance. Prior to unification southern women held greater social and political status than women in the north. Many served as judges, accountants, and other public officials.

register a formal letter of complaint against the government in Sanaa.[17] This letter claimed that the disturbances resulted from popular frustration at the continued northern military presence, and the generally lawless conditions in the province. Over the next few weeks, President Salih tried to ease the crisis by meeting with these and other prominent Hadramis in Sanaa.[18] After holding several meetings, Salih decided the best solution was to create special local councils in Hadramaut on a short-term basis.

Just as he had done after the 1994 war, President Salih used the subject of local government to serve his own political purposes. But in this case, his offer was rejected as insufficient. Shortly after Yemen's civil war in 1994, a group of civic and business leaders in al-Mukalla had proposed that President Salih establish an independent local government in Hadramaut. At the time, they were told this would not be possible because people in other provinces would want the same thing.[19] What was instructive about Salih's motives, after the shootings in al-Mukalla in June 1996, is that he did not invite the same civic and business leaders to join consultations in Sanaa. Salih first extended an invitation to the leading members of his GPC party in Hadramaut, including Hasan Salih Ba Awm, who directed Hadramaut's education office and was one of the board members who registered the original letter of complaint.

During consultations with the president in Sanaa, Hasan Salih Ba Awm spoke directly about the need to remove northern military and security forces, in order to establish a normal sense of law and order in the province.[20] But Salih was not satisfied with this advice. Shortly afterward, Ba Awm resigned his post in the GPC. Later the president brought a second delegation of "traditional" Hadrami leaders to Sanaa, including many of the province's top tribal shaykhs.[21] It was during the president's meeting with

---

[17] Interview with members of a charitable society and the chamber of commerce in al-Mukalla; January 1997.

[18] After the second shootings on June 10, Salih removed al-Dawraani and promised to investigate his actions. *Al-Ayyam* (in Arabic), June 16, 1996; p. 1. But no legal action was ever taken against al-Dawraani or the officer accused of rape.

[19] Interview with members of a charitable society and the chamber of commerce in al-Mukalla; January 1997.

[20] Interview with Hasan Ba Awm in al-Mukalla; January 26, 1997.

[21] Interview with deputy governor Muhsin Ben Shamlan in al-Mukalla; January 9, 1997. Ben Shamlan said that General Muhammad Ismail provided two military aircraft to fly more than eighty people to Sanaa. The deputy governor also said most of the province's tribal shaykhs were eager to have "the opportunity to show they could play a role in government." President Salih understood that these shaykhs from interior areas of the province, far from al-Mukalla, did not share the same sense of outrage about the rape case. President Salih was counting on their traditional customs and mores to alleviate his political problems.

these Hadrami shaykhs that he offered to create special local councils in the province. This was significant because it revealed President Salih's preference for dealing with the tribes, which he hoped to manipulate through the same divide and rule tactics he used in the north. During the second meeting in Sanaa on June 19, 1996, the president proposed nominating individuals from Hadramaut's "traditional" leadership to serve on a local council, which would then advise the northern governor, Salih al-Khawlani, and his staff. Some members of the tribal delegation supported the president's offer, but a majority eventually turned against the idea.[22]

The Hadrami community of Yemen is fairly cohesive, so it was not possible for President Salih to negotiate with "traditional" leaders without also involving other prominent Hadramis. Some members of the tribal delegation invited leading Hadrami businessmen, lawyers, and doctors in Sanaa to join the meeting with the president. The following weeks became an occasion for Hadramis to debate the president's proposal at the headquarters of the Hadrami Charitable Society. By rejecting the president's offer, members of the Hadrami society sent a clear message that the people of Hadramaut wanted genuine local government by law, as stipulated in the post-war constitution, and not by presidential whim.[23] They also wanted local government through popular elections, not presidential appointments. The president and his associates were caught by surprise at this rejection, and had to withdraw their offer.

The fact that President Salih responded to the crisis in al-Mukalla by attempting to establish weak, temporary local councils, with the help of newly recruited tribal allies, revealed much about his approach to decentralization. Salih and other elites in Sanaa, especially the "modernists" in the GPC, talked about the country's tribal structure as a major obstacle to decentralizing power. Some GPC "modernists" even proposed basic candidacy standards to exclude most tribal shaykhs.[24] Yet when the crisis in al-Mukalla erupted, Salih turned to the tribal shaykhs of Hadramaut as the foundation for a new local government system. This was clear evidence

---

[22] The choice to reject the president's offer was reached at a public meeting of the Hadrami Charitable Society in Sanaa on June 21, 1996.

[23] Interviews with a number of the prominent Hadramis who met with President Salih, or attended the discussions at the Hadrami Charitable Society in late June and July 1996. These interviewees included Hasan Ba Awm, Mahfouth Shamakh (the president of the HCS), Faisal al-Attas (a member of parliament), Shaykh Abdallah Salih al-Kathiri, Dr. Mohammed Ali al-Saqqaf (a prominent international lawyer in Sanaa), and others.

[24] Interview with GPC officials Abu Bakr al-Qirby and Muhammad al-Tayyib; March 19, 1997. They discussed the possibility of requiring candidates to have a university degree.

that Salih did not intend to create effective local government in Yemen. If he did, then he would have consulted the civic and business leaders of Hadramaut who were capable of creating such a system in al-Mukalla and other Hadrami cities.

THE PRESIDENT'S POSTWAR TRIBAL POLICY

Following the crisis in al-Mukalla, President Salih took some steps to ease the northern military occupation of Hadramaut and other areas in the south. He promised to require the main army commander in the eastern region, Muhammad Ismail, to pull his troops back from roadways leading into the Hadrami capital. He also agreed to allow one thousand Hadramis to serve in the local police force, and begin carrying personal weapons.[25] When these policies were not immediately implemented, there was a second round of larger and more violent protests in al-Mukalla at the end of September 1996.[26] The next month local policemen in Hadramaut, Aden, and other southern provinces were issued handguns for the first time since the 1994 war. All heavier firearms remained in the possession of northern military and security forces.[27] The minister of interior, Husayn Arab, was one of the leaders of the Ali Nasir group in Sanaa, so the partisans of Ali Nasir began to assume more police commands in the south, including Wadi Hadramaut.

President Salih's reliance on Ali Nasir partisans and tribal shaykhs was part of a dual strategy in the former south. As mentioned in the previous chapter, Salih recruited members of the Ali Nasir group, who opposed the YSP, to play roles as early as 1994. Likewise, he recruited members of the traditional southern ruling class, including the leading tribal shaykhs and family members of the former sultans, to do the same. But in some cases, Salih played one southern group against another. Many traditional southern leaders were as hostile toward the Ali Nasir group, as they had been to Ali Salem al-Bid and the YSP, because members of the Ali Nasir group had earlier participated in the same radical policies during the late 1960s and 1970s. Lingering resentment of these policies was something that President Salih was quick to exploit after 1994. For instance, the postwar minister of transportation, Ahmad Musaid Husayn, was one of the leaders of the Ali

---

[25] Interview with Hadramaut's deputy governor Muhsin Ben Shamlan, one of President Salih's most sympathetic supporters in the province; January 9, 1997.

[26] *Al-Ayyam* (in Arabic), September 29, 1996; p. 1. The protests were triggered by problems with utility services.

[27] Interview with a district manager in Aden; October 1998.

Nasir group from Shabwa province. His family became targeted in ways that resembled pre-1994 violence against YSP officials.

During the national independence movement in the late 1960s, Ahmad Musaid Husayn directed the old National Front's assault against the Aulaqi sultans in the "al-Sa'idi events." Following the 1994 civil war, President Salih appointed the son of one of these former Aulaqi sultans to be the local director of Husayn's home district, Nisab. In September 1996, there were fierce conflicts in Nisab between members of Husayn's family and supporters of the former sultan's son.[28] Before the end of the year, one of Husayn's sons was shot and killed. The circumstances of his murder were reminiscent of the attacks against the family members of Ali Salem al-Bid. In both cases, the shootings could be blamed on the settling of old political scores in the south due to conflicts in the 1960s. But the regime in Sanaa was well known for stoking local tribal disputes in order to weaken political rivals.[29]

After taking office in 1978, President Salih generally observed tribal customs in the north; and after 1994, he clearly preferred dealing with the tribal half of his southern alliance, since it provided an effective counterweight to Ali Nasir's partisans. The president's preference for tribal allies was on full display in November 1996, when he invited Ali Nasir Muhammad to return from exile, and join the anniversary celebration of southern independence from British rule. At a ceremony broadcast live on national television, Salih bestowed honorary medals on members of south Yemen's traditional ruling class, while cameras showed Ali Nasir sitting alone near the edge of the viewing stand. The former southern president appeared to be intentionally marginalized by those who organized the event. This was hardly the reception he expected during his first return to Aden in more than a decade.[30]

While President Salih sought closer ties to the south's prerevolutionary leaders, he did not align himself with the most prominent southern ruling families. The former al-Qu'ayti sultan of Hadramaut, Fadhl ben Ghanem, who once ruled the Hadrami coastal city of al-Mukalla, as well as the

---

[28] "Army and Security Forces Halt an Armed Clash in Shabwa," *al-Ayyam* (in Arabic), September 22, 1996; p. 1.

[29] Ahmad Musaid Husayn was also allegedly involved in a business dispute at Aden port involving individuals within the president's ruling circle. Interview with officials at the Aden Port Authority; December 1996.

[30] One month after his arrival, Ali Nasir left Yemen with no definite plans to return. Interview with a member of the Sanaa branch of Ali Nasir's Arab Center for Strategic Studies in Sanaa; March 1997.

inland Wadi cities of Shibbam and al-Qatn, made a return trip to the country in September 1996. Sultan al-Qu'ayti made a brief tour of Hadramaut, where he received a warm welcome from local citizens. But in Sanaa, President Salih was noticeably less receptive, making it clear the government would not welcome the return of any major sultans who sought to reclaim large land holdings like the territories of the former al-Qu'ayti sultanate.[31] Salih was willing to work with minor tribal shaykhs, and the regime returned small land holdings to families who lost property during the old regime's land appropriations. Some minor shaykhs were appointed to direct the new offices of "tribal affairs" in eastern and mid-southern regions. Local residents referred disparagingly to them as "the 1994 shaykhs" with foundations "built on sand rather than stone."[32] President Salih even appointed someone to direct "tribal affairs" in Aden, an appointment which city officials considered a bad joke.

President Salih's interest in building political alliances with regional elites was guided by a single principle: to ensure that he could keep potential rivals off balance. If an individual leader carried too much power or influence, such as former sultan Fadhl ben Ghanem, then Salih refused to develop any ties at all. He may have established alliances with lesser leaders who presented some degree of local opposition, but only if he could keep them off balance by undercutting their bases of power. For Salih, the tactic of divide and rule was critical, so he kept multiple alliances in every region around the country. If a political rival became too strong, then Salih would exploit factions in the individual's area, and create enough trouble to undermine the individual's base. This was especially true of Salih's approach to alliances with traditional southern ruling families in the area of Ali Nasir's hometown in northeastern Abyan province.[33]

After the end of the 1994 war, the regime in Sanaa encouraged multiple traditional figures in neighboring areas of Abyan and Shabwa provinces to

[31] Interview with Renaud Detalle, a French political researcher who accompanied the Qu'ayti sultan during much of his visit in Yemen; November 27, 1996. According to Detalle, the Qu'ayti sultan "very aggressively" put demands on President Salih to return his personal property in Hadramaut. However, the sultan left the country frustrated and feeling that he would never return to live in Yemen.

[32] Interview with a group of tribal leaders outside al-Mukalla, Hadramaut; January 1997. They derided the "1994 shaykhs," as lesser tribesmen.

[33] Perhaps the most prominent was a relative of Muhammad Ahmad al-Khader al-Seari, a well-respected, British-trained major in the former South Arabian Federation. The family of al-Seari is from the subdistrict of al-Maysari, whereas Ali Nasir is from al-Hasani sub-district.

play local leadership roles. This was a check on the power of Ali Nasir partisans. Individuals with anti-communist and Islamist credentials were favored over anyone with ties to the former YSP. Among these postwar alliances, the best known was between members of President Salih's inner circle and the son of the former al-Fadli sultan, Tareq ibn Nasir al-Fadli, who fought as a *mujahideen* in Afghanistan with Osama Bin Laden. Tareq al-Fadli was promoted after the 1994 war as a commander of security forces east of Aden. He was also supplied with arms and expensive vehicles registered with security clearances, even though he had been arrested in 1993 on charges of involvement in the bombing of two tourist hotels in Aden.[34] In Sanaa, Shaykh al-Fadli became a privileged member of the GPC permanent committee. His primary contact was General Ali Muhsin al-Ahmar, who married al-Fadli's sister.

Tribalism represents a powerful source of political-cultural hegemony for northern highland elites who, like President Salih and Shaykh Abdallah bin Husayn al-Ahmar, come from tribal backgrounds. They claim to be the main representatives of Yemen's tribes, the "sons of Qahtan," descendants of the original people in south Arabia. In the wake of Yemen's 1994 civil war, President Salih tried to extend this political-cultural hegemony through his tribal policy in the south. The advantage to the government in Sanaa was obvious because the revival of southern tribalism created new social divisions that could be exploited in the interest of the central governing authority. This became increasingly clear to the tribes of southern provinces, where many tribal shaykhs began organizing tribal solidarity conferences to prevent the regime in Sanaa from playing games of divide and rule.[35] Beginning in the fall of 1996, there was a series of tribal solidarity conferences in Hadramaut and other areas of the south. One of the first conferences occurred between the tribes of Nawah and Saiban, directly north and northwest of al-Mukalla.[36]

---

[34] Clark, 2010; pp. 158–165.

[35] In the 1990s, the regime in Sanaa described its tribal policy in the south as part of the country's liberalization, restoring the rights of tribal shaykhs who were oppressed under YSP rule. While many southern shaykhs were happy to see the YSP out of power, this did not necessarily translate into support for Salih's regime.

[36] The Nawah-Saiban conference was led by Shaykh Said Ba Husayn al-Sawmahi. Interview with officials of the League of the Sons of Yemen party in al-Mukalla; January 1997. At the conference, there were calls to remove northern military forces from the province. A news report was carried in the Saudi magazine, *al-Watan al-Arabi*, No. 1037, November 8, 1996; p. 24. Later tribal conferences were called for similar reasons in the central interior regions of Hadramaut, and Shabwa, as well as areas east of al-Mukalla. Tribes in these regions increasingly spoke about the need to "counter the president and his highland tribes."

After 1994, President Salih's regime had ample opportunities to foment tribal divisions and instigate local conflicts in Hadramaut and other southern provinces, as a result of its interference in land and housing affairs. While this created a modicum of control in Sanaa, it was not the most productive way to govern a newly unified nation like Yemen. Instead of uniting different communities under one flag, it tended to divide these communities. It was also wasteful of economic resources. President Salih spent enormous amounts of money catering to his tribal allies in the country's military and security forces, as well as highland tribal rivals who have their own powerful, well-equipped paramilitaries. In 1998, a member of the Yemeni parliament's financial and economic affairs committee claimed that many highland tribesmen receive military and security salaries without serving in any particular unit.[37] According to this member of parliament, there were roughly one hundred times more people in the northwest highlands who received some kind of military or security salary than actually served in Yemen's armed forces. After 1994, President Salih offered many southern tribal shaykhs the same opportunity to receive funds from the public treasury.

As a result of the regime's tribal strategy, it did not devote adequate funds to develop public services around the country. This is the primary problem with the hegemony of Yemen's highland tribal group. It does not foster beneficial public administration at local and regional levels. In the 1990s, officials in charge of municipal services around the country were required to send all revenues raised from local construction and building permits to Sanaa. Yet they received limited allocations from the central government to carry out projects. As a result, the directors of city services were forced to use irregular means to collect funds for basic municipal services.[38] Al-Mukalla was the first to innovate "municipal improvement" fees to raise funds for street cleaning and trash removal services.[39] Soon other provincial capitals began employing similar policies. All of these fees were collected from local business owners by technically illegal means

[37] Interview in Sanaa with a member of parliament who preferred to remain anonymous; March 1997. He said the fraud is committed when tribal shaykhs list "ghost" soldiers, or list the name of the same tribesman multiple times. While a single tribesman may get paid a soldier's salary, the shaykh keeps ten times the same amount.

[38] Interviews with officials in the provincial capitals of Sanaa, Hajja, al-Hudayda, and Taiz in the north, and Aden, Lahij, Abyan, and Hadramaut in the south; 1996–98.

[39] Al-Mukalla actually privatized its street cleaning services, when several unemployed municipal workers formed a company that operated on fees voluntarily donated by city merchants. Interview with Ahmad Ba Raoud, founder of the private company; January 1997.

because no taxes were supposed to be applied without an executive order from the president.

The ad hoc nature of municipal service fees was unavoidable because the regime in Sanaa did not establish effective rules to guide local government affairs. Government policy by ad hoc and illegal means was typical of government administrative standards in Sanaa. The irony of President Salih's postwar vow to decentralize government is that he would have been more successful if he had borrowed policies from the former south Yemeni system. The director of municipal affairs in Aden had more experience in municipal administration than officials in the north.[40] Ideally, President Salih could have learned and benefited from the expertise of southern government officials, instead of driving them from power.

TACTICS OF DIVIDE AND RULE

When Prime Minister Fareg Ben Ghanem resigned in early 1998, President Salih asked foreign minister Dr. Abd al-Karim al-Iryani to take his place. Dr. al-Iryani is one of the founders of the GPC party, who briefly served as prime minister during the 1980s. His family is part of the traditional highland ruling group. Thus, when Dr. al-Iryani replaced Ben Ghanem, it represented another failure of north-south power sharing. This was the second time that Salih called on a familiar hand from inside the GPC to serve as prime minister, as he did in late 1994 with Abd al-Aziz Abd al-Ghani. In 1998, President Salih also reshuffled the cabinet. The number of southern ministers dropped to seven, while the percentage of northern highland ministers rose to fourteen. For the first time since 1990, members of the dominant highland group held a majority of cabinet seats, and controlled not only the presidency, and the country's military and security forces, but also the prime minister's office.

On April 27, 1998, the fourth anniversary of the Yemeni civil war, the YSP and other opposition groups staged a memorial protest in al-Mukalla, Hadramaut. Northern troops entered the city, and responded to protestors with gunfire. Two citizens were shot and killed, while dozens of others

---

[40] By 1997, the government in Sanaa had restricted the municipality of Aden to a tightly controlled annual budget worth less than U.S. $80,000, an amount which was roughly one percent of Aden's municipal budget in 1985, five years before unity with the north. Between 1994 and 1996, district officials in Madinat al-Sha'ab (a suburb of Aden with a population of 250,000 people) said they functioned without a budget and received no allocations from the central government. Interview with a district official; August 1996.

were injured and arrested.[41] In the summer of 1998, the government in Sanaa implemented a new round of economic reforms required by the IMF's structural adjustment program. In reaction to prices rising 40 percent for basic state-subsidized goods like flour, grains, and fuel oil, there were violent protests in northern areas of the country, but not in the south. South Yemenis had grown wary of increasingly repressive actions by northern military and security forces. On June 20, 1998, thousands of demonstrators took to the streets in Sanaa, burning tires and throwing stones at government buildings.[42] Security forces used tear gas and live ammunition to disperse the crowds. The following day the capital seemed like it was under military occupation as dozens of armored vehicles patrolled the city's streets.

There were two government policies in 1998 that had particular impact on the politics of southern provinces. The first involved a series of dismissals of government personnel at middle levels of the bureaucracy. The regime called this an "early retirement" policy necessitated by IMF-backed reforms to cut the government's payroll. Northern as well as southern civil service workers were let go without adequate pensions. But many south Yemenis complained Salih used the forced retirements to target government workers from southern provinces. In particular, partisans of Ali Nasir, who joined the government and military services in 1994, were forced to retire after 1998. Abdul-Rabo Mansour Hadi remained as vice president, and two other partisans continued serving on the cabinet. Yet an unusually high percentage of workers among the Ali Nasir group became unemployed.[43] Following the second parliamentary election in 1997, President Salih had clearly rejected the idea of a deeper alliance with Ali Nasir. The alliance was always more cosmetic than real because Salih preferred working with tribal shaykhs and other traditional leaders.

---

[41] *Al-Shoura* newspaper (in Arabic), May 3, 1998, and May 10, 1998; p. 1 of both editions. Over the following days, there were solidarity marches in many southern cities, including Ali Nasir's hometown in Abyan. The leader of the YSP in Hadramaut, Hasan Ba Awm (seated at table in Photo 13; no relation to the former head of the GPC in Hadramaut), was charged with sedition for inciting riots. He was forced underground for more than a year until he resurfaced and was sent to jail in late 1999.

[42] Reuters news, June 21, 1998, accessed from CNN.com.

[43] In late 2001, the *Yemen Times* published an article based on interviews with Ali Nasir partisans who were dismissed from the government, claiming that sixteen thousand soldiers and eighteen thousand civil servants were forced into early retirement "for political motives." "Former Ministers Call for Justice," *Yemen Times*, Vol. XI, No. 51, December 17, 2001; p. 1.

At the end of the decade, the majority of Yemenis were struggling to sustain their standard of living in a deteriorating economy. This was true for people in northern and southern provinces. Nonetheless, there remained an identifiable difference between those in "early retirement" (or otherwise unemployed) in northern and southern provinces. Northerners were dismissed from civil service jobs by a government that they had known, and called their own, for decades. Southerners were dismissed by a government that they were still struggling to accept after eight years of turbulent union. Their experience was not unlike the experience of YSP members who were forced from government in 1993 and 1994. Through this shared experience, old southern rivals began organizing a nonpartisan lobby to represent southern interests. As early as 1997, there were rumors about Ali Nasir partisans opening lines of communication with their rivals in the YSP.[44]

The second government policy that had a significant impact on southern citizens in 1998 was the regime's plan to alter provincial boundaries, and create as many as four new provinces. Two areas in the south were targeted for consideration: Hadramaut in the east, which was intended to be split in half along an east-west line; and al-Dali' in the west, which indeed became a new province. The idea of dividing Hadramaut was first proposed in the early 1990s by citizens in Wadi Hadramaut who wanted their own administrative center so they would not have to travel to the coast to conduct business in al-Mukalla. The local writers' union in Saiyun organized a seminar on this topic in 1992, and several prominent citizens spoke in favor of dividing the province.[45] But as the unity crisis in Sanaa grew in 1993, the question of dividing Hadramaut became entangled in the larger north-south political contest. Public opinion quickly turned against the proposed division. When President Salih visited in September 1993 to celebrate the start of oil production at Canoxy's Wadi al-Masila field, he felt obligated to play to local opinion by pledging he would never divide the Hadrami province.[46]

Five years later, Salih broke his pledge and revived plans to divide Hadramaut. Besides Hadramaut and al-Dali' north of Aden, Salih also wanted new provinces in Amran north of Sanaa, and Zabid west of Taiz and south of al-Hudayda. The plan for four new provinces first surfaced when Dr. Ben Ghanem was prime minister. But Ben Ghanem strongly

---

[44] Interview with senior YSP officials in Sanaa; July 2002.
[45] Interview with Awadh Muhammad al-Sabaaya and other civic leaders in Saiyun who presented papers at the 1992 seminar; January 1997.
[46] *Al-Ayyam* newspaper, September 29, 1993; p. 1.

opposed the idea of a new province in Wadi Hadramaut.[47] As a native
Hadrami, Ben Ghanem was particularly interested in the local affairs of his
home province. He supported the idea of keeping Hadramaut united and
strong. This placed him in direct conflict with top officials inside the regime
who were determined to cut Hadramaut in half. The GPC tried to appeal to
the separate cultural identity of Wadi Hadramaut by suggesting that the
new province be called by its old name in the Quran, *al-Ahqaf*.[48] This was
clearly an attempt to win support of conservative religious elements in the
Wadi, while driving a wedge between them and people living along the
coast where the YSP was stronger. Former southern leader Ali Salem al-Bid
was part of a tribal group east of al-Mukalla along the sea coast.

In general, local government units are more successful when they retain
significant size and revenue-raising capabilities, in order to function independently of the central government. Yet political elites within the central
government, who were wary of decentralization, tended to favor splitting
local government units in order to keep them weak and dependent on central
government assistance. In Yemen, this was particularly true after the 1994
civil war. President Salih and Dr. Ben Ghanem's replacement, Prime Minister
al-Iryani, were concerned about the size and strength of Hadramaut, and the
possibility that it could become independent of the central government in
Sanaa. Dr. al-Iryani acknowledged this in 1996 when he said that people in
the highland region would become jealous of Hadramaut's success if it were
allowed to develop independently.[49] Highland elites in Sanaa are generally
aware that outlying regions of the country are more capable of developing
on their own. Thus, ruling groups in Sanaa look for ways to constrain
developments in regions like the western midlands, west coast, southwest,
and east, by keeping them divided. This retards the country's development,
while serving the interests of the most influential highland elites.

---

[47] Interview with a top southern ministry official; October 1998.
[48] Interview with Sadeq Amin Abu Ras, minister of local administration; August 8, 1996.
[49] Interview with Dr. Abd al-Karim Al-Iryani at his home in Sanaa; June 14, 1996. When he
      addressed this subject, Dr. al-Iryani also referred to the greater potential of economic develop-
      ment in al-Hujjariyya, Taiz and al-'Udayn, Ibb. These are two Shafi'i areas in the western
      midlands, which were the greatest concern for northern highland elites after the 1962
      republican revolution. Former deputy prime minister Abd al-Wahab al-Ansi, a member of
      the Islah party from Sanaa who chaired the postwar committee on local administrative policy,
      acknowledged this "list of concern" in a separate interview on November 7, 1996: "Marib
      and Hadramaut have oil, Aden and al-Hudayda generate revenues from trade at their ports,
      Taiz has other economic resources ... if these areas were given autonomy in a federal state,
      they would grow and prosper at the expense of other regions."

Ideally, for government decentralization to be successful in Yemen, there would only need to be five or six regional units. Each region could be encouraged to develop on its own, while sending representatives to a federal government council. Sanaa, Taiz, al-Hudayda, Aden, and al-Mukalla, Hadramaut, are the most appropriate locations for regional capitals in a federal system, perhaps adding the oil region of Marib or Shabwa as a sixth regional capital. What President Salih and Prime Minister al-Iryani proposed in 1998 was to add four new provinces to a collection of seventeen preexisting provinces, in addition to the Sanaa capital zone, creating twenty-two weak local governing units. The local opposition in Hadramaut was ultimately too strong for Prime Minister al-Iryani to advance the plan to divide the eastern province. Several thousand citizens joined massive street rallies and sit-ins in Wadi Hadramaut and al-Mukalla along the coast.[50] Local activists organized mass sit-ins, and gathered tens of thousands of signatures on a petition sent to the president in Sanaa.

PHOTO 13. Hadramaut protest led by Hasan Ba Awm and Omar al-Jawi (at mic), 1998

[50] The local opposition in Hadramaut considered it a great political victory when President Salih cancelled the plan in 1998. Interview with members of the political opposition in al-Mukalla; November 1998. Afterward, Salih formalized a separate deputy governor's office in Saiyun. Thus, it was still possible for government officials in Sanaa to exercise control over Wadi Hadramaut without going through al-Mukalla.

After widespread protest in Hadramaut, the government decided only to create two new provinces in Amran and al-Dali'. The idea of a new province at Zabid was shelved, but later in the 2000s the government created a new province near Zabid in al-Rayma, southwest of Sanaa. The new province of Amran was welcomed by local residents north of Sanaa, since it gave prestige to the Hashid tribes under Shaykh Abdallah bin Husayn al-Ahmar. Al-Dali' was the only new province that caused political problems for President Salih. It was formed along the old north-south border, combining territories of Lahij province in the south with Taiz and Ibb provinces in the north. For central government officials, the main purpose was to erase the former north-south borderline, thus reducing the chances of southern separatist activities. Yet in June 1998, a few weeks before the new provincial offices opened, a military encampment of northern soldiers outside the town came under artillery bombardment.[51]

Following the 1994 civil war, southern military officers in the areas surrounding al-Dali' retained some heavy artillery from their old army divisions. This artillery was used in the June 1998 attack, the opening salvo in a running battle through the end of the year. Residents of al-Dali' province had been preparing for battle since they organized a series of tribal solidarity conferences, modeled after the conferences in Hadramaut and Shabwa in 1996 and 1997. Throughout the fall of 1998, al-Dali' witnessed nearly continuous bombings and clashes between surrounding tribal groups and the government's army, both inside and outside the new provincial capital.[52] The clashes continued into 1999 and 2000, as government forces responded in an increasingly violent and repressive manner.[53] This was a prelude to events in the late 2000s, when the southwest region experienced active rebellion.

Before the end of 1999, President Salih faced his first personal campaign for office. The amended constitution in 1994 limited the president to a

---

[51] *Al-Ayyam* (in Arabic), June 3, 1998; p. 1. According to *al-Ayyam*, before the initial artillery attack, the army had held people in surrounding areas under a five-day curfew. Afterward government troops responded with their own artillery attack.

[52] In its October 14, 1998, issue, *al-Ayyam* reported that the director of political security in al-Dali' was targeted and injured by a bombing attack. In late November, the army imposed a blockade around the region; "Military Forces Impose a Blockade around the Zabid district of al-Dali'," November 29, 1998; p.1.

[53] On June 4, 2000, *al-Shoura* newspaper reported that YSP officials in al-Dali' accused the army of a campaign of assassinations in the province; p. 1. Following the Palestinian uprising at al-Aqsa mosque in early October 2000, youth in al-Dali' drew parallels to their own uprising. A committee of "families of victims of government violence in al-Dali'" called for a march of solidarity with Palestinians. *Al-Shoura* (in Arabic), October 8, 2000; p. 1.

maximum of two five year terms in office, while requiring a direct nationwide vote. It was important for Salih to observe the constitution, and hold the country's first presidential election on schedule, because he staked his legitimacy on democratic principles. There was no risk that Salih would lose the 1999 election, since the constitution stipulated that candidates could only be nominated by parliament. The Islah party was the only legitimate opposition in parliament because the YSP had boycotted the vote in 1997. As leader of Islah and speaker of parliament, Shaykh Abdallah placed President Salih in a slightly embarrassing predicament by refusing to nominate a candidate from his party. Shaykh Abdallah vowed that he would vote for President Salih, and encouraged his party's followers to do the same.

Shaykh Abdallah refused to nominate a candidate because Islah had been dropped from the cabinet in 1997, when the GPC refused to allow Islah members to serve as government ministers. This was Shaykh Abdallah's way of sending a signal to President Salih that if he wanted to govern on his own, then he could campaign for president by himself as the only candidate. Salih was placed in a bind because he needed to avoid the appearance of monopolizing power in a fraudulent democratic system. After his party's landslide victory in 1997, the GPC now had to sponsor its own rival presidential candidate, just to create the appearance of an open democratic contest. It nominated a southern politician who was the son of the first president of south Yemen, Qahtan al-Shaabi.[54] When it came time to vote in July 1999, many southerners boycotted the election, either refusing to show up or leaving their ballots blank. Ali Abdallah Salih won the no-contest election with more than 96 percent of all ballots.

EVOLUTIONS IN LOCAL GOVERNMENT

After seeing the danger of possessing too much authority in a divided country like Yemen, President Salih and other officials in the GPC party began taking more seriously the need to devolve local government power. This was one way to defuse growing voices of opposition, particularly in southern and eastern regions.

Years after the civil war in July 1994, when President Salih promised to hold local elections within a single year, he and other highland elites still

---

[54] The political opposition lampooned the contest between Salih and al-Shaabi. *Al-Shoura*, the newspaper of the Yemeni Popular Forces party, ran a front page cartoon portraying two election ballot boxes: the first with the symbol of the GPC, a white stallion on its hind legs; and the second with the stallion's tail. *Al-Shoura*, July 25, 1999; p. 1.

regarded the advocates of local elections as potential secessionists and traitors to the union.[55] For example, when the GPC deliberated on a draft law for local government in late 1998, a clear regional division arose between GPC ministers from the north, and the remaining cabinet members from the south. Minister of legal affairs Abdallah Ghanem (no relation to former prime minister Fareg Ben Ghanem) was the leading southern cabinet member who worked on the draft law. In one cabinet meeting, he and another southern minister were accused of being "separatists," plotting against the interests of the nation.[56]

The cabinet discussions in 1998 became so divided that there were even disagreements about what the new law should be called. The term "local government" (*al-hukm al-mahali*) was used in the former south Yemen, but was considered too radical by northern GPC officials who felt it implied that provinces would enjoy political autonomy. They preferred a term used in the former north, "local administration" (*al-idara al-mahaliyya*), which meant the provinces would remain mere extensions of the central bureaucracy. Eventually a compromise was reached in 1999 to call the draft law "local authority" (*al-sulta al-mahaliyya*). President Salih retreated from his earlier promise to allow elections of provincial governors and directors at the district level. According to the new law, the president would retain powers to appoint top local authorities, while giving citizens a limited right to elect members of local consultative councils. This contradicted an article of Yemen's post-war constitution requiring elections of all local leaders. A few members of parliament noted this fact, and several southern representatives voted against the legislation, saying it "sanctifies central control."[57]

The "local authority" law was finally adopted on February 10, 2000, nearly two years after Dr. Ben Ghanem's resignation and six years after the civil war. The long delay indicated the political sensitivity of central-local government relations. Later in the year, when President Salih set the date

---

[55] In the late summer of 1996, conservative members of the GPC, and members of its coalition partner Islah, scrapped the idea of holding elections for governors because they believed "these elections would give strength to 'separatist' forces in the south." Interview with former minister of interior Yahya al-Mutawakkel; October 22, 1996.

[56] Interview with minister of legal affairs Abdallah Ghanem at his home in Sanaa; October 21, 1998. *Al-Ayyam* ran a short story about these cabinet debates; "Harsh Discussion in the Cabinet–Accusations that Some Members Are Working against the Nation," *al-Ayyam* (in Arabic), September 6, 1998; p. 1. According to this article, the northern ministers of finance and housing accused Abdallah Ghanem and southern minister of interior Husayn Arab of being "separatists."

[57] Al-Mikhlafi, 2000; pp. 93–95.

for local elections on February 20, 2001, he also arranged simultaneously for a national referendum on a package of seventeen constitutional amendments. One of these amendments was designed to eliminate the contradiction between the postwar constitution and the new "local authority" law by granting the central government control over all local affairs. When Yemenis finally went to the polls in February 2001, there was great irony in their exercise of voting rights. This was the first time they could select their representatives at a local level. But the referendum meant that voters were also choosing to withdraw their local representatives' constitutional right to govern. The referendum was virtually guaranteed to pass because all the amendments were grouped together for a yes/no vote. The government made little effort to educate the public about the content of the amendments. Radio and television simply encouraged citizens to vote yes.[58]

The political campaign prior to the referendum and local elections witnessed a great escalation in violence. Kidnappings, bombings, shootings, and assassinations became daily occurrences. The competition was intense among thirty thousand candidates vying for more than seven thousand local council seats because the YSP and other opposition parties chose to join the campaign. The GPC demonstrated tremendous power as it employed political leverage in government, promising local development projects and other bribes in exchange for votes. In addition, it used the SEC to tilt voter registration and balloting procedures in its favor. Days before the vote, every opposition party denounced the election as a fraud.[59]

Local publishers of the *Yemen Times* newspaper described February 20, 2001, as "one of the deadliest election days in the history of Yemen." President Salih had deployed more than seventy thousand troops to patrol streets around polling stations.[60] The violence and illegal practices were so extensive that two hundred electoral centers (roughly 12 percent of the

---

[58] The *Yemen Times* conducted a survey of radio and television coverage of the constitutional referendum. It found that 86 percent of the air time was used to present propaganda encouraging citizens to vote "Yes," only 14 percent was devoted to informing citizens about the content of the constitutional amendments, and no air time was allotted for opposition parties to explain why the amendments should be opposed. "Initial Report of Media Coverage Reveals GPC Campaigning Dominated Official Media," *Yemen Times*, February 19, 2001.

[59] Several small parties announced a formal boycott, and many candidates withdrew from the race. Some of Islah's local branches were also inclined to join the boycott. Nine days before the vote a group of lawyers representing the opposition parties filed law suits in Sanaa to try to stop the elections. *Al-Ayyam* (in Arabic), February 12, 2001; pp. 1 and 8.

[60] "As Election Hysteria Dominates the Scene in the Last Days of Election Campaigning 70,000 Troops to Secure Local Elections," *Yemen Times*, February 19, 2001; p. 1.

total) had to cancel or postpone balloting. In several northern and southern districts, the GPC and opposition accused each other of carrying out murderous attacks. Government sources reported a total of eleven deaths and twenty-three injuries, but independent sources put the numbers at forty killed and more than one hundred injured.[61] The violence was worst in the western midland province of Ibb, where partisans of the GPC and Islah continued fighting for several days. On February 25, the president's Republican Guard used tanks to attack several villages of Islah supporters in Ibb's al-Radma district. According to the international daily *al-Hayat*, government sources reported nine killed in al-Radma (five from Islah plus four members of the Republican Guard) and eleven injured, while local independent sources said the casualties were much higher.[62]

Once the first ballots were counted, top GPC officials were quick to claim a sweeping victory with 80 percent of local council seats. Official vote counts later showed the GPC won 62 percent of seats.[63] But this still represented another landslide victory for President Salih. The public referendum on seventeen constitutional amendments passed with just under 75 percent of votes. When the new local councils met to choose their leaders, the GPC proved its strength by gaining directorship of every provincial council except two, Hadramaut in the east and Marib in the central interior region. In both of these provinces, independents and representatives of Islah held sway. The GPC was challenged by the YSP in Lahij, al-Dali', and Aden in the southwest.[64] In Aden, the YSP complained that its popular female candidate from Shaykh Othman district held a majority of support on the provincial council. But behind the scenes, the GPC tipped the selection process in favor of its chosen candidate. Once the local councils began their work in the spring of 2001, the overall experience proved highly disappointing. Most councils functioned as mere "talk shops" with little authority.

---

[61] "Preliminary Results: Violent Incidents," *Yemen Times*, February 26, 2001. In an article for *Middle East International* on March 9, 2001, Brian Whitaker reported approximately one hundred violent incidents around the country and "at least 45 people died on election day or during the prolonged and turbulent counting of votes." *Middle East International*, No. 645, March 9, 2001; p. 17.

[62] *Al-Hayat* (in Arabic), February 26, 2001; p. 1. Also see the more extensive reporting in the article by the *Yemen Times*, "Tanks Take Over," February 26, 2001; p. 1. Government sources claimed the fighting in Ibb started when several Islamic militants ambushed government forces. But reporters for *Yemen Times* interviewed local Islah supporters who say the conflict arose when the local GPC chair refused to release the election results, and then government forces were called in to carry the ballot boxes away.

[63] *Yemen Times*, February 26, 2001.

[64] In Aden's Crater district, the Islah party also outpolled the GPC.

The main problem was that the central government allotted few financial and technical resources to enable council members to carry out their limited duties. Council members received no salaries, and in most districts their central government subsidies amounted to a few hundred U.S. dollars per month. Later regulations allowed provincial and district councils to raise funds from traditional *zakat* taxes, special fees applied to electricity bills, and taxes applied to the sale of *qat*. But these revenues proved irregular since more powerful local officials already claimed them.[65] There was redundancy in Yemen's "local authority" system because the people's elected representatives sat idle, while the president's appointed staff carried out day-to-day affairs of government. During the first year, several district and provincial councils voted to withdraw their confidence from local officials appointed by the central government.[66]

Yemen's local elected councils lacked authority to hire and fire the staff appointed by the central government, yet the practice of "withdrawing confidence" soon spread around the country. This was the most significant democratic development after the 2001 local elections. Provincial and district councils found the "no confidence" vote to be the strongest means of gaining political influence. Eventually President Salih was compelled to take notice, and central government ministries began removing a few local officials who lacked public trust. As a result of these developments, and the heightened violence at election time, it was clear that local "elections" and regional politics presented more challenge to Salih's regime. National elections presented little difficulty because the ruling GPC party controlled vast resources to guarantee large majorities. In fact, the previous national elections in 1997 and 1999 proved that Salih's main dilemma was to limit the size of his victory, and ensure that the opposition had some political role to play.

During the late 1990s, President Salih and members of his inner circle felt they had sufficient control of the postunification government to manage regular elections, while preserving the GPC party's power. It appeared Salih was on the verge of regaining the kind of hegemony he once enjoyed in the former north Yemen years after founding the GPC. In 1999, many political observers thought President Salih might establish a system of patronage in southern provinces built on the same tribal alliances, and tactics of divide

[65] Interview with Taiz provincial council members; July 2002.
[66] This first occurred in Hadramaut, where Shibbam's district council voted against an assistant manager. Interview with Hadramaut provincial council members; July 2002. Photo 14 shows members of the Shibbam council (top) who took this critical stance.

PHOTO 14. Shibbam local council members (top) and Saiyun local council members (bottom) in Hadramaut province

and rule, that he employed in the highland mountains. But in the 2000s, the ground would shift dramatically under the president's feet.

SIGNS OF TROUBLES TO COME

An important moment of change came during the Islamic holy month of Ramadan in December 2001 and January 2002, following al-Qaeda's terrorist attacks on the United States and America's military response in the region, including greater pressure on Yemen due to the bombing of the USS *Cole* in Aden the previous year. During Ramadan, a group of prominent southern opposition figures held nightly meetings in Sanaa. The group included members of parliament, former cabinet ministers, activists in political parties and organizations, including the GPC, private business-men, as well as tribal shaykhs. Its real significance though was that the group included representatives from both sides of President Salih's "dual strategy" in the postwar south: namely, partisans of Ali Nasir Muhammad, and representatives of traditional southern ruling families.

Both sides of President Salih's "dual strategy" knew that, for years, top political elites in Sanaa had played them against each other, as competitors for the regime's support. They gradually realized that the president's "dual strategy" served his own interests in Sanaa more than it served the interests of their home regions. As a result, they came together to form the "Public Forum for the Sons of the Southern and Eastern Provinces."[67] The group's name recalled the first southern opposition party, the League (*al-Rabita*) of the Sons of South Arabia, which originated in Aden during British colonial rule. But the 2001 group was an informal association, not a political party. The Public Forum (*al-Multaqa al-'Amm*) was the best example of regional opposition coalescing around grievances outside the highland region. Its purpose was to represent citizens from Lahij and al-Dali' in the southwest to Hadramaut and al-Mahra in the eastern region, who complain of exclusion from political, social, and economic opportunities because north Yemenis, particularly the tribes of Hashid and Bakil, monopolize control of the country's resources.

The president of the Public Forum was a man born in Abyan province in the mid-southern region, named Ali Muhammad al-Qufaysh. Before uni-fication, al-Qufaysh lived in the northern YAR. He left his southern home in Abyan with other refugees who fled Marxist rule in 1969. During the 1970s, he joined one of the many militias sponsored by the YAR to fight

---

[67] Interview with the Public Forum's director at his home in Sanaa; July 3, 2002.

against the southern PDRY, serving in border regions of Taiz where Salih was a low-ranking army officer. Over time al-Qufaysh rose through the YAR's military ranks until he reached the level of commander. In the late 1980s, President Salih arranged for his friend to direct an organization for widows and children of martyrs killed in the country's 1960s revolutions. Thus, al-Qufaysh was someone who earned the personal confidence of the president, and could reach out to him on a private basis.

During the month of Ramadan, members of the Public Forum met in al-Qufaysh's spacious house in Sanaa. These were large *qat* sessions regularly attended by more than one hundred men, who met after breaking the fast each evening at sunset. Al-Qufaysh presided over each meeting with the assistance of Faisal Ben Shamlan, the independent member of parliament from Hadramaut who resigned as minister of oil in 1995. Under the leadership of such high-profile figures, the *qat* sessions held considerable prestige. The size of the group grew as al-Qufaysh, Ben Shamlan, and others reached out to people from southern and eastern regions who could help create a unified lobby to place pressure on President Salih. Socialists in the YSP were not major participants in the Public Forum. But some representatives of the party were in attendance.

Toward the end of the month of Ramadan in January 2002, after the Public Forum had compiled a list of its main grievances, Ali al-Qufaysh drafted a personal letter to President Salih in which he listed five requests for political change, including expanded local governance, equality of citizenship, access to jobs, and the safeguarding of land ownership and resource management. Al-Qufaysh addressed the letter to the president on a personal basis, as head of the new Public Forum. Thus, he encouraged President Salih to respond to the Public Forum in a private way, from one old friend to another. After a month of not hearing from the president, al-Qufaysh decided to publish the letter in a widely read newspaper, seeking publicity that would force the president's hand. In the following days, all independent and opposition newspapers picked up the story, and began speculating about the motivations and goals of this new group. Rumors flew in Sanaa, and across southern and eastern provinces.

The reaction of President Salih to the publicity and rumors was immediate and severe. He directed the government-run press to release damaging stories about his former friend, Ali al-Qufaysh, and other members of the Public Forum. Government newspapers accused members of the forum of treason, and demanded that they publish a formal retraction. Al-Qufaysh refused, but under pressure he ceased holding meetings at his house. Next al-Qufaysh's name was dragged through the mud of public scandal about alleged embezzlement of government funds during the 1980s. Government newspapers printed documents showing his signature and the amount of money that he allegedly appropriated from funds to aid widows and children of martyrs in the revolutionary wars.[68]

It was clear that political security officers had dug up files from Al-Qufaysh's past to tarnish his name, and shut down the Public Forum. This had previously been the standard practice of Zaydi imams throughout the history of north Yemen, when they appointed men of social influence to profitable posts, only to use corruption scandals to tear them down. Al-Qufaysh strongly denied the accusations made against him, and no criminal charges were ever filed. But the damage was done. The Public Forum could no longer function as a viable means to press southern demands for change. For other members of the Public Forum who participated in the group's brief activities, there were obvious lessons about the character of Salih's regime, and its resistance to redressing public grievances.

If President Salih was prepared to treat a longtime friend in such a callous way, then he would never respond to average citizens in southern and eastern provinces through the formal political process. Under al-Qufaysh's leadership, members of the Public Forum had tried by civil and democratic means to stir the president to action. But they failed. The ramification of this failure was felt in all southern regions, and many areas of the north. Citizens from all backgrounds, whether tribesmen or professionals, former military officers or civil servants, families of martyrs from the 1960s or refugees who fled Aden in 1986, felt the Public Forum had given expression to their voices. Now they knew that to resist President Salih's regime, they needed to form a larger, stronger, and more active opposition.

These developments in late 2001 and early 2002 occurred against the backdrop of events following September 11, 2001, in America. After al-Qaeda's terrorist attacks on the United States, President George W. Bush demanded that President Salih demonstrate greater cooperation in counterterrorism efforts. Some American government officials mentioned Yemen as a possible target of U.S. military actions, since Yemen had failed to track down the perpetrators of the USS *Cole* attack. Inside Yemen, observers speculated that, during Ramadan 2001, leaders of the Public Forum felt emboldened to lobby President Salih only because the

---

[68] This scandal was covered in all the major GPC and state newspapers in the early months of 2002.

Yemeni president was under external pressure from the United States. Many felt that Salih's behavior, during his campaign of intimidation against an old friend like Ali al-Qufaysh, appeared panicky and desperate. In practical terms, the president burned every bridge keeping Yemen united because the Public Forum included representatives of every southern faction. As Salih drove more of his allies into the opposition, and more members of the opposition united against him, the Yemeni president would find his room to maneuver shrinking fast.

7

Political Eruptions after 9/11

On October 12, 2000, the USS *Cole* pulled into Aden harbor to receive fuel on its way to the Persian Gulf, where it planned to join an ongoing operation enforcing decade-long economic sanctions against Iraq. A few boats from Aden's port authority helped the enormous American naval destroyer position itself along the fuel depot. Minutes later, as the USS *Cole* was tied to its moorings, two men in a small white watercraft, approximately twenty-five feet long, motored slowly toward the American ship. Sailors stood at ease along the USS *Cole's* deck. The two men aboard the skiff drew close to the ship's port side, waving at the sailors who stood high above them. The sailors waved back, and then there was a massive blast that completely destroyed the skiff and nearly sank the American destroyer.

It was later determined that this October 2000 blast came from a bomb estimated to weigh five hundred pounds. The bomb consisted of powerful C-4 plastic explosive material prepared by agents of al-Qaeda who shaped it around a projectile that was positioned in the bow of the skiff to cause maximum damage at the USS *Cole's* waterline. The thick steel hull of the *Cole* was designed to withstand more than fifty thousand pounds of pressure per square inch. The exploding bomb ripped through this steel, creating a jagged hole forty feet wide and twenty feet high. The force of the blast thrust the ship's lower decks upward, crushing a group of sailors who were eating lunch inside an onboard dining hall. Seventeen American sailors died, and nearly forty others were injured.[1] When seawater began

---

[1] "Blast Kills Sailors on US Ship in Yemen," *New York Times*, October 13, 2000; p. 1.

pouring into the gaping blast hole, the billion dollar destroyer listed slightly to its side. But it did not sink.

Residents of Aden report that the sound of the bomb's blast could be heard throughout the city, even in Crater district on the other side of giant volcanic Shamsan mountain, which protects Aden's harbor from the outer gulf.[2] In the first days after the bombing, Yemeni government officials refused to acknowledge the bombing was an act of terrorism. They claimed the blast resulted from an internal explosion aboard the U.S. naval destroyer. Few citizens in Yemen believed the official reports, echoing from government television and radio. Most knew that the attack on the USS *Cole* was likely conducted by local militants associated with Osama Bin Laden, who as early as 1997 publicly vowed to attack Americans on the Arab peninsula.

Immediate suspicions fell on a local group called the Aden-Abyan Islamic Army, whose members had joined Bin Laden's Afghan mujahideen during the 1980s, and later linked with the new al-Qaeda organization. In general, Yemen's population opposed American military policies that, in the fall of 2000, were associated with Israel's ongoing violence against Palestinians in the al-Aqsa intifada, as well as the continued suffering of Iraq's population. Thus many Yemenis were glad to see the American military attacked when the USS *Cole* was struck hard in Aden harbor. They believed that the United States was neither justified in its support of Israel, nor in its strangling of the Iraqi economy a full decade after the Gulf war.

To grasp the full meaning of the USS *Cole* bombing, and the general rise of militancy associated with al-Qaeda in Yemen, it is essential to consider these matters against the backdrop of the country's late Cold War and post–Cold War transformation. This transformation was generally conservative, Islamic-oriented, and officially considered a success of American Cold War policies developed in alliance with Saudi Arabia. Much like the political theater in Afghanistan and Pakistan during the 1980s, it is important to keep in mind that Yemen was also the site of a Cold War struggle between local Soviet-allied Marxist elements, on the one hand, and Saudi-allied Islamists, on the other hand. Just as militant Islamic forces rose to power in Afghanistan and Pakistan in the 1980s and 1990s, so, too, did Islamic militant forces arise in Yemen, especially following the defeat of the southern YSP-affiliated army in the 1994 civil war. In this sense, the 2000 bombing in Aden was "blowback" from earlier American and Saudi success in defeating the spread of Soviet-style Marxism on the Arabian

---

[2] Interviews with Aden provincial officials; July 2002.

peninsula. The same story of "blowback" was told after the rise of the Taliban government in Afghanistan.

Reactionary Islamic forces in Yemen are decades old, and well documented. At the beginning of Yemen's popular revolutionary era in the 1960s, Saudi Arabia, Britain, and the United States stood in alliance with reactionary elements from north Yemen's ousted Zaydi regime. Although the Kennedy administration initially recognized the new republican regime in Sanaa, the Johnson administration later joined Britain, Saudi Arabia, and secretly Israel, to finance, train, and supply conservative religious and tribal forces in the highland region. The aim was to prevent Egyptian and Soviet forces from establishing a united progressive Yemeni republic that would oppose vital Saudi and western interests on the peninsula. During the 1970s and 1980s, Yemen's leftist social forces were gradually worn down, as the forces of Islamic reaction and tribalism gained strength.

For decades, the U.S. and Saudi governments had been allied with north Yemen's regime, in support of a conservative religious trend that gave rise to groups like al-Qaeda. American and Saudi policies were similarly aligned in most regions of the Arab and Muslim worlds. The result of these Cold War orientations was the strengthening of reactionary puritanical Islamic groups inside Yemen and other countries. After Yemeni unity in the 1990s, the ultimate outcome of western Cold War politics on the southwest corner of the Arabian peninsula was the pressure cooker of political trouble that threatened to explode when al-Qaeda attacked New York and Washington on September 11, 2001.

Inside Yemen in the fall of 2001, President Bush demanded cooperation from Ali Abdallah Salih in targeting groups allied with al-Qaeda. The problem for Salih was that members of his inner circle were closely allied to militants in al-Qaeda, one of whom, Abd al-Rahim al-Nashiri, was involved in planning the *Cole* bombing.[3] Back in 2000, the Yemeni president stonewalled FBI investigators sent by the Clinton administration because he worried they would uncover evidence revealing criminal connections at the highest levels of Yemen's government.[4] President Salih had allied with al-Qaeda militants during his struggle with southern YSP leaders

---

[3] Clark, 2010; p. 174.

[4] After the USS *Cole* bombing, FBI investigators in Yemen faced resistance from Salih's regime during the fall of 2000. Wright, 2002. The U.S. ambassador in Yemen, Barbara Bodine, and top officials at the State Department in Washington, DC, intervened with the FBI, and requested that its agents not act as aggressively as they would inside the United States. The FBI felt it was being railroaded out of the country, and ended its investigation after only a few weeks. More details are presented in Lawrence Wright's 2006 book, *The*

in the early 1990s. Then after the 1994 civil war, President Salih promoted some of these militants, like Tareq al-Fadli, to privileged positions in the GPC. Al-Fadli and his allies in Abyan, less than twenty miles from Aden, possessed government vehicles registered with state security forces. There was never any evidence linking al-Fadli to the bombing of the USS *Cole*. But in 2000, he and other veterans of the Afghan *mujahideen* traveled freely in and out of Aden's port area with full government clearance.

The person in President Salih's regime with the closest ties to Tareq al-Fadli and other Afghan mujahideen was General Ali Muhsin al-Ahmar, the regime's strongman. Rumors inside the country said that al-Qaeda agents had telephone contact with Ali Muhsin before the USS *Cole* bombing.[5] Rumors like this run wild in Yemen, especially at daily *qat*-sessions. There is no way to know whether or not this particular rumor was true. Yet President Salih and his closest associates knew that al-Qaeda agents in Yemen might have been responsible for the *Cole* bombing. These associates certainly knew the names of individual suspects to interrogate, in order to find the specific planners and financiers of the bombing. But they did not want to upset interests at the heart of the Yemeni regime that could ignite more damaging explosions in the country.

By 2002, Salih agreed for the United States to send a covert team of American counterterrorism advisors to train a new elite unit of Yemen's Republican Guard. U.S. officials also persuaded Salih to allow the pilotless operation of Predator missile-carrying drones, which could target al-Qaeda members seeking sanctuary in Marib inside the desert interior region. On November 3, 2002, U.S. soldiers used a drone-fired missile to destroy a vehicle carrying the lead suspect in the *Cole* bombing, Qaed Sinan (Abu Ali) al-Harithi, who was traveling with five other people on the western edge of Marib's desert.[6] The official story inside Yemen, at the time of this attack, was that al-Harithi's car carried a bomb, which exploded when it hit a ditch. But in Washington at a Pentagon press briefing two days later, Deputy Defense Secretary Paul Wolfowitz bragged to the American media about the Bush administration's success in tracking and killing the lead Yemeni suspect in the *Cole* bombing.[7]

Looming Tower: al-Qaeda's Road to 9/11, and in the American *PBS Frontline* documentary film, "The Man Who Knew," first broadcast on October 3, 2002.

[5] A Yemeni diplomat, who headed the country's navy at the time of the *Cole* bombing and later sought asylum in Britain as a political refugee, claimed that General al-Ahmar had personal contact with the bombers of the USS *Cole*. "Britons' Killers 'Linked to Yemeni Army Chief'," *The Times of London*, May 8, 2005.

[6] Walter Pincus, "U.S. Strike Kills Six in al-Qaeda," *Washington Post*, November 5, 2002.

[7] Evan Thomas and Mark Hosenball, "The Opening Shot," *Newsweek*, November 11, 2002.

Before Wolfowitz's comments, there had been an understanding between the Yemeni and American governments that U.S. military presence in Yemen would be kept secret to avoid inflaming local anti-American sentiments. Yemeni government officials speculated that Wolfowitz intended to embarrass and destabilize Salih's regime by making public the U.S. military's role in Yemen. If this was Wolfowitz's intention, then his words had the desired effect when they were published in Yemeni newspapers. The immediate public reaction was severe condemnation of President Salih. Independent and opposition newspapers accused Salih of compromising the nation's sovereignty, and public anger arose because of U.S. operations on Yemeni territory.[8] The country's domestic politics had been boiling for a number of years. But the revelations from Washington blew the lid off, unleashing violent factions inside the political opposition as well as the regime.

In America and other Western countries, there is a mistaken perception that Islamic reactionary movements primarily target foreigners. But the truth is that these reactionary movements have long attacked liberal, progressive, left-wing, and secular Arabs and Muslims in larger numbers. This was true for decades during and after the Cold War, when American and British officials allied with Saudi Arabia to finance, train, and arm reactionary militants who used Islamic rhetoric to justify such political attacks. In reality, the lives of Arab and Muslim peoples have been more affected by Islamic militancy than the lives of Americans or westerners. The best evidence is what happened in Yemen in late 2002 when revelations about the Predator missile strike in Marib unleashed deep public anger. The first individual targeted in waves of violence was a senior Yemeni Socialist Party official named Jarallah Omar.

Jarallah Omar was assassinated near the end of December inside a large conference hall in Sanaa, just after he delivered a passionate speech about peace and reconciliation to supporters of Islah, Yemen's largest Islamic party.[9] It was an extraordinary speech, given at the invitation of Islah's leadership. The event signaled the possibility of a new era in Yemeni politics, if Islamists and socialists could reconcile and unite in opposition to President Salih's ruling GPC party. After finishing the speech and returning to his seat at the front of the conference hall near Islah's president, Shaykh Abdallah

---

[8] "Attack Reaction," *Yemen Times*, Vol. XII, No. 46, November 11, 2002. Also in the same edition, "Survey Shows Public Aghast." The Sanaa-based Arabic newspaper *al-Shoura* provided the best coverage of the upsurge of violent opposition in Yemen's capital during 2002, preceding the U.S. invasion of Iraq.

[9] "Assassinated," *Yemen Times*, December 24, 2002.

bin Husayn al-Ahmar, Jarallah was approached from the side by a stranger who asked to engage in conversation. This man pulled out a revolver, and fired two shots into Jarallah's chest, killing him instantly. During the early 1990s, when Jarallah's YSP was under attack by Islamists allied with Islah and President Salih's GPC party, hundreds of his colleagues were similarly targeted for assassination. Dozens died, and far more were injured in similar attacks.

Before pulling the trigger and firing his bullets, the assassin was overheard telling Jarallah "you are from the *Khawarij*," referring to the earliest splinter group that broke with the Muslim mainstream in the first decades of Islamic history. Thus it appeared the gunman had fundamentalist reasons for carrying out the assassination.[10] This was confirmed two days later when an associate of the assassin smuggled a weapon inside the American Baptist missionary hospital in the quiet town of Jibla, one hundred miles south of Sanaa not far from Jarallah Omar's hometown in the province of Ibb.[11] This man, Abed Abd al-Razzaq Kamil from Amran in the highland region, killed the hospital facility's head Australian physician and two American female staff, while severely injuring another American in the stomach. He told police that he and Jarallah's assassin plotted alone to kill Americans and "Yemeni infidels."

The link between Jarallah Omar's assassination and the killings at the American Baptist hospital was a tragic example of "blowback" from American government policies during the Cold War.[12] Few Americans fully consider the consequences of U.S. Cold War policies in the Arab Muslim world. But for secular, progressive individuals like Jarallah and countless members of the YSP, as well as similar political parties in other Arab Muslim countries, they were the primary targets of violence throughout the Cold War when American and other western governments aligned

---

[10] When Jarallah Omar was shot, there was pandemonium in the conference hall. Shaykh al-Ahmar's private security detained the assassin, and took him to the shaykh's house for interrogation. Islah leaders were concerned someone inside the regime had arranged this public assassination in order to derail the party's reconciliation with the YSP. During the videotaped interrogation at al-Ahmar's house, the assassin identified himself as Ali al-Hushayshi, a controversial mosque preacher from Amran where Shaykh al-Ahmar also has a home. Al-Hushayshi had earlier attended the Islah-affiliated al-Nur University. After 9/11, he was briefly arrested on suspicion of militant activities, but later released by the government.

[11] Neil MacFarquhar, "3 US Citizens Slain in Yemen in Rifle Attack," *New York Times*, December 31, 2002; p. 1.

[12] This concept is mainly associated with U.S. support, after 1979, for the decade-long *mujahideen* struggle in Afghanistan, and the consequent "blowback" after another decade in the 1990s when al-Qaeda plotted to attack New York and Washington, DC. Johnson, 2000.

PHOTO 15. Town of Jibla, Ibb, home of Islamic ruler Queen Arwa

strategically with the Saudi monarchy, and other conservative regimes, to foment militant fundamentalism. The "blowback" that America experienced after the Cold War was not generated by Marxists and other leftists, but rather the same forces of reaction that had targeted left-wing movements. In short, such violence is an old story, for which Arab Muslims like Jarallah's family and friends can hardly be expected to show sympathy toward the United States government.

The forces of reaction in Yemen and other Arab Muslim countries are not natural. Islamic militancy and extremism are certainly not inherent parts of Yemeni culture and society. The best evidence is the large numbers of Yemenis who turned out to show their respect at the funerals for Jarallah in Sanaa, and the American and Australian doctors in Jibla. Hundreds of thousands of people came to these funerals to express their grief and share condolences.[13] In Jibla, many mourners traveled hours through rough mountainous terrain. For weeks, they paid respect at a shady hilltop grave site near the hospital.

---

[13] "Hundreds of Thousands Bid Farewell to the Martyr Jarallah Omar," *al-Ayyam* (in Arabic); January 2, 2003.

In a remarkable tribute to the tolerance and respect that define Islamic traditions in Yemen, the families of the American and Australian doctors wanted their deceased loved ones to be buried in Yemen because they knew how much their loved ones cared about the Yemeni people, and how much the Yemeni people loved them in return.[14] Western midland communities around the Baptist hospital considered one of the American female staff physicians, Martha Myers, to be a mother figure, because she had delivered tens of thousands of babies during a career that spanned three decades. These American Christian missionaries were not hated by the Yemeni people, and they did not face prejudice or rejection from Yemeni society. To explain their deaths in such terms is false. They died at the hands of a lone extremist who acted for reactionary reasons in a climate of rising public anger over events inside Yemen and elsewhere in the world.

A BOILING CAULDRON

Following September 11, 2001, when American President George Bush first addressed world leaders in black-and-white terms, saying "you are either with us or against us," the Yemeni president's attention was powerfully drawn to U.S. terrorism concerns. Later when Bush and other American government officials spoke threateningly about removing regimes that sponsor or harbor terrorists, President Salih quickly fell in line with demands from Washington, DC. In late September and October, Salih initiated a campaign of arrests, sweeping up dozens of individuals, jailing those who were Yemeni, and "deporting whole planeloads of foreign Afghan war veterans."[15] He also arranged the earliest possible appointment to meet the American president in Washington, in order to enroll Yemen as an active supporter of the U.S. "war on terrorism."

On November 25–27, 2001, the Yemeni president met President Bush and other top U.S. officials at the State Department, Pentagon, and the CIA. During these meetings, which were held ten days after the American military took control of Kabul, Afghanistan, Salih promised full cooperation to track down individuals responsible for the USS *Cole* bombing in 2000. This led the following year to the killing of Abu Ali al-Harithi in Marib's desert. The Yemeni president's change in attitude between the fall of 2000, when Salih stonewalled FBI investigators, and the fall of 2001 can

---

[14] Phone conversation with the church pastor of one of the American families in Alabama; January 2003.
[15] Clark, 2010; p. 192.

be attributed to two factors. First, Salih remembered the consequences of his decision in 1990, when he resisted joining the first President Bush's coalition to remove Saddam Husayn's Iraqi troops from Kuwait. Afterward the senior President Bush terminated U.S. assistance to Yemen, and put severe diplomatic pressure on Salih's regime. Yemen also lost support from Saudi Arabia and many Gulf countries, setting off a decade-long economic crisis. The Yemeni president did not want a repeat in 2001.

Second, unlike in 2000 when he was pressured by FBI investigators, Salih now had genuine fears that he might be targeted by a U.S. military assault soon after the invasion of Afghanistan in early October 2001. If Salih had not pledged full cooperation in America's newest war, then Yemen might have been attacked even before Iraq in March 2003, or more likely later in coordination with U.S. operations in Somalia. President Salih was in such a rush to prove his loyalty to America that, less than a month after he returned from Washington in late November, he launched a poorly planned and misguided operation to arrest a group of men named as suspects in the USS *Cole* bombing.

In mid-December 2001, President Salih sent units of his Republican Guard troops into the interior desert, where shaykhs of the 'Abida tribe were accused of providing sanctuary for agents of al-Qaeda. The suspects came from regions outside Marib, including Shabwa in the mid-southern region and al-Hudayda on the west coast. When Yemeni ground forces approached the position of 'Abida's militia, Yemeni fighter jets buzzed the location at low altitude, intending to persuade the tribal shaykhs to give up the wanted men without a fight. Unfortunately, when the jets caused a sonic boom, it frightened the tribesmen into thinking they were under aerial assault. They opened fire on the Republican Guard troops, killing nearly twenty soldiers including the unit's commanding officer.[16] Government forces returned fire, killing three tribesmen, plus two local women and a young child. No al-Qaeda suspects were even detained, so the operation was a complete disaster.

This incident was the first to contribute to a growing climate of public discontent in Yemen due to perceived American pressure on Salih's regime. This pressure forced President Salih to act in ways that severely undermined his domestic legitimacy. Mass discontent initially peaked after details of Abu Ali al-Haritihi's killing were revealed in 2002. However, it did not reach its zenith until America invaded Iraq in 2003. When Salih remained firmly in alliance with the United States as American ground

[16] "What Went Wrong?," *Yemen Times*, December 24, 2001.

troops entered Baghdad in April 2003, and then stood shoulder-to-shoulder with President Bush as a "good Muslim" ally at a June 2004 G-8 summit meeting on Sea Island, Georgia, he knowingly loosened the already shaky foundations of his regime.

There is little doubt that the American invasion of Iraq is what finally caused the pressure cooker of Yemeni politics to explode. The vast majority of citizens considered it intolerable for their president to stand close to America at a time when U.S. soldiers occupied a fellow Arab Muslim country, especially when America's president lauded Israeli prime minister Ariel Sharon as a "man of peace" while Israel's forces reoccupied the West Bank and Gaza, continuing decades-long oppression of Palestinians. The public outrage unleashed in Yemen by American and Israeli military actions between 2001 and 2003, especially America's "shock and awe" bombing campaign in Baghdad, was unprecedented. When the first U.S. bombs fell on Baghdad on March 21, 2003, the streets of Sanaa witnessed waves of raw anger against the governments of America, Britain, and Israel. Tens of thousands of people marched on the American and British embassies, throwing stones, setting fires, and causing other vandalism.[17]

If President Salih had not called upon his security forces to defend western embassies, resorting to live ammunition in the end, then thousands of people may have climbed the embassy fences, stormed the buildings, and taken American and British hostages. At least four protesters were killed, and hundreds of others were injured and arrested. Although Jordan, Egypt, Pakistan, and Indonesia also witnessed anti-American protests on the same day, there was no other place in the Arab and Muslim worlds (except Iraq, Afghanistan, and Palestine) that witnessed as much bloodshed as Yemen. Over the following days, President Salih faced a roaring domestic firestorm as religious clerics at mosques across the country condemned him for killing citizens in the capital's streets.

At the famous Grand Mosque in the walled Old City of Sanaa, one of the oldest mosques in the world, clerics preached regular sermons against America, condemning the United States in fiery language in late March and April 2003. Later they also expressed criticism of the Yemeni president, calling his regime illegitimate as long as it stood with America against Iraq. These were words of rebellion that President Salih could not tolerate. Officers in Salih's political security typically operate by covert means with their ears to the ground, listening for any expression of dissent in private *qat*-sessions or other closed meetings. They are quick to harass anyone

---

[17] "It's War," *Yemen Times*, March 24, 2003.

who dares to hint of possible rebellion against the government. But in the spring and summer of 2003, there was no need for covert activities to catch hints of rebellion in Yemen. Rebellion was advocated openly in public. When political security officers began removing the leaders of mosques in Sanaa and other cities in August 2003, this created fertile ground for even greater political opposition in the future.[18]

Given the flood of rumors circulating around American, British, and Israeli actions in Iraq, Palestine, Afghanistan, and Pakistan, the majority of Yemenis perceived a "Western Zionist crusade" against Muslim interests. For the remainder of 2003, and throughout 2004 and 2005, many religious leaders in mosques throughout Yemen invoked *jihad* against the combined forces of the United States, Britain, and Israel.[19] Over a three-year span, there were hundreds, if not thousands of Yemenis who traveled to Iraq, primarily via Syria, to join the growing insurgency against U.S. occupation forces. Even female students signed up at their universities to become suicide bombers in Iraq.[20] Some of the Yemenis who actually ventured to Iraq did serve as suicide bombers and saboteurs for Abu Mussab al-Zarqawi's al-Qaeda cells. At this time, Yemeni youth identified with al-Qaeda and especially Osama Bin Laden, who always emphasized his Yemeni ancestry.

A significant percentage of Bin Laden's closest associates came from Yemen. The core leadership of al-Qaeda was Arab, even though its main base of operation had been Afghanistan. The organization was neither an Afghani nor a Pakistani creation, but distinctly Arab from the Arabian peninsula with close association to Egyptian Islamic Jihad leaders like Ayman al-Zawahiri. Much is made of Osama Bin Laden's connection to Saudi Arabia, since he was born there in 1957. But his father was a Hadrami from the eastern region of Yemen. In 1931, Muhammad Bin Laden arrived in Saudi Arabia as a young man with an entrepreneurial spirit. He built a business empire that would be worth billions of dollars to his sons. While

---

[18] "Tensions Rise Between GPC and Islah," *Yemen Times*, August 21, 2003. The Arabic-language party newspaper of the Union of Yemeni Popular Forces, *al-Shoura*, offered the best news coverage of the government's dismissal of preachers at Sanaa's mosques. This newspaper is not archived on the internet.

[19] Muhammad al-Qadhi, "Jihad Calls," *Yemen Times*, March 31, 2003. The political situation in Yemen was inflamed the week before the war started, when Shaykh al-Ahmar called for an obligatory *jihad (fard 'ayn)* to resist the U.S. attack on Iraq. *Al-Ayyam*, March 16, 2003, #3815; p. 1.

[20] "Women Stand in Jihad's Line," *Yemen Times*, March 31, 2003. The article described twenty young women carrying coffins marked with red paint, and quoted one student saying "I am prepared to go and perform martyrdom. ... I am prepared for death."

Osama grew up with close affiliation to the Saudi kingdom, he developed over time stronger personal ties to his father's ancestral homeland.

Osama Bin Laden and members of other wealthy Hadrami business families, who live in Saudi Arabia, are not original members of Saudi society. They are outsiders without status in the prevailing tribal order of the Najd region around the capital Riyadh in north-central Saudi Arabia. This is an important point about Osama Bin Laden's role in the formation of al-Qaeda. Osama particularly experienced his status as an outsider in Saudi Arabia when he opposed the kingdom's alliance with the United States during the first Gulf War to liberate Kuwait. In the fall of 1990, the young Osama lobbied the monarchy, and protested its invitation for American troops to enter the country and operate at bases near the Kuwait border. When Osama tried to mobilize radical Islamist opposition, the Saudi king restricted his activities. He left the country in 1991, and the king later revoked his citizenship.

Earlier in the fall of 1990, it is important to recall that the Saudi monarchy expelled nearly one million Yemeni migrant workers because the Yemeni government had also opposed the American-led coalition to remove Iraqi troops from Kuwait. At the time, Yemen held one of the ten rotating seats on the UN Security Council. Thus, its government's opposition to American war plans in early 1991 carried a high profile on the world stage, causing worse ramifications in Yemeni-American and Yemeni-Saudi relations. Crucially, Osama Bin Laden's outsider status in Saudi Arabia was reenforced simultaneously with several hundred thousand Yemeni citizens because of the coincidence of their expulsions from the oil-rich kingdom. This helped Bin Laden's ability to recruit among Yemen's wider population.

During al-Qaeda's early development in the 1990s, Yemenis volunteered with the organization as often as Saudi citizens, if not more frequently. The same was true of the anti-Soviet jihad in Afghanistan during the 1980s when Yemenis joined the mujahideen networks that were funded by the US and Saudi governments. When Osama Bin Laden transformed these networks into *al-Qaeda* ("the base," in the term's military sense), its base of support among Yemenis remained high. Many of Bin Laden's closest, most trusted assistants were Yemenis.[21] Furthermore, what some analysts consider

---

[21] For example, Nasir al-Wahayshi was with Bin Laden in Afghanistan on 9/11. He later emerged as the head of al-Qaeda on the Arabian Peninsula (AQAP) when this regional branch materialized in Yemen in January 2009. The best resource on AQAP's formation is Gregory Johnsen's blog with Brian O'Neill, *Waq al-Waq*, Islam and Insurgency in Yemen blogspot; and his many other publications including a book expected in 2012. A second key Yemeni member of al-Qaeda was Nasir (Abu Jandal) al-Bahri, Bin Laden's personal

al-Qaeda's first terrorist attack was the bombing of two tourist hotels in Aden in December 1992.

Before one of America's Blackhawk helicopters was shot down over the angry streets of Mogadishu, Somalia in 1993 or Americans were attacked in Riyadh, Saudi Arabia in 1995, and long before the bombing of the U.S. embassies in Kenya and Tanzania in 1998, there were the attacks on Aden's beach resorts where U.S. military servicemen had stayed in transit to and from Somalia. These attacks were carried out by individuals later associated with the Aden-Abyan Islamic Army. They missed their intended target because the U.S. military had stopped using the tourist facility the previous week. The only people killed were a European tourist and a local hotel staff member. The bomber mistook the European for an American soldier. Around the same time in 1992, Osama Bin Laden assisted other militant activities in Yemen, such as the assassination of numerous YSP officials.

Bin Laden funneled money into united Yemen to finance operations that were intended to ensure the ouster of the Yemeni Socialist Party. The head of the YSP, and vice president of the united Republic of Yemen, Ali Salem al-Bid, was from the same province as Bin Laden's father. Radical Islamists desperately wanted al-Bid and other YSP officials dead because of the roles they had played in south Yemen, during the late 1960s and early 1970s, when the ruling sultans and emirs were driven from the country. Many south Yemeni exiles, including al-Qaeda associates of Bin Laden, lived in Saudi Arabia and other countries on the Arabian peninsula during these decades. They bore deep grudges against southern YSP leaders, and many who joined the anti-Soviet mujahideen in Afghanistan during the 1980s returned to united Yemen in the 1990s intending to continue fighting Marxists in their own country.

When Osama Bin Laden first lived in exile in Sudan during the early 1990s, he supported the jihadis of Yemen with financing and manpower. This fact is worth knowing today, in order to understand political dynamics in the country. After Yemeni unity, there was clearly an antigovernment element inside local al-Qaeda groups that mirrored social, economic, and political frustrations among Yemen's religious conservatives. Both resented the continued presence of Marxist leaders inside the country.

bodyguard and director of al-Qaeda's guest house in Pakistan through which many Arab fighters transited to Afghanistan, including most of the 9/11 hijackers. On 9/11, al-Bahri was held in jail in Sanaa, and soon afterward interrogated by FBI officials who gained valuable intelligence about al-Qaeda's locations in Afghanistan before the U.S. invasion in October 2001. Nasir al-Bahri tells his story in the fascinating P.O.V. documentary, "The Oath," directed by Laura Poitras, and released on DVD by Zeitgeist Films in 2010.

Since Osama Bin Laden was expelled from Saudi Arabia simultaneously with Yemen's migrant workers in 1990–1991, there was also a shared animosity toward the Saudi monarchy. Just as Bin Laden opposed the political status quo on the Arabian peninsula – a status quo long defined by America's alliance with Saudi kings, most Yemenis shared the same sentiment. Yemenis have a love-hate relationship with Saudi Arabia. As devout Muslims, they turn in prayer on a daily basis toward Mecca. But they are also proud inheritors of an ancient civilization, once more wealthy and influential than any part of the Arabian peninsula. For this reason, Yemenis do not consider themselves beneath the Saudis even though their standard of living is lower.

In the twentieth century, Yemen was largely excluded from the great oil rush in Saudi Arabia and neighboring countries. Its population's standard of living declined relative to its neighbors. Former small towns on the Arab peninsula such as Riyadh, Dubai, and Kuwait City became sprawling urban centers with glass skyscrapers housing offices of major players in international commerce. Older and far larger centers of commerce in Yemen lagged behind, creating deep resentments about the imbalance of oil-financed development during the century of American dominance in world affairs and Saudi Arabian dominance in regional affairs. For all of these reasons, the social, economic, and political outlook of many Yemenis in the 1990s was similar to Osama Bin Laden's own outlook. The grievances and resentments motivating followers of al-Qaeda flourished inside Yemen.

Osama Bin Laden grew up with none of the privations experienced by Yemen's population. His father emigrated from the country as a poor man in the middle 1920s. After arriving in Saudi Arabia, he was fortunate to prosper from the kingdom's rapid economic growth once oil was discovered in the 1930s. Muhammad Bin Laden became the trusted building contractor of Saudi King Abd al-Aziz during the early boom years. Thus young Osama grew up in the 1960s and 1970s surrounded by wealth. During his time with the Afghan mujahideen in the 1980s, however, Osama developed an austere lifestyle that allowed him to identify with recruits from poor countries like Yemen and Somalia, Sudan and Egypt. When he proceeded to build al-Qaeda in the 1990s, he could effectively tap the grievances and resentments of these men. Before 9/11, when al-Qaeda's grand terror scheme required Saudi passport holders, who could more easily enter the United States to help hijack passenger airplanes, Osama Bin Laden looked to recruit men from a region of Saudi Arabia close to the Yemeni border, called 'Asir.

There are two districts in 'Asir, called Jizan and Najran, that were historically part of Yemen. Saudi King Abd al-Aziz seized these districts in the late 1920s and early 1930s, when he sought to continue expanding his territory following the first World War.[22] The residents of 'Asir sit at the bottom of the Saudi tribal hierarchy. They are generally poorer than citizens in the rest of the country, so many share the viewpoints of Yemenis across the border. Thus, even though Bin Laden recruited a team of hijackers from Saudi Arabia, many of the men on this team shared ancestral connections to Yemen. In the early 2000s, Yemen and its border region with Saudi Arabia provided fertile ground for al-Qaeda recruiters looking for young men to answer the call for *jihad*. This was especially true as the United States prepared to invade Iraq. The war in Iraq drew al-Qaeda militants away from Yemen, at least in the short term. Later in the decade, they would bring greater violence back to the country. Meanwhile, the forces destabilizing the country came from other domestic trouble spots.

REGIME POLITICS IN THE MID-2000S

Following Yemen's first local elections in February 2001, and the simultaneous constitutional referendum, President Salih rearranged the deck chairs of his government by appointing a new southern prime minister. One of the constitutional amendments in 2001 extended the term of president from five to seven years, and the term of parliament from four to six years. This allowed Salih to avoid holding the next parliamentary election until 2003, and he did not have to face reelection as president until 2006. The newly appointed prime minister was Abd al-Qader Ba Jamal, another Hadrami like Dr. Fareg Ben Ghanem. Unlike Dr. Ben Ghanem, Ba Jamal was a GPC insider who was more amenable to working within the regime's established patronage system. He previously served as minister of planning, and then foreign minister in the last half of the 1990s.

Ba Jamal's rise to the office of prime minister was another attempt by President Salih to create the appearance of north-south power sharing. But Ba Jamal did not truly represent the interests of the southern people. In Hadramaut and other southern provinces, Ba Jamal was neither as popular, nor as respected as Dr. Ben Ghanem. Most south Yemenis regarded Ba Jamal as a vain, verbose man, who preferred talking about his own accomplishments rather than the dire social and economic needs of the

---

[22] Dresch, 2000, pp. 30–35. The districts of 'Asir remained disputed territory until a Saudi-Yemeni treaty formalized the international border in 2000.

people. As prime minister, Ba Jamal was later suspected of embezzling millions of dollars to purchase an expensive home in London, where he retired soon after leaving government in 2007. The fact Ba Jamal could serve six years in the prime minister's office, while Dr. Ben Ghanem resigned after less than a year, shows that President Salih found it easier to work with individuals who were eager to serve their personal interests more than the public good. At the same time, corrupt and self-serving individuals like Ba Jamal found it easier to work with President Salih.

In late April 2003, during the first month of the U.S. military occupation of Iraq, the Republic of Yemen prepared its third parliamentary election. Despite severe international and national tensions at the time, the political campaigning and voting went forward as planned. Once again, there was violence in some electoral districts. But the disruptions were not as bad as the local elections in 2001. This was likely because public attention was absorbed by the dramatic events taking place in Iraq. The opposition parties, including Islah and the YSP, attempted to coordinate their campaigns against the GPC. Al-Ahmar had gradually learned that it was pointless to challenge Salih as head of a single opposition party. He needed partners in a stronger opposition coalition. Jarallah Omar had been the lead socialist interlocutor with Shaykh Abdallah's party until his assassination at the Islah conference hall in December 2002.

After the 1994 civil war, Jarallah Omar was one of the few YSP leaders who continued living inside Yemen. He was originally from north Yemen, and not associated with the southern secessionist effort. This made it easier for him to begin a dialogue with Islah party officials six years later. Once President Salih became aware of the ongoing talks between Islah and the socialists, he looked for ways to upset their chances of reconciliation. For instance, he chose in 2000 to rescind the earlier treason convictions against more than a dozen south Yemeni socialist leaders, and encouraged these men to return to the country. Former vice president Ali Salem al-Bid and prime minister Haider al-Attas remained outside the country. But Salem Salih Muhammad, al-Bid's former associate on the unity government's five-member presidential council, returned in January 2001, as did the former YSP speaker of parliament, Yasin Said Numan.

Local political observers speculated that President Salih's rehabilitation of old southern YSP enemies was a typical divide and rule tactic, pitting rival opposition factions against each other. Salih's earlier dual southern strategy, in which he sought to counter the Ali Nasir Muhammad group with traditional tribal leaders from the south, had already broken down. By driving a deeper wedge between northern and southern YSP leaders, he might find another means of keeping the opposition off balance. What happened instead is that Islah, the YSP, and other opposition parties took advantage of the president's unpopularity, due to his alliance with America in the "war on terrorism," and formalized their political reconciliation. This led to the creation of a broader anti-GPC coalition known as the Joint Meeting Parties (JMP).

Although Shaykh Abdallah and Islah were able to outmaneuver President Salih in forming a larger opposition bloc, the Islamic party's ideological differences with the socialists prevented them from effectively coordinating their 2003 electoral campaign, in order to compete against the ruling party's well-oiled political machine. As a result, the president's GPC party swept the vote by another landslide margin, winning just over 75 percent of the new parliamentary seats. The voting process was yet again marred by fraud, ballot stuffing, and stolen ballot boxes. Thus the official results were hardly deemed reliable.[23] Nearly 10 percent of electoral districts cancelled ballot counting because the level of fraudulent practices was so high. The primary problem existed in the Supreme Commission for Elections and Referendum (SCER), which operated under the GPC's control. In the end, the GPC won 226 of 301 seats in parliament. Islah won forty-seven seats; the YSP won seven seats; independent candidates and small parties combined to win nineteen seats; and two seats required a revote. Greater unity among JMP party members would happen later in the decade.

When the new parliament met in early June, a tribal group brought a sacrificial bull to the assembly grounds where they intended to settle a long standing dispute. Somehow the bull got loose, rampaged through the crowd, and gored four people.[24] Those in attendance took the accident as a bad omen of the country's future. The mood in the country was already dark because of the mysterious death of the deputy head of the GPC, Yahya al-Mutawakkil, in a car accident on January 13, 2003. From a traditional Zaydi ruling class family, al-Mutawakkil was a true hero of the 1960s revolution who fought for the new republic. A highly respected military officer, ambassador, and civil servant with decades of experience, he was the minister of interior in 1994 who tried but failed to rearm southern police officers after the civil war. Along with Dr. Abd al-Karim al-Iryani, he was one of the GPC's most prominent moderate, secular officials with close ties to America. In 2002, he fumed at the actions of Paul Wolfowitz because he

[23] Carapico, 2003. For a comprehensive analysis in Arabic, Dr. Muhammad al-Mikhlafi is the best source. al-Mikhlafi, 1999.

[24] Aref al-Maqtari, "Sacrificial Bull Rampages Through Parliamentary Compound, Injures 4," *Yemen Observer*, June 7, 2003.

foresaw the violence and instability that was unleashed after Wolfowitz revealed the truth behind the American drone missile attack in Marib.

In Yemen, there is a history of suspicious automobile and aircraft accidents taking the lives of influential political and military figures. Many observers speculated that Yahya al-Mutawakkil's death was arranged by unknown persons inside the regime. One and a half years later on November 17, 2004, a close associate of al-Mutawakkil, General Mujahid Abu Shawarib, died in another suspicious car crash near his home in Hajja province. The general was a powerful Hashid tribal shaykh married to a sister of Shaykh Abdallah. When President Salih first came to power in 1978, both the general and al-Mutawakkil were considered more capable candidates for the presidency. They had vastly more experience and stature, but decided to allow the younger Ali Abdallah Salih to play the lead role, while they operated behind the scenes. As Salih's family and clan from Sanhan acquired greater power and wealth, especially after 1994, al-Mutawakkil and Abu Shawarib lost their ability to direct politics in the country. Their mysterious deaths removed two of the primary obstacles to continued Salih family rule. At the same time, there were signs of division within the president's family and Sanhan clan.

Nervousness in Sanaa about dangerous rivalries inside President Salih's family and clan first arose in the late 1990s. At this time, the president began preparing a high profile role in government for his son, Ahmad, who was clearly being groomed to succeed his father. As early as 1996, there were rumors of violent confrontations inside the family when the president ordered his half brother, Ali Salih al-Ahmar commander of the Republican Guards, to step down in order for Ahmad Salih to replace him.[25] The commander's son, a nephew of the president and cousin of Ahmad, was alleged to have taken grave offense at how his father was treated. According to rumors, the nephew either threatened to kill the president, or attempted to kill him, with a weapon drawn. This nephew was never again seen in public. His father, the former commander of the Republican Guards, was alleged to have suffered an emotional breakdown. A short time later, Ahmad Salih emerged as the new commander of the Republican Guards, and his cousins, Yahya and Ammar, also began representing the family's younger generation in key command posts of central security and national security, respectively.

---

[25] Interview with a knowledgeable public official in Sanaa who spoke of an incident that was rumored to have taken place at the republican palace in the spring or summer of 1996; November 1996. This source preferred to remain anonymous.

More rumors of murderous intrigue circulated in August 1999 when President Salih's maternal uncle, Muhammad Ismail, died in a suspicious helicopter incident in Hadramaut. General Ismail was the long-serving regional military commander in Hadramaut whose actions after the 1994 civil war generated a backlash in the eastern region. The official story of the 1999 incident was that Ismail's army helicopter crashed due to poor visibility in desert terrain, killing him, another general, three colonels, and a dozen soldiers.[26] Some political observers wondered if local government opponents shot down the helicopter because of earlier disturbances in Hadramaut. Other observers speculated the helicopter had been sabotaged, perhaps by a bomb placed on board, since Ismail and his side of the family were obstacles standing in the way of President Salih's ability to pass the torch of leadership to his son. Ali Abdallah Salih rose to power in 1978 amidst deadly conspiracies that killed two former presidents. It appeared that he was paving the way for his son to become president in similar circumstances.

One year after the 2003 election, Salih's government suspended many of its economic reform efforts. During Prime Minister Ba Jamal's tenure, levels of corruption rose dramatically within the state bureaucracy. Local journalists who wrote about corruption in state institutions risked abduction and assault, as happened to the prominent journalist Jamal Amir in August 2005.[27] Later the same year, the World Bank suspended part of its aid program due to escalating complaints about the country. For the same reason, the United States removed Yemen from its Millennium Challenge program. Around this time, Dr. Robert Burrowes of the University of Washington, an American political scientist who had long admired President Salih as founder of the GPC, began describing the government of Yemen as a "kleptocracy."[28] Gradually, as more citizens considered President Salih's rule illegitimate, conditions in various regions of the country became ripe for rebellion. To the surprise of many inside and outside Yemen, the

---

[26] "Some 17, Including Two High-ranking Yemeni Army Officers, Killed in Plane Crash," arabicnews.com, August 16, 1999.

[27] "Yemen: Harassment of journalists must stop," Amnesty International, August 26 2005. Amnesty International's public complaint stated that Amer was arrested outside his home, driven to a remote location, beaten, and threatened with death, after he published news stories detailing corruption at top levels of Salih's regime.

[28] Dr. Robert Burrowes previously considered President Salih a successful nation builder who was responsible for developing democratic institutions and a constitutional foundation for the state. However, Burrowes changed his views during the mid-2000s. By "kleptocracy," Burrowes meant that President Salih, his family and tribal allies, were "stripping the country of its modest national wealth." Burrowes and Kasper, 2007.

region that first erupted in open rebellion was neither in the south nor in the east, but north of Sanaa inside the highland province of Saʿda.

THE REBELLION OF AL-HUTHI IN SAʿDA

The most volatile source of rebellion in Yemen during the mid-2000s came from the northwest province of Saʿda, deep in the heart of traditional Zaydi lands. A few miles southeast of Zaydism's old religious and political capital, which is located inside the massive mud-brick walls surrounding the historic square-mile city of Saʿda, the son of a Zaydi cleric launched an anachronistic and equally improbable drive to overthrow Salih's government in Sanaa. The leader was a former member of parliament named Husayn al-Huthi, son of an elderly Zaydi cleric, Badr al-Din al-Huthi, who was widely consulted on Zaydi religious law in Saʿda province.

During the last half of the 1980s, the family of al-Huthi and other traditional Zaydi clerics had been contacted by secular GPC officials concerned about the spread of Saudi-inspired *Salafi* groups in Saʿda and neighboring regions. In Arabic, the term *Salafi* refers to the "ancestors," or early followers of Islam, during the time of the prophet Muhammad. Like the state-sponsored al-Wahhabi clerics in Saudi Arabia, Yemen's *Salafi* advocate a return to original "pure" practices of Islam. They receive financial support

PHOTO 16. Husayn ibn Badr al-Din al-Huthi, member of 1993 parliament

from Saudi Arabia, where puritanical al-Wahhabi clerics draw massive government payouts from the kingdom's annual budget. Before Yemen's national unification, a few GPC officials became interested in blocking the spread of *Salafism*. They thought Badr al-Din al-Huthi's traditional Zaydi followers could be of assistance along the border with Saudi Arabia.

Beginning in the 1980s, a *Salafi* cleric named Muqbil Hadi al-Wadei, who died in 2002, sponsored religious training schools in Sa'da and other northwestern provinces. His main facility was called the Dammaj Center, where he instructed local youth to reject Zaydism and follow the original practices of Islam from the seventh century C.E. In the 1990s, students of the Dammaj Center vandalized Zaydi mosques, and the shrine tombs of famous Zaydi religious leaders. Across al-Wahhabi history since the eighteenth century, its clerics often ordered believers to attack the mosques and shrines of Shia Muslims in north Arabian areas along the Persian Gulf. Occasionally they raided deep into Iraqi territory, vandalizing the great Shia mosques of Karbala and al-Najaf. Yemen was largely spared this kind of sectarian violence until the early twentieth century. It was revived in the 1980s and 1990s with the spread of Muqbil's *Salafi* schools.

The zeal of Muqbil Hadi al-Wadei gravely concerned the senior Badr al-Din al-Huthi in Sa'da. It also concerned secular-minded officials in the GPC. Thus the family of al-Huthi and leaders of the GPC found reason to collaborate around the time of Yemeni unity. After unification in 1990, al-Huthi and other families formed a Zaydi religious party called *Hizb al-Haqq* (Party of Truth/Justice), which received encouragement, if not outright financial support from a few officials in the GPC. Hizb al-Haqq competed openly against the larger Islamic party, Islah, which was more popular among *Salafis*. During the political infighting and civil war in Yemen in 1993 and 1994, the younger Husayn al-Huthi refused to support the GPC's alliance with Islah against YSP socialists. For political reasons, Husayn al-Huthi briefly fled to Syria.[29] After returning to Yemen later in the 1990s, he formed a new, more radical youth movement in Sa'da with summer religious training camps.

The new movement was called "believing youth" (*al-shabab al-mu'min*). The summer camps focused primarily on giving young boys a greater appreciation of Zaydi beliefs and customs.[30] Some political analysts claim

[29] Paula Mejia and Atef Alshaer, "What it Means to be a Huthi," *Yemen Post* online, October 10, 2009.
[30] Hakim al-Masmari, "Muhammad Yahya Ezani, Founder of the Believing Youth," *Yemen Post* online, November 9, 2009.

that Husayn al-Huthi was inspired, during his exile in Syria, by the mass mobilization programs of northern Shia parties like Hizbullah in Lebanon, and perhaps also Iran's Shia regime. Others claim that he modeled his new movement after the Taliban regime in Afghanistan, where Pashtun Sunni leaders also started by offering religious training for young students (the *taliban; tullab*, plural). Whatever the influences on Husayn al-Huthi, he continued to find support among GPC officials until the events of 9/11. Afterward, the leader of the youth movement began preaching rebellion against President Salih's alliance with America. Later he advised his followers to stop paying traditional *zakat* taxes to the state, and instead give *zakat* to the Huthi-led movement.

The story told of Husayn al-Huthi's rebellion in Sa'da province begins in January 2002, when the young Zaydi leader encouraged his followers to shout "God is Great! Death to America and Israel!" at one of his religious schools.[31] This slogan had been commonly used for decades by Shia fundamentalist groups like Hizbullah in Lebanon and Iran's revolutionary regime. According to the story told about Husayn al-Huthi, his followers hesitated to shout the slogan due its obvious association with Hizbullah and Iran. Husayn al-Huthi continued shouting the slogan, over and over, with a louder voice, "Death to America and Israel!" He refused to stop, and then led his followers outside where they continued shouting until the slogan gradually faded away, as each person returned home. From this moment in January 2002, the Huthi rebellion became associated with shouting the slogan: "Death to America and Israel!" It also appeared on posters and banners carried by al-Huthi followers.

Gradually in late 2002 and early 2003, the leaders of other Zaydi mosques began using the same slogan. At the time of the U.S. invasion of Iraq, the slogan could even be heard rising from the Grand Mosque in old Sanaa: "Death to America and Israel!" This was one of the reasons why President Salih clamped down, and removed some mosque leaders after large demonstrations in the streets of the capital. The regime became gravely concerned that the slogan would galvanize mass opposition across the country. In many areas of the highland region, it captured the mood of people, and threatened to create popular religious forces beyond the Salih family's control. President Salih's family background is Zaydi like all highland tribesmen in Hashid and Bakil. But Salih's politics were decisively republican, not theocratic. His regime upheld the political principles of the 1962 revolution

---

[31] Khaled Fattah, "Yemen: A Slogan and Six Wars," *Asia Times*, October 9, 2009.

that overthrew the last Zaydi imamate. Thus, he and his family had no legitimacy as upholders of Zaydism.

The spread of "Death to America and Israel!" chants after March 2003 brought greater prominence to Husayn al-Huthi among highland groups opposed to America's war on Iraq. It also brought his name to the attention of political security officers inside the regime, especially when police discovered that Husayn was dissuading people from paying taxes to the state. In June 2004, there was a bloody clash in Sa'da between government forces and militia formed by al-Huthi's followers. More than twenty were killed, mainly on the government's side.[32] Local security forces were unable to arrest al-Huthi, so the Yemeni army began to pursue him with greater determination to take him dead or alive. In September 2004, troops cornered Husayn al-Huthi with a few of his followers in a remote mountainous region of Sa'da province. These troops targeted the group with heavy artillery, killing the young Zaydi leader in a massive bombardment.[33] In death, Husayn al-Huthi became a martyr with far more influence on his followers. This greatly advanced the cause of militant resistance to Salih's regime.

Over the following years, the religious movement engaged government armed forces in running battles on an annual basis. Commentators began referring to the Huthi war, or "war in Sa'da," as if it involved regular rounds of a boxing match.[34] Round One began in 2004. Round Two came in 2005, when fighting spread as government forces confronted tribal militias sympathetic with al-Huthi's movement, especially among the Bakil tribes of Sa'da and neighboring areas of al-Jawf province. Thereafter, the fight took on the characteristics of tribal warfare because hundreds of tribesmen sought revenge for earlier deaths of their kinsmen. On some occasions, groups allied with al-Huthi rebels initiated battles, and government forces were placed on the defensive. On other occasions, the Yemeni army pursued aggressive military campaigns to wipe out al-Huthi rebels.

In Yemen, the assumption among most political observers is that the Sa'da war dragged on for so long due to internal divisions inside Salih's regime. The fighting clearly involved more than a defense of the "believing youth" group, or the legacy of Husayn al-Huthi. There are well-known Yemeni arms merchants with strong ties to the government who profited

---

[32] Boucek, 2010.

[33] Mohammed bin Sallam, "Fighting against al-Huthi insurgency: More dead and wounded," *Yemen Times*, September 6, 2004.

[34] Boucek, 2010; p. 44 ff.

by selling weapons to both sides of the conflict. These arms merchants were threatened with arrest, but they had influential contacts inside the regime who protected them. Many Yemenis speculated there was a proxy war being fought between military elements aligned with General Ali Muhsin, who controlled the army's first artillery brigade in the north-western highlands, and other elements of the regime sympathetic with efforts to block the spread of *Salafism* or reduce the power of General Ali Muhsin.

Since Ali Muhsin was the most prominent member of the regime to be associated with the *Salafi* trend of Sunni fundamentalism in Yemen, and since this trend had been opposed in the 1980s by influential GPC members like the late Yahya al-Mutawakkil and Mujahid Abu Shawarib, it made sense that a proxy war could be fought between rival powers inside the regime. The mysterious deaths of al-Mutawakkil and Abu Shawarib in car accidents one year apart, the first before, and the second shortly after Husayn al-Huthi's martyrdom in September 2004, lend further credence to the idea of an intra-regime proxy war in Sa'da. Later in the decade, there were occasional confrontations between General Ali Muhsin's brigade and Republican Guard forces under the command of President Salih's son, Ahmad. When the Wikileaks website began releasing online copies of U.S. diplomatic cables in 2010, one document from the U.S. embassy in Riyadh revealed information about an incredible plot to kill General Ali Muhsin.

In 2009, the Huthi war briefly spilled across the border with Saudi Arabia when Yemeni armed forces sought to entrap rebel fighters from two sides. After al-Huthi militia fired artillery at positions inside Saudi Arabia, the Saudi air force began bombing al-Huthi targets in Yemen. The Wikileaks document reported that Saudi officials discovered President Salih had given them ground coordinates to target in Sa'da province, which turned out to be the location of General Ali Muhsin's command center just outside the area of fighting.[35] An accidental bombing was allegedly averted when Saudi pilots suspected something was wrong with instructions to hit the site. According to the document released by Wikileaks, Saudi officials surmised reckless intentions were behind this close call. They concluded that President Salih wanted General Ali Muhsin dead, and would have been happy to blame his death on a stray Saudi missile.

[35] Wikileaks, "Saudi Arabia: Renewed Assurances on Satellite Imagery," 10RIYADH159, February 7, 2010.

POLITICS AS USUAL

Yemen celebrated its fifteenth anniversary of national unity on May 22, 2005. For the first time, a site in Hadramaut was chosen for the official celebrations attended by President Salih and other members of his GPC-led government. In the seaside provincial capital al-Mukalla, the ruling party wanted to showcase the completion of a large public works project in the city's western al-Dees neighborhood, thus strengthening unionist sentiment in the eastern region. Because the central government depends on petroleum resources in Hadramaut and neighboring Shabwa province for most of its revenues, President Salih recognized the need to boost local support while maintaining at least the appearance of north-south, east-west power sharing with Hadrami prime minister Abd al-Qadr Ba Jamal standing by his side. The choice to mark the anniversary of unity upon the completion of a government project designed to resolve a terrible sewage problem in al-Mukalla was meant to dispel local impressions of political neglect. It was also meant to challenge wider public opinion that national revenues primarily served Salih's family and other political elites in Sanaa.

Generally speaking, residents of Hadramaut saw greater public works projects in the 1990s and 2000s than any other area of the country, except the national capital. Salih's regime clearly strived to serve public interests in Hadramaut, and coordinate business with wealthy Hadrami merchant families. Just three years before the 2005 anniversary celebration, a group of young businessmen at al-Mukalla's chamber of commerce reported feeling optimistic about their chances to expand the local economy through an upcoming trade mission to the UAE and other Arab Gulf countries.[36] Hadrami merchants have strong connections to countries in the Gulf Cooperation Council (GCC), as well as countries in southeast Asia. Thus, they are well positioned to benefit from any trade opportunities. Yet an older group of officials at al-Mukalla's chamber of commerce did not share the enthusiasm of their sons.[37] They spoke from experience about the risks and uncertainties in Yemen's future.

In 2005, the economy in most Yemeni provinces remained in critical condition. The national economy never fully recovered from its crisis in the 1990s, and regular unemployment problems meant severe hardship for

---

[36] Interview with a group of young men at the Hadramaut Chamber of Commerce in al-Mukalla; July 2002.

[37] Interview at a *qat*-session in a private home with fathers of the young businessmen cited above; July 2002.

most families. Two months after the anniversary celebration of national unity in al-Mukalla, violent riots erupted in many cities and towns, including the capital Sanaa, when the government attempted to lift subsidies on basic consumer goods in July. Riots had occurred for similar reasons in the past, but this violence was far more severe. The rioting in Sanaa lasted a few days, and President Salih was forced to implement martial law.[38] He ordered armored vehicles to patrol city streets until there was calm. Dozens of citizens were killed, and hundreds more injured and arrested.

These clashes in the streets of Sanaa were worse than the street clashes in March 2003 at the start of the U.S. invasion of Iraq. Given the wider political context in July 2005 with an ongoing rebellion by al-Huthi supporters in Sa'da, rumors circulated of a military coup in the capital. Some observers speculated that rioters turned violent with such force because they thought Salih's regime was on the verge of collapsing. The intensity of what happened in 2005 was due to the people's eagerness for a change in regime nearly six years before the Arab world's mass uprisings in January 2011. Citizens would have a chance to vote Salih out of office the next year, when the president was forced to stand for reelection in September 2006. But few Yemenis had any trust in the electoral process.

In the 2006 presidential campaign, Islah, the YSP, and other opposition parties were better prepared to unite under the banner of the new Joint Meeting Parties (JMP) coalition. In parliament, members of the JMP nominated a single candidate to compete against President Salih. They chose Faisal Ben Shamlan, the independent politician who briefly served as oil minister in 1994–1995, and helped direct the Public Forum for Sons of the Southern and Eastern Provinces in Ramadan 2001–2002. Ben Shamlan was acceptable to northern and southern Islah supporters in 2006, as well as members of the YSP, because he was widely regarded as a fair-minded politician with a clean reputation. During the political campaign, Ben Shamlan's public rallies drew large crowds in the hundreds of thousands.[39] Across southern provinces he obviously had a large following, especially in his native Hadramaut, and in Aden where he lived for many years. But large numbers in Taiz, al-Hudayda, and Sanaa, even inside Amran and other northwestern provinces, began to express enthusiastic support for his campaign in the summer of 2006.

---

[38] "Yemeni Cities on Alert," *Yemen Times*, July 25, 2005.
[39] "Yemeni president faces his first real challenger in elections Wednesday," *International Herald Tribune*, September 18, 2006.

For a brief time, it appeared Yemenis would finally have a genuinely competitive electoral race, similar to the first parliamentary election in 1993. At an outdoor rally in Amran on September 5, two weeks before the election, Hamid al-Ahmar, son of Hashid's paramount shaykh and a successful businessman within the Islah party, gave a rousing introduction for Bin Shamlan in front of a large audience. The crowd responded with such exuberance that the demonstration of support "frightened Salih and openly raised the question of violence on the street if Bin Shamlan were to win."[40] Days after the Amran rally, President Salih would resort to every means possible to ensure the success of his candidacy.

The president contacted many influential religious and tribal shaykhs, appealing for their support. The old Islah cleric, Shaykh Abd al-Majid al-Zindani, was persuaded to break his commitment to the JMP candidate. Soon al-Zindani appeared at rallies calling on his followers to vote for Salih and the GPC. Even Shaykh Abdallah al-Ahmar, Hamid's father, came out in support of Salih.[41] In a field study during the 2006 elections, which also included a vote for the second term of local councils, American researcher April Longley found that most businessmen in the highland region feared incurring financial costs if they supported the JMP candidate.[42] The president's campaign resorted to the usual bribery and coercion, and even used a few new dirty tricks.

GPC campaign managers planted a security officer with former ties to al-Qaeda among a group of body guards working for Bin Shamlan, and then photographed the man standing near the JMP candidate at one of his public rallies. Government newspapers published the photograph one day before voters went to the polls, and state television quickly ran stories about Bin Shamlan's alleged association with Osama Bin Laden and international terrorism.[43] This was shameful stereotyping of Faisal Bin Shamlan as a citizen born in Hadramaut, similar to Osama Bin Laden's father. The regime sought to scare voters about Bin Shamlan's Hadrami roots. On the eve of the election, it used this ploy to portray JMP supporters as people who

---

[40] Longley, 2007; p. 247.
[41] Johnsen, 2006(a).
[42] Longley, 2007; pp. 256–257.
[43] "Saleh says arrested terrorist was a Bin Shamlan electoral companion," *Yemen Times*, September 21, 2006. Bin Shamlan's campaign managers explained that they suspected the man in question, and had fired him prior to the scandalous photograph being published in GPC newspapers. "Opposition campaign says Yemeni president trying to scare people with al-Qaida allegations," *International Herald Tribune*, September 19, 2006.

would jeopardize national security by allegedly increasing the risk of direct American military intervention.

During GPC campaign rallies in 2006, the president often used public funds to pay students and workers to attend large venues and hear him speak. The aim was to create scenes with masses of people, larger than JMP rallies, in order to have dramatic video footage to run on Yemen's only government-backed television channel. At one venue in Ibb province, the GPC crowd grew so large and boisterous that it caused a stadium retaining wall to collapse. This caused more than fifty deaths and many more injuries as people were crushed under falling debris and a pile of bodies.[44] During the president's campaign stops, he repeated propaganda about security and stability to sway voters.

Following the day of voting on September 20, 2006, SCER once again declared a landslide victory for Salih and the GPC, claiming that the president had won by a 77 percent to 22 percent margin. There is good reason to believe the actual voting result was closer than indicated by these percentages. Judging from massive turnouts at Bin Shamlan's campaign rallies, and considering the regime's history of tampering with ballots, it is possible that Bin Shamlan drew as much as 30–40 percent of the popular vote. Nonetheless, few political observers genuinely believed that Bin Shamlan could have outpolled the president. The short coming of the JMP's campaign was clear before the voting took place, as senior highland elites, like al-Zindani and Shaykh Abdallah, switched allegiances to support President Salih in the GPC.

The political reality was that regional solidarities still mattered in 2006. Strong loyalties among tribes of the highland region, and among conservative religious and business figures in and around Sanaa, made it difficult for them to support a political leader from another region of the country, especially a southern or eastern region. The mentality of highland elites is that individual leaders from the highland region deserve to rule the country, much as the Zaydi imams ruled Yemen in earlier centuries. When the 2006 electoral campaign tightened, and Bin Shamlan's candidacy appeared to gain greater momentum than the GPC campaign, highland elites became wary of disrupting the status quo. They did not want to risk a possible shift of political power, so they fell in line with President Salih.

President Salih's personal popularity was likely below 50 percent in the 2000s. Yet he managed to exert enormous influence over elections by

---

[44] "Stampede breaks out at campaign rally for Yemeni president, killing at least 51 people," *International Herald Tribune*, September 13, 2006.

controlling all television and radio broadcasts, and using state funds to buy the support of influential people in different regions. The ruling GPC party did not compete on a level playing field with its opposition. This became increasingly clear to members of the JMP. Despite all their efforts in four different national and local electoral campaigns since 1993, the combined parties of the JMP never cut the GPC's ruling majority below 70 percent. The opposition was not competing against a party that temporarily happened to be in charge of the government, yet was willing to step aside if it failed to win a majority of votes. The opposition was competing against a permanent ruling party, equivalent to the state itself, which possessed all of the government's financing and facilities.

The too close association between the GPC and state institutions, especially after the 1994 civil war, hindered the development of democracy in the Republic of Yemen. In 1994, President Salih expanded his powers as president, and the Yemeni parliament became a weak legislative body that provided poor cover for Salih's mismanagement of the country. In times of economic crisis or social upheaval, Salih could blame the parliament due to its constitutionally required support for the prime minister and cabinet. Many members of the opposition claimed that, since Salih exercised full executive powers of decree, he alone was responsible for the failure of state policies. If necessary, according to the opposition, Yemen's constitution should be amended to create a pure presidential system, instead of blending parliamentary and presidential features. Otherwise, Salih would continue to dodge responsibility for the country's depressing social and economic conditions.

During electoral campaigns, President Salih tended to equate the nation with his GPC party. He appealed to voters by generating sympathy not with a political party or ideology, but with Yemeni national unity and defense of the homeland. Salih placed himself above the country's economic crises, wrapping himself in the flag and Yemen's historical virtues. Anyone who challenged his right to rule was subject to being framed as a traitor, similar to the ploy used in 2006 to destroy the late Faisal Bin Shamlan's reputation by absurdly linking him to al-Qaeda. During that presidential campaign, the Iraqi insurgency reached a peak of violence against the American military. Members of al-Qaeda were suspected of carrying out deadly suicide bombings in Baghdad, Samarra, Mosul, and other Iraqi cities and towns. President Salih was able to play on the fears of voters, who did not want to see the same violence on the streets of Yemeni cities and towns.

In the summer of 2006, President Salih emphasized that he alone could protect the nation, and defend it against foreign invasion and the chaos of al-Qaeda. According to this rhetorical line, the JMP opposition threatened to turn Yemen into an al-Qaeda haven, or a Taliban state. The president showed a flair for political word play, erasing the public's memory of his own association in 2001 and 2002 with President Bush's "war on terrorism," and the invasion of Iraq in 2003. Once the American occupation of Iraq descended into chaos, and proved to be an obvious policy failure for the Bush administration, Salih backed away from his support of the U.S. "war on terrorism." He also backed away from his commitment to track and arrest al-Qaeda suspects living inside Yemen.

Between 2002 and 2004, the Yemeni government operated a rehabilitation program for militants held in jail, called the "Religious Dialogue Council" under the direction of Minister of Justice Hamoud Hitar. Those jailed could be released for good behavior, if they met with Hitar to receive instruction in the proper meaning of the Quran, and the proper practice of Islam.[45] When some of the released men showed up on the battlefields of Iraq after rejoining al-Qaeda, the rehabilitation program was wound down. But inside Yemen, there remained few problems with al-Qaeda. As late as 2005, there had been no major terrorist strike since the October 2002 bombing of the French-flagged *Limburg* oil tanker off the south Yemeni coast. There was even a decline in tribal kidnappings, previously considered the country's main security problem. The domestic scene changed dramatically in 2006, after violence in Iraq exploded and President Salih came under internal pressure to break his alliance with America.

During the middle 2000s, more members of President Salih's inner circle sympathized with al-Qaeda and the goals of jihad in Iraq. Even Justice Minister Hitar began to question whether or not the conditions in Iraq called for jihad. Powerful elements of the regime began willfully supporting militants associated with the terrorist organization. In February 2006, seven months before President Salih's campaign against the JMP's Bin Shamlan, twenty-three al-Qaeda members managed to escape a high security prison in Sanaa run by President Salih's political security agency.[46] The escape reportedly happened when the men dug a tunnel more than

---

[45] Johnsen, 2006(b).
[46] The best coverage of al-Qaeda's development in Yemen, during and after 2006, can be found at a weblog run by Gregory D. Johnsen and Brian O-Neill called "*Waq al-Waq.*" islamandinsurgencyinyemen.blogspot.com. Johnsen also published many articles about Yemeni al-Qaeda in the online journal of West Point's Combating Terrorism Center, *CTC Sentinel*. In 2010, the Carnegie Endowment for International Peace in Washington, DC, published a book, *Yemen on the Brink*, which included two chapters about al-Qaeda by Sarah Phillips and Alistair Harris.

one hundred meters from their prison cell to the women's bathroom of a neighboring mosque. Most observers inside the country ridiculed the official story, assuming Salih's political security force intentionally allowed the men to run free.

Following this February 2006 prison break, al-Qaeda became far more active in Yemen. First, in the spring of 2006, there was a string of bombings at oil and gas facilities in Marib and Hadramaut. The group quickly expanded by recruiting a younger, more radical generation with combat experience fighting U.S. forces in Iraq. In June 2007, al-Qaeda formally announced its reemergence in Yemen with a video statement by a man named Qasim al-Raymi from the new northern province of al-Rayma between Sanaa and the western Red Sea coast. The person who eventually emerged as leader of the group is Nasir al-Wahayshi, originally from Shabwa province in the former south Yemen. He had previously served as Osama Bin Laden's personal secretary in Afghanistan. Al-Wahayshi was one of the twenty-three "escapees" from the political security prison in Sanaa. This prison break proved that al-Qaeda was not linked to Faisal Bin Shamlan's presidential campaign. Months before the 2006 election, the group likely had support inside the state's political security force.

8

The Return of Yemeni Regionalism

During a late March 2009 interview with *al-Hayat* newspaper, President Ali Abdallah Salih spoke metaphorically about what it is like to govern Yemen: "it is like dancing on the heads of snakes."[1] The comment revealed more about his own approach to ruling the country than it did about the countrymen living under his rule. When the president spoke, he still had support from cross-sections of the population. Some praised his long record as leader. Others marveled at his ability to survive times of crisis, seeming always to emerge on top of his rivals. Nonetheless, by the end of the decade, most influential actors had grown tired of the president's perpetual grip on power. They refused to consider any possibility that the president's son might replace him in office. The fact Salih wanted his sons and nephews to play more active roles in national affairs created space for ever more violent forms of opposition, and the consequent breakdown of law and order.

In truth, there are a number of reasons for the breakdown of the Yemeni state during the last half of the decade. In 2003 state revenues from oil started to decline because of falling levels of production. Not only did this deepen the country's economic crisis, but it diminished the president's ability to buy off contenders for political power. Since Yemenis had lived with economic crisis for many years, this factor alone could not account for the country's implosion. Backlash from the U.S. invasion of Iraq in 2003, when the public rejected Salih's close alliance with the Bush administration in

---

[1] Quoted in the foreword of Victoria Clark's book, *Yemen: Dancing on the Heads of Snakes*, 2010.

Washington, was clearly a contributing factor. The suspicious deaths of moderate nationalist figures, Jarallah Omar, Yahya al-Mutawakkil, and Mujahid Abu Shawarib, produced heightened cynicism. The absence of these three men's voices of reason, and their skills at negotiating compromise, left a void on the political stage. This was undoubtedly an important factor in Yemen's breakdown. More important was the spread of regional factionalism across broad stretches of the country.

After 2005, the Huthi rebellion in the northwest highlands had a broad demonstration effect about the possibility of resisting the regime's armed forces. The next year groups in the southwest region around Aden discussed ways to reconcile with Ali Nasir partisans in the mid-southern region, in order to confront Salih's regime through peaceful protest and civil disobedience. From these efforts was born a broad southern protest movement known as the peace movement of the south (*al-haraka al-salmiyya lil-junub*) or what eventually was called *al-Hirak*, simply "the Movement." Al-Hirak spread quickly beyond southwestern and then mid-southern provinces to the eastern region of Hadramaut and al-Mahra. Due to south Yemen's history as a separate state, this protest movement presented a different challenge than al-Huthi rebels in Sa'da. It presented the risk of a breakup of the Republic of Yemen.

The activities of al-Hirak dramatically altered Yemen's political climate, so it is important to trace its development to understand the later collapse of President Salih's regime in 2011. Why al-Hirak arose, and how it challenged the regime between 2007 and 2010, are crucial questions in Yemeni politics. What they reveal is how regionally fractured the country remained after twenty years of national unity. The new Republic of Yemen was constructed on a very poor foundation in 1990. After two decades, it remained weak largely because President Salih had obstructed the development of genuinely representative institutions of government, and badly failed to mediate conflicts across divided lands. In general, the president was more proficient at prolonging conflict, and driving deeper wedges into multiple divisions, than he was at mending divisions and resolving conflict.

RISE OF THE SOUTHERN MOVEMENT

There are five precedents to the rise of the southern movement in the late 2000s. First, the outcome of the 1994 civil war, and the postwar policies of Salih's regime, created grievances among people in provinces of the former south Yemen. Once the civil war ended, the vast majority of southerners were too tired of conflicts, extending back at least eight years to 1986, to organize active opposition. During the initial post–civil war years, opposition was mainly expressed in passive terms. But the seeds of resistance existed from an early point in time. Mass opposition only surfaced on rare occasions in 1996 at the time of the prosecutor's trial in al-Mukalla, and again in 1998, when al-Dali' became the capital of a new province intended to erase the old north-south borderline.

Second, the forced early retirements of civilian and military employees during and after 1998, especially among partisans of Ali Nasir Muhammad, increased economic discontent while broadening southern opposition to the regime in Sanaa. Third, the activities of the Public Forum for the Sons of Southern and Eastern Provinces during Ramadan 2001–2002 showed, for the first time, the intention of southern elites to organize in opposition to President Salih's policies. Fourth, the surprising public support for the 2006 presidential campaign of Faisal Bin Shamlan encouraged people in the south to think that political change was possible, and perhaps more importantly, that it was possible to work across ideological lines to mobilize a larger opposition bloc. While leaders of Islah in the northwest highland region betrayed the JMP coalition in 2006, Islah supporters in southern and eastern regions stood with Bin Shamlan's candidacy. This signaled that Islamists and socialists could work together in the south, and perhaps also the western midlands.

Fifth, citizens across the south interpreted the 2005–2006 success of Huthi rebels as a sign that President Salih's military had grown weak during the last ten years. In 2006, groups in the southwest and mid-southern regions began a reconciliation process that led directly to the campaign of peaceful protests. The inaugural rally for "reconciliation and forgiveness" (*tasalah wa tasamuh*) was held in al-Dali' on January 13, 2007, the anniversary of the bloody intraregime warfare in 1986 that divided the YSP and led to the exile of President Ali Nasser and his partisans. The 2007 event only drew a small crowd. But over the next two months, there was a series of peaceful sit-ins in Aden and surrounding provinces following a dispute at the port city's Tariq military base.[2] The dispute arose when local retired officers insisted on better protection at a base cemetery for martyrs of the January 13, 1986, fighting.

By the middle of May 2007, an Aden coordinating council for the newly formed "local association for military retirees" announced plans for massive sit-ins across the region, one day before the seventeenth anniversary of

---

[2] "Peaceful Sit-ins in Aden, al-Dali', Lahij and Abyan," *al-Ayyam* (in Arabic), February 25, 2007.

Yemeni unification, May 22.[3] This was the event that launched al-Hirak. Hundreds of former southern military officers began holding weekly sit-ins to demand jobs and greater compensation than their virtually worthless pension funds. Some of these officers faced early retirement in 1998. But most had been forced from work as early as 1994, despite their young age and qualifications. It is significant that al-Hirak started with former military officers because they symbolized south Yemen's loss of statehood. It is also significant that they rallied around important anniversary dates and locations, which held significance in the history of the former south Yemen.

The head of the coordinating council for southern military retirees, Nasir Ali al-Nuba, emphasized the need for peaceful sit-ins without firearms. He and members of the group did not seek a violent confrontation with the regime. In the summer of 2007, President Salih acted in haste to squash the protest movement when he ordered that al-Nuba be arrested due to fears the protests would spread. Other members of the southern opposition were also arrested at this time, including the longtime opponent of the government in Sanaa, Hasan Ba Awm, leader of the YSP party in Hadramaut. These arrests drew more attention to the rapidly evolving protest movement, as more citizens began participating in daily sit-ins and rallies.

At first, there were dozens who attended the sit-ins, then hundreds and eventually thousands. In the fall of 2007, on the eve of the October 14 holiday commemorating the start of south Yemen's revolt against British colonial rule in the 1960s, there was a fateful clash in Lahij province between government security forces and activists in the protest movement. Local activists in Radfan district were preparing for holiday ceremonies the next day in the town of al-Habilayn, the same town where soldiers of the former British colonial authority shot and killed seven men on October 14, 1963. It was this incident in 1963 that ignited south Yemen's revolution against Britain, eventually forcing its withdrawal in November 1967. Each year, south Yemenis hold ceremonies commemorating the event, called "the martyrs of al-Habilayn." On the night of October 13, 2007, President Salih's security forces clashed with activists in al-Habilayn, opening fire with live ammunition and killing four young residents of the town.[4] The deceased quickly became martyrs for a new generation of southerners.

---

[3] "Coordinating Council of the Military Retiree Associations Sets May 21 as the Date for Mass Sit-ins," *al-Ayyam* (in Arabic), May 12, 2007.

[4] "One of the Injured Tells about the Incident of Four Killed and 15 Wounded at al-Habilayn Stage Site," *al-Ayyam* (in Arabic), October 16, 2007.

The political symbolism of the October 2007 deaths in al-Habilayn was enormous because the young men were killed on the exact spot where young men of an earlier generation had been gunned down by British forces. The parallels to more revolutionary times in the 1960s are what sparked truly massive antigovernment protests, which President Salih was unable to stop. Salih became so concerned about the potential negative fallout from the shootings in al-Habilayn that he offered compensation to the families of the four deceased men, and fifteen others who were injured. Government spokesmen referred to the four deceased as "martyrs" who were betrayed by "foreign agents" allegedly seeking to destroy the country's unity.[5] Yet numerous eyewitnesses saw government forces shoot directly into a crowd of people preparing for ceremonies the next day. Salih often portrayed local opposition as a foreign-inspired threat to national security, as he did during the 2006 presidential campaign. This was the regime's standard playing card after the civil war in 1994. Political opponents were often labeled as traitors "plotting to break apart Yemeni unity."

The killings in al-Habilayn spurred al-Hirak to draw support from hundreds of thousands of citizens. It was shortly afterward in early 2008 that activists began using the name *al-Hirak*, instead of the previous name "military retirees association." Students were the most active participants in al-Hirak. They joined members of earlier generations who lived through revolutionary times in the 1960s. Throughout the fall and winter of 2007–2008, there were sit-ins and rallies on a daily basis in cities and towns across southern and eastern provinces. These were peaceful events, where participants held protest signs denouncing government corruption and regional discrimination. They called for equality of citizenship, more jobs for southern workers, and releasing from jail leaders of the retirees association.

Organizers of al-Hirak were careful to instruct members not to use violence, and not to respond to provocations. They did not want their movement associated with the violence of al-Huthi in Sa'da, or the terrorism of al-Qaeda. They knew that any violence would give President Salih an excuse to drive them from the streets. The peaceful southern protesters clearly had popular momentum, capturing the imagination of people living

---

[5] The daily newspaper associated with the Yemeni military, 26 *September*, published a list of individuals it accused of being responsible for the incident, and inciting sedition in the country. These individuals were mainly from Yemen's socialist party including Ali Munasir Muhammad of the YSP's politburo; Ali Salih Ubad Muqbil, the former secretary general of the YSP; YSP members of parliament and independent activists like Aden human rights lawyer, Badr Ba Sunaid. 26 *September* newspaper (in Arabic), October 14, 2007, Sanaa, Yemen.

across the former border. Northern citizens began holding rallies in support of the southern movement, especially leaders of the JMP coalition from western midland and coastal regions. There were also a few JMP-led rallies in Sanaa. The largest outpouring of southern public support happened in mid-December 2007, during the funeral procession of the four men killed in al-Habilayn sixty miles north of Aden.

Families of the al-Habilayn martyrs did not want their sons buried the day after their deaths, as is Muslim custom. They requested the corpses be kept in a hospital freezer, awaiting an official inquiry to prove that their sons were killed by bullets fired by government forces. President Salih had no intention of investigating the killings, or holding anyone accountable inside the government. After nearly two months, the families decided to proceed with the funeral on December 10. The day of the funeral, mourners streamed into al-Habilayn. Lines of cars, and masses of people on foot, stretched as far as the eye could see across rolling hills of Radfan district There were estimates that hundreds of thousands of people trekked to the site of the funeral. The Arab satellite network, *al-Jazeera*, had a camera crew on the ground prepared to broadcast live images around the world.

PHOTO 17. Crowds at 2007 al-Habilayn Funeral (Photo credit: *al-Ayyam*, Aden)

But President Salih ordered his security to prevent *al-Jazeera* from filming under threat that their camera equipment would be confiscated.[6]

The possibility that images from the funeral procession in al-Habilayn could be broadcast on television gravely concerned the Yemeni president. These images held the potential to inspire political opposition in every province of the country. Al-Habilayn holds tremendous symbolic meaning for all Yemenis, including north Yemenis, many of whom fought against the British in the southern revolution. The anniversary date of October 14 was regularly celebrated in Sanaa before unity in 1990, and the tradition continued after the civil war in 1994. The dates of the northern and southern revolutions on September 26 and October 14 make an extended national holiday season in Yemen. But the 2007 shooting in al-Habilayn risked recreating the country's old division. Shortly after the December 2007 funeral, President Salih's military command staged tank maneuvers in the desert north of Wadi Hadramaut. This was intended to send a signal that the regime remained capable of fighting on two fronts, despite the Huthi rebellion in the north.[7] Salih next ordered his security to disrupt a follow-up rally planned for the next January 13 anniversary.

The second "reconciliation and forgiveness" rally in 2008 was expected to be larger than the event in al-Dali' in 2007, so organizers shifted the location to Hashemi Square in Aden's northern district, Shaykh Othman. This location offered easy access for people traveling by land from neighboring provinces. The daytime rally was intended to resolve any feelings of ill will among southerners who fought each other in January 1986. But the organizers also wanted the rally to resolve bitter feelings from even earlier political conflicts in the 1960s. In other words, the rally represented a comprehensive effort to build a new alliance among all south Yemenis. In effect, it continued work started by the Public Forum during Ramadan 2001–2002.

President Salih obviously wanted the Aden rally stopped because he sent additional security forces to disrupt incoming traffic, and harass participants once they arrived at Hashemi Square. Early in the rally shots were

---

[6] "The Country Witnesses an Unprecedented Funeral Procession," *Al-Ayyam* (in Arabic), December 11, 2007. This was neither the first time, nor the last that the regime harassed *al-Jazeera*'s reporters. The regime reserved worse treatment for local independent and opposition journalists who suffered regular abuse at the hands of security forces and secret police. President Salih's record of denying press freedoms was documented by Amnesty International in its annual reports on Yemen. Reporters Without Borders also filed regular reports on Yemen's lack of press freedom.

[7] "Ba Jamal: We Can Never Again Listen to Those Charlatans that Time Forgot," *al-Ayyam* (in Arabic), December 16, 2007.

fired, killing two demonstrators and injuring more than ten, while causing a riot as people reacted to police firing tear gas and rubber bullets.[8] One thing was certain after this bloody anniversary of Aden's 1986 violence, yet another example of tragic history repeating itself: the incident played to the disadvantage of President Salih. The shootings only strengthened the cause of nonviolent street demonstrators, who continued holding daily sit-ins in the following weeks. Afterward they drew even larger crowds inside Aden, as well as Taiz and other northern provinces.[9] Thus al-Hirak would not necessarily redivide the nation. It always held a potential to unite people around the country in support of peaceful opposition to the regime in Sanaa.

At the time of Aden's Hashemi Square incident, there was no central leadership behind al-Hirak. Instead, multiple groups across southern and eastern regions directed their own local activities in what was a loose body of political opposition. As late as 2009, there were five or more similarly named organizations in different areas, each claiming to speak for southern citizens.[10] The most radical groups used the word "revolution" within their names. Through the end of 2008, senior leaders of opposition parties and the military retirees associations called on young activists to practice nonviolent discipline. Their intent was to avoid armed clashes with the regime's military and security forces.

DANGEROUS GAMESMANSHIP

In late January 2008 President Salih acknowledged the strength of the peaceful southern opposition when he conceded to some of their demands. He offered concessions to retired southern military officers by rehiring some men and increasing the pension payments of others. He also stressed

---

[8] "Killings, Injuries, and Arrests on the January 13th Anniversary," *al-Ayyam* (in Arabic), January 14, 2008. *Al-Ayyam* later printed a story quoting people at the scene who claimed the initial shots came from windows of a hotel facing Hashemi Square. "The Lawyer Representing Families of Deceased Blames Five Sources for the Killing of the Martyr at al-Hashemi," *al-Ayyam*, January 23, 2008.

[9] One man killed in Hashemi Square was an Islah supporter from Taiz. His killing further united north and south members of the JMP. The 2006 presidential candidate, Faisal Bin Shamlan, attended the Aden funeral ceremony for the Taiz victim before his casket was transported home for burial at the front of a long line of cars. "Today Aden Pays Respect to the Reconciliation Martyr in Taiz," *al-Ayyam* (in Arabic), January 20, 2008.

[10] Stracke and Heydar, 2010. Nicole Stracke and Mohammed Saif Heydar listed the names of seven different groups involved in protest activities. These groups used names referring to "Independence of the South" and "Liberation of the South," as well as "Peaceful Struggle" and "Peaceful Revolution."

the importance of settling land disputes in Aden and other southern provinces, promising local military officers that they could reclaim hundreds of properties previously taken from them.[11] Yet the next month, Salih's security forces continued harassing protest leaders and their lawyers, as well as journalists who reported on the peace movement. This included the publisher of *al-Ayyam*, the popular independent daily newspaper in Aden, whose staff started their own sit-in. Due to the president's reputation for gamesmanship, most southern observers realized that he desired neither a continuation of the peaceful protests, nor the start of genuine political reform. Instead, most expected the president to stage yet another "dirty trick."

In late March 2008, the regime in Sanaa extended an invitation to hundreds of young men from al-Habilayn, Radfan, and al-Dali', to attend an army recruitment conference in Dhamar, halfway between the sprawling capital in the northwest highlands and the western midland city of Taiz. Dhamar sits just inside the historical Zaydi region of Yemen, north of the more populous areas of Ibb, Taiz, and Aden. President Salih, his extended family, and the strong shaykhs of the Hashid tribe share a common cultural heritage in the Zaydi highlands. But the youthful recruits, who were invited to attend the Dhamar conference, came from different backgrounds. The invitation to these young supporters of al-Hirak extended across a social, cultural divide running throughout Yemeni history. This is important for comprehending what happened next, when the youth were sternly lectured at the recruitment conference, insulted for supposedly lacking the strength and loyalty necessary to serve the nation, and then sent home without jobs.[12]

Returning to their homes at the end of March 2008, the youth reacted in frustration by rioting in cities and towns of Lahij and al-Dali' provinces.[13] This was a noticeable break from the disciplined peace protests. The town of al-Habilayn in Radfan district became the site of widespread violence when President Salih deployed his army in operations not seen since the 1994 civil war. These operations seemed scripted, as if the government had

---

[11] "Minister of Defense: Comprehensive Measures to Be Taken to Resolve the Problem of Retirees," *al-Ayyam* (in Arabic), January 20, 2008. In addition to these concessions, President Salih pursued discussions in February 2008 with exiled leaders abroad like Ali Nasir Muhammad and former prime minister Haider al-Attas.

[12] "Young Demonstrators in Radfan Demand Employment in the Military," *al-Ayyam* (in Arabic), March 30, 2008.

[13] "Radfan and al-Dali' Witness Angry Youth Demonstrations," *al-Ayyam* (in Arabic), March 31, 2008.

looked for an excuse to crack down on peaceful protesters. Some members of the southern opposition referred to a "second war on the south." Fighting continued through the first week of April 2008 with the army using tanks, artillery, and fighter aircraft.[14] There is no accurate count of the numbers killed and injured, since press coverage was restricted due to the military's encirclement of areas of fighting. At least one soldier died in the first week of April, while several civilians were killed and dozens injured.[15] Some reports said as many as three hundred al-Hirak activists were arrested and beaten. Other reports claimed local security forces abandoned their posts, and joined the fight against the army.

Throughout the deadly clashes in the first week of April, and the weeks that followed, supporters of al-Hirak continued their peaceful sit-ins and marches in Abyan, Shabwa, Hadramaut and al-Mahra.[16] In northern cities like Taiz, Ibb, and al-Hudayda, citizens rallied in solidarity with those who died, or were injured and arrested. The largest northern opposition rally occurred on April 6 in Taiz, where thousands of citizens were angered by the arrest of a local writer and performance artist, Fahd al-Qarni, who produced popular satirical recordings criticizing President Salih.[17] Al-Qarni was a strong supporter of al-Hirak, and he claimed to have been silenced because of this support. During a later trial, he took a principled stand defending his right to free speech, and refusing government promises of leniency if he admitted his guilt. Many residents of western midland cities like Taiz shared southern feelings of marginalization by political elites who hold power in Sanaa. Inside the capital, there were small sympathy demonstrations in April 2008 organized by JMP supporters. But government propaganda depicting southern al-Hirak members as "disloyal to the nation" penetrated tribal areas of the northern highlands.

After using a heavy stick in Radfan and al-Dali', Salih tried offering a "carrot" by agreeing to hold the Republic of Yemen's first election of provincial governors. Voting occurred on May 17, 2008, and the GPC

---

[14] "Rise in Protests in Response to the Arrests Amidst a Heavy Military Deployment," *al-Ayyam* (in Arabic), April 2, 2008.

[15] "Over 200 Detained Over Riots," *Yemen Times*, April 10, 2008. In its next issue the *Yemen Times* printed a summary of the government's view that external elements sought to destabilize Yemen, and that the President and parliament were the properly elected leaders who could alone define what is and is not the democratic will. "Don't Play With State Security, Saleh Warns," *Yemen Times*, April 14, 2008.

[16] "Protest Marches in Shabwa and Hadramaut," *al-Ayyam* (in Arabic), April 5, 2008.

[17] "Protest in Support of Arrested Singer," *Yemen Times*, April 7, 2008.

once again proved its dominance by winning outright control in seventeen of twenty-one provinces. These local elections did not involve citizens voting at the polls. The regime did not have time to organize a direct popular vote because of its decision to hold elections on such short notice. In any case, President Salih did not want to allow a direct vote because of the momentum building behind the southern protests. Instead, he and his advisors arranged indirect elections among members of the weak provincial councils, first established in 2001.[18] What is noteworthy about the provincial governor elections in 2008 is the suddenness of the regime's decision to advance a process that the political opposition had been demanding in the south since the early 1990s.

GPC officials knew that local elections were a persistent demand of political opponents in southern and eastern provinces, so the decision to allow indirectly elected provincial governors was a way to dangle a "carrot" in front of its main regional opposition. The plan for elections was announced just a few days after the intense fighting in Lahij and al-Dali' provinces, when President Salih called an extraordinary meeting of Yemen's National Defense Council on April 9, 2008.[19] The president and members of his regime were clearly panicked by the size and resilience of the southern opposition. They initially acted in haste, declaring that the election of governors would take place before the end of the month. After a few days, the regime postponed the date until May 17. But members of the JMP opposition coalition did not reach for the dangling carrot.

After the initial announcement of an election date in late April, the JMP declared a boycott, and asked its members on provincial councils to ignore the voting procedures. The JMP protested the elections because citizens were not given a chance to vote directly for their governors. It also opposed the extraordinary means by which the elections were arranged.[20]

---

[18] A second round of local elections had previously been held at the time of the 2006 presidential contest between Salih and Bin Shamlan. Thus, the provincial council members who selected new governors in May 2008 were the victors of elections two years earlier. Longley, 2007; pp. 259–260. At the end of April Longley's article, she provides two tables showing the official results released by SCER. According to these tables, the GPC improved its control of provincial councils between 2001 and 2006, from 62 percent to 85 percent of the seats, giving added assurance that President Salih's ruling party could control the outcome of the indirect voting for provincial governors in 2008.

[19] "NDC approved speeding up governors election," *Almotamar.net*, April 9, 2008. "Calls for Comprehensive Reforms: JMP opposes gubernatorial elections," *Yemen Times*, April 17, 2008.

[20] "JMP Representatives and Independents Reject the Reforms," *al-Ayyam* (in Arabic), April 17, 2008.

Opposition leaders understood that President Salih was on the defensive because of the strength of al-Hirak and the rebellion of al-Huthi followers in Saʻda. They felt Salih was attempting to weaken this political opposition, and undercut the expanding protest movement, by appearing to make concessions on local government. But it was also true that the JMP lacked control of provincial councils, and would be unable to affect the outcome of voting. It controlled only one council in al-Daliʻ province, where the GPC held just 20 percent of the seats.[21] The Islah party held 40 percent of the seats in al-Daliʻ, and the YSP held 33 percent. Thus, the JMP boycott denied the required quorum in this southwestern province. Nonetheless, the regime ordered voting to proceed the following day.

Elsewhere in the country, the selection of governors proceeded on schedule. In the central interior region, where the GPC controlled barely half of the seats in Marib and al-Jawf provinces, two independent candidates were victorious. Also in the western midland province of al-Bayda, an independent candidate defeated the GPC candidate. In fourteen other provinces, the ruling party's candidates ran unopposed.[22] Thus the selection of governors did not require a vote in two-thirds of Yemen's twenty-one provinces. In some northern provinces, council members representing Islah failed to observe the JMP boycott. For instance, they turned out to vote in Sanaa, Amran, and Hajja, often supporting GPC candidates. This was a repeat of what happened in 2006, when Islah's leaders, Shaykh al-Ahmar and Abd al-Majid al-Zindani, broke with the JMP and supported Salih's candidacy for president.[23] For the remainder of 2008, al-Hirak continued its peaceful protests in the south, coordinating rallies in different towns on specific days of the week, in order to maintain the appearance of steady opposition to the regime. For its part, the regime continued using repression to break up the protests.

President Salih resorted to his old tactic of divide and rule when his regime created "committees for defense of unity" among local client groups in Lahij, al-Daliʻ, and Abyan. These committees were often supported by irregular military forces from northern tribes. Their main purpose was to harass al-Hirak activists, organize counterdemonstrations,

[21] Longley, 2007; pp. 259–260.
[22] Mohammed Bin Sallam, "Ruling party wins majority of governor seats amid absent rivalry," *Yemen Times*, May 19, 2008.
[23] In Yemen's northwest highland region, where tribal connections matter more than partisan loyalties, Islah was not a consistent ally of other opposition parties. This was the main reason why the JMP faced difficulty building stronger opposition across the country's primary division between highland and midland/coastal regions.

and serve as spies for the regime by naming government opponents and passing along other information.[24] This created greater tensions, which led to violent clashes in urban and rural areas, driving politics in more extreme directions. In November 2008, the Yemen Observatory on Human Rights (YOHR) filed its first annual report detailing government repression of al-Hirak.[25] The report offered a detailed picture of al-Hirak's activities and the means of repression used by the regime in Sanaa.

The YOHR report catalogued 623 peaceful protests between January and mid-November 2008, roughly two protests per day; the number of occasions security forces used physical repression against protestors (85, or 14 percent of occasions when protests were held); and the number of protestors killed (7), injured (75), and arrested (860). These numbers mean that each time security forces physically intervened, they arrested more than ten protestors, while injuring one person on average. Among the seven protestors killed in 2008, the report lists four in al-Dali' and three in Lahij. Aden was the province with the highest number of arrested protestors (402, or 46 percent of the total 860). Lahij was second with 230 (26 percent), and al-Dali' was third with 124 (14 percent). The report also cited hundreds of other human rights violations, including the denial of legal representation in court and illegal seizure of property. It counted tens of thousands of private claims against the government for failing to compensate citizens for employment and pensions. This was the original impetus for al-Hirak in 2007.

Aden's popular daily newspaper, *al-Ayyam*, provided the most extensive coverage of al-Hirak protests in 2008. On a regular basis, its pages were filled with stories about sit-ins and rallies across southern and eastern regions. As the government used more repression, *al-Ayyam* published more detailed stories with graphic color photographs of the dead and injured. The newspaper and its website helped maintain political momentum for opposition forces by providing information about future protests. The Bashraheel family publishes *al-Ayyam*. Since the middle 1990s, its owner and publisher, Hisham Bashraheel, was widely known to sympathize

[24] Longley Alley and al-Iryani, 2009. April Longley Alley and Abd al-Ghani al-Iryani describe the "committees for defense of unity" carrying out illegal activities like seizing bundles of newspapers published by nongovernment sources. *Asharq Alawsat* newspaper published a February 2010 interview with one al-Hirak leader who described the "committees for defense of unity" as vigilante groups, similar to the Janjawid forces in Darfur, Sudan. http://www.aawsat.com/english/news.asp?section=1&id=19791

[25] "Facts about the Peaceful Rallies" (in Arabic), Yemen Observatory for Human Rights, Sanaa, Yemen, November 2008. http://www.yohr.org

with the political opposition. In the late 1990s and early 2000s, he faced constant harassment by political security officials.[26] In 2008, he and his reporters received physical threats from government agents who accused the newspaper of harming national security. Similar threats were made during the previous two years against Sanaa-based reporters covering the war in Sa'da.

The journalist Abd al-Karim al-Khaiwani was arrested for reporting about the suffering of civilians during the Huthi war. In June 2008, al-Khaiwani was sentenced to six years in prison.[27] Throughout his trial in Sanaa, Abd al-Karim al-Khaiwani's lawyers openly challenged the state's ability to rule against a journalist who merely reported domestic news. The problem for al-Khaiwani, the Bashraheel family in Aden, and many other journalists in Yemen was the lack of legitimacy of state institutions. Later the state empowered extraordinary courts to process criminal charges against journalists.[28] This clearly violated Yemen's constitutional guarantees of press freedom. Around the same time, the regime ordered the closure of seven independent newspapers, including the Bashraheel family's *al-Ayyam*. But the regime multiplied its problems each time it adopted a new "emergency measure."

Political observers inside and outside Yemen recognized that President Salih was becoming increasingly paranoid. In 2008, Round Five of the Huthi war spread beyond Sa'da, and reached the northern suburbs of Sanaa. In the fall, Salih appointed an official mediator to negotiate an end to the war with al-Huthi leaders. This mediator was Abd al-Qadr Ali Hilal, minister of local administration, and member of a prominent ruling class family from the highland region. Hilal is a respected politician, and he was a good choice to mediate with al-Huthi leaders because of his family's proud Zaydi legacy. Hilal made progress in his work. Yet when he offered concessions to resolve the northern rebellion, he was accused by President Salih of sympathizing with al-Huthis, and trying to undermine the regime. Hilal was bewildered by the president's reaction, so he ended his mediation

[26] Personal interviews with Hisham Bashraheel, his brother Tamam and son Bashar, at *al-Ayyam* headquarters in Sanaa and Aden; December 22, 1996, October 25, 1998, and June 22, 2002.

[27] "Yemeni journalist sentenced to 6 years in prison," Amnesty International UK, June 17, 2008. At al-Khaiwani's sentencing in Sanaa, one of his colleagues, Muhammad al-Maqaleh, broke out laughing when he heard the judge try to justify the long prison sentence. The judge then ordered al-Maqaleh's arrest inside the courtroom.

[28] Khaled al-Hilaly, "Journalists further protest 'illegal' press court," *Yemen Times*, June 11, 2009.

efforts and resigned his post as minister of local administration.[29] This incident typified the Yemeni president's behavior. Instead of listening to wise counsel from individuals representing different interests in society, Salih acted jealously of his own interest to stay in power.

On urgent matters like equitable sharing of national revenues and decentralization, President Salih should have advanced reforms a full decade earlier in order to relieve pressures on the central government. His refusal of legitimate power sharing created an inevitable clash of interests in the 2000s because as the formal game of politics was corrupted, citizens looked for other means to pursue their agendas. Salih and his highland cronies had long divided the spoils of state business among themselves, and their primary response whenever regional outsiders complained was to raise charges of treason and disloyalty to national unity. Following President Salih's landslide victory in the 2006 presidential election, even highland members of the JMP questioned the value of continuing to play the game. As in the past, Salih sought to form a governing coalition in 2006, but no opposition member had wanted to negotiate a power-sharing deal. The JMP candidate, Faisal Bin Shamlan, even refused to congratulate the president.

Before the end of 2008, the space for political compromise and power sharing was virtually nonexistent in Yemen. The JMP refused to coordinate voter registration for any future election until voting procedures were completely overhauled at SCER. All member parties of the JMP declared a boycott of the next parliamentary election in April 2009. In the past, Salih could persuade at least some parties to join an electoral campaign by offering financial incentives. But on this occasion, every member of the opposition stuck to the planned boycott. On November 26, 2008, the JMP organized a massive street demonstration in Sanaa, calling attention to their demands to end fraudulent elections.[30] More than one hundred thousand people marched peacefully through the streets with banners: "No to the Coup against Democracy! No to Forging the Will of the People!" Police responded with tear gas and clubs, beating several people including five journalists. Some called these events Yemen's "November Intifada." Twenty-three people were injured in the melee, three seriously, while twenty-one others were arrested.

[29] "The government has no place for honest people: Hilal's severance pay," *Yemen Times*, November 27, 2008.
[30] "Arrests and Abuse of Journalists during their Reporting of Protest Marches in Sanaa," *al-Ayyam* (in Arabic), November 29, 2008.

Members of the JMP had labored in negotiations with the GPC for several years, trying to restrict the ruling party's control of voter registration and other electoral procedures. But the JMP no longer held any hope of reforming SCER. For his part, President Salih realized that holding an election without parties in the JMP, as he did in 1999, would expose his monopoly control over the state. Members of the JMP effectively forced President Salih to cancel the 2009 parliamentary elections, thus ending Yemen's nearly two decades experiment with electoral democracy.[31] Like the peaceful protests of al-Hirak in 2007 and 2008, the "November Intifada" in Sanaa offered a glimpse of the massive street protests that would bring down President Salih's regime in 2011. In the interim two years, conditions in the country turned very violent.

A VIOLENT YEAR

In 2009 political violence soared across the country. This was Yemen's most violent year since the civil war in 1994. In the spring and early summer, following sporadic clashes between the army and Huthi rebels in the northwest highlands, President Salih launched "Operation Scorched Earth" in August 2009. During full-scale military operations involving more than forty thousand government troops, the president sought to crush the Huthi rebellion.[32] Hundreds of thousands of civilians fled their homes, swarming into refugee camps that were understaffed and overflowing. In one horrendous incident, an air force jet dropped a bomb on a refugee camp, killing more than eighty people, mainly women and children.[33] In September, UNICEF expressed "deep concern" about the rising civilian death toll. But the army launched a massive assault on October 11, and a second major assault followed on November 4. It seemed that Salih wanted to drive every civilian from the land in order to deprive the rebels of local support networks. One foreign journalist raised the specter of future war crime charges against President Salih.[34]

The "Scorched Earth" policy multiplied the regime's foes because larger numbers of Bakil tribesmen joined the insurrection without any prior

---

[31] "Discerning Yemen's Political Future," *Viewpoints*, The Middle East Institute, No. 11, June 2009. In this publication, the author contributed an essay entitled "Yemen Postpones Its April 2009 Parliamentary Elections."
[32] Boucek, 2010.
[33] Brian Whitaker, "War crimes in Yemen?," *The Guardian*, England, September 18, 2009.
[34] Ibid.

affiliation to al-Huthi.[35] Over the years, the Sa'da war had become a regional uprising that involved at least half of the highland mountain territories. This was disastrous for President Salih's standing inside his own tribal region. Far from being a creative problem solver in the customary Yemeni sense, as a leader looking for admirably clever means of resolving conflict, Salih increasingly resorted to brutal aggression. The military operation in 2009 dealt a severe blow to al-Huthi rebels, but it did not stop their armed insurrection. Meanwhile, in the country's southern regions, armed rebels began carrying out frequent attacks against government targets in al-Dali', Lahij, Abyan, and Hadramaut, even inside the crowded port city of Aden.

Low-level violence in the south started in late 2008, during the JMP's boycott of upcoming parliamentary elections. A few SCER offices were vandalized in southern provinces. In al-Dali' and Lahij, local SCER workers were prevented from conducting voter registration. On November 14, 2008, the SCER office in Ja'ar, Abyan was bombed; no deaths or injuries occurred because the bombing occurred at night. Ja'ar sits in the lower Yafi' tribal area, near Abyan's capital Zinjibar. This area was a center of militancy in the 1990s, when local members of the Islamic Army of Aden and Abyan bombed tourist hotels in late 1992, and then kidnapped a group of sixteen foreign tourists in late 1998. The latter ended badly when a poorly planned rescue operation triggered a firefight at a rural location outside Aden.[36] Three British citizens and one Australian died, while two others were injured. In the past, nearly all kidnappings of foreigners were resolved peacefully, so the killings in 1998 were a bad sign for the future.

In November 2008, when the SCER office in Ja'ar was bombed, it was not clear whether this was the work of the same Islamic militants, possibly allied with al-Qaeda, or the work of radicalized members of al-Hirak. Similar attacks in 2009 against military, security, and civilian government

---

[35] Mohammed al Qadhi, "Yemen conflict 'no longer internal issue," *The National*, UAE, October 21, 2009. Al-Qadhi quotes Gregory Johnsen: "What was once a three-sided conflict between the government, its Salafist allies and the Huthis has become much more complex. Now, tribesmen and other interest groups have been brought into the fighting on the side of the Huthis not out of any adherence to Zaydi theology or doctrine but rather as a response to government overreaching and military mistakes. In effect, after five rounds of fighting, the government's various military campaigns have created more enemies than it had when the conflict began."

[36] Brian Whitaker, "Kidnap Terror Ends in Death," *The Guardian*, December 30, 1998. Sheila Carapico, "Yemen and the Aden-Abyan Islamic Army," *Middle East Report Online*, October 18, 2000.

offices in southern provinces also added to the ambiguity. Earlier attacks in other regions were relatively easy to blame on al-Qaeda. For instance, when al-Qaeda reemerged following the Sanaa prison break in early 2006, there were a few attacks resembling terrorist operations in Iraq, Afghanistan, and Pakistan. In July 2007, a suicide bomber detonated a car load of explosives in Marib province, next to two tourist vehicles parked at the entrance of an archeological site believed to be the legendary temple of the Queen of Sheba. Al-Qaeda claimed responsibility for this attack, as well as a March 2007 assassination of a Marib criminal investigator who earlier assisted the U.S. drone strike that killed Abu Ali al-Harithi in 2002.

The suicide bombing in Marib killed eight Spanish tourists and two Yemeni drivers. This was followed by more than a dozen similar, well-prepared attacks, including a deadly suicide mission on September 17, 2008, when the U.S. embassy in Sanaa was hit by a coordinated assault involving six men carrying automatic weapons and grenade launchers in two bomb-laden trucks.[37] The trucks were used to destroy a high-security perimeter wall. The assailants then entered the grounds firing their weapons. All U.S. staff were safely protected inside the embassy building, which had been constructed in the 1980s at great expense, precisely for added protection, on the northern outskirts of Sanaa. But more than a dozen people died outside the embassy building.[38] Between 2006 and 2008, al-Qaeda mainly struck foreign targets, such as tourists, embassies, and oil facilities. In its pronouncements, the group spoke critically of Salih's regime. But it rarely used violence against Yemeni government personnel or facilities.

This pattern changed in July 2008, when al-Qaeda members struck central security forces in Saiyun, the administrative center of Wadi Hadramaut.[39] A suicide bomber, who was later identified as Ahmad al-Mushjari, drove a vehicle packed with explosives into a local base that housed central security forces. During the following days, the government hunted down a group of militants in Wadi Hadramaut who had assisted

---

[37] Ellen Knickmeyer, "Attack Against U.S. Embassy in Yemen Blamed on Al-Qaeda," *The Washington Post*, September 18, 2008.

[38] Among the dead was one U.S. citizen, a young Yemeni-American woman named Susan al-Baneh who was visiting relatives in the country, and had just married a young Yemeni man. Minutes before the attack, she entered the embassy's outer gate with her husband, seeking a visa for him to travel to the United States. The young couple and five other civilians were caught in the crossfire. Tragically, they died beyond the protection offered by the main embassy building. Also killed were six Yemeni security guards and government police who helped defend the outer compound.

[39] Aqeel Al-Halali, "Al-Qaeda's war in Yemen," *Yemen Times*, August 7, 2008.

the attack. Six months later in January 2009, al-Qaeda in Yemen announced its formal merger with the international organization's Saudi network, forming a new regional branch called al-Qaeda on the Arabian Peninsula (AQAP). The leader of AQAP was Nasir al-Wahayshi, who fled Osama Bin Laden's side in Afghanistan after 9/11. Al-Wahayshi's trail of escape from American bombs in 2001 passed through Iran, where he was arrested by authorities in Tehran, and then extradited to Yemen.[40] He was jailed until the mass prison break in February 2006. By 2009, al-Wahayshi led the most active regional wing of al-Qaeda.

Before the announcement of AQAP in January 2009, it was assumed that the Yemeni group's base of operations was Marib in the central interior desert, not in southern or eastern regions of the country. For instance, between August 2008 and April 2009, al-Wahayshi's men carried out three assassination operations in Marib, where al-Qaeda maintained a vendetta against security officials and criminal investigators since 2002. Then in July 2009, AQAP ambushed and killed three Yemeni soldiers in Marib province. Throughout the year, however, there were more armed attacks in southern provinces, raising the possibility that AQAP had moved its base of operations to Abyan or Shabwa in the mid-southern region, which is al-Wahayshi's homeland. There existed at least two other possibilities: first, the violence in the south could have been carried out by radicalized members of al-Hirak who abandoned the discipline of peaceful protest; and second, radicalized members of al-Hirak may have found common cause with AQAP to attack Salih's regime.

In January 2009, the state prosecutor's office in Lawdar district of Abyan province was sprayed with gunfire. There were no injuries or deaths in this incident. On March 8, the local security director's office in the Abyan capital, Zinjibar, was sprayed with gunfire. Before the end of March, the deputy director of a local security office in Lahij province was shot and killed. Then on April 12, a judge's house was bombed in al-Dali'. These low-level attacks were not likely the work of AQAP. But other violence was clearly associated with the terrorist group, either because it followed traditional patterns of al-Qaeda or the terrorist group publicly claimed responsibility. For instance, it was known that AQAP attacked a group of Korean tourists visiting Shibam in Wadi Hadramaut in March 2009, killing four Koreans and their Yemeni tour

---

[40] Detailed information about Nasir al-Wahayshi's background can be found at the weblog run by Gregory Johnsen and Brian O-Neill called "*Waq al-Waq*."

guide.[41] The same was true of an incident in early November 2009, when AQAP claimed responsibility for killing the director of political security in Hadramaut and two of his colleagues at a remote site near the Saudi border.

In 2009, some al-Hirak activists had undoubtedly started to fight back against government forces. One of their tactics was to block major roads passing between southern provinces. The same tactic is often used by rebellious tribes in northwest highland mountains. Traditionally, whenever tribesmen of Hashid and Bakil have an unresolved grievance with the regime in Sanaa, they set up blockades by dropping large stones onto major roadways, thereby disrupting traffic and commerce, and creating an impression that the government lacks control over the tribe's territory. This compels government officials to negotiate with the local tribal shaykh until the dispute is resolved in a peaceful manner. Inside the highland region, Salih's regime had long tolerated this process of dispute resolution, and rarely resorted to military force. But in southern regions, the regime did not show the same restraint.

In January 2009, al-Hirak activists blocked the main road through al-Dali', which provides the most direct route between Aden and Sanaa. Again in March 2009, activists in Abyan blocked the main route between Aden and Hadramaut. Both of these incidents led to violent clashes between al-Hirak protestors and government forces. In April, more violent clashes occurred between government forces and al-Hirak supporters in Radfan district of Lahij province, when protestors challenged army forces at checkpoints on mountain access roads. Local al-Hirak activists claimed the government had violated an earlier agreement after the clashes in April 2008, when the state vowed not to establish checkpoints overlooking al-Habilayn and other towns and villages. The clashes in 2009 continued for more than a month. Local reports counted eighteen people killed, including five from the government's side.[42]

The most significant development in southern provinces happened in early April 2009, when Shaykh Tareq al-Fadli announced that he was joining al-Hirak. This surprising news further blurred the line between al-Hirak and Islamic militants tied to al-Qaeda, since Shaykh al-Fadli had once been a leader of the Arab-Afghan mujahideen with personal ties to Osama Bin

---

[41] "Tourists die in Yemen explosion," BBC News, March 15, 2009. The previous year in January 2008, a Yemeni al-Qaeda cell targeted a group of European tourists in Shibam. Two Belgian citizens were killed, along with two Yemeni tour guides.

[42] "Citizens Killed and Injured during Security Force Crackdowns in al-Habilayn," Yemeni Observatory for Human Rights, April 15, 2009.

Laden.[43] When al-Fadli announced his support for al-Hirak, it generated
doubts among peaceful protesters who questioned whether or not he represented a "Trojan horse" sent by President Salih to destroy the movement's
strategy of peaceful civil disobedience. But the majority of al-Hirak leaders
welcomed al-Fadli's declaration of support. In the following days, *al-Ayyam*
newspaper printed numerous favorable replies from opposition leaders in all
southern provinces.[44] Likewise, exiled southern leaders, Ali Salem al-Bid, Ali
Nasir Muhammad, and Muhammad Ali Ahmad, the governor of Abyan
until January 1986, sent their approval.

This development in Abyan was surprising because Shaykh Tareq
al-Fadli had been allied with President Salih for nearly two decades. The
entire al-Fadli family was ideologically opposed to the former socialist ruling
party of south Yemen because its Marxist leaders had nationalized the
family's property and forced them into exile during the late 1960s. Before
the emergence of al-Hirak in 2007, al-Fadli had fought against the same
individuals who organized the movement, such as al-Nuba and Ba Awm.
Now in April 2009, Shaykh al-Fadli was joining southern protests against
the government in Sanaa. Soon he became one of the most vocal advocates of
southern independence. President Salih and members of his inner circle were
especially disturbed by this development. They fired rhetoric against "secessionists" in the south, and denounced a regional "culture of hatred" that was
harmful to national unity.[45] The president accused al-Fadli of ties to foreign
interests, just like the old sultans of south Arabia who signed protection
treaties with Britain. Shaykh al-Fadli countered by saying that, even though
he and his tribesmen fought to preserve national unity in 1994, they had
been denied equal opportunities with political elites in Sanaa.[46]

---

[43] During the 1980s, Tareq al-Fadli acknowledges fighting alongside Osama Bin Laden's
mujahideen forces in Afghanistan. He also acknowledges receiving support from Bin
Laden to help defeat Ali Salem al-Bid's break away southern state in Yemen's 1994 civil
war. British author Victoria Clark provides a detailed biography of Tareq al-Fadli, based
on personal interviews she conducted with him in Abyan. Clark, 2010; pp. 155–166.

[44] "All Sides of the Peace Movement in Eight Districts of Yafi' Welcome Shaykh Tareq al-
Fadli's Statement on the Southern Cause," *al-Ayyam* (in Arabic), April 3, 2009.
"Widespread Consultations among Shaykhs and Sultans of the South to Join the Peace
Movement," *al-Ayyam*, April 4, 2009.

[45] "Presidential directives call for creation of a national alignment against hatred cult,"
Almotamar.net, April 23, 2009. "Enough Abuse of Unity," *22 May* online news, April
25, 2009.

[46] "Al-Fadli: The issue is not Yemen's unity for which we paid with our blood, but the South
and its well-being," *al-Ayyam* (in Arabic), April 2, 2009. A long interview with al-Fadli
appeared on April 15, 2009. Ahmad Yaslim Salih, "In a First Press Interview: Shaykh
Tareq bin Naser al-Fadli Talks to al-Ayyam," *Al-Ayyam*, April 15, 2009.

In the middle of April 2009, top ruling party officials in the GPC revived promises of political decentralization, hoping to persuade Shaykh al-Fadli and other influential southerners that the government would gradually devolve more political power.[47] Al-Fadli set a date near the end of April to address a large outdoor audience in the center of Zinjibar, and clarify his stance on key political issues. There was great anticipation across southern provinces, as well as in Sanaa, to hear what al-Fadli had to say. He chose April 27 to deliver his speech, since it is an important date in the history of united Yemen. On this date, the country's first parliamentary elections were held in 1993. Subsequent elections in 1997 and 2003 were also held on this date, and the government began referring to it as "Democracy Day." But April 27 also marked the start of Yemen's civil war in 1994, one year after the first parliamentary elections. Thus the date carries a double meaning in Yemen.

On the morning of April 27, 2009, hundreds of people streamed into Zinjibar from surrounding areas. Security forces patrolled the city, and army helicopters circled over head.[48] A peaceful crowd of thousands packed into a small stadium on the city's main road. Al-Fadli appeared on a canopied platform with a number of supporters, including former southern general Ali al-Saadi, one of the organizers of the military retirees association in 2007. But this was not an assembly of unarmed peace activists like those at early rallies in Aden. Shaykh al-Fadli came attired in the traditional clothing of his father, the former sultan of al-Fadli territory. He wore a colorful turban with a silver dagger tucked into the front of his belt, and a revolver on his side. Surrounding al-Fadli, there stood several armed guards with AK-47 machine guns slung over their shoulders. Al-Fadli opened his remarks with a solemn tone, "Oh, Sons of the Free, Noble South." As his speech progressed, he became more bitter and defiant as he explained his decision to join the opposition. Without mentioning President Salih by name, or referring to the government in Sanaa, he spoke of how "sons of the south are arrested and held in prisons far from our land, while those who sit in palaces steal our wealth."[49]

---

[47] Many of these matters were addressed in a long speech that President Salih delivered on April 25, 2009. The government's 22 *May* newspaper provided texts of the speech in Arabic and English. "President calls for strengthening the values of tolerance, unity," 22 *May* online, April 25, 2009.

[48] "Zinjibar Lives under a Security Fist, While Helicopters Circle Above," *al-Ayyam* (in Arabic), April 27, 2009.

[49] "Shaykh Tareq al-Fadli: Today We Stand Together in One Line to Restore Southern Ties," *al-Ayyam* (in Arabic), April 28, 2009. This article reproduced al-Fadli's full speech.

Everyone in attendance knew the meaning and importance of Shaykh al-Fadli's words. His primary demand was political independence for "sons of the south" (*ibna`a al-junub*). He addressed the need for solidarity among all southern people, in order to stand united against government oppression. He called on foreign leaders to support the southern people, and requested that the United Nations Security Council fully apply its 1994 resolutions, Nos. 924 and 931. Parallels between Shaykh al-Fadli's remarks, and political positions adopted by exiled southern leaders like Ali Salem al-Bid, were no accident due to increased coordination between members of the southern opposition inside and outside the country. In a most surprising twist one week after al-Fadli's speech, he declared his acceptance of Ali Salem al-Bid's return to southern lands, vowing to support al-Bid as president of a new southern state.[50] As ideological contests from the 1960s faded from memory, the hands of time had finally come full circle. If al-Fadli and al-Bid could stand together, then the reconciliation of old southern rivals was nearly complete.

While the rally in Zinjibar ended peacefully, al-Hirak supporters clashed with government security forces across southern and eastern regions in the days that followed. Hundreds were arrested in al-Mukalla, Aden, as well as cities and towns of Lahij and Abyan. A YSP member of parliament representing Radfan in Lahij province, Dr. Aidrous Nasr Nasir, stated that the government's army had "launched an undeclared war."[51] Local newspapers printed stories about government repression of protestors. The next week on May 4–5, the regime shut down seven independent presses, including *al-Ayyam* and *al-Nida* in Aden, *al-Mukalla* in Hadramaut, and four others, including *al-Masdar*, a popular online news source.[52] On May 12, there was an exchange of fire between security guards at the Bashraheel home in Aden after government security forces attempted to arrest *al-Ayyam*'s publisher. One bystander was killed. On May 21, four civilians were killed and scores injured, during protests at Aden's port. More than two hundred people were arrested at this site, one day before anniversary celebrations of Yemen's national unity.

---

[50] "Interview: Al-Fadli Affirms His Blessings for Ali Salem al-Bid," *al-Wasat* (in Arabic), May 13, 2009.

[51] "Parliament Member Aidrous: What the Districts of Radfan Are Witnessing is an Undeclared War," *al-Ayyam* (in Arabic), April 29, 2009.

[52] "Major crackdown on independent media," Reporters Without Borders, May 5, 2009.

LOOKING INTO THE ABYSS

In the middle of May, President Salih and other GPC officials conducted a public relations blitz, attempting once again to persuade southern citizens that leaders in Sanaa would share political power. On May 17, Salih pledged to allow elections at the city level, empowering municipal governments in Aden, al-Mukalla, and other urban centers.[53] He spoke of new constitutional amendments that would grant "broad powers" to all local districts. Between June 3 and June 16, the GPC conducted local government conferences throughout the country with sixteen thousand people in attendance. The conference in Abyan was met with protestors who tried to shut down the event. Elsewhere in the south, citizens did not protest because elected council members shared the same doubts that President Salih would fulfill his promises. Meanwhile, street violence escalated. At the end of May, there was an especially violent clash in Lahij province, where three civilians and one policeman were killed.

No reliable reports exist of the total number of al-Hirak protestors killed, injured, and arrested in 2009. But the number was undoubtedly many times higher than the 2008 statistics reported by the Yemeni Observatory for Human Rights. On June 7, two people died in Radfan district of Lahij, when young activists came to a hospital to collect the corpses of friends who had been killed by police at an earlier demonstration. Police opened fire, killing two young leaders of al-Hirak.[54] In reaction, elected members of the district council resigned in protest of government oppression. Then in the middle of June, protestors again blocked main roads, and clashed with security forces. On June 15, nine people were arrested for blocking a road in al-Mukalla, Hadramaut, and on June 17 hundreds of protesters in Lahij's capital, al-Hawta, blocked the main access road into Aden. Dozens were injured and arrested in al-Hawta. On June 24, five protestors were killed in the capital of al-Dali', and dozens more injured.

July 7 is the date Salih celebrated his victory in the 1994 civil war. Leading up to July 7, 2009, police arrested suspected leaders of al-Hirak. This fanned the flames of opposition to a regime that still celebrated, after

---

[53] "Yemeni president pledges reforms after violence in southern areas," *Yemen Post*, May 17, 2009.

[54] There was a revealing profile of the family of one of the deceased in the English-language *Yemen Times* in late July 2009. The article aptly describes the motivation of many young activists in al-Hirak. Fuad Musaed, "Desperate Youth Challenge State at the Cost of their Lives," *Yemen Times*, July 22, 2009.

fifteen long and bitter years, a divisive civil war. *Mareb Press* and *Yemen Post* gave the most complete accounts of the street violence on July 7, 2009. One person was killed, and nine injured in Aden, including three police officers, while dozens were arrested. Rallies in Lahij, al-Dali', Abyan, and Shabwa saw similar numbers. Unexpectedly, al-Mukalla, the capital of Hadramaut, witnessed greater disturbances than any other southern city. Protesters in al-Mukalla began burning stores of merchants and traders from northern provinces. This started a horrific trend in the following weeks, as radicals targeted anyone from a northern background.

On July 11, a northern merchant was stopped while driving on a road through al-Dali'. He was murdered beside his vehicle, along with one of his sons and a brother-in-law.[55] A second son managed to escape, and notify police. On July 25, a grocer from Taiz who ran a store near Zinjibar, Abyan, was murdered. Before the end of the month, senior leaders in al-Hirak condemned these killings, pleading with youth to stop targeting northern civilians. There was a three-month lull, but the practice briefly resumed in late October, and then again in early December. During the last half of 2009, northern residents in the south reported fearing for their lives. Many returned to their homes across the old borderline.

The single worst incident of violence in the south occurred on July 23, when security forces engaged a three-hour battle with Shaykh Tareq al-Fadli's tribal militia in Zinjibar.[56] According to government sources, the fighting started on the street before moving to Shaykh al-Fadli's house, where his tribesmen barricaded themselves with heavy arms including shoulder-fired missiles. The government claimed that al-Fadli's tribal militia had first demanded the release of members held in jail, and then threatened to storm the jailhouse. This led to an exchange of fire between security forces and tribesmen using automatic weapons and RPG launchers. Some reports claimed as many as twenty people died, including six security personnel, and thirty others injured. Among the dead was the assistant chief of police in Zinjibar. When Shaykh al-Fadli refused to surrender, and tribesmen continued fighting from his property, President Salih called off government operations. Negotiations allowed medical treatment for the injured, but in

---

[55] "Three dead in Yemen attack", *Albawaba.com* (in Arabic), July 11, 2009. Leaders of the Southern Movement denied that their followers were involved in the attack. *Aleshteraki. net* (in Arabic), July 11, 2009. Beginning on July 21, 2009, the online news source, *Yemen Post*, ran a two-part series on the deadly politics of al-Dali'.

[56] "Alert Lifted in Abyan after Clashes Continued for More than Three Hours," *News Yemen* (in Arabic), July 23, 2009. "16 Killed, 30 Wounded In Yemen Clashes- Witnesses," Reuters agency, July 23, 2009.

the end the shaykh remained blockaded inside his house.[57] In late September 2009, a new round of fighting occurred at al-Fadli's property. He was confined there through the end of the year.

During the weeks after the first clash in Zinjibar in July 2009, fighting in other southern provinces resembled warfare in Sa'da the previous year. In Lahij province, reports surfaced in August of an unprecedented collapse of security. Many police stations simply ceased operations, and closed down. Locally employed police left their posts because they refused to side with the government. Northern policemen feared that if they stayed on the job, they would be killed by local residents. This was the same month President Salih unleashed "Operation Scorched Earth" in Sa'da and other highland provinces. None of the fighting in southern and eastern provinces compared to the level of violence in the highlands during the last half of 2009. Nonetheless, the violence in the south was just as threatening to Salih's regime. In fact, before the end of the decade, the regime made less distinction between its three main domestic challengers: al-Huthi, al-Hirak, and al-Qaeda. All three ultimately turned to militant activities, seeking to sabotage, and if possible incapacitate, the government in Sanaa.

President Salih preferred to lump the rebels of al-Huthi and activists of al-Hirak into the same threat matrix with al-Qaeda. He frequently described confrontations with his domestic opponents as part of a common battle against terrorists, saboteurs, and anyone who opposed the status quo. Anytime the Yemeni president could play up the threat of al-Qaeda it helped to gain foreign backing, while undermining the position of his domestic critics. In reality, President Salih feared al-Qaeda less than he feared either al-Huthi or al-Hirak. This was because al-Qaeda represented a fringe element without a strong regional constituency in Yemen. Meanwhile, both al-Huthi and al-Hirak carried the potential of spreading popular resistance to Salih's regime inside strategic regions of the country. In May 2009, AQAP leader Nasir al-Wahayshi declared his unsolicited support for al-Hirak and its goal of creating an independent south Yemeni state.[58] Yet those rallying for southern independence did not share

[57] Clark, 2010; pp. 256–257.

[58] Abdul Hameed Bakier, "Al-Qaeda in Yemen Supports Southern Secession," *Terrorism Monitor*, Volume 7, Number 16, June 12, 2009. After al-Wahayshi's declaration of support, various leaders of al-Hirak distanced themselves from al-Qaeda, and denied any linkage with AQAP's leader. Later there were also reports that al-Qaeda's senior leadership in Pakistan rejected the idea of redividing Yemen, since their goal had always been to unite the wider Muslim world. AQAP served as a model for the terrorist group, combining supporters from Yemen and Saudi Arabia without respect to political boundaries.

the agenda of international terrorism. More paradoxically, al-Wahayshi's followers tended to support President Salih's war against al-Huthi rebels in Sa'da.

Devout supporters of al-Huthi advocate Zaydism as a branch of Shia Islam. Generally speaking, they are ideological rivals of Sunni-based *Salafi* associated with al-Qaeda. Between 2005 and 2009, there were numerous reports of al-Qaeda supporters and sympathizers enlisting in the government's battles with al-Huthi rebels. In some cases, the Yemeni army even hired southern mercenaries to fight the war in Sa'da.[59] Thus, it was just as difficult to draw a solid line between the terrorist group and the regime's opponents, as it was to separate al-Qaeda from elements inside the regime. In a country like Yemen with complex tribal and regional identities political alliances and affiliations have a tendency to shift as individual interests are recalculated in changing circumstances. One thing was certain in the late 2000s: President Salih was rapidly losing control of the country as sources of opposition grew in number and strength.

In the last half of 2009, there were rampant rumors in Sanaa that Salih's regime was on the verge of being overthrown. His political security force acted with great paranoia toward anyone suspected of working against state interests. In late July, the spokesman for the JMP coalition in Sanaa, Nayif al-Qanis, began receiving death threats in person and over the phone. On July 30th, he went public with one phone call from a person claiming to be President Salih. The caller warned al-Qanis to stop speaking about JMP opposition to the regime, and threatened that if he did not stop, then his death would be arranged in a "car accident." The latter reference played upon widespread suspicions that prominent individuals, such as former interior minister Yahya al-Mutawakkel and Hashid shaykh General Mujahid Abu Shawarib, had been killed the same way.[60] Months later on November 2, 2009, al-Qanis was abducted in Sanaa, beaten up, and thrown on the street where a passing motorist took him to a hospital.

There is little doubt that Yemen teetered on the edge of becoming a failed state at this time. The western midlands and west coast had not yet entered a stage of rebellion. But there was clearly an unstable environment in every other region. This was true from Sa'da in the northwest to Marib

---

[59] Victoria Clark mentions a cousin of Tareq al-Fadli among the mercenaries in Sa'da. Clark, 2010; pp. 251–252.

[60] During the late 1990s, the founding publisher of *Yemen Times*, Abd al-Aziz al-Sakkaf, died when he was struck by a reckless driver while crossing a street in Sanaa. Friends and family members suspected that this "accident" was arranged by government figures.

and al-Jawf in the central interior desert, and from Lahij and al-Dali' in the southwest to Abyan and Shabwa in the mid-southern region, and even further east to Hadramaut. Various elements of the political opposition certainly had reason to think that President Salih could be overthrown. People in Aden, Hadramaut, and many other areas envisioned a popular uprising like the 1960s, when the British were expelled, the last Zaydi imam was ousted, and all Yemenis embraced a vision of political change. But if Salih's regime were removed from Sanaa, it was not certain that Yemen would remain a united state. There were so many rebellious parts in the country, it seemed unlikely that all of the centrifugal forces could be constrained from tearing the country apart.

In the first week of November 2009, a Syrian writer for *al-Quds al-Arabi* newspaper wrote a plaintive essay entitled, "Is Yemen still a state?"[61] This question weighed heavily on the minds of many Arab leaders. Saudi officials became particularly concerned on August 29, 2009, when an AQAP terrorist nearly assassinated deputy interior minister Prince Muhammad bin Nayef bin Abd al-Aziz at a personal meeting in the Red Sea coastal city of Jidda. Later in the fall, when Yemen's war with al-Huthi rebels briefly spilled across the northern border, the Saudi army and air force both engaged in the fighting. In the first week of October, Amr Musa, head of the Arab League, travelled to Sanaa for a meeting with the Yemeni president. During his visit, thousands of al-Hirak activists poured into the streets of provincial capitals in al-Dali', Lahij, Abyan, and Aden, waving the old south Yemeni flag and holding posters of exiled southern leaders Ali Salem al-Bid and Ali Nasir Muhammad.[62] The crowds wanted the Arab League and United Nations to support southern independence. But Egyptian president Husni Mubarak and other Arab heads of state supported a united Yemen, fearing the consequences for the entire region if Yemeni unity were to fail.

The turmoil in Yemen also weighed heavily on western leaders concerned about the correlation between state failure and the spread of

---

[61] Ammar Dayub, "Is Yemen Still a State?," *al-Quds al-Arabi* (in Arabic), November 7, 2009.

[62] Ahmed al-Haj, "Protests Sweep Across South Yemen," Associated Press agency, October 6, 2009. "South Yemenis Rally for Self-Rule," *al-Jazeera.net*, October 8, 2009. From Germany, Ali Salem al-Bid championed the cause of national independence for southern regions. Ali Nasir Muhammad issued a more cautious statement from Syria, saying that "political change is needed, not secession." *Yemen Post* online provided English translations of interviews with Ali Salem al-Bid on October 5, 2009, originally conducted by the Lebanese newspaper *al-Akhbar*, and with Ali Nasir Muhammad on October 11, 2009, originally conducted by the UAE newspaper *al-Khaleej*.

al-Qaeda. During the fall of 2009, many western leaders reacted with their own calls of support for Yemeni unity. The newly elected U.S. president Barack Obama rushed emergency economic and military aid to President Salih, fearing his government might collapse and al-Qaeda gain strength.[63] A few months later on Christmas day, it became clear that AQAP had been planning to strike targets on American soil when a terrorist attack was thwarted aboard an American passenger aircraft. As Northwest Airlines Flight 253 neared Detroit, Michigan, after a transatlantic trip from Amsterdam, Holland, a student traveling from Yemen attempted to ignite a bomb. The student, Umar Farouq Abd al-Mutallab, had trained and prepared for his mission with AQAP in Yemen. Yet he was originally from Nigeria, the son of a wealthy businessman who had earlier tried to warn American officials in Africa about his son. Traveling with a Nigerian passport, the student bomber managed to evade airport security in Amsterdam by carrying a chemical explosive inside plastic in the underwear of his pants. Crew and passengers aboard the aircraft were fortunate to disarm the bomb when the chemical failed to detonate.

Following the bombing attempt on Christmas day, British Prime Minister Gordon Brown called a special meeting in London, England, for January 27, 2010, to address growing international security concerns about Yemen. President Obama welcomed Prime Minister Brown's plan to hold the meeting on the eve of an earlier scheduled London conference about multinational operations in Afghanistan. British Foreign Minister David Miliband led the Yemen talks with U.S. Secretary of State Hillary Clinton and representatives of other countries, including Yemen's new prime minister Ali Muhammad Mujawar and foreign minister Abu Bakr al-Qirby. The urgency with which this meeting was arranged on short notice reflected Yemen's rise to the top of global security concerns. Miliband and Clinton used the meeting to form a new "Friends of Yemen" group, calling for political reform inside the country and greater foreign assistance to help stimulate its economy.[64]

Before the London meeting adjourned, a second meeting of potential financial donors was announced the next month in Riyadh, Saudi Arabia. At this second meeting of "Friends of Yemen" during late February 2010, representatives from GCC states balked at Yemen's requests for new

---

[63] "US Yemen Assistance Increased," Yemen Embassy in USA, Press Office, September 15, 2009. "Yemen Signs Military Deal with US," Reuters agency, November 11, 2009.

[64] Jonathan Marcus, "Can Friends of Yemen bring about stability?," *BBC News*, January 28, 2010. Karen DeYoung, "Hillary Clinton among those praising Yemen's efforts against al-Qaeda," *Washington Post*, January 28, 2010.

financial aid. Earlier in 2006, GCC states pledged Yemen a combined $5.5 billion. During the interim four years, only 10 percent of these funds was disbursed because Yemen lacked transparency to prove the money would be spent on legitimate social welfare programs.[65] At the meeting in Riyadh, Yemeni Prime Minister Mujawar presented a five-year spending request (2010–2015) totaling an amount several times larger than what the GCC offered in 2006. GCC members demanded that the Yemeni government first prove its ability to spend the 2006 funds before making any new requests. If such proof could not be demonstrated, then the GCC members asked the Yemeni government to allow their own national relief organizations to operate inside the country.

There is a perception in the international aid community, among countries of the GCC as well as Western countries, that money donated to Yemen disappears into the pockets of corrupt politicians. Among some observers, there was also a belief that President Salih instigated security problems solely for the sake of alarming his neighbors on the Arab peninsula, and drawing attention from the United States and Western countries. Salih and his closest associates undoubtedly stirred up troubles inside the country. They held hardened, cynical outlooks toward foreign aid programs, and were aware that foreigners took interest in Yemen only during times of crisis. But in 2010, the reasons why Yemen needed foreign aid were not manufactured. Yemen faced deep political, social, and economic troubles at this time. These troubles had boiled below the surface for nearly a decade. In the mid-2000s, they started to boil over. And in 2009, they erupted with full force.

One of the problems with giving foreign aid directly to President Salih's government was the public perception that external powers wanted to prop up an unpopular and failing regime. This was the trouble with the bulk of American foreign aid in 2009 and 2010. The Obama administration dramatically increased U.S. military assistance from less than $5 million shortly before coming to office to $155 million in 2010 (and a proposed $1.2 billion in the coming six years). The United States was criticized, both inside and outside Yemen, for sending the wrong signal by rushing greater military aid to Sanaa, as well as military trainers and advisors, while offering much less social and economic assistance. The military aid reinforced the idea that Americans were mainly motivated by matters of high security, instead of Yemen's more prevalent problems of poverty, government corruption, and internal regional divisions.

---

[65] Mohammed al Qadhi, "Bureaucratic red tape blocks foreign aid to Yemen," *The National*, UAE, March 1, 2010.

9

Yemen's Political Meltdown

Following the terrorist incident in the skies over Detroit, Michigan in December 2009, American media referred to Yemen as al-Qaeda's "new safe haven." According to one theory at the time, when U.S. and coalition forces increased their operations in Afghanistan and the border region with Pakistan in 2008–2009, al-Qaeda fighters fled the mountains and deserts of South Asia for a similar, yet more secure environment on the southwest corner of the Arabian peninsula. Western journalists descended on Sanaa in droves, seeking the latest secrets and mysteries of this obscure land. In January 2010, news headlines about threats emanating from Yemen splashed across American television screens, newspapers, and political magazines. For the first time since the USS *Cole* bombing in 2000, Yemen was back in the public spotlight.

Inside Washington, DC, some commentators described President Barack Obama as "caught off guard" by the attempted terrorist attack aboard Northwest Flight 253. There was renewed talk of U.S. intelligence officers "failing to connect the dots" before al-Qaeda reached American soil. A few members of Congress fed a growing public hysteria by portraying the president as weak on national security. Connecticut Senator Joseph Lieberman called for a ground invasion of Yemen to wipe out al-Qaeda's base of operations.[1] Despite the panicked reaction on Capitol Hill and in the media, President Obama already had his sights on Yemen. Over the preceding year, his counterterrorism advisor John Brennan, and military

[1] Sam Stein, "Lieberman: The United States Must Preemptively Act in Yemen," *Huffington Post*, December 27, 2009.

commanders like General David Petraeus, made repeated visits to the country, in order to discuss the need for greater coordination with President Salih.[2] Furthermore, prior to the Christmas Day incident, U.S. military forces carried out two attacks inside Yemen, although these operations were denied at the time by White House officials.

Working with Yemeni authorities, President Obama approved two separate missile strikes on suspected AQAP bases in mid-December 2009. This followed discovery that a Yemeni-American cleric with ties to AQAP had an indirect link to an attack the previous month at Fort Hood, Texas. On November 5, 2009, a lone gunman of Jordanian descent, Major Nidal Malik Hasan, killed more than a dozen American military personnel at the U.S. army base. U.S. investigators learned that Hasan had been in contact with the cleric Anwar al-Aulaqi, who was then living in Yemen.[3] Al-Aulaqi provided Hasan with the *fatwa*, or religious ruling to justify the attack, that he had sought by email. After the shootings, al-Aulaqi wrote a message on his Internet website praising "the heroic act of brother Nidal."[4] In jihadist circles around the world, Nidal Hasan became a champion of al-Qaeda's cause, while Anwar al-Aulaqi developed a reputation as a guide for Muslims wanting to target America.

The next month President Obama sent Brennan to Sanaa to meet Yemen's president, and coordinate an attack against Anwar al-Aulaqi and other suspects in AQAP. Two days later on December 8, the U.S. Senate passed a resolution, requesting the Obama administration "use all

---

[2] "US Says it Helps Yemen Get Rid of al-Qaeda Threats," *News Yemen* Online, October 5, 2009.

[3] Anwar al-Aulaqi's relationship with AQAP leader Nasir al-Wahayshi was unclear. Both men came from families of Shabwa province in the mid-southern region. But this may be their only personal connection, since Anwar al-Aulaqi was born and raised in America. In the late 1960s, Anwar's parents fled Shabwa under Marxist rule in the former PDRY. He attended school in New Mexico, while his father completed a doctoral degree in agricultural sciences. When Anwar's father was appointed to be agricultural minister in north Yemen, the family relocated to Sanaa where Anwar attended high school. He returned to the United States for university studies in the 1990s, and began working as an imam at mosques in the United States after completing a Masters degree. The official "9/11 Report" found that two of the 9/11 hijackers from Saudi Arabia had earlier attended Anwar al-Aulaqi's mosque in Falls Church, Virginia, as well as his mosque in San Diego, California. Kean and Hamilton, *The 9/11 Report*, "Chapter 7: The Attack Looms," footnote 33. Due to extensive police surveillance and pressure after 9/11, al-Aulaqi left the United States for England, and later Yemen. U.S. officials pressed the Yemeni government to arrest him, and he was tortured before being released from jail. The experience radicalized his views of America, and over the Internet he began to advocate jihad against the United States.

[4] Michael Isikoff, "Imam Anwar al Awlaki Calls Hasan 'Hero'," *Newsweek*, November 9, 2009.

appropriate measures" to confront threats in Yemen, and prevent it becoming a failed state. The first American missile strike came nine days later on December 17, when an American cruise missile slammed into an area of Abyan province in Yemen's mid-southern region. The second U.S. missile strike occurred on Christmas eve in neighboring Shabwa province, the home of al-Aulaqi's family, just one day before the failed bombing in Detroit. Before President Obama came to office, he had pledged to target al-Qaeda on fronts like Yemen. The airstrikes in December were his first effort to fulfill a campaign pledge.

THE INTERSECTION OF AMERICAN
AND YEMENI INTERESTS

When AQAP's bomb failed to detonate on Christmas day, President Obama fortunately did not overreact. Still in his first year on the job, he refused to order a military invasion of Yemen like the previous administration's mistaken raid into Iraq. The new White House leader realized that a heavy U.S. military presence in Yemen would have disastrous consequences by increasing support for al-Qaeda throughout the region. The likely consequences would be far worse than the impact of the earlier American invasion of Iraq, where the presence of U.S. troops served as a tremendous recruitment tool for al-Qaeda between 2003 and 2007. President Obama keenly understood that the dangers in Yemen were greater than one radicalized Nigerian student. On American television, comedians like Jon Stewart and Stephen Colbert lampooned the public hysteria about the "underwear bomber," and focus on Yemen quickly faded until the next year when a second AQAP plot was revealed. In late October 2010, plastic explosives were found hidden in printer ink cartridges shipped from Yemen aboard cargo airplanes bound for the United States. None of the bombs exploded.

Meanwhile inside Yemen, there was a severe backlash against the earlier U.S. missile strikes in Abyan and Shabwa, as well as the subsequent British plan to hold an international conference on Yemeni security issues in London. Following the first cruise missile strike in Abyan's Mehfed district, President Salih claimed responsibility and denied any American involvement. The Obama administration only admitted providing technical assistance to Salih's regime. Yemeni and American officials claimed the first strike killed as many as twenty-four AQAP terrorists at a rural training facility in the small village of al-Ma'ajala. But residents of nearby towns and villages reported innocent civilians died in the attack. During rescue operations at the site, digging through rubble of a few collapsed mud-brick homes, they uncovered more than forty corpses, mainly poor women and children who died in their sleep.[5] An official Yemeni parliamentary delegation visited the site. It concluded that those who died were not part of *tantheem al-Qaeda* – the "organization of al-Qaeda," but rather *tantheem al-fuqahaa* – the "organization of the poor."[6]

Despite government denials in Sanaa and Washington, local residents correctly identified an American warship off Yemen's southern coast as the source of the first attack. In the early morning sky, they saw a missile contrail coming from the direction of the sea. They also found identifiable fragments of a U.S.-manufactured Tomahawk cruise missile on the village grounds. In the spring of 2010, Amnesty International sent a team of investigators to inspect collected evidence in al-Ma'ajala. It released its findings in June: at least one American cruise missile, plus hundreds of cluster bombs, killed dozens of civilians.[7] According to one Amnesty International official in London, "the fact that so many of the victims were actually women and children indicates that the attack was grossly irresponsible, particularly given the likely use of cluster munitions."

Later in the year, Wikileaks released a U.S. embassy document that summarized a meeting in Sanaa between President Salih and General David Petraeus three weeks after the airstrike on al-Ma'ajala. During the meeting, Salih and his deputy prime minister, Rashad al-Alimi, joked about the lies they told Yemeni parliament members seeking information about the Abyan airstrike: "We'll continue saying the bombs are ours, not yours," al-Alimi laughed as he spoke with Petraeus.[8] When this quote appeared on Wikileaks's website in December 2010, it confirmed long held suspicions among Yemen's general public, while fueling deep distrust of Salih's regime. But this was not the only news fueling public distrust.

---

[5] "Fifty-eight Killed in the Assault on *al-Ma'ajala*" (in Arabic), *al-Masdar* Online, December 17, 2009. This and other Yemeni news sources published horrific photographs of the dead, but later reduced the number of fatalities to forty-three. The fact that civilians died due to an American missile was later reported by the *New York Times* in an August 14, 2010, story, "Secret Assault on Terrorism Widens on Two Continents."

[6] The elected governor of Abyan issued a statement refuting official stories that supporters of al-Hirak in al-Ma'ajala had ties to al-Qaeda. "Breaking News: Abyan's Governor Refutes, via *al-Jazeera*, Any Relationship between al-Hirak and al-Qaeda," *Aden Press* Online, December 21, 2009.

[7] "US Missile 'Used in Yemen Raid'," *BBC News*, June 7, 2010. Days after the strike, al-Hirak held a solidarity rally at the bombing site. Tragically, someone stepped on a cluster bomb that resulted in more deaths and injuries.

[8] Wikileaks, "General Petraeus' Meeting with Saleh on Security Assistance," #10SANAA4; January 4, 2010.

Prime Minister Brown's announcement of plans for the London meeting set off alarm bells in Yemeni society. The thought of Western powers holding an emergency meeting about the country fed wild speculation of hidden agendas in London and Washington. Some asked if the failed airliner bombing over Detroit was being used as an excuse for military intervention. During the first weeks of the new year, rumors of a pending American invasion leapt between *qat*-sessions in the private salons of Sanaa, Taiz, Aden, and other cities. Some rumors spoke of a new "Sykes-Picot agreement" with Western leaders planning a revived colonial mandate on Arab lands, placing Yemen under an international trusteeship.[9] Other rumors spoke of American and British designs to partition Yemen into multiple states, similar to what happened to Greater Syria after World War I.

Since 9/11, Yemen had long been mentioned as a potential target of the American military. Following the invasions of Afghanistan and Iraq, there was ample reason for Yemenis to suspect that they could be next. Once U.S. forces became bogged down in Iraq's civil war between 2004 and 2007, fears of an American invasion diminished. But after President Obama was elected in November 2008, pledging to leave Iraq and focus on al-Qaeda in Pakistan and other countries like Yemen, some found new reason for concern about American aggression. Following the missile strikes in December 2009, it did not help matters when Senator Lieberman advocated putting "boots on the ground," and spoke of Yemen as "America's next war." These comments, and other inflated rhetoric on the internet, did nothing to dampen rumors about a new "Sykes-Picot" plan to divide Arab lands.

A couple of weeks prior to the London meeting, more than 150 Islamic clerics, headed by Islah leaders, organized a public conference in Sanaa. On January 14, 2010, they declared their intentions to urge militant *jihad*, if the London meeting resulted in sending foreign troops to their country.[10] This

---

[9] These rumors were reported in a number of local Arabic newspapers, including *al-Masdar*, which quoted Hashid's new paramount shaykh Sadeq al-Ahmar, son of the late Shaykh Abdallah al-Ahmar, warning of American and British plans to impose a "Sykes-Picot agreement and partition of Yemen." A reporter for *al-Ahram* in Egypt picked up the story of Shaykh Sadeq al-Ahmar's rumor. Mohamed Hafiz, "First Guns, Then Butter," *al-Ahram Weekly* Online, Issue No. 94, February 4, 2010. As early as July 2009, Shaykh Abd al-Majid al-Zindani had warned of internal and external plots to enable foreign colonization of Yemen. Husayn al-Jarbani, "al-Zindani Accuses Some Yemenis of Calling for the Foreign Invasion and Colonization of Yemen," *Asharq Alawsat* (in Arabic), #11181, July 9, 2009.

[10] Yusuf Qadi, "Al-Zindani: The London Conference Intends to Impose a Type of Trusteeship on the Country," *al-Masdar* Online (in Arabic), January 14, 2010.

was no idle threat. It was a public statement reflecting the feelings of a broad segment of Yemen's twenty-five million citizens. The individuals who endorsed the conference's final statement were not radical fringe elements, hiding in the shadows with al-Qaeda. In attendance were sons of the late paramount shaykh of the Hashid tribal federation, Abdallah bin Husayn al-Ahmar, the Salafi religious leader Shaykh Abd al-Majid al-Zindani, and many others. These men represented the tribal and religious establishments of Yemen, all of whom were capable of rallying hundreds of thousands, if not millions of trained fighters. The mood in Yemen was turning dark in an already desperate and dangerous environment.

It is important to bear in mind that Yemen's Islamic politics is broader than a single organization like al-Qaeda. Beginning in the early 1990s, Islah operated as a fully functional political party with its own social and economic platforms, strategies of elite recruitment, and public interest representation.[11] Between 1994 and 1997, Islah briefly served in a coalition government with the General People's Congress. Afterward it stood in opposition to President Salih's ruling GPC party. Other formal religious parties exist in the country, including some representing the traditional Zaydi ruling class. Each of these parties is more influential in Yemeni society than Osama Bin Laden's al-Qaeda group. Due to the country's complex, conservative, and highly traditional social system, it does not lend itself to easy equations between Islamists and terrorists. Expressions of anti-American sentiment, by religious clerics or regular citizens, certainly do not equate with motivations to join al-Qaeda.

Like most Arab countries, the main source of anti-American sentiment comes from US support of Israeli policies that deny Palestinian national rights. This is true of Yemenis who claim political affiliation with Islamic parties, as well as Yemenis who support socialist and secular nationalist parties. In this sense, anti-American sentiment is largely political, and unrelated to the radical agendas of al-Qaeda. Only a small percentage of the population ever supported al-Qaeda, but this support grew whenever U.S. missiles killed civilians, or U.S. politicians called for military invasion. After the missile strike on al-Ma'ajala, supporters of al-Hirak from Aden to Hadramaut rallied in the streets, angrily chanting the village's name. During this time, there is no way to know how many supporters of the movement were radicalized to take up arms and fight the Yemeni and U.S. governments.

President Salih's cooperation in America's "war on terrorism" contributed to a confluence of political turbulence in Yemen. Without the

---

[11] Schwedler, 2007.

widespread public rejection of President Salih's commitment to President Bush's policies between late 2001 and 2004, a strong domestic opposition may never have emerged between 2005 and 2008. This points to an important lesson: a too close association between the American and Yemeni governments, particularly on military and security affairs, undermines domestic politics in the country. This remained true under the Obama administration. Far from making Yemen more stable, and diminishing its problems with terrorism, the American missile strikes in December 2009 fostered greater insecurity. And if the United States ever sent an invasion force to prop up the Yemeni government, it would destabilize broad sections of the country, creating a state of anarchy similar to Iraq between 2003 and 2007, or Somalia since the 1990s.

MYTH AND REALITY OF YEMEN'S POLITICAL VIOLENCE

Before the first U.S. cruise missile slammed into al-Ma'ajala village, a Pandora's box of troubles had already been opened in Yemen. This was due to President Salih's use of brutal force against al-Hirak and al-Huthi during the preceding three years. After the December 2009 missile strike, the new dynamic meant supporters of al-Hirak in southwestern and mid-southern regions began employing tactics similar to al-Qaeda. In Salih's mind, if U.S. missile strikes could provoke violent confrontations with al-Hirak, then it would serve his ultimate goal of waging warfare against his most worrisome opposition in the south. Indeed, this was the outcome of events in the spring and summer of 2010, when the Yemeni president launched a full-scale war in Lahij, al-Dali', and Abyan. Although this may have pleased members of Salih's regime who sought American backing under the cover of fighting al-Qaeda, it also pleased AQAP leaders who suddenly multiplied their recruitment of young men enraged by the deaths at al-Ma'ajala.

Before al-Hirak's peaceful street protests commenced in 2007, many of its rank and file, especially among YSP members and retired southern military officers, soldiers, and policemen, were the perceived enemies of al-Qaeda. Earlier in the 1990s, these rank and file members faced regular attacks by the former mujahideen who had fought with Shaykh Tareq al-Fadli and other southern exiles tied to Osama Bin Laden in Afghanistan. Shaykh al-Fadli and most members of traditional southern ruling class families previously considered the YSP, and its members who founded al-Hirak, to be "infidel" Marxists. Yet President Salih's repression of al-Hirak, combined with outside pressure from the U.S. government, now forced more members of al-Hirak into the same camp with the newly formed AQAP. From al-Hirak's perspective, since the U.S. missile attacks in December 2009 preceded Salih's warfare on southern provinces, America had merely enabled the continuation of a military occupation spanning fifteen years.

The danger of Yemeni al-Qaeda in southern and eastern provinces is real. On occasion, when Yemeni and American forces targeted AQAP leaders, they had success capturing or killing its members. On the day of the fateful cruise missile strike in al-Ma'ajala, President Salih's forces carried out a simultaneous raid northeast of Sanaa at a site in Arhab. This is the home district of the elderly religious leader and former spiritual advisor to Osama Bin Laden, Shaykh al-Zindani. Yet it was not clear whether Salih's motive involved threats from AQAP or rival tribes in the highland region. A pattern of mixed success continued one week later, when the second U.S. missile strike in Shabwa province killed two low-level AQAP recruits. In the middle of March 2010, there was a third American missile strike in a small Abyan village called al-Qashaber, killing an al-Qaeda member named Jamil al-Anbari.[12] Two months later, yet another U.S. missile mistakenly killed the popularly elected deputy governor of Marib province, Shaykh Jaber al-Shabwani. President Salih had previously tasked Shaykh al-Shabwani to negotiate a truce with local tribal supporters of AQAP. While returning from a meeting with the tribe, al-Shabwani died when his vehicle was struck by a drone-fired missile. This gross error did nothing to dissuade local tribesmen to cease acts of violence. In angry retaliation, they bombed a section of oil pipeline in the area.

Prior to the worst fighting in 2010, one development on the ground in Abyan revealed Yemen's often perplexing side. Shaykh Tareq al-Fadli, who remained confined to his home in Zinjibar since the previous summer, used the internet in early February to circulate video of himself standing at attention while the American flag was raised in front of his house as "The Star-Spangled Banner" played on loudspeakers.[13] This former ally of

---

[12] Local reports claimed a total of seven people were killed and twenty-three others injured. Scott Shane, Mark Mazzetti, and Robert F. Worth, "Secret Assault on Terrorism Widens on Two Continents," *New York Times*, August 14, 2010.

[13] "Followers of Tareq al-Fadli Raise the American Flag in Abyan," *Mareb Press* (in Arabic), February 2, 2010. Later the *New York Times* ran a long profile of Tareq al-Fadli, telling the story of how he raised the stars and stripes banner. Robert Worth, "Is Yemen the Next Afghanistan?," *New York Times*, July 6, 2010. In the meantime, Shaykh al-Fadli had released another video of himself burning the U.S., British, Yemeni, and PDRY flags. This second act, taken in frustration at the American and Yemeni governments, and perhaps responding to local critics who did not approve the first video, symbolized the traditional tribal ambivalence to nation-states.

Osama Bin Laden, and late convert to al-Hirak's cause, was using the new media to send a message: he and other members of the southern opposition could oppose the regime in Sanaa without intending any hostility toward America. In all likelihood he also wanted to avoid U.S. cruise missiles raining down on his family home, if someone in the regime chose to give the geographic coordinates of his house to U.S. commanders. Nonetheless, Shaykh al-Fadli clearly intended to demonstrate friendly motives. In the following days, protestors waved the U.S. flag and the former flag of south Yemen.

During interviews in January and February 2010, Shaykh al-Fadli claimed that President Salih had used Western fears of al-Qaeda to justify attacks against domestic political opponents. Leaders of the two main parties in the JMP coalition, Yasin Said Numan of the YSP and Abd al-Wahhab al-Ansi of Islah, both expressed similar views.[14] Evidence indicated they were right because after the second U.S. missile strike in December 2009, President Salih's initial operation in the south was not against AQAP. Instead, he ordered security forces to invade the home and office of *al-Ayyam* newspaper's publisher, whose main infraction had been reporting opposition activities. On January 3, 2010, troops surrounded the Bashraheel family compound in Aden's southeastern Crater district, overlooking the bay at Sera island. They came to arrest Hisham Bashraheel on trumped up charges from an old property dispute in Sanaa. It was obvious that Salih sought to silence the independent media prior to his upcoming military campaign against al-Hirak.

During the initial clash at the Bashraheel compound, one of the newspaper's security guards was shot and killed, while a few government troops were injured by return gunfire.[15] Two days later, after a long siege, the publisher and two of his sons were taken into police custody, and sent to prison in Sanaa. *Al-Ayyam* had been a thorn in President Salih's side since the middle 1990s. More than any other southern institution, the newspaper weakened his regime and strengthened political opposition. There was always a risk that AQAP could benefit from the political instability generated by al-Hirak, and fanned by *al-Ayyam*'s news coverage. Perhaps

---

[14] Mohamed bin Sallam, "The GPC and JMP Exchange Accusations of Terrorism and Instigating Disorder in the South," *Yemen Times*, February 2, 2009. Mohammed al Qadhi, "Yemeni Government and Secessionists Trade Blame for Deaths," *The National*, UAE, December 4, 2009. Both reports quote YSP member and al-Hirak leader, Nasir al-Khabji, making the strongest charges against the regime in Sanaa.
[15] "One Killed and Three Injured Among the Guards of al-Ayyam Newspaper; Six Injured among the Security Forces," *al-Masdar* online (in Arabic), January 4, 2010.

government officials in Sanaa imagined that this justified their crackdown on Aden's largest newspaper. But the greater risk was that it would drive social forces in a more violent direction.

Across the first six months of 2010, antigovernment violence steadily increased in southwestern and mid-southern provinces. In late January and early February, violent attacks against government personnel and facilities in Abyan, Lahij, and al-Dali' became so frequent and severe that security forces acknowledged their complete loss of control. On February 17, President Salih spoke in belligerent tones about secessionists seeking to break up the country. The next month, he amassed armed forces outside large towns and cities, vowing to "crush al-Hirak with an iron fist," just as he had sought the previous year to squash al-Huthi forces in Sa'da during "Operation Scorched Earth."[16] In early 2010, President Salih shifted to pursue a peace settlement with armed rebel leaders in Sa'da. This led to a truce, which held reasonably well through the end of the year, as the army more aggressively confronted al-Hirak in southern and eastern provinces. For the first time since 2005, there were more killed and injured in southern provinces than in Sa'da and other provinces north of Sanaa.

The clearest sign that al-Hirak's tactics were starting to merge with AQAP was two prison breaks in the spring of 2010. First, near the end of March, someone used a hand grenade to blast open the main prison in al-Dali'. This allowed the escape of more than forty leaders of al-Hirak. Then in the middle of June, a group of AQAP fighters attacked a prison in Tawahi district on the south side of Aden's harbor, killing eleven people including seven soldiers, and releasing all prisoners at this high security facility. The next week, after a broad campaign of arrests inside Aden, street clashes broke out following reports that one of the new detainees died while being tortured in jail. An even more brazen attack occurred in Abyan's capital, Zinjibar, on July 14, when multiple motorcycles and cars were used in a well-coordinated attack on the local police headquarters and political security building. More than twenty men armed with RPGs and machine guns took part in the assaults.[17] After more than two hours of fighting, there were dozens of deaths and injuries on all sides.

The latter attack in Zinjibar bore all the hallmarks of an al-Qaeda operation with the goal of hitting more than one target at a time. But

[16] "Salih Declares War on the South" *Aden Press* (in Arabic), March 7, 2010. Mohammed al-Qadhi, "Yemeni President 'Will Crush Activists' but Welcomes Talks," *The National*, UAE, March 9, 2010.

[17] Mohammed al-Qadhi, "Al Qaeda Ramps Up Attacks in Yemen," *The National*, UAE, July 14, 2010.

al-Qaeda typically operates clandestinely with teams of militants working in small, isolated cells where attacks are usually planned months or years apart. This was generalized violence against government targets, and it seemed to occur on a biweekly basis amidst a complete breakdown of law and order. The wave of violence in 2010 more closely resembled the violence in Iraq before the "awakening" of the Sunni Arab triangle northwest of Baghdad in 2007. Between 2004 and 2007 in Iraq, there was little difference between the attacks of al-Zarqawi's "al-Qaeda in Iraq" group and the more numerous assaults by members of the Iraqi resistance. Similarly, the violence in southern Yemen reflected resistance by a region-wide opposition that was greater than a few isolated terrorist cells. Earlier AQAP attacks in Sanaa and Marib were more typical of al-Qaeda. The violence in 2010 reflected the actions of a people who felt they had been living under military occupation since 1994.

The main cause of political instability in Yemen was clearly coming from sources of regional opposition, not al-Qaeda. Between 2004 and 2009, the government's war with al-Huthi rebels led to far greater violence than either al-Qaeda or the southern opposition. Nearly ten thousand people were killed during the fighting in the northwest highlands.[18] This included more than a thousand fatalities on the government's side, as well as the side of al-Huthi rebels, with innocent civilians making up the largest percentage of deaths. By comparison, barely a couple hundred members of al-Hirak were killed between 2007 and 2009, with less than twenty fatalities among government forces in southern provinces. Al-Dali' province was the center of most of the early southern violence. Between April 2007 and March 2010, there were thirty protestors killed and 320 injured in al-Dali', with hundreds more arrested.[19] The number of people killed by AQAP during the same years was only a fraction of al-Hirak's death toll.

Between 2006 and 2009, al-Qaeda terrorists killed no more than fifty people in the entire country, including just fourteen foreigners. Despite two attacks on the American embassy, and other assaults on compounds where westerners worked and lived, Susan al-Baneh was the only American citizen killed by Yemeni al-Qaeda after the October 2000 bombing of the USS *Cole*. The danger of AQAP was obviously exaggerated in comparison to the horrific loss of life during the Yemeni government's battles with al-Huthi and al-Hirak rebels. Americans certainly had little reason to fear

---

[18] "Armed Conflict in Northern Yemen," Human Rights Watch, 2009.
[19] "More than Thirty Killed and 320 Injured," *Mareb Press* online (in Arabic), March 19, 2010.

AQAP, since neither the organization's Christmas 2009 bombing attempt in the skies over Detroit, nor its November 2010 cargo bombs, caused a single fatality or serious injury.

VOICES OF REGIONAL OPPOSITION

Back in the early fall of 2009, the *Yemen Times* published a story highlighting the regional characteristics of Yemen's political opposition at the end of the decade. On September 7, 2009, the chief editor Nadia al-Sakkaf described three new regional opposition formations in Shabwa, the Tihama, and Taiz.[20] She referred to al-Hirak as the original and largest opposition group without mentioning al-Huthi rebels in the northwest highlands. A group called the "Desert Alliance" was formed in May 2009. Its leadership in northern Shabwa province demanded a new federal division of powers in Yemen, allowing interior desert communities to keep 50 percent of all revenues from the extraction of petroleum on their lands.[21] Next came the "Tihama Coastal" movement in al-Hudayda province, followed by the "Central (Midland) Plateau" movement formed the same month of al-Sakkaf's article.

Nadia al-Sakkaf described the Desert Alliance as a movement formed in the central interior region, including Marib, al-Jawf, and desert areas of Shabwa and Hadramaut, thus straddling the old north-south border. She mentions two leaders of the movement, al-Sharif Abd al-Rab Salih bin Soud and Shaykh Salih Fareed al-Suraima, president of the Shabwa Council for Just Development. The latter brought together "intellectual and social leaders" representing economic interests similar to the interests of citizens in Marib, who complained about the regime in Sanaa exploiting petroleum resources without providing adequate local development funds. "All we are asking for is a fair, decent life, knowing that our (province) has been providing the whole republic with oil and gas," Shaykh al-Suraima was quoted saying. "It is only fair that some of our own resources be used for the benefit of the locals."

A member of parliament from Taiz organized the "Central Plateau" movement with help from supporters in al-Bayda, al-Rayma, and parts of Ibb province. This area covers the entire midlands, which is another possible

[20] Nadia al-Sakkaf, "Popular Movement Demands Rights for Central Yemen," *Yemen Times*, September 7, 2009.
[21] "Following the Formation of the Movement of Sons of the Desert, al-Sharif Demands Federal Government and Fifty Percent of Oil Revenues," *Mareb Press* online (in Arabic), July 14, 2010.

translation of the Arabic for "central plateau." The head of the group, Sultan al-Samie, described multiple preparatory meetings in 2009, including coordination of activities with the "Tihama Coastal" movement. In June 2010, al-Samie also led a solidarity campaign with members of al-Hirak in al-Dali' province.[22] He and more than seventy people from Taiz drove a "peace convoy" loaded with food and supplies south to al-Dali', in order to break a two months army siege of the city. According to al-Samie, a major reason for regional opposition movements was public frustration with formal politics. "The parliament is a joke, and its decisions are ready-made elsewhere. We, as parliamentarians, can't even demand our own rights, let alone the rights of the people whom we represent," he said. "This is why such popular movements have succeeded as an alternative to demanding people's rights."

When Nadia al-Sakkaf asked al-Samie if his group was prepared to face violence from President Salih's regime, he replied: "We can't lose more than we are already losing today, and all we want is to be treated as equal citizens and enjoy the wealth of our own country." The newspaper editor also interviewed local supporters in Taiz, and one outside supporter from Hadramaut province. The latter individual stated: "It is time that the brave men of Taiz wake from their sleep and join others in their revolutionary efforts to oust the corrupt regime. Taiz was the starting place of the revolution in 1962, and it is time for a new one." A revolutionary climate was forming in Yemen months before the first street protests in the Tunisian town of Sidi Bouzid, where Muhammad Bouazizi's desperate act of self-immolation on December 17, 2010, ignited passions across the Arab world.

In Taiz, Nadia al-Sakkaf quoted two people who mentioned the political and economic dominance of highland tribes around Sanaa as one of the main reasons for the growth of regionally based opposition. One professor at Taiz University commented: "we run companies and teach at universities. We are the engineers, doctors, and professionals, yet we don't even get the minimal percentage of decision-making positions because of the way things are today: merit is not how qualified you are, it is from which tribe you come from." A female professional in Taiz said, "we aim to liberate our country from the control of corrupt tribal oppressors. It will be an Islamic, leftist revolution that works to spread peace and justice in a civilized way." This statement foretold the larger popular uprising in early 2011, when massive street protests swept through the country. The forces of revolt in Yemen were not yet ripe in 2009 and 2010 primarily because of the fragmentation

---

[22] Mohamed Bin Sallam, "Taiz Peace Convoy Moves to Break Blockade on Al-Dali'," *Yemen Times*, June 17, 2010.

PHOTO 18. Family home in Tihama near Zabid

of regional opposition to President Salih and other powerful figures in the highland mountains.

Citizens in Tihama along the Red Sea basin arguably had the greatest reasons to feel aggrieved. They were worse off than citizens from Taiz who generally enjoy better educational and health institutions, as well as a more industrialized economy. People living in the sweltering heat of the western coastal region have long complained about discrimination and poor revenue sharing by government officials in Sanaa.[23] Tihama is one of Yemen's most impoverished regions with very high unemployment and rising malnutrition among children. In 2009, there were disturbing reports of child trafficking and slavery in Tihama and neighboring al-Wussab south of al-Rayma on the western slopes of Yemen's mountains.[24] On June 24, 2009, Islah's newspaper *al-Sahwa* ran a profile of al-Wussab that described 60 percent unemployment.[25] Citizens complained of racial discrimination, and spoke of regular harassment by soldiers from the

---

[23] "Poor People of al-Hudayda Complain in silence: Influential Officials and Military Leaders Pillage al-Hudayda Lands," *Yemen Post*, August 31, 2009.

[24] "Story of Slavery in Yemen Disclosed," *News Yemen*, February 21, 2009. Omar al-Omqi, "The Untold Story of Slavery in Yemen," *Yemen Times*, July 8, 2010.

[25] "Wossab Trapped in Marginalization, Discrimination," *Sahwa.net*, June 24, 2009.

highland region who often arrest them without cause, only to demand bribes for their release.

Tihama and al-Wussab continue to suffer from the highland tribesman's legendary "horizontal rifle," which is still in use today. There is a popular saying inside Yemen, *hamihu harambu*, "the one who (supposedly) protects is the one who causes harm." This applies to the experience of most citizens who interact with the government's military and security forces. Since 1994, it describes the experience of citizens in southern and eastern regions. But in Tihama, it describes the experience of citizens as far back as the 1920s. In late 2009, government forces clashed with local residents defending their homes in the Tihama market town of Bayt al-Faqih.[26] Troops were sent to a neighborhood where an outside investor had swindled ownership of property for the purpose of commercial development. Hundreds of people were being evicted. When bulldozers began destroying cinderblock and corrugated metal dwellings, local residents threw stones as did protesters in al-Dali' in 2000, when they drew inspiration from the simultaneous Palestinian intifada.

The evidence of grievances fragmenting Yemen's population into ever more violent regional opposition movements was on display in May 2010. During preparations for what should have been a grand celebration of Yemeni national unity's twentieth anniversary, there was a string of assassination attempts against members of President Salih's cabinet. The motor convoys of two deputy prime ministers, Sadeq Amin Abu Ras who was responsible for local administration, and Rashad al-Alimi who was responsible for internal security, were attacked in Shabwa and Lahij, respectively, during the first two weeks of May.[27] Both men escaped without injury, but three security officers were killed and four others injured. Around the same time, the government's television broadcast station in Aden was bombed, injuring the local director of political security affairs. The anniversary celebration was held without incident on May 22, but the mood in the capital and elsewhere in the country carried little enthusiasm for the national holiday. Most Yemenis sensed their country was unraveling, and they blamed Salih's regime for wasting national revenues on extravagant ceremonies.

Three months later, the single worst incident of political violence happened in Abyan during the month of Ramadan between August 19–24,

[26] "Clashes Between Security Forces and Hundreds of Citizens in Bayt al-Faqih," *Al-Masdar Online* (in Arabic), November 21, 2009.

[27] "Senior Official Escapes Second Assassination Attempt in Southern Yemen," *News Yemen*, May 15, 2010.

2010. Fighting in Lawdar, one of the mid-southern region's main cities, started on a Thursday when two soldiers chased a group of youth attempting to blockade a main road leading into the city. When the youth ran toward the main *suq*, the soldiers entered narrow streets where they were ambushed by gunmen and killed. An armored military vehicle responded, but it was quickly hit by an RPG. This ignited a fire that engulfed the vehicle, killing eight more soldiers.[28] Local news sources blamed AQAP fighters as the only ones capable of such attacks. Over the following days, army troops surrounded Lawdar, and began a massive sweep through the city. This led to street-to-street fighting in which more than thirty people died, including at least three bystanders and nineteen men whom government sources linked to al-Qaeda. One of the dead was identified as AQAP's deputy commander in Abyan.

On August 21, the army distributed leaflets advising more than eighty thousand people to flee their homes. This caused a flood of refugees similar to conditions in Sa'da during "Operation Scorched Earth." The fighting continued for two more days, when armed bands of fighters were seen fleeing the city for refuge in rural areas. One of the leading Yemeni analysts, Muhammad al-Qadhi, who writes for the UAE's English-language *The National* newspaper, described the fighting in Lawdar as the clearest example of AQAP merging with activists in al-Hirak.[29] In the same article, Al-Qadhi quotes an independent analyst in Sanaa saying that the Yemeni government's habit of "blurring the lines between the (AQAP) extremists and the (al-Hirak) secessionists would only serve al-Qaeda."

Once the city of Lawdar was pacified, President Salih spoke at a mosque outside the city on Saturday, August 28, calling al-Qaeda the country's greatest threat. Salih appealed for religious clerics and citizens to "stand by the side of the state," and stop the terrorists who are "harming the nation's and the citizens' interests."[30] A few hours before the president spoke, AQAP claimed a brutal slaying of eight soldiers on patrol in Ja'ar, Abyan, closer to Aden than Lawdar.[31] The corpses were mutilated. One report described the soldiers piled together and set on fire. This signaled growing regional hatred between north and south Yemenis due to Salih's extended military campaign in the south. Three days later on September 1, 2010, a case of fratricide

[28] "Al-Qaeda Fighters Killed in Yemen," *al-Jazeera*, August 21, 2010.
[29] Mohammed al-Qadhi, "Al Qaeda 'Allied with Separatists' in Yemen," *The National*, UAE, August 26, 2010.
[30] Ahmed al-Haj, "Yemen Says al-Qaida Is Government's Main Challenge," Associated Press, August 29, 2010.
[31] Ali Saeed, "Eight Soldiers Killed in Abyan," *Yemen Times*, August 30, 2010.

occurred between two soldiers posted together in Lawdar. According to *al-Masdar* newspaper, the soldiers were guarding the outskirts of the city, when they argued about regional differences in the country.[32] The deceased soldier came from the northwest highland province of Dhamar, while the soldier who fired the fatal shot came from the southwest province of Lahij. *Al-Masdar* described the Lahij soldier taking offense at his Dhamar colleague's prejudice against the southern population.

One week later on September 8, 2010, *al-Masdar* reported that a group of tribal shaykhs in Lahij called upon all soldiers and security personnel from Radfan, Yafiʻ, and al-Daliʻ to quit their posts and return home.[33] Three years earlier in 2007, when retired southern army officers started their peaceful sit-ins and rallies in Aden, their main demand had been to get their old jobs back. The youth who demonstrated in early protests of al-Hirak also demanded more jobs in state institutions. In other words, there was a greater desire in 2007 and 2008 for inclusion and integration into the army and other state institutions. Now in 2010, hard separatist feelings were once again surfacing among the southern population, similar to the time before civil war in 1994.

During speeches to the nation in 2009 and 2010, President Salih often spoke against the spread of regional bias and bigotry. He regularly vilified the southern opposition for spreading a "culture of hate."[34] But the problem of regional intolerance and bigotry was not limited to areas of the south. Ruling elites from northwest provinces had long discriminated against citizens from areas outside the highland mountains. This was true of how they treated citizens with African ancestry in Tihama, marginalizing them as *Habashi* or "people from Ethiopia." It was also true of weaker tribes in coastal and midland regions, not to mention the *Akhdam* at the bottom of Yemen's social hierarchy.[35] Inequality and failing unity among citizens were ultimately the responsibility of President Salih and his

---

[32] "Soldier Killed in Lawder, Shot by a Colleague During an Argument About Regionalism," *al-Masdar* online (in Arabic), September 1, 2010.

[33] Ghazi al-Alawi, "The Shaykhs of Subayha in Lahij Give an Order to the Sons of Radfan to Leave the Region," *al-Masdar* online (in Arabic), September 8, 2010.

[34] "Presidential Directives Call for Creation of a National Alignment Against Hatred Culture," *Almotamar.net*, April 23, 2009.

[35] "Yemen: Girls, Poor and Black Children Most Discriminated Against," *Yemen Online*, March 16, 2009. In the summer of 2009, Nadia al-Sakkaf, chief editor of the *Yemen Times*, wrote about deep-rooted social discrimination in Yemen. Nadia al-Sakkaf, "The Class System in Yemen," *Yemen Times*, July 29, 2009. The 2010 Booker Prize winning author from Yemen, Ali al-Muqri, also published a work about the *Akhdam*, entiled *Black Taste, Black Smell (Taʻam Aswad, Raʼiha Sudaʼa)*.

inner circle. Since his rise to power in 1978, official rhetoric about "the sons of Qahtan" had lost value because Salih allowed a small group of elites to monopolize command posts in the military and security forces, prior to promoting his own sons and nephews once they reached adulthood in the 1990s.

THE YEAR OF UPRISINGS, 2011

On the eve of the mass uprisings that swept the Arab world in 2011, shortly after Muhammad Bouazizi's self-immolation sparked a revolution in Tunisia in mid-December, President Salih's advisors prepared legislation to extend his time in office. Weeks earlier between November 22 and December 5, Yemen successfully hosted its first Gulf Cup games. A few Arab football officials had sought to cancel the tournament at stadiums in Aden, due to widespread fears that al-Hirak or AQAP would disrupt the games with protests and violence. But Salih insisted on going forward, assuring tournament organizers that he could guarantee the safety of teams and fans from Saudi Arabia, Oman, the UAE, Qatar, Bahrain, Kuwait, and Iraq. By holding the games in Aden, Salih wanted to prove that his rule of southern provinces was firm, and that all Yemenis, north and south, could unite around a sporting spectacle.

Amidst tight security measures, including many restrictions on traffic inside and around Aden, the tournament proceeded without a problem. Players from Kuwait emerged as Gulf Cup champions. President Salih considered the games to be a personal triumph, vindicating his leadership. In his mind, the tournament completely rehabilitated his domestic and international image, so he asked Yemen's parliament to allow him another term as president after 2013. During the last week of December, Salih pushed a new set of constitutional amendments that would have entirely eliminated term limits, paving the way for him to serve as president for life.[36] In response, the JMP opposition coalition held rallies in Sanaa, decrying the political maneuver as a coup that would force the country into "a dark tunnel leading to totalitarian rule."

American diplomats in Sanaa cautioned President Salih about employing questionable means to extend his time in office, especially when his ruling party had not amended voting procedures after the JMP forced a cancellation of parliamentary elections in 2009. The United States was

---

[36] "Parliament Agrees for Constitutional Amendments; Opposition Shocked," *Yemen Post* online, January 1, 2011.

274 Yemen's Political Meltdown

concerned that the continued suspension of democracy in Yemen would undermine the country's stability, leaving it more vulnerable to radical forces. During the previous five months, AQAP claimed to have carried out 49 assaults, while the Yemeni government reported 178 of its troops were killed in 2010 and more than 800 injured.[37] In early 2011, the army faced continued losses in Lawdar, Abyan, where militants killed at least twelve soldiers on January 6. In mountainous terrain of al-Jawf province northeast of Sanaa, rebel tribesmen trapped an entire unit of Yemen's elite central security force, denying food and water to sixty soldiers for more than a week. Around the same time, the United States announced it would begin training new counterterrorism units in four Yemeni provinces presumed to have the closest ties to AQAP: Abyan, Shabwa, Marib, and Hadramaut.[38] In the new year, the number of U.S. military trainers was expected to rise above one hundred.

On January 11, 2011, U.S. Secretary of State Hillary Clinton visited Yemen to meet with President Salih and other GPC officials, as well as leaders of the JMP. She told Salih that the U.S. partnership with Yemen "goes beyond counterterrorism" to include the government sector, emphasizing how officials in the Obama administration "support an inclusive political process that will in turn support a unified, prosperous, stable, democratic Yemen." The next day Clinton met with the JMP in a closed conference lasting more than two hours. Afterward, a JMP member noted that "Mrs. Clinton showed strong support for the opposition and clearly mentioned the need for change."[39] Despite American diplomatic efforts to dissuade the Yemeni president from revoking constitutional limits on his time in office, Salih refused to budge from his demand that parliament approve new constitutional amendments.

A few days later Shaykh Muhammad Abu Luhum, a top member of the GPC and a powerful Bakil tribal leader, won JMP support for a plan to break the political impasse. He managed to reach agreement on a set of reforms to the voting law that would prepare the way for new parliamentary elections. Yet Salih maintained his desire to continue serving as

---

[37] "Al-Qaeda Says it Carried out 49 Assaults During Five Months," *al-Masdar* online (in Arabic), January 1, 2011. "1,030 Yemeni Security Force Members Killed or Wounded in 2010," *Yemen Post* online, January 21, 2011.

[38] Ali Saeed, "US and British Forces to Train Yemen's New Anti-terrorism Units," *Yemen Times*, January 10, 2011.

[39] "Washington Wants Change in Yemeni Regime, JMP leader," *Yemen Post* online, January 12, 2011. Embassy of the United States, Yemen, "Remarks with Yemeni President Saleh after Their Meeting," January 11, 2011.

president beyond 2013. The timing of this matter could not have been worse for the president because, within just a few weeks, he would be desperate to halt the spread of the largest political protests he had ever faced. The futility of his task was clear because Salih's best hope was to persuade his countrymen that he had no intention of staying in office beyond his term limit. In short, just before the Arab uprisings, the Yemeni president undermined his future credibility by destroying an essential bargaining position. In the coming months, no one would believe that he truly intended to leave office as required under the Yemeni constitution.

The Arab uprisings of 2011 started in Tunisia when peaceful street protesters forced President Zayn al-Abidin Ben Ali into exile on January 14. From this date, a spirit of revolt spread quickly to Egypt, where massive crowds in Cairo bravely and passionately demanded the ouster of President Husni Mubarak. Egypt has long been the political and cultural center of the Arab world. Soon Yemenis, Bahrainis, Algerians, and Libyans borrowed the chants, slogans, songs, and practices that Egyptian street protesters copied from Tunisia. Lively satellite television broadcasts showing millions in Cairo's *Maidan al-Tahrir* (Liberation Square) were the primary means by which the spirit of the times spread, eventually reaching Syria, Jordan, and Morocco. Nearly every Arab regime, including the Saudis and Emiratis, faced some level of protest in the spring of 2011.

The uprisings in the Arab world were a testament to three factors unrelated to internet telecommunication, which was the faulty basis of analyses made by many U.S. commentators who sought to explain the "democratic spring" in terms of western technology. Only a tiny percentage of Yemenis used cell phones and tablets for internet access in 2011, so neither Facebook nor Twitter could possibly rank with the following three factors. First, an abiding sense of Arab solidarity allowed citizens across the Middle East and North Africa to share common aspirations to oust corrupt autocratic rulers, even though the pan-Arab era ended in the 1970s.[40] Second, a single demonstration effect in a region long resistant to political change, namely, Ben Ali's panicked departure to Saudi Arabia, allowed neighboring citizens to think the same was possible in their own countries. Third, inspired by Palestinians and Iraqis who had resisted forces of repression for decades, a new generation of Arab youth were willing to

---

[40] The best analysis of the 2011 uprisings appeared on the Arab American academic website *Jadaliyya*. Bassam Haddad wrote two early, influential essays on January 14 and 15, 2011, including "Why, What, Where to, and How: Tunisia and Beyond." In addition, Mohammed Bamyeh wrote about the Tunisian effect on January 17 and 21, and "The Egyptian Revolution" on February 11.

suspend their fears, and bravely stare down the gun barrels of their own regimes.

Yemen's mass uprising began one day after Tunisians overthrew Ben Ali. On January 15, university students marched through the streets of Taiz and Sanaa. In practical terms, the entire country was already protesting against President Salih. Thus, it is unreasonable to assign a definitive starting part for what was to transpire in Yemen. Compared to Tunisians and Egyptians, as well as citizens of other Arab states involved in the 2011 uprisings, Yemenis were at an advanced stage of rebellion in 2009 and 2010 due to al-Hirak in southern provinces, al-Huthi in northwestern provinces, as well as the protest and boycott activities of the JMP. The change after mid-January was clearly driven by Yemeni youth under age twenty-five who made up more than half of the population. Millions of young people arrived at a stage of political awareness with dreams of a better future, and they were eager to lift their country from its abyss.

As young Yemeni protesters were quick to point out, President Salih had been in office longer than either Ben Ali or Husni Mubarak. Only Muammar al-Qadhafi of Libya and the Sultan of Oman had ruled longer than Salih. In addition, the youth noted that their nation's poverty level was higher than Egypt and Tunisia. Yemen is the poorest Arab country with a per capita income less than U.S. $100 per month. One of the organizers in Sanaa and Taiz was Tawakul Karman, the brave director of an organization called "Female Journalists without Chains," which had long campaigned on problems of poverty and human rights. On January 15, Karman helped rally a large group of Sanaa University students who marched to the Tunisian embassy in solidarity. In this opening phase, the Yemeni police did not obstruct street demonstrators but instead helped divert traffic around them. Early student rallies expressed progressive national politics. In Taiz, many youth carried posters of Che Guevara. Most were fed up with Yemen's old parties, so they chanted: *"No partisanship! And no parties! Our revolution is a revolution of youth!,"* which has good rhyme and meter in Arabic (parties = *ahzab*; youth = *shabab*).

Recipient of the 2011 Nobel Peace Prize, Tawakul Karman is a liberal Islamist, human rights activist, and proponent of the tactics of peaceful protest first introduced in 2007 by al-Hirak in Aden. She is originally from Taiz, a mother of three young girls, and daughter of a former cabinet minister from the Islah party who served in government during the mid-1990s. Tawakul Karman is a smart, eloquent, and outspoken street organizer who conveys confidence and trust to her young followers. In the past, her political activities and writings drew the attention

PHOTO 19. Tawakul Karman and daughters, 2011 (Photo credit: *Yemen Times*, Sanaa)

of Salih's political security force. On January 23, she was arrested and held for thirty hours without outside contact or legal counsel. She was released unharmed the next day along with JMP activist Nayif al-Qanis, who was also arrested in January after previously being beaten by political security officers in 2009.

Following Karman's release, she did not stop leading street protests. On February 3, she appeared at a "Day of Rage" rally in Taiz. A video briefly circulated on *YouTube*, showing Karman on stage in front of tens of thousands of people, some clinching Che Guevara photos and many more holding posters of Ibrahim al-Hamdi. In the new political climate, members of al-Hamdi's family revived accusations that Salih and his tribal clan were the ones who murdered President al-Hamdi and his brother in 1977. Many members of the northern political opposition revived memories of al-Hamdi's populist rule, denouncing Salih's thirty year "detour from the road of progress." At one point in the video of Tawakul Karman's speech in Taiz, she asked the crowd to recite the famous poetic lines by the early twentieth century Tunisian Abu al-Qasim al-Shaabi, which became the anthem of mass uprisings in Tunis and Cairo: "One day, if the people desire to live, then destiny must prevail, darkness will dissipate, and chains will break."

In the previous week, the JMP coalition had organized a massive nation-wide rally modeled after Egypt's street protests. On January 27, hundreds of thousands of demonstrators stepped onto the streets of Sanaa, Taiz, al-Hudayda, Aden, and other cities. Before this event, President Salih was on the telephone with his friend Husni Mubarak, lending moral support and exchanging ideas on how best to silence the rising voices of dissent. Sanaa has a central public square called *Maidan al-Tahrir*, just like the one in Cairo. It is named for north Yemen's 1962 revolution, which itself was inspired by Egypt's 1952 revolution. President Salih followed Mubarak's advice not to allow protesters to build camps on sites symbolic of earlier revolutions. But destiny still prevailed, and chains were broken in both Cairo and Sanaa.

One day before the JMP event in late January, President Salih's GPC planned a massive public rally in *Maidan al-Tahrir*. This began a series of dueling protests in Sanaa that took place every Friday from February through late May. Salih packed *Maidan al-Tahrir* with his own supporters, many of them tribesmen of Hashid and Bakil, who were supplied with mounds of free *qat* to chew beneath large tents erected by the regime. Consequently, JMP leaders were forced to hold their rally in another part of the city, eventually settling near Sanaa University's new campus where the spirit of the times was more likely to spread among the youth. Afterward youth began to camp at the same site renamed "Change Square." Outside the main entrance to Sanaa University, there is a tower-ing obelisk covered with Arabic calligraphy of the words attributed to the Prophet Muhammad: "Yemen is faith; Yemen is wisdom." The lines of calligraphy ascend until they come together in a point that touches the sky. In the months to come, students regularly met at the foot of this pure white obelisk, reciting the poem by Abu al-Qasim al-Shaabi, as well as other lines from chants first heard on the streets of Tunisia and Egypt, or later popularized in Yemen.

After the JMP demonstration, Salih pledged to meet the JMP's demand to reform the country's election law. But it was too late. Sensing Salih's panic, and believing that events in Tunisia and Egypt had already shifted the balance of power, youth in the streets hardened their bargaining positions. Salih initially responded like his fellow authoritarian leader in Egypt, using a combination of "carrots and sticks." When the standard instruments of repression, teargas and bully clubs, failed to prevent daily protests, both Salih and Mubarak hired street thugs, "*baltagiyya*," to assault protesters with sticks and stones, camel-back riders carrying whips in Egypt, and in Yemen's case, the traditional *jambiyya* or curved dagger.[41] The "carrots" included a 50 percent tax break and promises of a 30 percent wage increase for public employees, both military and security personnel as well as civil servants, in an effort to prevent defections. President Salih also exempted students from paying university fees in 2011, and pledged to create more jobs for graduating seniors. The latter was a feeble attempt to buy off young revolutionaries because wages in Yemen's public sector are barely above poverty level.

In late January and February, great tension surrounded street protests in northern cities like Sanaa, Taiz, and al-Hudayda, especially during clashes with *baltagiyya* at "Change Square" on the capital's northwest side. Dozens of students and other protesters were severely injured by stones, clubs, and knives, but there were few gunshot wounds and even fewer deaths. The number of armed clashes rose after February 11, when Husni Mubarak was forced to step down in Egypt. The next day protestors in the streets of Sanaa chanted "A Yemeni revolution after the Egyptian revolution," and for the first time, President Salih genuinely feared that he could be next. While Salih's sons and nephews were too young to know the significance of pan-Arab sentiments from the 1950s and 1960s, when Yemenis closely followed political trends in Egypt, the president's generation certainly understood the power of these sentiments.

One week after Mubarak's removal from power in Cairo, three protesters in Taiz died, and more than eighty were injured, when someone threw a hand grenade into a crowd of tens of thousands rallying at this midland city's new "Freedom Square." Then on March 8 in Sanaa's "Change Square," a protester was killed and dozens injured when government troops fired into a large crowd. The same day in Sanaa, dozens of protesters experienced convulsions and spasms caused by tear gas allegedly containing a poisonous gas. Doctors at makeshift field hospitals could not diagnose the source of the neural disorders, but all patients were fortunate to recover. Except for these disturbing incidents, the atmosphere at most of the early protests in Sanaa and other northern cities was similar to a street carnival. Between late January and early March 2011, families attended the protests with small children who often had their faces painted with

---

[41] "Who Directs the Baltagiyya in Yemen," *al-Masdar* online (in Arabic), February 24, 2011. National security forces, and specific ruling party offices, formed a new "crisis management" unit (*wihdat idarat al-azmaat*) to silence the street protests, using men in plain clothes from specially trained riot control and counterterrorism units.

bright colors (Yemen's flag and the word *Irhal*, "Leave!," were favorite themes). When it was time for the call to prayer, the crowds bowed in unison sharing powerful, solemn moments together.

In contrast to the north's carnival atmosphere, early street protests in southern cities were met by government soldiers who did not hesitate to fire live ammunition. Even areas controlled by al-Huthi supporters in the northwest highlands, where fierce battles were fought between 2005 and 2009, remained relatively quiet in comparison to Aden. In fact, many al-Huthi supporters joined the street carnivals in Sanaa during February and early March, raising banners with calligraphy expressing their standard religious messages and denunciations of America and Israel. On at least one occasion, JMP members from the Islah party clashed with al-Huthi members at "Change Square." But differences were quickly resolved, in order to maintain solidarity among the opposition. Meanwhile, there was little peace in the streets of Aden and other areas of the south.

Soon after the start of Yemen's uprising in 2011, government forces acted ruthlessly toward southern youth using many of the same slogans heard in Sanaa and Taiz, Tunisia and Egypt. At first, Aden's youth were wary of protesting due to the regime's violent repression of al-Hirak demonstrations in 2009 and 2010. But they took their cue from "Day of Rage" protests in the north. Al-Hirak activists announced their own "Day of Rage" in Aden on Friday, February 11. When city youth began chanting "the people want the downfall of the regime," police opened fire with live ammunition. The violence continued through the week with eleven protesters killed and scores injured.[42] Government troops used heavy weaponry, including high-calibre machine guns mounted on armored vehicles. Horrific photos and video from streets in al-Mansoura and Shaykh Othman districts were posted on the internet, showing young men carrying dead friends with severe head wounds. In other districts, such as al-Tawahi, al-Ma'ala, and especially the wealthier district of Khormaksar, young protesters chanted the same slogans. Yet security forces responded with tear gas, water cannons, and only occasional live fire. There was no excuse for the heavy firepower used against protesters in Aden's poorest neighborhoods.

Local council members in Aden called for the prosecution of the city's northern director of security, Abdallah Qairan. Nonetheless, shootings resumed on Friday, February 25, when eight young Adenis were killed in a single day. The tall apartments lining both sides of al-Ma'ala district's main thoroughfare were shrouded by thick clouds of smoke from burning

---

[42] "11 Dead in Aden's Protest Jump in Four Days," *Yemen Post* online, February 19, 2011.

buildings and tires set alight by protesters. In late February 2011, Aden looked like a war zone as youth attacked government offices. In surrounding areas of Lahij, al-Dali', and Abyan, armed groups attacked military and security bases, in one case kidnapping the base commander and a number of his soldiers. Before the end of the month, when the regime lost control of a few police stations and other bases of operation, President Salih sent reinforcements to Aden in four military aircraft. Then on March 1, he removed five elected governors who were presumably unwilling to order stiffer security measures against protesters.[43] This included the governors of Aden and Lahij in the southwest region, Abyan in the mid-southern region, Hadramaut in the eastern region, and al-Hudayda province along the west coast.

The regime's deadly crackdown on street protesters eventually reached Sanaa on March 18, a date thereafter known as "Bloody Friday." As tens of thousands gathered in streets near "Change Square," several plain-clothes snipers fired into the crowd from strategic positions atop buildings outside the campus of Sanaa University. At least fifty-two people were killed in a shooting spree that lasted more than one-half hour. Hundreds of other people were injured, many of them in critical condition with head, neck, and chest wounds.[44] Volunteer doctors were overwhelmed by the high number of casualties, and even Sanaa's government hospitals had difficulty treating all the victims. It was widely assumed that well-trained marksmen from one of the national security branches acted on orders from high inside the regime. Public revulsion to the killings in Sanaa signaled the beginning of the end for President Salih.

THE REMOVAL OF ALI ABDALLAH SALIH

After "Bloody Friday" on March 18, 2011, levels of violence in Yemen, north and south, east and west, reached greater equilibrium as street protesters around the country confronted a regime willing to resort to armed force. In April and May, the city of Taiz witnessed some of the worst repression by state forces. Protesters in Taiz, Sanaa, al-Hudayda, and other northern cities showed remarkable commitment to peaceful tactics, whereas government forces used deadly fire power. Days after the "Bloody Friday" massacre, President Salih tried to dampen the protests by

---

[43] "President Salih Removes 5 Governors," *al-Masdar* online (in Arabic), March 1, 2011.
[44] Mohammed al-Qadhi, "Killings Galvanize Yemeni Opposition," *The National*, UAE, March 20, 2011.

dissolving the cabinet, and announcing a month long state of emergency. The latter was employed to impose a curfew meant to keep protesters off the streets. But in the weeks to come, the protests grew in size. The dissolution of the cabinet was meant to preempt resignations by ministers who had turned against the president.

"Bloody Friday" had three major consequences. The first was the mounting number of defections from the regime, including ruling party members, ambassadors overseas, and even military commanders. The most significant defection came on March 21 when Brigadier General Ali Muhsin al-Ahmar, commander of Yemen's first armored brigade and military strongman who stood behind President Salih for three decades, declared support for the opposition. He vowed to protect street protesters from future attacks. The commander of Yemen's eastern region in Hadramaut and al-Mahra, General Muhammad Ali Muhsin, also defected the same day. Thus President Salih lost control of two vital areas of the country. As a member of the Sanhan tribe, and widely assumed to be a distant relative of the president, the Brigadier General caused the first crack within the regime's inner circle. It appeared that Ali Muhsin wanted to position himself as a transitional leader of the country. But in a rare interview with the press, he stated that he had no desire to rule, and would gladly step down if Salih would do the same.[45]

Before "Bloody Friday," there were earlier defections from the GPC party, including several members of parliament and top Hashid tribal shaykhs like Husayn al-Ahmar and his elder brother Sadeq, the paramount shaykh of Hashid. Hashid's top shaykhs offered to use their tribal militias to protect demonstrators at Sanaa's "Change Square." Bakil's shaykh Muhammad Abu Luhum also quit the GPC, and later in April he formed a new party named "Justice and Development" after the popular ruling party in Turkey. While there were early defections from military and security forces, they tended to be low-ranking soldiers. Like the protesters in Tunisia and Egypt, protesters in Sanaa appealed to soldiers with flowers and sweets, chanting slogans of national solidarity. On February 21, a soldier named Adam Ahmed Amin al-Hamiri joined protesters in Sanaa's "Change Square." *Al-Masdar* newspaper printed a photograph of him in uniform, receiving roses and well wishes from student protesters.

Adam al-Hamiri said he decided to join the protesters because of "the neglect that soldiers suffer in the security and armed forces, where they are

---

[45] "Yemen General is Feared Player – WikiLeaks," Reuters news agency, March 26, 2011.

used as spearheads in wars that only benefit the state's leadership."[46] He referred specifically to battles in Sa'da province and other areas north of Sanaa, where thousands of soldiers died or were injured in battles against fellow countrymen. "I, as a simple soldier in the army, declare my stand in solidarity with the protests that are demanding the fall of this corrupt regime, which steals Yemen's valuable resources. And I want to inform you that all of the soldiers in the armed forces are standing with you, even though they may wear the army's uniforms." The next week it was reported that Adam disappeared, presumably arrested or killed by government forces.

The second major consequence of Sanaa's "Bloody Friday" was how it helped build new solidarity among opposition groups across the country. The young martyrs who died on the streets of Sanaa were eulogized in every province of Yemen, and more citizens joined the protests in order to hold President Salih accountable for the bloodshed. Evidence that the regime might soon collapse created the possibility of overcoming divisions between citizens in different regions of the country. In particular, young supporters of al-Hirak began organizing in solidarity with students in the north. Before March 18, protestors marching through the streets of Aden, and other southern and eastern provinces, typically did not carry Yemen's unity flag. Instead, they marched under the banner of the former PDRY with its red star inside an inner-quadrant, light blue triangle. But after March 18, it was more common to see young southern protesters rallying in the streets of Aden, Lahij, Abyan, Shabwa, and Hadramaut, while carrying the unity flag's standard red, white, and black stripes.

Leaders of the JMP coalition considered this a positive development because they wanted to encourage unionist sentiments at street demonstrations. Waving the unity flag was an effective way of countering President Salih's frequent claim that if he resigned, and the GPC lost power, then the country would collapse in civil war, perhaps redividing into multiple states. In the spring of 2011, the president's opponents began turning the tables as southern street protesters gradually realized it was in their interest to wave the union flag, and join northern students in demanding President Salih's resignation. A national protest organizing committee based in Sanaa started to assign a theme for each Friday rally, so protesters in every region could rally in solidarity. March 25 became "Departure Friday" for President Salih's pending exit from power. April 22 was "Last

---

[46] "Soldier Joins the Protest Rally in Sanaa," *al-Masdar* online (in Arabic), February 21, 2011.

Chance Friday" when protesters gave Salih two weeks to leave. After this date, youth leaders planned to escalate their protests by surrounding government buildings, including the prime minister's office in Sanaa and governor offices in Taiz and Aden. This led to worse repression by state forces. April 29 became "Martyrs Friday," and each succeeding Friday commemorated the area with the most martyrs. May 6 became "Loyalty with Southern People Friday," and May 13 "Loyalty with Taiz Friday."

The third major consequence of Sanaa's "Bloody Friday" was that the Gulf Cooperation Council (GCC) became directly involved in negotiating a political transition in Yemen. Prior to March 18, President Salih maintained that he alone had constitutional legitimacy as the leader of Yemen. He denied the demands of protesters calling for his resignation, vowing to fight to "the last drop of blood," and stating that he would only leave office after his final term ended in 2013. After March 18, Salih signaled his willingness to consider an early departure by the end of 2011. In the first week of April, Qatar's prime minister Shaykh Hamad bin Jassim al-Thani took the lead role when he announced the GCC sought a deal for the Yemeni president to leave the country. GCC Secretary General Abd al-Latif al-Zayani began meeting with Yemeni government officials, as well as representatives of the JMP, inside Yemen and Saudi Arabia. A plan quickly took shape for President Salih to resign after one month in exchange for full immunity from prosecution for any wrongdoings during his time as head of state.

In late April leaders of the JMP coalition agreed to the GCC plan, but student protesters refused to recognize GCC involvement in the country's politics. Sensing a foreign plot to hijack Yemen's revolution, the youth demanded the prosecution of President Salih and other members of his regime responsible for killing scores of people since January 2011. The most ardent youth leaders in Sanaa, Taiz, al-Hudayda, Aden, and other cities distrusted the leadership of the JMP, especially the senior tribal and religious figures in Islah, whom they accused of exploiting the sacrifices of street protesters in order to gain power. According to these youth, any future rule by Islah leaders like Hamid al-Ahmar or Abd al-Majid al-Zindani, each of whom had patrons in Saudi Arabia, would be as bad or worse than the rule of Ali Abdallah Salih. The same was true of General Ali Muhsin or Hashid's paramount shaykh Sadeq al-Ahmar. All of these influential figures were highland rivals to the president, hardly representatives of genuine political change.

President Salih agreed to sign the GCC plan at the end of April, but at the last minute he changed his mind, demanding instead to sign as head of

PHOTO 20. Friday protest rally in Sanaa, May 2011 (Photos credit: al-Masdar, Sanaa)

the GPC party along with heads of the JMP. This was the beginning of a game of brinksmanship, as Yemen's president sought to manipulate the JMP and GCC into dropping demands for his resignation. The next month JMP leaders agreed to sign the GCC plan, but twice again Salih reneged on his commitment. At the final signing ceremony arranged on May 22, a bizarre drama played out when President Salih's armed supporters blockaded the GCC secretary general, and the ambassadors of United States and Europe, inside the UAE embassy in Sanaa. An army helicopter had to airlift the diplomats to President Salih's palace, but Salih still refused to sign, insisting that representatives of the JMP sign in his presence.

All sides were exasperated by President Salih's behavior, and the GCC secretary general departed the country with no plan to return. Western embassies ordered nonessential staff to leave the country, as fears of warfare spread amid rising tensions in Sanaa. Leaders of the JMP refused to meet the president in his palace because they feared being arrested, or perhaps executed. Their fears were justified. Two days later on May 24, Hashid's top shaykhs of the Ahmar family were targeted for assassination. The home of Sadeq al-Ahmar was struck by heavy artillery in the same al-Hasaba compound on Sanaa's north side where the late Shaykh Abdallah once lived in counterbalance to Salih in the presidential palace on the city's south side. The two sides exchanged missiles and mortar fire over four days, damaging many government buildings, including the headquarters of Yemenia Airlines, the Yemen press agency, and the ministries of interior, local administration, and tourism, each of which changed hands between combatants.

A truce between the president, his soldiers, and central security forces, on the one hand, and Hashid tribal militias loyal to al-Ahmar families, on the other hand, was finally reached on Friday, May 27. Over the following days, a shaky peace held in what had amounted to tribal war on an urban landscape. Thousands of refugees fled to rural areas, and there were unconfirmed reports of one hundred dead. Meanwhile, intense fighting spread to other parts of the country, especially Zinjibar, Abyan where armed bands with alleged ties to AQAP invaded the city on May 28. Militants entered Zinjibar after the army withdrew its checkpoints in the city. This led to speculation that the president wanted AQAP to seize control as proof his resignation would spread anarchy and terrorism. At the beginning of June, the army reentered Zinjibar, while air force jets bombed locations still held by militants. Tens of thousands of residents, nearly the entire population of Abyan's capital, fled to Aden and safe zones in Lahij.[47] Journalists described scenes from hell with dozens of decaying

---

[47] Anees Mansour, "Mareb Press Throws Light on the Tragedy of Abyan Refugees in Aden and Lahij," *Mareb Press* online (in Arabic), June 7, 2011. This lengthy article provides detailed information about the tens of thousands of refugees staying in local school buildings of Aden and Lahij.

bodies strewn on the ground, and wild dogs roving deserted streets. These reports surfaced after even more shocking news in Sanaa, where President Salih and his top political associates had been struck down.

On June 3, 2011, the president attended a small mosque on his palace grounds to perform Friday prayers with his prime minister, Ali Mujawar, two deputy prime ministers, the president of the upper assembly, Abd al-Aziz Abd al-Ghani, and a number of other top GPC officials like Numan Duwayd, governor of Sanaa and a leading Bakil shaykh. These men were unaware that someone inside the mosque had planted a bomb set to detonate as the men bowed on the front row. The explosion blew out windows in the building, sent shrapnel flying, and ignited a fire ball that killed the mosque leader. The president suffered a puncture wound near his heart, and severe burns on his face, hands, and half of his body. He survived along with other officials who had similar injuries.[48] The most seriously injured, including President Salih, were stabilized before being evacuated to hospitals in Saudi Arabia, where they stayed for several weeks of surgical procedures.

Initial reports from the president's office described a missile or mortar shell striking from outside the palace grounds. Officials blamed Sadeq al-Ahmar for launching the attack with heavy artillery in the possession of his tribe. This led to renewed fighting around his family's compound in al-Hasaba, as well as the house and offices of Hamid al-Ahmar in Hadda district on Sanaa's southwest side. But evidence indicated the explosion originated inside the small palace mosque, not outside by a projectile. Although evidence from the site did not absolve Sadeq al-Ahmar of responsibility, it cast suspicion on potential culprits on the president's staff who had access to the mosque. The attempted assassination of Yemen's president was more likely an "inside job." Regardless of how the attack originated, President Salih temporarily became the third Arab leader, after Ben Ali of Tunisia and Mubarak of Egypt, to be forced from power in 2011. One month later on July 7, he made a brief television appearance from a Saudi hospital, where he appeared badly burned and scarred with bandages covering his head and hands. He intended to return to Yemen, but it seemed unlikely he could resume his standing as head of state because of earlier pledges to accept the GCC plan.

---

[48] A few presidential bodyguards died at the mosque, but there was later speculation that they had been shot after the bomb blast due to suspicions of their responsibility for the bombing. In August, Abd al-Aziz Abd al-Ghani died of his injuries in a Saudi hospital.

The larger question in the summer of 2011 concerned the future role of President Salih's son, Ahmad, as well as nephews who remained in charge of elite branches of the military. The fighting in the capital largely represented an internal power struggle among highland tribal elites who were accustomed to holding political, military, and economic power in the country. According to the Yemeni constitution, the long serving vice president Abd al-Rabo Mansour Hadi, an old Ali Nasir partisan from the mid-southern region, was the rightful successor to President Salih during his recovery outside the country. But Ahmad Salih, commander of the Republican Guards, moved into the presidential palace, and began acting as a substitute for his father. In this way, Yemen was not like Egypt or Tunisia, where the removal of the president brought a quick change in government. Egyptian president Mubarak's son, Gamal, actually fled Cairo before his father's downfall. The professionalism of the Egyptian military helped ensure relatively peaceful change along the Nile River.

The difference in Yemen was that elite military and security forces were commanded by Salih's sons and nephews, all from the Sanhan region of Sanaa. In this sense, the Yemeni state more closely resembled the Saudi monarchy, where the king's many brothers, cousins, and nephews also command the nation's armed forces. During Salih's absence, JMP leaders and young street protesters called on Vice President Abd al-Rabo to take charge of the state, in order to form a transitional governing council which could prepare a new constitution before sponsoring parliamentary elections. Thus, the streets of Sanaa and Aden, Taiz and al-Mukalla, soon heard a new chant: "The people demand a transitional governing council." But Abd al-Rabo did not have power to assume control because he was an outsider to Sanaa's highland ruling group.

One telling Yemeni newspaper cartoon in mid-June 2011 depicted the vice president with a military officer's gun to the back of his head. Playing on the meaning of Abd al-Rabo's last name, "calmly" or "gently," the cartoon's caption depicted a faceless figure behind the vice president saying, "okay, *Hadi*, lets make your next move." As long as the president's sons and nephews commanded powerful branches of the armed forces with the intention of holding office until Salih's recovery was complete, it was impossible for Abd al-Rabo to assume presidential command, or act with executive power. The primary challengers for power were General Ali Muhsin and Shaykh Sadeq al-Ahmar. Yet these two highland tribal elites who were little different from the president. If either man came to power, then it would be a counterrevolutionary thrust. This was understood by youthful street protesters, who may have appreciated the early security provided by Ali Muhsin and Shaykh Sadeq, but wanted neither man to replace the Salih family.

An additional factor complicating the political transition in Yemen was international concerns about the growing threat from AQAP, and lingering uncertainties about the country's unity. These matters troubled leaders of the GCC, as much as American and Western heads of state. After Salih was evacuated to Saudi Arabia, vast regions of the country fell beyond state control. Parts of Abyan and Shabwa in the mid-southern region, as well as Marib and al-Jawf in the central interior, became virtually ungoverned by the state. In Taiz, local militias came to the defense of protesters after an especially brutal army crackdown on the night of May 29–30. More than sixty people were killed as army troops rampaged through the makeshift tent city, burning it to the ground with sleeping youth and handicapped trapped inside. Afterward al-Maddhaj tribesmen, led by Hamoud al-Mikhlafi, expelled the army by force of arms. In Aden, citizens formed district security committees, and began policing their own neighborhoods. Earlier in May, a group of southern exiles, including former president Ali Nasir and former prime minister Haider al-Attas, met in Cairo, Egypt, calling for a new federal constitution that would allow citizens in southern and eastern regions to govern their own local affairs.[49] Compared to Tunisia and Egypt, the effort to change Yemen's government was more complicated due to regional divisions inside a troubled twenty-year experiment with national union.

---

[49] The Cairo conference was held between May 9–11, 2011, "for the sake of uniting visions among the Sons of the South to resolve the southern issue in the context of the youth revolution for change in Yemen."

Conclusion

The removal of Ali Abdallah Salih as Yemen's head of state was not made official until late November 2011, following sixteen weeks of medical treatment in Saudi Arabia and then his surprise return to Sanaa in September. On November 23, President Salih finally fulfilled his months-long commitment to sign the GCC-sponsored deal transferring real executive power to Vice President Hadi. The signing ceremony required Salih to make a second trip to Riyadh, where he relinquished his powers under the watchful eye of Saudi King Abdallah. Hadi refused to join the disgraced president on his final state visit. Over the past seven years, Salih had shown terribly bad form as the primary contestant in a form of politics where honor and respect can only be won by keeping the peace through clever and confounding ways. The president's spectacular failure was made painfully clear by a population of millions voicing disapproval in the streets, carrying signs of protest and chanting slogans against the "murderous tyrant." Until the end, Salih treated the street protests with derision. He felt the same way about the GCC agreement, which he called a *coup d'etat* and violation of Yemen's democratic constitution. Over the decades, of course, he had rewritten this constitution to serve his own interests, using powers of decree with questionable backing from parliament and fraudulent public referenda.

Sitting next to the Saudi monarch in Riyadh, Salih joked when a royal aide handed him a pen to sign the GCC document. The simple tribesman from Sanhan, a man short-of-stature who envied the much taller Saudi king's autocratic powers, smiled sarcastically as he scribbled his name. He behaved similarly in 1994 when signing the "document of pledge and accord" in front of King Hussein in Amman, Jordan. Technically, Salih retained an honorary title of president for a few more months until a new government could be formed in Sanaa. This arrangement was added to the

GCC deal because Salih insisted upon it before traveling back to Riyadh. Some of his domestic opponents suspected a trick, wondering if Salih sought a symbolic departure from office, only to plot his return if the country descended into further chaos, perhaps by Salih's own design. Yemenis had good reason to suspect Salih's intentions. During 2011, he proved more cagey and difficult to remove than other Arab dictators, such as Ben Ali in Tunisia and Husni Mubarak in Egypt, both of whom were quickly ousted. In the end, Salih outlasted Libya's Muammar al-Gaddhafi, who also endured active rebellion after the middle of February. Al-Gaddhafi was eventually chased from Tripoli by rebel forces, then captured in the Libyan desert and quickly executed on October 20, 2011. Salih will forever be known as the fourth Arab president overthrown by street protests more dramatic than the region had ever seen.

There was another reason why the political opposition's wariness of the GCC deal was justified. Following the signing ceremony in Riyadh, more violence by armed forces erupted in Sanaa as well as north of the capital and inside Taiz. Al-Huthi fighters clashed violently with their Salafi rivals, massacring more than twenty in Dammaj of Sa'da province before the end of November. Activists in independent youth groups in Sanaa, Taiz, and other cities vociferously rejected the GCC deal because it immunized Salih from prosecution for war crimes, while allowing him and his family to keep much of their wealth. Moreover, Salih's son Ahmad and nephews Yahya and Ammar still retained their military commands. According to the GCC deal, Vice President Hadi would appoint a committee to restructure the nation's armed forces in late 2011 and early 2012. Yet few among the street protesters believed the military could be rebuilt free of Salih's influence as long as his sons and nephews remained in control of key units. When youth protesters took to the streets on November 23 and 24, they were met with bullets fired by the same forces that had killed more than 2,000 and maimed another 10,000 since the beginning of the year.

Some of Yemen's most deadly violence occurred two months earlier in September when fierce military assaults coincided with President Salih's surprise return from Saudi Arabia on Friday, September 23. These assaults began in Sanaa on the preceding Friday, and continued through the week. For the first time inside the capital, military forces under the command of General Ali Muhsin were drawn into battles with Republican Guard troops loyal to Salih's son. More than one hundred civilians died in intense fighting. The worst violence occurred along the city's main street, al-Zubayri, especially at the crowded "Kentki" intersection named after a nearby popular fast food restaurant. Once Salih arrived home by private jet, calling for a ceasefire and looking ghoulish with his face blistered, head bandaged, and hands covered by oversized medical gloves, citizens realized the terrible bloodshed in Sanaa's streets had been meant to secure Salih's safe return. On the same day Salih's supporters in the armed forces unleashed massive celebrations with anti-aircraft guns. This caused more civilian casualties when heavy ammunition fell from the sky, sparking even worse fighting over the following days.

Long before the GCC deal was signed in late November, Salih's sons and nephews developed a pattern of using military and security forces with murderous intent to preserve the president's post. As early as July 2011, they militarized the confrontation with political opponents. Gone were the days of peaceful protests met by teargas and only rare gunfire. Some neighborhoods in Sanaa and Taiz took on the appearance of war zones, similar to earlier conditions in Aden in February. Military check points were established, restricting traffic patterns in daylight and forcing most residents to stay indoors at night because of random gunfire. The risks of full scale warfare were clear because of the large number of soldiers who had defected once General Ali Muhsin declared his support for protesters back on March 21. One reliable report in early July claimed that 2,000 Republican Guards had defected since May; this followed the defection of 12,000 soldiers in April, adding to the 30,000 army troops already under Ali Muhsin's command.[1] By early August, the urban warfare around Shaykh Sadeq al-Ahmar's residence in Hasaba district became so intense that the main airport had to be closed. All flights, domestic and international, were temporarily diverted to Aden.

Taiz remained the beating heart of the political opposition through the summer and fall of 2011. It witnessed more regular conflict than any other location in the country. Salih's sons and nephews frequently tried to retake the city by military force, but protesters effectively defended their positions with help from armed al-Maddhaj tribesman under Mahmoud al-Mikhlafi's command. This overcrowded city in the midland region saw nightly exchanges of small arms fire, occasionally interrupted by tank and anti-aircraft fire.[2] War planes frequently circled overhead. On occasion, the scale of fighting in Taiz was surpassed by rural clashes north of Sanaa in two tribal districts, Arhab and Nihm, where tribesmen attempted to seize

---

[1] Hakim al-Masmari, "Yemeni Soldiers Defecting, Says Official," *The National*, U.A.E., July 3, 2011.

[2] The best reporting from Taiz was offered by independent commentator and well known local physician, Dr. Abdulkader al-Guneid, via his Twitter account @alguneid.

camps of Republican Guards. Some reports indicated that tribes from Marib and al-Jawf joined an effort to persuade the Guards to surrender. When members of Salih's family learned of the pending surrender at one camp, they sent fighter jets to bomb the location. Journalists described more than two hundred killed, mainly among defecting troops.[3] In late July, similar reports came from the mid-southern region where officers loyal to Ali Muhsin enlisted al-Fadli tribal support against AQAP in Zinjibar. Air force jets commanded by Ali Salih "accidentally" bombed the tribesmen, killing more than a dozen. In a September interview, two months after the incident, Shaykh Tareq al-Fadli said he had tried to dissuade tribal members from participating because he feared deceit by Salih's family.[4]

On top of escalating military clashes, Yemen's economy hit rock bottom in 2011. Losses due to fuel shortages and power outages were estimated in the billions.[5] During the month of Ramadan, when the faithful fasted through a long hot August, skyrocketing inflation raised prices forty to sixty percent on basic food items, 200 percent on drinking water, and an astonishing 900 percent on car fuel.[6] Many families could no longer cope under severe social and economic hardship, so the post-Ramadan feast *Eid al-Fitr* was a bleak occasion. Most unfortunately, the children of poor families were recruited as soldiers on one or the other side of the ongoing military conflict. The problem of child soldiers first surfaced during the Huthi wars.[7] By 2011, news reports indicated as much as fifty percent of combatants in some areas were under the age of eighteen.[8] Youth were also susceptible to being recruited into al-Qaeda's AQAP branch, which expanded its activities in as many as five provinces beyond state control.

---

[3] "Yemen Air Force Kills at Least 200 of Its Own Forces in Arhab District," *Yemen Post* online, August 3, 2011. Later in the summer, reports surfaced that Yemeni pilots began refusing orders to fire missiles on their countrymen, so the air force command in Sanaa allegedly recruited Iraqi and Syrian pilots who were less apt to refuse orders.

[4] Wajdi al-Shaabi, "Interview with al-Fadli: The Two Armies of the Regime and Revolution Are Combining Forces to Destroy Abyan," *al-Umanaa* (in Arabic), Aden, Yemen, September 21, 2011. Also reprinted the next day on the Arabic website, *NewsYemen*, under the title "al-Fadli: The President Contacted Me."

[5] "Losses in Private Sector in Unrest-crippled Yemen over $7 Billion, Official," *Yemen Post* online, July 28, 2011.

[6] "The Rising Temperature of Yemen's Political Situation Sets Prices on Fire," *al-Masdar* online (in Arabic), July 30, 2011.

[7] James Reinl, "UN Tries to Save Child Soldiers," *The National*, U.A.E., June 17, 2010. The recruitment of child soldiers during the wars in Sa'da and other highland provinces included children born of Somali refugees who had endured destitution for nearly two decades.

[8] "Yemen: Conflict Generating More Child Soldiers," United Nations IRIN news, July 20, 2011.

A young, restless, and hungry population makes an explosive combination anywhere in the world, but particularly one located in al-Qaeda's heartland.

In the summer of 2011, AQAP carried out regular assassinations of military and civilian officials in Marib, al-Jawf, Abyan, Shabwa, and Hadramaut. The United States also escalated its use of pilotless drones to target individuals suspected of ties to the group, especially in Abyan. According to American officials, these drones were launched from Djibouti across the narrow *Bab al-Mandab* at the mouth of the Red Sea. Most Yemenis suspected they actually came from inside their territory or neighboring Saudi Arabia. On September 30, exactly one week after President Salih's return to Yemen following his recuperation in Saudi Arabia, American drones fired on a car in al-Jawf province carrying the Yemeni-American imam Anwar al-Aulaqi. Al-Aulaqi was instantly killed with three other men, including a Pakistani-American associate named Samir Khan who edited al-Qaeda's online English magazine, *Inspire*. Although American officials refuted the matter, many Yemenis believed the attack succeeded due to new intelligence that Salih had only agreed to share with the United States after his return. Ever wary of Salih's survival skills, the public saw yet another ploy to relieve some of the growing pressure for his resignation by proving his continued value to the U.S. government.

What finally led Salih to sign the GCC agreement on November 23, giving up his executive powers? There is little evidence that the Obama administration ever ceased demanding a transfer of political power in Yemen. If anything, American officials grew more convinced that Salih's presence undermined security in Yemen and the wider region. On October 21, 2011, the United States cosponsored resolution #2014 at the UN Security Council, calling for Salih's immediate transfer of power to Vice President Hadi based on the GCC plan. When Salih again bluffed about signing in late October, U.S. and European diplomats signaled their intention to reconsider the matter at the Security Council before the end of November, if necessary by applying sanctions against the president's regime. This second action at the Security Council was postponed when Salih requested time to arrange his trip to Riyadh on November 23. After seeing what happened to Muammar al-Gaddhafi when the UN Security Council took action against the Libyan regime, Salih wanted to avoid the same fate. Further evidence of the important role played by the United Nations is the critical late work by UN envoy Jamal Ben Omar who shuttled tirelessly between the U.S., Europe, Sanaa, and Gulf Arab capitals to ensure that Salih signed the GCC deal.

Another reason Salih decided to quit is undoubtedly the rising domestic pressure on his regime. The true champions of Yemen's protests were the youth who courageously took to the streets, day after day, for ten months. Videos uplinked to websites on the internet in September and October showed some youth in Sanaa and Taiz practically daring Salih's military and security forces to shoot at them. One video from Sanaa showed rock-throwing youth defying a barrage of bullets, as one young man danced the traditional highland *bara'a* while using his cell phone camera as an imaginary curved dagger raised high above his head.[9] A second video from Taiz showed lines of unarmed, shirtless young men at the front of a march, openly challenging the regime's soldiers to fire into their bare chests. The public's determination to oust Salih was unshakeable. Women were very active in the protest rallies and street demonstrations. Following Tawakul Karman's early lead, they often appeared on the front lines to shame soldiers firing on unarmed civilians. In a horrific incident in Taiz at a mass Friday demonstration on November 11, Salih's artillery fired directly into the female prayer section, killing three women. On the same day, other military attacks in Taiz killed another thirteen people, including five children. Scores more were injured.

Amid the regime's perfidy, there was one bright spot in the fall of 2011 when Tawakul Karman was awarded the Nobel Peace Prize during the first week of October. She shared the prestigious international award with two other female advocates of peace and human rights from Liberia, West Africa. Karman became the first Arab woman to win the award, and the youngest person at just thirty-two years of age. Nearly every Yemeni citizen celebrated her accomplishment, which brought much needed positive attention to the country from around the globe. Karman humbly accepted the award on behalf of all Yemenis protesting peacefully against the regime's armed forces. Salih shamelessly tried to take credit for the Nobel prize, claiming that his ruling party had promoted women's rights for decades and enabled peaceful protests in 2011 by "not resorting to military force." In reality, back in April when the size of street demonstrations first reached mass levels, Salih had tried to halt them by using Islamic admonitions against women appearing in public with men. Many female protesters were Islah activists. They pressed onward with women

---

[9] "Yemeni Dancing on Battles, Sana'a, Yemen," uploaded on YouTube by "noname1824" on October 17, 2011. http://www.youtube.com/watch?v=BKu_4G8XKP0&feature=related

from other political streams by asserting their human and Islamic rights to be as publicly active as men.[10]

President Salih had absolutely no chance of ending such open defiance of his authority because he lacked any means of responding to massive peaceful street protests without resorting to massacres. Much earlier in 2011, he could hire thugs, *baltagiyya*, to do his dirty work, thereby avoiding bad publicity whenever his uniformed troops used live fire. Evidence that his regime hired *baltagiyya*, as well as snipers responsible for "Bloody Friday" at Sanaa's Change Square on March 18, surfaced in late November when someone posted a revealing online video.[11] The video shows the head of Salih's ruling party bloc in parliament, Yahya al-Ra'ei, addressing a group of highland tribesman in what appears to be his home. The video was made shortly after Ali Muhsin's defection because al-Ra'ei mentions this fact in the video. He instructs the tribesmen to confront street protesters with a good "slapping" after the "slap" given to them at Change Square. This new evidence proved what no longer needed any proof. Earlier in the month, when the religious "feast of sacrifice," *Eid al-Adha*, followed the Hajj season on November 6, the same *baltagiyya* rioted against the government because GPC officials refused to pay their holiday bonuses. Salih was completely discredited. Unwilling to pay his brutal enforcers, he had little choice but to resign.

During the middle 1990s, political and economic analysts warned President Salih about the approaching collapse of his state authority. This collapse was anticipated by analysts inside and outside Yemen, despite the country's celebrated national unification in 1990 and its earlier discovery of oil in the 1980s. After gaining entry to valuable oil markets, President Salih and members of his inner circle behaved as if their small share of the Arabian peninsula's great petroleum prize afforded them an opportunity to live like Saudi royals. They spent extravagantly on palaces, airplanes, and cars, as well as military instruments of control, while handing out just enough money, to as few local clients as necessary, in order to guarantee their survival. The nation could ill afford such extravagances and debts because the land and people of Yemen were never meant to be ruled like the Saudi monarchy.

---

[10] A YouTube video entitled "Yemen's Brave Women Revolutionaries," which was uploaded with English subtitles by "luminessential" on October 17, 2011, shows an articulate young Sanaa woman responding to President Salih's remarks. She sternly lectures him about women's rights under Islam. http://www.youtube.com/watch?v=A9XrP7nx2iM

[11] "Video Segment of al-Ra'ei Inciting a Tribal Group," *al-Masdar* online (in Arabic), November 25, 2011.

For more than three decades, President Salih headed one of the most corrupt governments in the world. In 2010, the organization Transparency International, which ranks countries on fair government and business practices in order to create a global index of the best political and economic climates, placed Yemen near the bottom of its list. The Republic of Yemen tied for 146th with Haiti and Cameroon, slightly behind Zimbabwe.[12] Between 1990 and 2010, there had been terrible mismanagement of the Yemeni economy. Given the state's rising production of oil, this should have been a time of economic advancement with new public investments to improve infrastructure, develop better health and education systems, and encourage expansion into secondary industrial fields. Instead, Yemen declined in nearly every socioeconomic category.

According to the UNDP's 2010 *Human Development Report*, Yemen ranked 133rd among 169 countries, placing it behind Bangladesh and barely ahead of the poorest countries of sub-Saharan Africa.[13] Yemen was obviously not in the position of a vastly rich country like Saudi Arabia or other members of the GCC organization. Ruling Yemen through a centralized patronage system, as President Salih tried to do, was not the best way to develop its modest economic potential. Yemen has one of the fastest growing populations in the world due to its perpetuation of traditional family practices. During the 1990s, the average Yemeni woman would give birth to nearly seven children in her lifetime. From thirteen million people in 1990, the national population doubled in little more than twenty years. By 2011, there were already more Yemenis born since unification than those who lived through the creation of the new republic.

In the middle 2000s Yemeni society started to show uncustomary signs of stress with increased suicide rates among men, and prostitution among women. These are strong taboos in Yemen, proving how severe the social and economic crisis had become years before the political upheaval in 2011. Begging on the streets had steadily increased, and most citizens faced a daily struggle trying to meet the basic needs of life. In September 2010, Britain's Ambassador for UNICEF, Martin Bell, stated that Yemen's humanitarian crisis should receive the highest priority, calling for more economic assistance, not military weapons and counterterrorism training.[14] With twenty-six million people today and growing fast, Yemen is

---

[12] Corruption Perceptions Index, 2010 Results; Transparency.org.
[13] *Human Development Report 2010*, United Nations Development Program.
[14] Martin Bell, "What the world doesn't know about, it will not care about or do anything to remedy," *The Daily Mail Online*, London, England, September 1, 2010.

trapped in a perfect storm of political, social, economic, and environmental crises. Severe water shortages cripple Sanaa, where one million people live at mountain elevations difficult to reach by pumping desalinated sea water from the coast. There are nearly as many people in Taiz who live on the slopes of a massive mountain called *Sabr* ("Patience"), halfway to the southern port of Aden.

The water shortage in Taiz is worse than Sanaa, but in the midlands it would be easier to pump water from the coast. The main barrier to supplying Taiz with good, clean drinking water is lack of funds required for the engineering effort. Yet if the citizens of Taiz could administer their own local affairs, independent of tribes around Sanaa, then they would likely generate the necessary funds based on simple revenue sharing. The same is true of local government in other regions. The empowerment of local government, allowing elected officials to keep more tax revenues at the municipal and provincial level, should be a point of emphasis in Yemen's new era. President Salih and his ruling GPC party ignored this matter for too long. One of the best means to stimulate economic growth more evenly around the country, especially after the country's severe collapse since the mid-2000s, is to decentralize decision-making powers outside the capital. This could also help ease regional political grievances toward the government in Sanaa. There remain political sensitivities between regions on opposite sides of the old north-south border, as well as unique sensitivities inside the eastern region of Hadramaut. All of these demand careful attention.

When Abd al-Rabo Mansour Hadi assumed executive powers in late November 2011, he headed a transitional government to be administered by a joint cabinet of JMP and GPC ministers. A 50:50 power-sharing arrangement between the two parties recalled the failed structure of Yemen's government during the dysfunctional, stalemated transition after unity in 1990. Similar to that arrangement in 1990, the new power-sharing formula was meant to serve until multiparty democratic elections could determine the government's next phase. Based on previous experience, this was not a propitious beginning to the post-Salih era. Hadi announced early presidential elections for February 2012. Most observers expected the GPC and JMP to accept Hadi as their chosen candidate, in order to avoid destabilizing competition. His background from the southern Ali Nasir group in the PDRY before 1986, combined with years of service in the GPC as Salih's vice president, made him tolerable to a maximum number of political elites in major opposition and ruling parties. Yet large numbers of citizens wanted the right to choose among other candidates.

The more difficult political issues in Yemen's 2011–2012 transition to a new government concerned the prime minister's post; the election of a new parliament to choose the next prime minister; the creation of more transparency and safeguards in voter registration and voting; and the larger question of whether or not the Yemeni constitution should be amended to create a purely parliamentary model of government based on proportional representation. Each of these points had been demanded by the JMP since at least 2008. They also gained support in 2011 among independent street protesters. The independent youth in the streets did not approve Hadi as head of state because of his association with the military under Salih, and his responsibility for atrocities during Salih's absence in Saudi Arabia. The JMP was granted the right to choose a transitional prime minister to direct the joint JMP-GPC cabinet. It selected another southern personality, Muhammad Ba Sindwa, a senior politician who briefly served as foreign minister in the unity government between 1993 and 1994, and later minister of information. He was acceptable to most independent youth as an elder representative of their interests.

Born in Aden to a Hadrami family, Ba Sindwa had lived in Sanaa since the late 1960s, often serving in northern governments. His elevation as head of the transitional cabinet was yet another sign that political elites from the highland region were aware of the need to win support among south Yemenis, especially active supporters of al-Hirak. A major concern after 2011 was how to keep the twenty-one-year-old republic intact, and avoid a new secession in the south. In this sense, it was noteworthy to find Abd al-Rabo Mansour Hadi from the mid-southern region and Muhammad Ba Sindwa, with a family background from eastern and southwestern regions, as leading figures during the post-Salih transition. No one from north Yemen, especially the top shaykhs of Hashid and Bakil such as members of the al-Ahmar family or the Abu Luhum family, but also political elites from densely populated western midlands in Taiz, Ibb, and al-Bayda, appeared to challenge the lead of Hadi and Ba Sindwa. In the interests of the country's unity and a restoration of social peace, it was not deemed acceptable for Sadeq, Husayn, or Hamid al-Ahmar to position themselves as successors to President Salih. This was even more true of General Ali Muhsin al-Ahmar. The political status of highland tribal and military figures was at a remarkable low point because they were not perceived as unifying figures among the wider population.

In the summer of 2011, when opposition groups first proposed a transitional government after Salih's evacuation to a hospital in Saudi Arabia, there had been a number of different political ideas put forth. Tawakul Karman and leaders of Sanaa's independent youth group were the first to suggest a transitional governing council. On July 16, they produced a list of seventeen individuals, including southern exiles such as former president Ali Nasir Muhammad and the first prime minister of united Yemen Haidar al-Attas, to head a government of technocrats until elections could be held nine months later.[15] In addition, their plan called for a 501-member national assembly to draft a new constitution, which would include proportional representation and political decentralization. Other individuals in Sanaa soon proposed their own transitional plans. This included everyone from Bakil shaykh Muhammad Abu Luhum, and his new party modeled after the Turkish Justice and Development party, to Hashid's top shaykh Sadeq al-Amar, as well as leaders of the main opposition parties in the JMP. Abu Luhum's proposal included an opening to al-Huthi leaders; and he was open to the idea of reforming government along federal lines, in order to appeal for support among southern al-Hirak leaders.[16]

The most serious step toward producing a transitional government occurred at the new campus of Sanaa University on August 17, when more than one thousand delegates met to nominate a 143-member National Council.[17] Like the earlier effort by Tawakul Karman, the individuals chosen for this council included prominent southern exiles, Ali Nasir Muhammad and Haidar al-Attas. However, no one asked these men if they wanted to be nominated. In the following days, they announced their refusal along with more than twenty percent of individuals on the list. This indicated a continuing split between politicians and activists in Sanaa, on the one hand, and politicians and activists from outlying regions, on the other hand. In particular, political activists from Yemen's southern and eastern provinces rejected efforts in Sanaa to form a new government. On August 25, a leader of al-Hirak in al-Dali' province, Salah al-Shanfara, claimed the street rebellions in Sanaa only concerned citizens in the north; in his words, "we

---

[15] "Yemeni Protesters Form Council to Run Country," *al-Jazeera* website, July 16, 2011.

[16] Mohammed bin Sallam and Nadia al-Sakkaf, "Popular Roadmaps for a Transition of Power," *Yemen Times*, July 28, 2011.

[17] Mohammed al-Qadhi, "National Council Formed to Run Yemen Revolution," *The National*, U.A.E., August 18, 2011. Woman from Yemen, "The Newly Formed National Governing Council: Will it Govern in a New Way?," *Jadaliyya* website, August 18, 2011. "Members Reject Participation in Yemeni Opposition National Council," *Yemen Post*, August 20, 2011.

demand a separate southern state."[18] Once Salih signed the GCC deal, the founder of the military retirees association in Aden, Nasir al-Nuba, also voiced support for southern self-determination. He and other opposition leaders organized a massive street rally in Aden on November 30, 2011, celebrating the official holiday of southern independence.[19] More than one hundred thousand crowded onto the main thoroughfare in al-Ma'ala, stretching for miles and carrying the old southern flag.

Back in late summer and early fall 2011, when Sanaa and Taiz bore the costs of great violence, some northern street activists complained that southern citizens had not done enough to organize similarly large street rallies, especially at a time when northern youth were sacrificing their lives on a daily basis. Meanwhile, the public perception in southern and eastern provinces was different. Most citizens living in areas of the former south Yemen viewed Salih as a monstrous leader who had exploited southern and eastern provinces since 1994, traumatizing the local population. Since Salih was originally created in the interests of Sanaa and Taiz, it was the responsibility of Sanaa and Taiz to get rid of him and initiate a better government. Through the fall of 2011, southern exiles Ali Nasir Muhammad and Haidar al-Attas continued holding public conferences in Cairo, Egypt. They developed their own proposal for a transitional government based on a federal state structure for two to three years, after which south Yemenis could vote by referendum on whether or not to remain united with the north.[20] There is little doubt that the success or failure of rebuilding Yemen's government will depend on how the country's complex regional dynamics are managed, and how the issues of federalism and local government power are handled.

Before Salih resigned, leaders of the protests in Sanaa wanted to believe that people from all regions of the country could work together and move forward to build a brighter, common future. To admit otherwise risked creating a political advantage for Salih, who always claimed that he was

[18] "Salah al-Shanfara to al-Khaleej: The Present Revolution Means the North; Our Demand Is the Return of the Southern State," *Aden Press* online (in Arabic), August 25, 2011.

[19] "Aden: Supporters of al-Hirak Cheer for the Celebration of November 30 in al-Ma'ala, Demanding Disengagement (from the North)," *Mareb Press* online (in Arabic), November 30, 2011.

[20] Mustafa Anbar, "The First Southern Conference for Sons of South Yemen Debates Today the Achievement of a Federal Union," *Aden Press* online (in Arabic), November 21, 2011. The best English-language analysis of earlier transition proposals by Yemen's southern exile groups, as well as proposals by southerners inside the country, was prepared by April Longley for the International Crisis Group. "Breaking Point?: Yemen's Southern Question," crisisgroup.org, October 20, 2011.

the only person capable of maintaining Yemeni unity via his old divide and rule tactics. Sanaa's protest leaders were justified in their fears that Salih might use regional divisions to stay in power. Most members of the southern opposition shared these fears, and before November 23, they had willingly dampened their calls for independence in order to deny Salih any advantage. Yet Yemen's internal divisions remain an undeniable fact, which must be addressed by the country's future political leadership. Even UN diplomat Jamal Ben Omar admitted this point after his successful shuttle diplomacy succeeded in getting Salih to sign the GCC deal. When pressed to explain why a political settlement in Yemen had taken so long compared to Tunisia and Egypt, he had a prepared answer based on long experience. Unlike the latter two countries, where the 2011 protests mainly pitted a united opposition against an unpopular regime, Ben Omar said, "There are multiple dimensions to Yemen's political problems."

Analysts of Yemeni politics rarely give enough attention to the persistence of regional divisions as a source of ongoing political turmoil and economic mismanagement in the country. This is particularly true of Western counterterrorism analysts who look at Yemen, and only see the threat of al-Qaeda. Between 2001 and 2010, there was a tendency among American analysts to emphasize the dangers presented by al-Qaeda due to Yemen's weak state institutions and the fragility of its national unity. A chorus of experts regularly warn about Yemen's "state failure," which is expected to create fertile soil for terrorists to take root. For this reason, Yemen's central government, and the military strongmen behind this government, are perceived as key allies. The idea of decentralization and local control is typically viewed as a threat to political stability. It is primarily for this reason that President Salih was considered the best option for so long. Yet there had long been a problem with this option, due to a dangerous conflation between Salih's domestic rivals and AQAP. For example, US cooperation with the Yemeni military in targeting areas of Abyan after 2009 led to the provincial capital falling into the hands of Islamic militants in 2011. Without a clear means of distinguishing between AQAP and domestic opponents of the regime, joint U.S.-Yemeni military operations were bound to create greater instability.

Simple unilinear assumptions that "failed states" cause terrorism have serious flaws. Given that Yemeni unity is relatively new, and given the state's near constant instability over the last two decades, it begs the question: did western leaders and counterterrorism experts focus on the right issue when they made decisions based on the fear of Yemen becoming a failed state? The problem of Yemen's national unity, and the weakness of its state institutions, preceded the rise of al-Qaeda. Since these were nearly contemporaneous events, there was a tendency to regard al-Qaeda and Yemeni national unity as two sides of the same coin: either Yemen overcomes its internal weaknesses, and its national union succeeds; or al-Qaeda prevails on the Arabian peninsula. But Yemeni unity is weak due to historically strong regional divisions. Since the time of political unification between north and south Yemen in 1990, multiple internal divisions have badly undermined the central government in Sanaa. AQAP is able to flourish in this environment due to grievances about corruption and abuses of power inside Sanaa and the highland region.

If Yemen descends into further anarchy like nearby Somalia, located just across the Gulf of Aden from Yemen's southern coast, then there is the potential for it to become fertile soil for al-Qaeda to deepen its roots and expand. In this scenario, militant extremists in AQAP might coalesce into something far worse. But conditions of anarchy depend upon the future Yemeni government's handling of the country's internal divisions, not AQAP as an independent actor capable of determining the country's future. AQAP is neither the only danger, nor the greatest danger emanating from Yemen. The greatest danger is a continued mishandling of the country's regional divisions. This will happen if there is a too narrow focus on central government powers in Sanaa, due to the false equation between "state failure" and terrorism. Western intervention to prevent state failure will likely lead to the replacement of one military strongman with yet another military strongman such as Ali Abdallah Salih's son, Ahmad, or Ahmad's cousin, Yahya, both of whom worked with U.S.-trained counterterrorism units.

Counterterrorism analysis of Yemen ignores many critically important matters, such as the highly troubled process of national unification after 1990, and the country's civil war in 1994. Counterterrorism chronologies typically start with the bombing of the USS *Cole* in Aden in 2000. Yet the country's political violence started long before this incident, and the grievances of its citizens extend to the original formation of the new Republic of Yemen. Yemenis never fully recovered from the crises of their early unity years. The wounds inflicted by the 1994 civil war left deep scars across the face of the population. Just as the Yemeni landscape is scarred by impressive geological features, towering mountains and vast canyons, the Yemeni people have always been divided along regional lines. This has been true for thousands of years, and it will remain true for the near future. The best hope is to build on new solidarities among the population during the 2011 uprising against President Salih's regime, in order to restart Yemeni national unity on more favorable terms.

When north and south Yemen united in 1990, the politicians and average citizens were in denial about the multiple divisions across their nation. During the next two decades, President Salih eagerly exploited these divisions in order to strengthen his hold on power. As shown throughout this book, the balancing of different regional and tribal groups, and playing games of divide and rule, were standard practices in Sanaa throughout the twentieth century. This was true before 1990 when Salih ruled the northern YAR. It was also true during the reign of the Zaydi imams before the 1962 revolution. But something profound changed in 1990, when unification nearly tripled the size of territory administered by the central government in Sanaa. President Salih immediately stumbled into a costly civil war in 1994. Then in the last half of the 1990s, he struggled to legitimize his military control over southern and eastern regions. During the next decade, he ultimately proved incapable of governing united Yemen. Like a crude caricature of the 1990s comedy television show *Dahbash*, he acted in embarrassingly irresponsible ways. The old snake charmer had badly lost his way.

The problem President Salih had with national unification after 1990 was that unity increased the number of regional groups vying for pieces of the political pie, which consist of various national resources. This brought additional pressure on Salih to satisfy a larger set of political demands. "Dancing on the heads of snakes" was much easier before 1990, when he was only concerned about two or three regional groups, and the occasional rebellion by subtribes of Hashid and Bakil. National unification with the south added at least three more groups to the political mix: stalwarts of the Yemeni Socialist Party in the southwest region around Aden; various disgruntled elements in the mid-southern region of Abyan and Shabwa provinces; and influential, highly resourceful individuals in the eastern region of Hadramaut. But the strongest indication President Salih lost his way in the 2000s was not his mishandling of relations with any of these groups. Instead, it was the rise of powerful opposition inside his own highland region, originating with traditional Zaydi interests in Sa'da during the rebellion of Husayn al-Huthi's "believing youth" organization.

For decades, Zaydism slept as a spent force in Yemeni politics because both highland tribal federations, Hashid and Bakil, had supported the new republican order established in the 1960s. For more than forty years, Zaydi religious leaders in Sa'da (and al-Mahwit province west of Sanaa, especially the spectacular cliff-top town of Kokaban) complained about their marginalization within the republican order in Sanaa. After 1970, this order was built on highland tribal dominance with Bakil playing the role of Hashid's weak partner and rival. The arrangement worked with reasonable effectiveness until unification with south Yemen opened the door to a different kind of politics, pluralist and more competitive with shifting group alliances. When President Salih lost the ability to balance different regional players, and keep his rivals off guard, it exposed four-decade-old fissures among highland tribes inside the mountains of Sanaa. Inside these fissures, the rebellion of a-Huthi became a major threat to the regime.

When the rebellion by al-Huthi's followers led to full scale warfare after 2004, it knocked President Salih off his center of gravity. Zaydi leaders of al-Huthi had no natural allies among other regional groups, except the tribes of al-Jawf province in the central interior region. Nonetheless, they could exploit old Hashid-Bakil rivalries in the highlands, which extend centuries back in time. Between 2006 and 2008, just as al-Hirak launched its mass street protests in the south, Zaydi elites began drawing greater support from disgruntled tribal members of Bakil. This was especially true of Bakil shaykhs who resented playing a minor role to the top Hashid shaykhs who dabbled in Saudi al-Wahhabi religious ideas. Some Bakil shaykhs shared these religious sympathies. But a larger number had never invested in al-Wahhabi trends, which swept the country before and after national unification. In 2005, when Zaydi leaders of al-Huthi called for a wider insurrection, these Bakil shaykhs were more willing to respond.

Al-Huthi rebels represented the greatest threat to President Salih between 2005 and 2009 because they struck at the heart of the regime's core constituency among highland tribes. Salih's regime staggered under the pressure of al-Huthi until 2007. But thereafter the president was completely overtaken by multiple regional oppositions, especially al-Hirak in southern and eastern regions. Although al-Hirak and al-Huthi supporters share some attributes, there is an important difference between the two. They arose for similar reasons, such as objections to President Salih's leadership, and resentments over political marginalization and poor economic development. Yet in the end, al-Hirak raised basic questions of national identity, clamoring for independence from the regime in Sanaa. This is something unique to al-Hirak. Unlike al-Huthi members in Sa'da, who dreamed of capturing Sanaa and restoring Zaydi influence over the capital city's politics, al-Hirak activists in the southern movement sought to express their political identities separate from Sanaa.

Citizens in southern and eastern regions of Yemen, as well as western midland, coastal, and central interior regions around Taiz, Zabid, al-Hudayda, Marib, and Shabwa, realize they could make greater social and economic progress, if they did not live under the controlling influence of highland elites in Sanaa. This is true because Yemen's most valuable resources are the oil and gas fields in Marib, Shabwa, and Hadramaut, and the port facilities at Aden, al-Hudayda, and al-Mukalla. President Salih gradually tried to placate the demands of political opponents inside these regions through political decentralization, granting greater power to elected local leaders at provincial, district, and municipal levels. He first agreed to these measures, following heated debates about federalism in late 1993 and the eventual signing of the "document of pledge and accord" in February 1994. But it took him until 2008 to implement the measures, and by then it was too late.

Issues of decentralization and local government have a long history in Yemen. But their meaning varies from region to region. Inside the highland mountains, members of the political opposition do not view decentralization as a question of political identity. For them, it is strictly a matter of administrative reform between central and local government bodies. Meanwhile outside the highlands, the same subject concerns identity issues in multiple regions of the country. This is the challenge of decentralization for political elites in Sanaa. Following the 1994 civil war, President Salih made a mistake by delaying the election of local governors, which he had promised to arrange within one year. When the national law on "Local Authority" was passed in 2000, it appeared Salih had promised something for six years that he was ultimately unwilling to deliver. Dissatisfaction with the first local council elections in February 2001 deepened opposition in many outlying regions because people no longer trusted the regime in Sanaa to allow fully democratic elections. This lack of trust made it more difficult for President Salih to placate al-Hirak activists later in the decade, when he abruptly arranged indirect elections for governors in May 2008, and then offered to allow the election of municipal mayors in 2009.

At a time of relative stability in the last half of the 1990s and early 2000s, the president should have encouraged an expansion of locally elected government. This may have built more confidence in the unification process, relieving Sanaa of some burden of responsibility for the nation's troubles, while possibly stimulating economic growth in outlying regions of the country. Instead, the regime made a forgery of decentralization between 1994 and 2008, retaining central government powers to appoint provincial officials and control local revenues. Unfortunately, the violence in southern and eastern provinces between 2008 and 2011 makes it difficult to restore trust in the central government. The same is true in all regions of the country. On the eve of the 2011 uprising, all regional opposition groups spoke of their marginalization by political and economic elites living in palatial homes in Sanaa, and driving luxury four-wheel-drive vehicles purchased with state funds. These elites included Hashid shaykhs from the al-Ahmar family, as well as General Ali Muhsin. Jealousy of wealth concentrated in Sanaa, and resentments toward elites inside the highlands, fanned opposition around the country.

Across Yemeni history, Sanaa was an isolated urban center in the mountains cut off from the outside world by rulers who preferred keeping the city gates locked. It is still an insular city, where many customs are unchanged after hundreds of years. In Sanaa, there is an assumed pattern to life that resists change, and fosters conformity. By comparison, the city of Aden was always more open to the outside world, and better able to manage social and cultural diversity. Since the united Republic of Yemen requires a government capable of addressing diverse identities across multiple regions, it would be better served if power were placed in the hands of government technocrats in the former southern capital. The late Faisal Bin Shamlan, and the earlier prime minister from Hadramaut, Fareg Bin Ghanem, could have served as fair-minded rulers of Yemen. There are other potential leaders from communities in Taiz and al-Hudayda, who possess broader visions of Yemeni national unity. Generally speaking, people living nearer Yemen's coasts are more open-minded than tribal and military elites in Sanaa.

One sign of the narrow vision of Sanaa's ruling class came during the tribal looting of Aden in July 1994. When northern military and tribal leaders from the president's family, as well as the family of the late Hashid shaykh Abdallah bin Husayn al-Ahmar, took possession of vacant houses and lands in the southern port city, they initially denied property rights to Adeni families of Indian and Somali ancestry.[21] In the 1990s, many northern elites in Sanaa could be heard dismissing former south Yemeni leader, Ali Salim al-Bid, as a "Hindi" because of his physical likeness to people in India. Measured by Yemen's "Qahtan" standard, anyone from India or Somalia, Ethiopia or even Iraq and Syria, does not belong to the nation. The rhetoric about Qahtan no longer serves a constructive purpose. It originated in the 1950s and 1960s as an effective means of overcoming north Yemen's sectarian divide between Zaydis and Shafi'is. It was a way for early republicans to combat the prejudices of highland tribesmen toward people of Shafi'i backgrounds. Once these tribesmen began

---

[21] Interview with municipal government officials in Aden; July 1998.

dominating the politics of Sanaa in the 1970s and 1980s, the Qahtan rhetoric provided only a thin veneer beneath which existed bigotry and exclusion of people from nonhighland regions.

According to leading Hashid tribal shaykhs, and a few allies from Bakil, they alone represent the strengths and virtues of Qahtan's descendants. This belief is particularly strong among the family of al-Ahmar, members of President Salih's family, and General Ali Muhsin.[22] In their minds, they are most capable of ruling Yemen, and keeping the national union intact. Yemenis from other regions are considered either too weak or untrustworthy. The idea of Qahtan excluded the Zaydi religious aristocracy in the middle twentieth century. Today it still excludes al-Huthi family members from Sa'da. This was one reason for the 2004–2009 warfare north of Sanaa, where traditional Zaydi ruling class families felt marginalized by the central government. The rhetoric of Qahtan is now more divisive than the past because it largely serves the interests of groups in Sanaa that maintain power by military means. In regions outside the highland mountains, especially areas where valuable resources are located, such as Hadramaut, Marib, Shabwa, and Aden, it is little wonder that locals feel animosity toward ruling elites in Sanaa. It is also unsurprising that they seek greater local control, including the right to manage their own resources.

The main source of Yemen's political instability since 1990 has been a competition over scarce resources among different regional groups. Due to the disjuncture between concentrated political power in Sanaa and valuable economic resources in outlying regions, President Salih had to expend excessive energy and state revenues to maintain control of areas beyond his home region in the highland mountains. During his wars in the south, his primary concern was sources of wealth in the oilfields of Hadramaut and Shabwa, and the southern port in Aden. The president openly acknowledged the country's divided character when he warned protesters that their rebellion, if successful, would result in the formation of multiple small

---

[22] In the late 1990s, the author sat in a social gathering with President Salih's nephew, Yahya Muhammad Abdallah Salih, later commander of Yemen's central security forces and American-trained counterterrorism units. At this gathering, Sanhan's rise to prominence in Yemen's political order was a topic of conversation. The young man, and future "general" accused of brutal crackdowns on street protesters in 2011, described a mythological story about an ancient gathering of south Arabian tribal shaykhs, who sat around a large fire. According to his story, the leading shaykhs of Yemen were challenged to place a heavy, red-hot piece of iron across their shoulders to prove their capability of ruling Yemen. Many shaykhs of Hashid and Bakil tried, but failed, until the leader of Sanhan was successful at the task. In reality, all highland tribes of Yemen tell similar versions of this legend.

states. His government's fiscal policies had always revealed regionally differentiated spending patterns. In addition, every election since 1993 showed regionally differentiated results along multiple, distinct lines.

The primary axis of Yemeni politics in the twenty-first century is not religious or ideological, partisan or class-based. Earlier struggles between Arabists and tribal traditionalists, Islamists and socialists have faded. Today Yemen is returning to a much older pattern of regionalism separating people in the highland mountains from people living in the western midlands around Taiz, and others living along the west coast of Tihama, the southwest region around Aden, the mid-southern and central interior regions, and the eastern regions of Hadramaut and al-Mahra. Yemen remains a fragmented country, where politics is largely defined by the competing interests of groups in multiple regions across a topographically complex landscape.

The political system of Yemen is correctly defined as "primordial federalism." This is how former U.S. ambassador to Yemen, Barbara Bodine, described the country's politics during her testimony to the U.S. Senate Foreign Relations Committee on January 20, 2010, nearly a month after the attempted bombing of Northwest Flight 253 in the skies over Detroit, Michigan. Ambassador Bodine referred specifically to President Salih's granting of autonomy to traditional tribal leaders in highland and central interior regions of the country. If there is a way to save Yemeni national unity, and avoid a breakup of the country into multiple states, then it may come by formalizing this "primordial federalism" in all regions. The same autonomy given to leading shaykhs of Hashid and Bakil should be extended to elected governors in other regions who are more capable of lifting their people from the economic abyss. Yemen needs the talents of good statesmen who can negotiate the sharp differences exposed by regional opposition groups, and set a new course for the united republic.

Elsewhere on the Arabian peninsula, the United Arab Emirates developed a federal structure of government in the 1970s. This structure has worked reasonably well for Emiratis, and it should not be taboo for Yemenis to admit their own proclivity toward federalism. Yemen's political system needs drastic updating for the twenty-first century. The future goal should be to establish equitable power sharing among self-governing regional groups in a strong federal government. Confederalism would risk breaking the national union. But strong federalism could lead to better long-term results. The country is likely to endure as a fractured landscape, regardless of who cames to power in Sanaa. No member of the ruling class in Sanaa, or other potential leaders from regions outside the highland mountains, can erase the country's regional divisions. These divisions persist more than twenty years after Yemeni unification, just as they have for centuries.

Any redesign of Yemen's constitution must come from inside the country, by representatives of the Yemeni people, not outside actors. If Yemen's government is restructured along federal lines, yet this is perceived to be imposed from the outside, then it will doom any prospects of success. The American government should avoid involvement in such a process because of the generally negative perception of America's role in establishing federal rule in Iraq. Unfortunately, many Yemenis associate federalism with the 2003 American invasion of Iraq, and the continuing problems Iraqis have trying to resolve disputes between different regional groups in their country. This is unfortunate because federalism could help alleviate regional divisions in Yemen, and bring an end to violent opposition to the government in Sanaa. Ironically, Yemen needs a strong federal order like the United States, not the weak federal or confederal system imposed in Iraq by Ambassador Paul Bremer and other officials serving under President George W. Bush.

Leaders of the UAE and other members of the GCC could provide incentives to restructure Yemen's government along strong federal lines by making it a condition for Yemen's future entry into the GCC. But Gulf leaders must avoid fomenting divisions in Yemen, pitting northerners against southerners, or sowing conflict along other regional lines. It will be disastrous for Yemen, if outsiders take sides between different regional groups. The result would bring prolonged fighting, which could spill over into the Gulf countries. At the same time, political elites in Sanaa must stop denying the existence of regional divisions, many of which they are responsible for inflaming. There is one simple, yet significant step to take: end celebrations of the northern army's July 7 victory at the conclusion of the 1994 civil war. No nation with difficulties achieving unification can afford to hold festivities commemorating a civil war. Each July 7 holiday is an occasion for opposition rallies in southern and eastern provinces, so the official ceremonies should be cancelled as a show of good will.

There is clearly a need for outside actors to be engaged with Yemen, in order to help resolve its many political and economic problems. But the manner of international engagement should avoid domestic backlash against imagined foreign conspiracies. Yemenis should be encouraged to resolve their own problems, as much as possible, with assistance from neighboring Arab governments in the GCC and the Arab League. Arab diplomats must work with exiled Yemeni leaders who should be included in all talks and negotiations. Over the decades, several Yemeni heads of state and members of various cabinets fled domestic turmoil for exile in Egypt and Syria, Saudi Arabia and the UAE. There cannot be peace and stability in Yemen until the country reconciles with every exiled leader willing to participate in talks. As long as there remain exiled leaders, and groups loyal to them inside the country, there will be plots to destabilize Yemen. Saudi Arabia has a special responsibility to encourage national reconciliation in Yemen because, during the Cold War, al-Wahhabi religious influence undermined centuries-old moderate customs among the Yemeni people.

It is important for Saudi Arabia, the United States, and other influential actors to help finance the rebuilding of Yemen. But questions about who leads the country, and what structure its future republic takes, can only be answered by citizens on the inside. It would be a mistake for American and Saudi policymakers to intervene in Yemen's domestic affairs, seeking to predetermine a political outcome. In early 2010, when American and British officials called the first "Friends of Yemen" meeting in London, they were wise to set a calm diplomatic tone, and refuse to intervene overtly in a country that remains as enigmatic and perplexing as any in the world. Although an end to the regime of President Salih, his family, and the Sanhan group may lead to new problems and divisions, it will not mean the failure of Yemen. Yemen will endure as a fragmented polity, just as it has for millennia.

Appendix

The survey used to compile the data in Tables 2.5 through 2.7, and Tables 5.2 through 5.4, was designed in coordination with staff members at two Yemeni institutions, the National Institute of Administrative Sciences, and the Yemeni Center for Studies and Research, both located in the capital Sanaa. This 1996–1997 survey aimed to record the personnel changes in Yemen's various provincial administrative bodies before and after the country's national unification in May 1990. Due to the lack of effective public recordkeeping in Sanaa, and the loss of south Yemeni government files in Aden after the 1994 civil war, it was necessary to conduct this first-of-its-kind survey to discover changes in the country at the provincial level. For this purpose I designed a survey with the help of the late astute professor Othman Said al-Mikhlafi, who was one of Yemen's leading experts on local administrative affairs, and Dr. Abduh Ali Othman, a former minister of local government in north Yemen and current professor of sociology at Sanaa University.

In consultation with Professor al-Mikhlafi and Dr. Othman, it was agreed that the best means of collecting the desired information was to draw up a detailed survey form, which I could take on research trips to several of Yemen's most important provinces. During these research trips, I would interview the relevant local administrative officials who could complete the information on the survey form. Dr. Othman arranged a letter of sponsorship from the head of the Yemeni Center for Studies and Research, the esteemed national poet Dr. Abd al-Aziz al-Maqaleh. In addition, Professor al-Mikhlafi helped arrange a separate letter of introduction to all provincial governors signed by the deputy minister of local administration in Sanaa. This letter requested assistance from each governor's staff during my stay in the provincial capitals. Both of these letters were instrumental in giving me the proper entry to conduct research throughout the country at a time of relative stability.

I decided to conduct the survey in at least half of Yemen's then eighteen provincial units, including the capital zone in Sanaa. I sought to spend enough time in each province, in order to gain a full understanding of local administrative practices, achievements, and shortcomings. For this reason, I knew that it was impractical to visit every province of the country. I chose to visit an even number of provinces in the former halves of the country, five in the north and five in the south. I also wanted to visit the largest and most populous provinces, which held the greatest political significance. In the north, I selected the capital Sanaa, as well as the provinces of Sanaa, Hajja, Taiz, and al-Hudayda. In the south, I selected Aden, Lahij, Abyan, Hadramaut, and Wadi Hadramaut, which was then being considered as a possible nineteenth province in the country. Hadramaut is vast in size, and the political significance of its coastal and wadi regions is greater than many smaller provinces of Yemen.

The five provinces I chose to visit in the north represent three of the seven geographic regions of Yemen described in Chapter 1: Sanaa and Hajja are in the highland region; Taiz is in the western midlands; and al-Hudayda is on the west coast. In the south, the five areas I chose to visit represent three additional regions in the country: Aden and Lahij are in the southwestern region; Abyan is located in the mid-southern region; and Hadramaut and its wadi make up a large part of Yemen's eastern region. There was only one of Yemen's seven regions that I did not visit for the purpose of research: the sparsely populated central interior desert. However, I did travel through this region on two occasions, while traversing the desert between Sanaa and Wadi Hadramaut. This included a one-day and overnight visit in Marib.

In designing my survey form, I decided in consultations with my Yemeni advisors to record four key pieces of information about each local administrative employee: the person's name; his or her regional origin; educational background; and last previous employment. The survey form consisted of seven pages listing the various provincial administrative positions from governor and deputy governor to director of finance, health, agriculture, and youth sports.[1] The survey form asked the interviewees to

---

[1] A sample copy of the survey form appears in the appendix of the author's Ph.D. dissertation at Georgetown University, "Power Sharing and Hegemony: A Case Study of the United Republic of Yemen," August 2001.

provide information from 1985 to 1996, the later being the year in which the survey was initiated. The starting year of 1985 was chosen in order to provide information about the local administrative practices of the former north and south Yemen several years before unification in 1990. It would also provide information about the administrative changes in the former southern PDRY following its intraregime warfare in January 1986, when tens of thousands of people from the mid-southern region were forced into exile or killed.

In consultation with my Yemeni advisors, I decided to divide the various provincial administrative posts into three categories: first, the "Top Four" posts, which are most critical to local authority (governor, deputy governor, and the two directors of public and political security); second, the "Ten Major" posts, which combine the "Top Four" with six additional key posts in the critical areas of financial and judicial affairs (namely, the directors of the central bank branch, finance, taxation, customs, audit and control, and criminal prosecution); and third, numerous "Minor" administrative posts, which are not as critical to political power in the provinces, including health, education, agriculture, industry, housing, supply and trade, planning, information, civil service, legal service, religious affairs, culture and tourism, social insurance, communications, transportation, water, electricity, and youth sports.

Where possible the survey was completed by referring to local records in the governor's office. But these records were only available in Aden and Hadramaut. More often I relied on two or more senior officials who were familiar with their province's local administrative history, and could recall the information based solely on memory. Often I sat with groups of five to ten local administrators as they enjoyed a "brainstorming" game, trying to recall who served in which administrative posts during the previous twelve years. This became a topic of widespread conversation for several days, since I stayed in each province for at least a week, and usually two to three weeks. In nearly every case, provincial officials were generous with their time, and took an interest in my research. On a number of occasions, I joined customary afternoon *maqil al-qat*, or qat chewing sessions, where the stimulant of the plant helped strengthen the memory capacity of those completing the survey form. The Yemeni custom of meeting for hours after lunch to chew qat is an aid to anyone conducting social research in the country.

After "brainstorming" sessions with provincial administrators, I typically found other independent reviewers who could confirm the accuracy of the information collected. Professor al-Mikhlafi's connections with staff at branch offices of the National Institute of Administrative Sciences were particularly helpful with this cross-checking process. In addition, I occasionally found retired local administrators who agreed to serve the same function. While this method of completing each provincial survey is not flawless, it was the best method available given the lack of official record-keeping in the country.

The results of the administrative survey provided hard data previously unavailable in the study of Yemeni politics. This data offers the best indication of the regional distribution of power in the country for the critical six years before national unification, and after national unification. In the provinces where I did not have a chance to conduct research, I later received help from the minister of civil service in Sanaa to fax the seven-page survey to his provincial directors in Sa'da, al-Jawf, Marib, Dhamar, Ibb, al-Bayda, al-Mahwit, Shabwa, and al-Mahra. The minister requested that his local staff complete and return the survey forms. By this means, I was able to conduct the survey in nearly every province of the country. Only the civil service staff in al-Jawf and Dhamar provinces of the former north Yemen did not return the information. I had no way to confirm how the faxed surveys were completed. I could only assume that staff used similar "brainstorming" and cross-checking methods. Nonetheless, I consider the faxed survey forms to be less reliable because I did not control how they were completed.

Bibliography

Abd al-Salam, Muhammad (possible pseudonym of Dr. Abu Bakr al-Saqqaf), *al-Jumhuriyya bayn al-Sultana wa al-Qabila fi al-Yaman al-Shamali*, ("The Tribal-Sultanate Republic of North Yemen"), al-Ahl Press, Yemen, 1988.

Abu-Amr, Ziad Mahmoud, *The People's Democratic Republic of Yemen: The Transformation of Society*, Unpublished Ph.D. Dissertation, Georgetown University, Washington, DC, 1986.

Abu Ghanem, Fadhl Ali Ahmad, *Al-Qabila wa al-Daula fi al-Yaman* ("The Tribe and State in Yemen"), Dar al-Minar, Cairo, Egypt, 1990.

Abu Taleb, Hasan, "The Future of Yemen after the Civil War," in E. G. H. Joffe, ed., *Yemen Today: Crisis and Solutions*, Caravel Press, London, England, 1997.

Anderson, Benedict, *Imagined Communities: Reflections on the Origin and Spread of Nationalism*, Verso Books, New York, 1993.

Arabishe Republik Jemen: Politik, Munzinger-Archiv./IH-Landeraktuel, Heft 12–13/88; pp. 1–2.

al-Audi, Hamud, "Development and the Experience of Cooperative Work in Yemen" (in Arabic), *Kitab al-Ghad* ("The Book of Tomorrow"), Series No. 2, Sanaa, Yemen, 1975.

Badeeb, Saeed M., *The Saudi-Egyptian Conflict over North Yemen 1962–1970*, Westview Press, Boulder, Colorado, 1986.

al-Bakr, Bashir, *Harb al-Yaman: al-Qabila Tantasar `ala al-Watan* ("Yemen's War: The Tribe Triumphs over the Nation"), al-Mu'asasa al-Arabiyya lil-Dirasaat wa al-Nashr, Beirut, Lebanon, 1995.

al-Baradduni, Abdallah, *al-Thaqafa wa al-Thawra fi al-Yaman* ("Culture and Revolution in Yemen"), Sana'a, Yemen, 1992.

Barth, Fredrik, *Ethnic Groups and Boundaries: The Social Organization of Culture Difference*, Little Brown & Co., New York, 1969.

al-Batati, Abd al-Khali bin Abdallah bin Salih, *Ithbat Ma Laysa Mathbut* ("Confirming What Has Been Unconfirmed about the Yafe`a History in Hadramaut"), Dar al-Bilad Publishing, Jidda, Saudi Arabia, 1989.

Bawazir, Said Awadh, *Safhat min al-Tarikh al-Hadrami* ("Pages from Hadrami History"), Maktab al-Thaqafa, Aden, Yemen, 1957.

Bidwell, Robin, *The Two Yemens*, Westview Press, Boulder, CO, 1983.

al-Bishari, Ahmad, ed., *al-Baraamij al-Intikhabiyya lil-Ahzab wa al-Tanthimaat al-Siyasiyya* ("The Election Programs of Political Parties and Organizations"), al-Thawabit Journal, Sanaa, Yemen, 1993.

al-Bishari, Ahmad, ed., *Mustaqbil al-Hukm al-Mahali fi al-Jumhuriyya al-Yamaniyya* ("The Future of Local Government in the Republic of Yemen"), Thawabit Press, Sanaa, Yemen, 1996.

Boucek, Christopher, "War in Saada: From Local Insurrection to National Challenge," in Christopher Boucek and Marina Ottaway, *Yemen on the Brink*, Carnegie Endowment for International Peace, Washington, DC, 2010.

Bujra, Abdullah, *The Politics of Stratification: A Study of Political Change in a South Arabian Town*, Clarendon Press, Oxford, England, 1971.

Burrowes, Robert, *The Yemen Arab Republic: The Politics of Development, 1962–1986*, Westview Press, Boulder, Colorado, 1987.

Burrowes, Robert, "Prelude to Unification: The Y.A.R., 1962–1990," *International Journal of Middle East Studies*, Volume 23, 1991; pp. 483–506.

Burrowes, Robert, "The Yemen Arab Republic's Legacy and Yemeni Unification," *Arab Studies Quarterly*, Volume 1, No. 4, Fall 1992; pp. 41–68.

Burrowes, Robert, *Historical Dictionary of Yemen*, The Scarecrow Press, Lanham, Maryland, 1995(a).

Burrowes, Robert, "The Yemeni Civil War of 1994: Impact of the Arab Gulf States," in Jamal S. al-Suwaidi, ed., *The Yemen War of 1994: Causes and Consequences*, Saqi Books, Abu Dhabi, UAE, 1995(b).

Burrowes, Robert and Catherine M. Kasper, "The Salih Regime and the Need for a Credible Opposition," *Middle East Journal*, Volume 61, Number 2, Spring 2007.

Carapico, Sheila, Walker, S. Tjip, and John Cohen, Local Organization, Participation and Development in the Y.A.R., Cornell University, 1983.

Carapico, Sheila, "From Ballot Box to Battlefield," *Middle East Report*, Volume 25, No. 1, September–October 1994.

Carapico, Sheila, "Yemen Between Civility and Civil War," in Augustus Richard Norton, ed., *Civil Society in the Middle East*, Volume Two, E. J. Brill, New York, NY, 1996.

Carapico, Sheila, *Civil Society in Yemen*, Cambridge University Press, Cambridge, England, 1998.

Carapico, Sheila, Lisa Wedeen, and Anna Wuerth, "The Death and Life of Jarallah Omar," *Middle East Reports* Online, December 31, 2002.

Carapico, Sheila, "How Yemen's Ruling Party Secured an Electoral Landslide," *Middle East Reports* Online, May 16, 2003.

Carapico, Sheila, "Counter-Proposal from Yemen's Revolutionary Youth," *Jadaliyya* website, May 26, 2011.

Caton, Steven, *Yemen Chronicle: An Anthropology of War and Mediation*, Hill and Wang, New York, NY, 2005.

Chaudhry, Kiren, *The Price of Wealth: Economies and Institutions in the Middle East*, Cornell University Press, Ithaca, New York, 1997.

Clapp, Nicholas, *Sheba: Through the Desert in Search of the Legendary Queen*, Mariner Books, Boston, Massachusetts, 2002.

Clark, Janine, *Islam, Charity, and Activism: Middle Class Networks and Social Welfare in Egypt, Jordan, and Yemen*, Indiana University Press, Bloomington, Indiana, 2004.

Clark, Victoria, *Yemen: Dancing on the Heads of Snakes*, Yale University Press, New Haven, Connecticut, 2010.

Coll, Steve, *Ghost Wars: The Secret History of the CIA, Afghanistan, and Bin Laden*, Penguin Books, New York, 2004.

Coll, Steve, *The Bin Ladens: An Arabian Family in the American Century*, Penguin Press, New York, 2008.

Cooley, John, *Unholy Wars: Afghanistan, America, and International Terrorism*, Pluto Press, London, England, 1999.

Dahlgren, Susanne, *Contesting Realities: The Public Sphere and Morality in Southern Yemen*, Syracuse University Press, Syracuse, NY, 2010.

Day, Stephen W., "Barriers to Federal Democracy in Iraq: Lessons from Yemen," *Middle East Policy*, Volume XIII, No. 3, Fall 2006; pp. 121–139.

Day, Stephen W., "Updating Yemeni National Unity: Could Lingering Regional Divisions Bring Down the Regime?," *Middle East Journal*, Volume 62, No. 3, Summer 2008; pp. 417–436.

Day, Stephen W., "Yemen Postpones Its April 2009 Parliamentary Elections," *Viewpoints*, The Middle East Institute, Number 11, June 2009.

Day, Stephen W., "The Political Challenge of Yemen's Southern Movement," in Christopher Boucek and Marina Ottaway, *Yemen on the Brink*, Carnegie Endowment for International Peace, Washington, DC, 2010.

Day, Stephen W., "Who Will Be Next to Fall? AAS of Yemen," *Jadaliyya* website, February 2, 2011.

Day, Stephen W., "Yemen's Popular Uprising in Photos," *Jadaliyya* website, March 2, 2011.

Despres, Leo, *Ethnicity and Resource Competition in Plural Societies*, Mouton Publishers, The Hague, Netherlands, 1975.

Detalle, Renaud, "The Political Economy of Reforms," in E. G. H. Joffe, ed., *Yemen Today: Crisis and Solutions*, Caravel Press, London, England, 1997.

Deutsch, Karl, "The Growth of Nations: Some Recurrent Patterns of Political and Social Integration," *World Politics*, January 1953, pp. 168–195.

Douglas, Leigh, *The Free Yemeni Movement*, American University Press, Beirut, Lebanon, 1987.

Dresch, Paul *Tribes, Government, and History*, Clarendon Press, Oxford, England, 1989.

Dresch, Paul, and Bernard Haykel, "Stereotypes and Political Styles: Islamists and Tribesfolk in Yemen," *International Journal of Middle East Studies*, No. 27, 1995(a); pp. 405–431.

Dresch, Paul, "The Tribal Factor in the Yemeni Crisis," in Jamal al-Suwaidi, ed., *The Yemeni War of 1994: Causes and Consequences*, Saqi Books, Abu Dhabi, UAE, 1995(b).

Dresch, Paul, *A History of Modern Yemen*, Cambridge University Press, Cambridge, England, 2000.

Dunbar, Charles, "The Unification of Yemen: Process, Politics, and Progress," *Middle East Journal*, Volume 46, Number 3, Summer 1992; pp. 456–476.

Dunbar, Charles, "Internal Politics in Yemen: Recovery or Regression," in Jamal al-Suwaidi, ed., *The Yemeni War of 1994: Causes and Consequences*, Saqi Books, Abu Dhabi, UAE, 1995.

Gause, Gregory, "The Idea of Yemeni Unity," *Journal of Arab Affairs*, Volume 6, No. 1, 1987.

Gause, Gregory, *Yemeni-Saudi Relations*, Columbia University Press, New York, 1990.

Gavin, R. J., *Aden Under British Rule, 1839–1967*, C. Hurst and Company, London, England, 1975.

Geertz, Clifford, "The Integrative Revolution: Primordial Sentiments and Civil Politics in the New States," in Clifford Geertz, ed., *Old Societies and New States*, Free Press, London, England, 1963.

Ghaleb, Mohammed Anam, *Government Organizations as a Barrier to Economic Development in Yemen*, National Institute of Public Administration, Sanaa, Yemen; April 1979.

Haddad, Bassam, "Why, What, Where to, and How: Tunisia and Beyond," *Jadaliyya* website, January 14, 2011.

al-Haddad, Muhammad Yahya, *Tarikh al-Yaman al-Siyasi*, ("The Political History of Yemen"), Beirut, Lebanon, 1986.

Halliday, Fred, *Arabia Without Sultans*, Penguin Books, Harmondsworth, England, 1974.

Halliday, Fred, "Catastrophe in South Yemen," *Middle East Report*, March–April 1986.

Halliday, Fred, *Revolution and Foreign Policy: The Case of South Yemen 1967–1987*, Cambridge University Press, Cambridge, England, 1990.

Halliday, Fred, "The Third Inter-Yemeni War and Its Consequences," *Asian Affairs*, Number 26, 1995; pp. 131–139.

al-Hamdani, Abd al-Hadi Husayn, *al-Tanmiyya al-Idariyya fi al-Jumhuriyya al-Yamaniyya*, ("Administrative Development in the Republic of Yemen"), Dar al-'Asar Publishing, Sanaa, Yemen, 1990.

al-Harbi, Ahmad, *Tanthim al-Idara al-Mahaliyya wa al-Tanmiyya al-Thatiyya*, ("The Organization of Local Administration and Self-Development"), General Secretariat for Local Councils and Cooperative Development, Sanaa, Yemen, 1989.

Harris, Alistair, "Exploiting Grievances: al-Qaeda in the Arabian Peninsula," in Christopher Boucek and Marina Ottaway, *Yemen on the Brink*, Carnegie Endowment for International Peace, Washington, DC, 2010.

Haykel, Bernard, *Revival and Reform in Islam: The Legacy of Muhammad al-Shawkani*, Cambridge University Press, New York, 2003.

al-Hibshi, Abdallah Muhammad, *Hawaliyyat Yamaniyya: al-Yaman fi al-Qarn al-Tasi' Ashar* ("Yemeni Annals: Yemen in the Nineteenth Century"), Dar al-Hikma al-Yamaniyya, Sanaa, Yemen, 1991.

Hill, Ginny, and Gerd Nonneman, "Yemen, Saudi Arabia, and the Gulf States: Elite Politics, Street Protests, and Regional Diplomacy," *Chatham House Briefing Papers*, May 2011.

Hoffman, Stanley, *Chaos and Violence: What Globalization, Failed States, and Terrorism Mean for U.S. Foreign Policy*, Rowman & Littlefield Publishers, Inc, Lanham, MD, 2006.

Hudson Michael, "Unhappy Yemen: Watching the Slide Toward Civil War," *Middle East Insight*, May-August 1994; pp. 10–19.

Hudson Michael, "Bipolarity, Rational Calculation, and War in Yemen," in Jamal S. al-Suwaidi, ed., *The Yemen War of 1994: Causes and Consequences*, Saqi Books, Abu Dhabi, UAE, 1995.

Ismail, Tareq and Jacqueline, *The Peoples Democratic Republic of Yemen: Politics, Economy, and Society*, Lynne Rienner Publishers, Boulder, Colorado, 1986.

al-Jawi, Omar, "We are the Opposition," in E. G. H. Joffe, ed., *Yemen Today: Crisis and Solutions*, Caravel Press, London, England, 1997.

al-Jifri, Abdul-Rahman, "Yemeni Unification," in E. G. H. Joffe, ed., *Yemen Today: Crisis and Solutions*, Caravel Press, London, England, 1997.

Joffe, E. G. H., ed., *Yemen Today: Crisis and Solutions*, Caravel Press, London, England, 1997.

Johnsen, Gregory D., and Brian O'Neill, *Waq al-Waq*, "Islam and Insurgency in Yemen," blogspot.com.

Johnsen, Gregory D., "Reprogramming the Imagination in Yemen: Hamoud al-Hitar and the Religious Dialogue Council," unpublished paper; Middle East Studies Association conference, Washington, DC, November 2005.

Johnsen, Gregory D., "The Election Yemen Was Supposed to Have," *Middle East Report Online*, October 3, 2006(a).

Johnsen, Gregory D., "Yemen's Passive Role in the War on Terrorism," *Terrorism Monitor*, Volume 4, Issue 4, Jamestown Foundation, Washington, DC, February 23, 2006(b).

Johnson, Chalmers, *Blowback: The Costs and Consequences of American Empire*, Henry Holt & Company, New York, 2000.

Katz, Mark, "External Powers and the Yemeni Civil War," in Jamal S. al-Suwaidi, ed., *The Yemen War of 1994: Causes and Consequences*, Saqi Books, ABu Dhabi, UAE, 1995.

Kean, Thomas, and Lee Hamilton, *The 9/11 Report: The National Commission on Terrorist Attacks Upon the United States.*, St. Martin's Press, Boulder, Colorado, 2004.

Khobani, Anise, *A Study on Local Government Councils in the PDRY*, Unpublished academic dissertation, Budapest, Hungary, 1989.

Kostiner, Joseph, *The Stuggle for South Yemen*, Croom Helm, London, England, 1984.

Kostiner, Joseph, *South Yemen's Revolutionary Strategy*, Westview Press, Boulder, Colorado, 1990.

Kostiner, Joseph, *Yemen: The Tortuous Quest for Unity*, Chatham House, London, England, 1996.

Lackner, Helen, *P. D. R. Yemen: Outpost of Socialist Development in Arabia*, Ithaca Press, London, England, 1985.

Longley, April, "The High Watermark of Islamist Politics? The Case of Yemen," *Middle East Journal*, Volume 61, Number 2, Spring 2007, pp. 240–260.

Longley Alley, April, and Abdul Ghani al-Iryani, "Discerning Yemen's Political Future," *Viewpoints*, The Middle East Institute, Number 11, June 2009.

Longley, April, "Breaking Point?: Yemen's Southern Question," International Crisis Group, October 20, 2011.

Lutz, Eberhart, "The Local Development Associations and their Socio-Political Relevance," in Muhammad al-Saidi, *The Cooperative Movement of Yemen*, Professors World Peace Academy, New York, New York, 1992.

Mackintosh-Smith, Tim, *Yemen: Travels in Dictionary Land*, John Murray Publishers, London, England, 1997.

al-Madhagi, Ahmed, *Yemen and the United States: A Study of a Small Power and Super-state Relationship, 1962–1994*, I.B. Tauris Publishers, New York, 1996.

Mahairez, Abdallah Ahmad, "Can a Generation Write Its Own Modern History?" (in Arabic), *al-Thaqafa al-Yamaniyya* (Yemeni Culture: Futuristic Viewpoints), Part One, Sanaa, Yemen, 1991; pp. 51–56.

al-Manea, Ilham, *al-Ahzab wa al-Tanthimaat al-Siyasiyya fi al-Yaman, 1948–1993* (Political Parties and Organizations in Yemen: An Analytical Study, 1948–1993), Al-Thawabit Publishing, Sanaa, Yemen, 1993.

al-Mansoub, Abd al-Aziz Sultan, *Intikhabat 1993 al-Niyabiyya fi al-Yaman* ("The 1993 Parliamentary Elections in Yemen"), Mutaba'a al-Yaman al-Asriyya, Sanaa, Yemen, 1995.

Mardini, Ramzi, *The Battle for Yemen: al-Qaeda and the Struggle for Stability*, Jamestown Foundation, Washington, DC, 2010.

al-Mikhlafi, Muhammad Ahmad Ali, "The Requirements and Dangers of Political Pluralism" in Arabic, *al-Thawri* newspaper, January 23, 30, and February 13, 1997, No. 1458–1460; p. 5, all editions.

al-Mikhlafi, Muhammad Ahmad Ali, *Qadiyat Dawlat al-Qanun fi al-Azma al-Yamaniyya* ("The Issue of the Rule of Law in the Yemeni Crisis"), *Dar al-Kunuz al-Adabiyya*, Beirut, Lebanon, 1999.

al-Mikhlafi, Othman Said Qasim, "Local Government: The Means for Equality of Citizenship," *an unpublished Arabic paper presented at Yemen's National Institute of Administrative Sciences*, 1998.

al-Mikhlafi, Othman Said Qasim, "The Law of Local Authority in Yemen," ("*Qanun al-Sulta al-Mahaliyya fi al-Yaman*"), *Al-Masar* in Arabic, Volume 1, Number 2, Bethesda, MD, Summer 2000.

al-Mujahid, Muhammad Muhammad, *Madinat Taiz* ("The City of Taiz"), al-Ma'amal al-Fanni lil-Taba'a, Taiz, Yemen, 1997.

Muller, Walter, "Outline of the History of Ancient South Arabia," in *Yemen: 3000 Years of Art and Civilization in Arabia Felix*, Pinguin-Verlag, Innsbruck, Austria, 1988.

al-Muqri, Ali, *Ta'am Aswad, Ra`iha Suda`a* ("Black Taste, Black Smell"), Dar el-Saqi, Beirut, Lebanon, 2008.

Nagi, Sultan, "The Genesis of the Call for Yemeni Unity," in B. R. Pridham, ed., *Contemporary Yemen: Politics and Historical Background*, St. Martin's Press, New York, New York, 1984.

Nonneman, Gerd, "Key Issues in the Yemeni Economy," in E. G. H. Joffe, ed., *Yemen Today: Crisis and Solutions*, Caravel Press, London, England, 1997.

Numan, Ahmed, *al-Anna al-Oula* ("The First Sound of Agony"), Yemeni Foundation for Research, Sanaa, June 1995.

Omar, Jarallah, "We are the Opposition," in E. G. H. Joffe, ed., *Yemen Today: Crisis and Solutions*, Caravel Press, London, England, 1997.

Pape, Robert, *Dying to Win: The Strategic Logic of Suicide Terrorism*, Random House, New York, NY, 2005.

Peterson, John, *Yemen: The Search for a Modern State*, Johns Hopkins University Press, Baltimore, Maryland, 1982.

Peterson, John, "Nation Building and Political Development in the Two Yemens," in B.R. Pridham, ed., *Contemporary Yemen: Politics and Historical Background*, St. Martin's Press, New York, New York, 1984.

Phillips, Sarah, *Yemen's Democracy in Regional Perspective*, Palgrave Macmillan, New York, NY, 2008.

Phillips, Sarah, "What Comes Next in Yemen? al-Qaeda, the Tribes, and State Building," in Christopher Boucek and Marina Ottaway, eds., *Yemen on the Brink*, Carnegie Endowment for International Peace, Washington, DC, 2010.

Piepenburg, Fritz, "The Cooperative Movement of Yemen: Developments after 1985," in Muhammad al-Saidi, *The Cooperative Movement of Yemen*, Professors World Peace Academy, New York, 1992.

Pridham, B.R., ed., *Contemporary Yemen: Politics and Historical Background*, St. Martin's Press, New York, 1984.

Pridham, B.R., *Economy, Society, and Culture in Contemporary Yemen*, Croom Helm, Kent, England, 1985.

al-Qasim, Khalid Muhammad, *Yaumiyyat wa Watha`iq al-Wihda al-Yamaniyya, 1972–1986* ("A Diary and Some Documents of Yemeni Unity"), The Yemeni Center for Studies and Research, Sanaa, Yemen, 1987.

Rotberg, Robert I., *State Failure and State Weakness in a Time of Terror*, Brookings Institution Press, Washington, DC, 2003.

Safran, Nadav, *Saudi Arabia: The Ceaseless Quest for Security*, Cornell University Press, Ithaca, New York, 1985.

al-Saidi, Muhammad, ed., *The Cooperative Movement of Yemen*, Professors World Peace Academy, New York, 1992.

al-Salami, Khadija, *The Tears of Sheba: Tales of Survival and Intrigue in Arabia*, John Wiley and Sons, England, 2003.

al-Saqqaf, Abu Bakr (under possible pseudonym, Muhammad Abd al-Salam), *al-Jumhuriyya bayn al-Sultana wa al-Qabila fi al-Yaman al-Shamali* ("The Tribal-Sultanate Republic in North Yemen"), al-Ahl Press, Yemen, 1988.

al-Saqqaf, Abu Bakr, "Tribal Power in Yemen" in Arabic, *al-Thawri* newspaper, three-part series from October 1996.

al-Saqqaf, Abu Bakr, "Yemeni Unity: Crisis in Integration," an unpublished paper presented at the Hamburg Institute of Orientalism, Hamburg, Germany, April 4, 1997.

Schwedler, Jillian, *Faith in Moderation: Islamist Parties in Jordan and Yemen*, Cambridge University Press, New York, 2007.

al-Shamiri, Abd al-Wali, *Alf Sa'at Harb* ("One Thousand Hour War"), Dar al-Kutub, Sanaa, Yemen, 1995.

al-Sharjabi, Qaid Numan, *Al-Shara`ih al-Ijtima'iyya al-Taqlidiyya fi al-Mujtima' al-Yamani* ("Traditional Social Slices of Yemeni Society"), Markaz al-Dirasaat wa al-Buhuth al-Yamani, Sanaa, Yemen, 1986.

Stookey, Robert, *Yemen: The Politics of the Yemen Arab Republic*, Westview Press, Boulder, Colorado, 1978.

Stookey, Robert, *South Yemen: A Marxist Republic in Arabia*, Westview Press, Boulder, Colorado, 1982.

Stracke, Nicole, and Mohammed Heydar, "The Southern Movement in Yemen," online paper by Gulf Research Center, Dubai, UAE, April 2010.

al-Suwaidi, Jamal S., ed., *The Yemen War of 1994: Causes and Consequences*, Saqi Books, Abu Dhabi, UAE, 1995.

Swagman, Charles, *Development and Change in Highland Yemen*, University of Utah Press, St. Lake City, Utah, 1988.

Warburton, David, "The Conventional War in Yemen," *Arab Studies Journal*, Spring 1995.

al-Waysi, Husayn Ali, *al-Yaman al-Kubra* ("Greater Yemen"), al-Irshad Publishing, Sanaa, Yemen, 1962.

Wedeen, Lisa, *Peripheral Visions: Publics, Power, and Performance in Yemen*, University of Chicago Press, Chicago, Illinois, 2008.

Wenner, Manfred, *The Yemen Arab Republic*, Westview Press, Boulder, Colorado, 1991.

Whitaker, Brian, "National Unity and Democracy in Yemen: A Marriage of Inconvenience," in E. G. H. Joffe, ed., *Yemen Today: Crisis and Solutions*, Caravel Press, London, England, 1997.

Wright, Lawrence, "The Counter-Terrorist," *New Yorker*, January 14, 2002.

Wright, Lawrence, *The Looming Tower: al-Qaeda's Road to 9/11*, Viking-Penguin, New York, 2006.

al-Zhahiri, Muhammad Muhsin, *Al-Dur al-Siyasi lil-Qabila fi al-Yaman, 1962–1990* ("The Political Role of the Tribe in Yemen, 1962–1990," in Arabic), Madbuli Press, Cairo, Egypt, 1996.

English Language News Sources

al-Ahram Weekly (Egypt)
Asia Times (Thailand)
Associated Press
BBC News (UK)
The Daily Mail (UK)
The Guardian (UK)
Huffington Post
International Herald Tribune
al-Jazeera (Qatar)
The National (UAE)
Newsweek
New York Times
Reuters agency
The Times of London (UK)
Washington Post
Wikileaks website
World Bank website
Yemen Observer, semiofficial (English language), Sanaa
Yemen Post online, independent (English language), Sanaa

Yemen Times, independent (English language), Sanaa
Yemen Update, semiannual by U.S. academic AIYS

Arabic Language News Sources from Yemen

14 October, official, Aden
22 May online, GPC ruling party, Sanaa
26 September Net, official army, Sanaa
Aden Press online, independent, Aden
al-Ayyam, independent, Aden
Aleshteraki Net, YSP party, Sanaa
al-Ghad online, independent, Sanaa
al-Jumhuriyya, official, Taiz
Mareb Press online, independent, Marib
al-Masdar online, independent, Sanaa
al-Mostaqbil, YSP party, Aden
Almotamar Net, GPC ruling party, Sanaa
NewsYemen online, independent, Sanaa
al-Sahwa & *Sahwa Net*, Islah (Islamic) party, Sanaa
al-Shoura, Union of Yemeni Popular Forces party, Sanaa
Taghyeer Net, independent, Sanaa
al-Tajammu'a, Unionist Grouping party, Aden
al-Tariq, independent, Aden
al-Thawra, official, Sanaa
al-Thawri, YSP party, Sanaa
al-Wahdawi, Unionist Nasserist party, Sanaa
al-Wasat, independent, Sanaa
al-Wihda, GPC ruling party, Sanaa
Yemen Observatory for Human Rights (yohr.org), Sanaa

Other Arabic Language News Sources

Asharq al-Awsat (UK; Saudi owned)
al-Hayat (UK)
al-Mostaqilah (UK)
al-Quds al-Arabi (UK)
al-Watan al-Arabi (Lebanon)

Index

Abd al-Aziz Abd al-Ghani, 66, 84, 135, 145,
    155, 168, 179, 287
Abd al-Nasser, President Gamal, 38, 62, 114
Abd al-Rabo Mansour Hadi, 134, 169, 288,
    290, 294, 298, 299, 306, 307
Abd al-Raqib Abd al-Wahhab, 91
Abu Luhum, Muhammad, 301
Abu Shawarib, Mujahid, 62, 126, 212, 218,
    227, 252
Abyan. *See* Yemen's mid-southern region
ACC (Arab Cooperation Council), 115
Adam Saif, 152
Aden. *See* Yemen's southwest region
Afghan mujahideen, 133, 196, 198, 208, 245
Afghanistan, 4, 15, 101, 102, 113, 177, 196,
    202–07, 216, 225, 243, 244, 246, 254,
    256, 260, 262
    comparison with Yemen, 23, 196,
    197, 200
agriculture, 10, 25, 27, 47, 50, 53, 159
al-Ahmar, Abdallah bin Husayn (Shaykh),
    94, 95, 99, 103, 110, 125–27, 132, 149,
    156–58, 163, 164, 166, 168, 169, 177,
    184, 185, 200, 205, 210–12, 221, 222,
    237, 260, 286, 299, 307
al-Ahmar, Hamid, 221, 284, 287, 299
al-Ahmar, Sadeq, 149, 260, 284, 286–88,
    292, 299, 307
Akhdam, 44, 272
Ali Muhsin al-Ahmar, General, 89, 102,
    103, 113, 137, 177, 198, 218, 284, 288,
    293, 299, 307, 308
    2011 defection by, 282
    president's plot to assassinate, 218
Ali Nasir Muhammad, President, 51, 73, 74,
    76, 77, 80, 133, 141, 175, 176, 234,
    246, 253, 289, 300–02, 307

partisans of, 120, 133–35, 137, 138, 141,
    142, 168, 174, 175, 177, 180, 191, 210,
    227, 228, 288
    return to Aden, 175
al-Alimi, Rashad, 259, 270
AQAP(al-Qaeda on the Arab Peninsula), 3,
    206, 244, 245, 251, 253, 257, 261–66,
    271, 274, 286, 289, 293, 294, 298, 302,
    303, 304
    2009 attacks in US, 3, 58, 256–61
    2009 declaration of support for
    al-Hirak, 251
    formation in 2009, 244
    targeted by Obama administration, 4,
    258, 262, 263, 294, 298
Arab uprisings in 2011, 1–2, 4–6, 273–76
assassinations. *See* political violence
'Asir, 29, 30
al-Attas, Haider, 210, 234, 289, 299, 301,
    307
al-Aulaqi, Anwar, 58, 257, 258, 294, 298
authoritarianism, 278
    denial of, 144

Ba Awm, Hasan (YSP member in
    Hadramaut), 180, 229, 246
Ba Awm, Hasan Salih (GPC member in
    Hadramaut), 172
Bakil tribe, 13, 21, 31, 34, 37, 44, 47, 61,
    67, 68, 86, 88, 94, 95, 104, 138,
    131–47, 191, 216–17, 241, 278, 299,
    304–05, 307
    shaykhs of, 35, 42, 60, 62, 68, 70, 84, 86,
    91, 92–98, 113, 126, 149–51, 274, 282,
    287, 305, 307–10
al-Baneh, Susan 242, 265
Bashraheel, Hisham, 238, 248, 264

List of Books in the Series